Customer Service

Building Successful Skills for the Twenty-First Century

Office Technology Product List (2002–2005)

Customer Service

**Building Successful Skills
for the Twenty-First Century**

Third Edition

Robert W. Lucas

McGraw-Hill
Irwin

Boston   Burr Ridge, IL   Dubuque, IA   Madison, WI   New York   San Francisco   St. Louis
Bangkok   Bogotá   Caracas   Kuala Lumpur   Lisbon   London   Madrid   Mexico City
Milan   Montreal   New Delhi   Santiago   Seoul   Singapore   Sydney   Taipei   Toronto

CUSTOMER SERVICE: BUILDING SUCCESSFUL SKILLS FOR THE TWENTY-FIRST CENTURY
Published by McGraw-Hill/Irwin, a business unit of The McGraw-Hill Companies, Inc., 1221 Avenue
of the Americas, New York, NY, 10020. Copyright © 2005, 2002, 1996 by The McGraw-Hill
Companies, Inc. All rights reserved. No part of this publication may be reproduced or distributed in
any form or by any means, or stored in a database or retrieval system, without the prior written
consent of The McGraw-Hill Companies, Inc., including, but not limited to, in any network or other
electronic storage or transmission, or broadcast for distance learning. Some ancillaries, including electronic and print components, may not be available to customers outside the United States.

This book is printed on acid-free paper.

1 2 3 4 5 6 7 8 9 0 DOW/DOW 0 9 8 7 6 5 4

ISBN 0-07-293805-6

Editorial director: *John E. Biernat*
Sponsoring editor: *Doug Hughes*
Developmental editor I: *Anna M. Chan*
Marketing manager: *Keari Bedford*
Producer, Media technology: *Damian Moshak*
Project manager: *Marlena Pechan*
Production supervisor: *Gina Hangos*
Design coordinator: *Mary E. Kazak*
Photo research coordinator: *Ira C. Roberts*
Senior digital content specialist: *Brian Nacik*
Cover design: *Lodge Design*
Cover images: *©GettyImages*
Interior design: *Ellen Pettengell*
Typeface: *10/12 Palatino*
Compositor: *Carlisle Communications, Ltd.*
Printer: *R. R. Donnelley*

Library of Congress Cataloging-in-Publication Data

Lucas, Robert W.
    Customer service : building successful skills for the twenty-first century / Robert W.
Lucas.-- 3rd ed.
        p. cm.
    Includes bibliographical references and index.
    ISBN 0-07-293805-6 (alk. paper)
     1. Customer services. I. Title.
    HF5415.5.L83 2005
    658.8'12--dc22   2004044880

www.mhhe.com

Personal Biography

Robert (Bob) W. Lucas

Bob Lucas holds dual roles as President of *Creative Presentation Resources*—a creative training and products company—and founding Managing Partner for *Global Performance Strategies*, LLC—an organization specializing in performance-based training, consulting services, and life planning seminars.

Bob has extensive experience in human resources development, management, and customer service over the past three decades in a variety of organizational environments. This background gives him a real-world perspective on the application of theory he has studied and used for several decades. He is certified in a variety of programs from various national and international training organizations. He is also an Inscape Publishing (formerly Carlson Learning) product distributor and instructor.

Bob focuses on assisting organizations and individuals in developing innovative and practical strategies for improved workplace performance. His areas of expertise include presentation skills, training and management program development, train-the-trainer, interpersonal communication, adult learning, customer service, and employee and organizational development.

Currently, Bob serves on the board of directors for the Central Florida Safety Council. Additionally, he is a former President of the Central Florida Chapter of the American Society for Training and Development and served on the board for the Metropolitan DC and Suncoast chapters of that organization.

In addition to giving regular presentations to various local and national groups and organizations, Bob serves as an adjunct faculty member for Webster University. In that position, he teaches organizational and interpersonal communication, diversity, and Introduction to Training and Development.

Listed in the *Who's Who in the World, Who's Who in America,* and *Who's Who in the South and Southeast* for a number of years, Bob is also an avid writer. Published works include *The Creative Training Idea Book: Inspired Tips and Techniques for Engaging and Effective Learning; The BIG Book of Flip Charts; How to Be a Great Call Center Representative; Customer Service Skills and Concepts for Success; Job Strategies for New Employees; Communicating One-to-One: Making the Most of Interpersonal Relationships; Coaching Skills: A Guide for Supervisors; Effective Interpersonal Skills; Training Skills for Supervisors;* and *Customer Service: Skills and Concepts for Business.* Additionally, he has been a contributing author for the *Annual: Developing Human Resources* series by Pfeiffer & Company since 1992 and to the HRHandbook by HRD Press.

Bob has earned a Bachelor of Science degree in Law Enforcement from the University of Maryland and a Master of Arts degree with a focus in Human Resources Development from George Mason University in Fairfax, Virginia. He is currently enrolled in the Master of Arts program in Human Resource Management at Webster University.

A Quick Look at the New Edition

Customer Service, by Robert Lucas, covers the concepts and skills needed for success in business careers at every level of every corporation and industry. This text covers the essential service skills for anyone working in business today—crucial skills that include listening techniques, verbal and nonverbal communication, and use of technology. The third edition has also been updated to provide insights and tips for customer service supervisory personnel.

Chapter Openers

Each chapter begins with a two-page opener of learning tools that help set the stage for chapter content.

- **Opening Quotes** prompt student thinking related to the chapter topic and guide students to the focus of the chapter.

- **Chapter Objectives** summarize the chapter's goals and focus. These major concepts provide a path for students to follow as they complete the chapter.

- Each chapter is introduced with interviews with customer service professionals, called **From the Frontline.** These insightful profiles answer questions about careers in customer service, give tips for new professionals, and provide knowledge on how to provide excellent customer service.

- **Quick Previews** give students an opportunity to assess their knowledge before reading each chapter and alerts them to important topics.

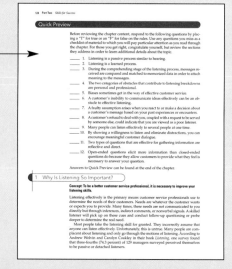

Chapter Pedagogy

- **Concept Checks** appear throughout the chapter, introducing students to the key issues of each section before the material is explained in detail.

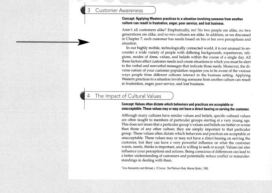

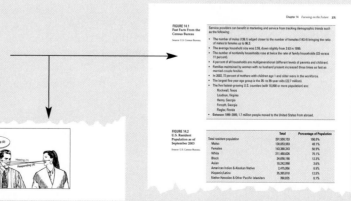

- **Work It Out** activities provide an opportunity for students to work through questions and exercises on learned customer service topics. These activities provide a basis for individual or small group work and help students to extend their learning to the next level.

- **NEW Leadership Initiative boxes**—the third edition features expanded customer service leadership coverage. These boxes highlight the leadership qualities managers of customer service groups exude. These insightful examples are valuable because they demonstrate different leadership styles and provide insights into how to manage effectively.

- **Figures and tables** effectively expand discussions and support the text material. They are reader-friendly and accessible for both instructors and students.

Chapter Review

The end-of-chapter features wrap up key concepts and encourage students to apply what they've learned in a variety of activities.

- A **Chapter Summary** sums up the major points of each chapter.

- **Service in Action** sections present an overview of internationally known organizations that are successfully implementing service philosophies. Featured companies include FedEx, Starbucks, and Southwest Airlines.

- **Chapter Review Questions** stimulate thinking on how certain situations might be handled using information gained in the chapter.

- **Search It Out** activities encourage students to expand their knowledge of customer service facts and figures that can be used in group activities, presentations, or discussions. New to the third edition is an accompanying list of links to customer service resources on the text's OLC.

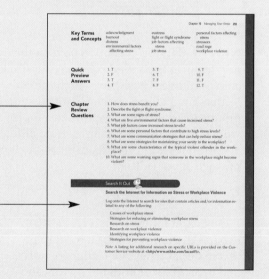

- **Collaborative Learning** activities provide an opportunity for students to join forces with their peers and work through a customer service problem. These group activities not only reinforce key concepts, but help to strengthen necessary customer service skills to better understand and relate to others.

- **Face to Face** exercises allow students to role-play and act out customer service scenarios. These active participation exercises examine realistic customer service problems and help students build people skills crucial in the business world.

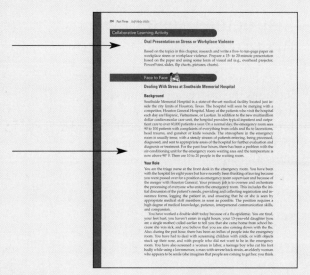

- **Planning to Serve** features encourage students to develop a strategy to apply what they've learned to real-world service environment.

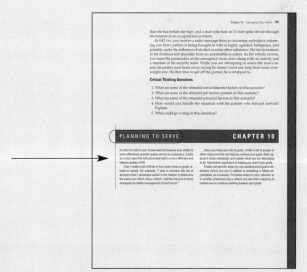

A Wealth of Supplements

Instructor's Resource CD-ROM

This valuable teaching resource includes the Instructor's Manual, Test Bank, and a PowerPoint presentation for each chapter. It includes teaching tips and questions for class discussions, as well as a computerized Brownstone test generator.

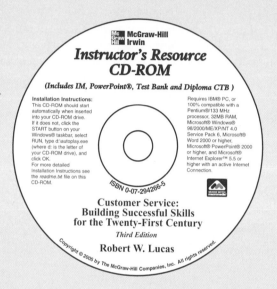

NEW Customer Service Hot Seat Videos

This interesting video collection captures real-life customer service managers in the "hot seat," responding to critical real-world situations. These excellent discussion starters allow viewers the opportunity to see learned concepts in action.

NEW Online Learning Center

Exclusive to the OLC is the Business Writer's Workshop. This web-based workshop emphasizes the importance of written messages in business. Students will learn how business relationships can be enhanced through a formal exchange of ideas and thoughts.

Numerous resources available for both Instructors and Students are online at **<www.mhhe.com/lucas05>**. Instructor resources include downloadable versions of the Instructor's Manual, PowerPoint presentation, and Instructor Notes to accompany the videos. Student study tools include Chapter Quizzes, Worksheets that provide the opportunity to act on information provided in the chapters and serve as student study tools or instructor assigned activities, and a list of Customer Service Resource links that provide students with a platform to complete Search It Out exercises from the text.

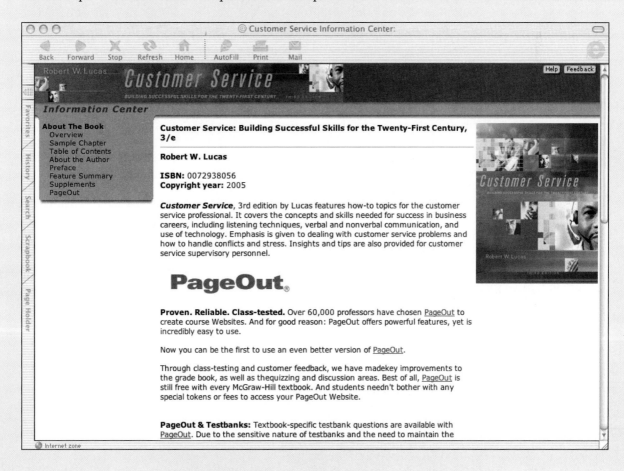

Preface

Welcome to an exciting journey through the wonderful world of customer service into the twenty-first century. The last century was challenging, but hold onto your hats, because, as Dorothy said in *The Wizard of Oz*, "Toto, I don't think we're in Kansas anymore."

The business world, society, and the worldwide demographics have changed dramatically in recent decades. The pace of these changes is greatly accelerating and more changes will come. Further, with advances in technology, change is happening in the business world at a phenomenal pace.

So let's explore the dynamics occurring at every level of every organization in every industry and organization as we examine the people, practices, and events that make the world of customer service what it is today and will be tomorrow.

As you read this book, you will discover that it provides a thorough introduction to a crucial skill set for anyone working in business today—people skills, or the skills to better understand and relate to others.

Our intention is to raise your awareness, prompt your thinking, give you many step-by-step suggestions for improvement, and provide you with a valuable reference for information on how you and your organization can deliver service excellence. The information contained herein will benefit you whether you are new to dealing with others in a business setting or are more experienced with internal customers (e.g., coworkers or other employees) and external customers (e.g., consumers, vendors, or other end users of products).

Although the terms *customer service professional* and *customer service organization* are used throughout the book, they are not meant to be exclusive. Everyone in business, government, or industry today has internal and/or external customers to whom they must provide products, services, information, or other deliverables.

The skills, strategies, and techniques outlined in this book are valid in any organization because they are directed toward identifying customer needs and then satisfying those needs.

Text Features

Customer Service: Building Successful Skills for the Twenty-First Century uses a wide variety of text and activities to gain and hold your interest while providing insights into the concepts and skills related to customer service.

The text begins with an overview of what customer service involves, then focuses on specific skills and related topics, and finally provides insights into future customer service trends and issues.

The book contains 14 chapters divided into five parts. The parts focus on different aspects of customer service: Part 1, "The Profession," Part 2, "Skills for Success," Part 3, "Self-Help Skills," Part 4, "Enhancing Customer Relationships," and Part 5, "Customer Service for the Twenty-First Century." Along with the valuable ideas, guidance, and perspectives offered in this book, you will encounter real-world cases about experts in today's business world, as well as activities to challenge your thinking on the topics discussed.

As you move through each chapter, you will find many helpful tools to enhance your learning experience and assist you in transferring your new knowledge to the workplace.

Each chapter starts with a quote from a famous person—to prompt your thinking related to the chapter topic and focus.

Also, note the behavioral-based **Chapter Learning Objectives,** the main concepts that a learner should know or be able to put into use by the end of a chapter. The **Chapter Learning Objectives** direct your focus and give you a way to measure your success in grasping the chapter concepts, once you have completed the chapter.

Before you begin each chapter, you will do a self-assessment of your current skills and knowledge levels. This is the **Quick Preview,** which is a list of brief questions related to providing customer service that you answer and score yourself. Your incorrect answers help you focus on chapters and parts of chapters as you read the book; your correct answers help you determine which chapters and parts of chapters you should turn to for reinforcement.

From the Frontline features appear at the beginning of most chapters. They provide insights into customer service in a variety of businesses, industries, and organizations. Told in the words of experts in the fields, these candid snapshots describe what it is like to provide service in an ever-changing world.

Worksheets are provided on the website for this book <http://www.mhhe.com/lucas05> to correspond to chapters in the text and to give you an opportunity to act immediately on what you have learned. In some cases, you will create samples based on information provided in the chapter, and in others you will develop an action plan or a list of valuable information for future use on the job.

Leadership Initiatives are short, quick tips for implementing concepts outlined in a chapter. They are designed to assist peer coaches, managers, supervisors, and others in leadership positions to create a powerful service environment.

Work It Out activities are provided in all chapters to challenge your knowledge and provide an opportunity for individual and/or small group work on a specific topic or issue.

The end-of-chapter features begin with a **Chapter Summary** that brings together the key concepts and issues.

Service in Action presents overviews of internationally known organizations that are successfully implementing service philosophies.

Key Terms and Concepts are listed at the end of each chapter to assist readers in identifying important elements they should have learned.

Chapter Review Questions are given at the end of each chapter to stimulate thinking on how certain situations might be handled using information gained in the chapter. They also can be used as a discussion vehicle to share ideas with others.

Search It Out activities give you an opportunity to expand your knowledge of customer service and your research skills on the Internet. In each chapter, you will be asked to explore the Internet to obtain a variety of customer service facts, figures, and related information that you will use in group activities, presentations, or discussions. You will also have an opportunity to participate in **Collaborative Learning** activities, in which you and one or more of your peers can work through a customer service problem to practice your skills and find answers to your questions.

Face to Face exercises are customer service scenarios in which you assume the role of an employee and use the information provided to determine how you would solve a customer service problem.

Planning to Serve action planning forms are provided at the end of each chapter. These can be used by readers to develop a strategy for applying what they learned in each chapter to the real-world service environment.

The Appendix, Reader's Customer Service Survey, helps the author—by providing your feedback on how you view this book. In addition to filling out an actual customer survey to tell us what you liked and did not like, you will also receive a gift for completing and returning the form.

A Glossary, Bibliography, and Index follow the Appendix.

Basis for Content

This book draws from my 32 years of management, human resources, and service experience. Some research and theoretical material appear in the book, but much of the information is derived from personal experience, research, and the reflections of other people who have experienced customer service encounters.

Whether you are new to business and wish to expand your knowledge of customer service or are more experienced and are able to describe your efforts in dealing with people through customer service, customer relations, or customer encounters, your goal in using this text should be to improve your knowledge and skills. This can lead to total customer satisfaction.

I'm confident that this book will help you reach your goals.

Robert William Lucas

Acknowledgments

Throughout the years, my wife, friend, and life partner M. J. and my mother Rosie have sacrificed much while I have dedicated time and effort to developing this text and others. Their support and love have been invaluable assets in helping me reach my goals and are much appreciated.

I also thank Doug Hughes, Anna Chan, Marlena Pechan, and other members of the publishing team at McGraw-Hill/Irwin for their expertise and patience as they guided me through the process of bringing this book to fruition. They are all true professionals and have been a great help.

Special thanks also go to the following educators who reviewed the last edition and offered suggestions, critique, and guidance in the refinement of the book content and format. I believe that their time, expertise, and valuable input have resulted in an enhanced product.

A. Murlene Asadi
Scott Community College

Blake Beck
Idaho State University

Claudia Browning
Mesa Community College

Gary Corona
Florida Community College at Jacksonville

Margaret A. Fisher
Florida Community College at Jacksonville

Linda Harris
Florida Metropolitan University

Heidi Hutchins
GateWay Community College

Lea Ann Kremer
McCann School of Business & Technology

Albert Mastromartino
Sir Sandford Fleming College

John Moonen
Daytona Beach Community College

Jacqueline Nicholson
Holyoke Community College

Shelly Rex
York Technical Institute

Paul Ricker
Broward Community College–North Campus

Carl Stafford
Manchester Community College

Kathleen Wachter
University of Mississippi

Joyce Walsh-Portillo
Broward Community College

Michael Wierzbicki
Scottsdale Community College

Callie P. Williams
Florida Community College at Jacksonville

Richard Williams
Nashville State Community College

Contents

The Profession

What Is Customer Service?

Quick Preview

Before reviewing the content of the chapter, respond to the following statements by placing a "T" for true or an "F" for false on the rules. Use any questions you miss as a checklist of material to which you will pay particular attention as you read through the chapter. For those you get right, congratulate yourself, but review the sections they address in order to learn additional details about the topics.

_____ 1. The concept of customer service evolved from the practice of selling wares in small general stores, off the back of wagons, or out of the home.

_____ 2. The migration from other occupations to the service industry is a recent trend and started in the late 1970s.

_____ 3. One of the reasons for the shift from manufacturing to customer service is that society has changed.

_____ 4. As more women have entered the workforce, the demand for personal services has increased.

_____ 5. Advances in technology have created a need for more employees in manufacturing businesses.

"Concentrate your strength against your competitor's relative weakness." Bruce
Henderson, CEO, Boston Consulting Group, Inc.

Chapter Learning Objectives

After completing this chapter, you will be able to:

- Define customer service.
- Identify the socioeconomic and demographic changes that have influenced customer service.

- Recognize the factors responsible for a shift to a service culture.
- List the six major components of a customer-focused environment.

_____ 6. Workers in the United States have more disposable income now than at any other time in history.

_____ 7. As a result of deregulation in a variety of industries, competition has slowed.

_____ 8. There are six key components that can be identified in a customer service environment.

_____ 9. An organization's "culture" is what the customer experiences.

_____ 10. Quality customer service organizations recruit, select, and train qualified people.

_____ 11. Customers are happy when they receive quality and quantity as promised.

_____ 12. To determine whether delivery needs are being met, organizations must examine industry standards, customer expectations, capabilities, costs, and current and projected requirements.

Answers to Quick Preview can be found at the end of the chapter.

1 Defining Customer Service

Concept: Customer-focused organizations determine and meet the needs of their internal and external customers. Their focus is to treat everyone with respect and as if they were special.

Many attempts have been made to define the term *customer service.* However, depending on an organization's focus, such as retailing, industry, manufacturing, or service, the goals of providing customer service may vary. In fact, we often use the term **service industry** as if it were a separate occupational field unto itself; in reality, most organizations provide some degree of customer service. For the purposes of this text, **customer service** is defined as the ability of knowledgeable, capable, and enthusiastic employees to deliver products and services to their internal and external customers in a manner that satisfies identified and unidentified needs and ultimately results in positive word-of-mouth publicity and return business.

Many companies specialize in providing only services. Examples of this type of company are banks and credit unions, consulting firms, Internet service providers, utility companies, call centers, brokerage firms, laundries, plumbing and electrical companies, transportation companies, and medical facilities. Some organizations provide both products and services. Examples are businesses such as car dealerships, retail stores, and manufacturers that have support services for their products, supermarkets, theaters, and restaurants.

The term **service sector** as used by the Census Bureau and the Bureau of Labor Statistics in their reports and projections typically includes:

Transportation, communication, and utilities

Wholesale trade

Retail trade

Finance, insurance, and real estate

Other services (including businesses such as legal firms, barbershops and beauty salons, personal services, housekeeping, and accounting)

Federal government

State and local governments

In addition, there are people who are self-employed and provide various types of services to their customers and clients.

Customer-Focused Organizations

Some common characteristics for **customer-focused organizations** are described below.

They have internal customers (for example, peers, coworkers, bosses, subordinates, people from other areas of their organization) and/or external customers (for example, vendors, suppliers, various telephone callers, walk-in customers, other organizations, others not from within the organization).

Their focus is on determining and meeting the needs of customers while treating everyone with respect and as if they were special. Information, products, and services are easily accessible by customers. Policies are in place to allow employees to make decisions in order to better serve customers.

Management and systems support and appropriately reward employee efforts to serve customers.

Reevaluation of the way business is conducted is ongoing and results in necessary changes and upgrades to deliver timely, quality service to the customer.

Build relationships through **customer relationship management (CRM)** programs.

Before distribution systems were modernized, peddlers went from house to house, particularly in rural areas, to deliver merchandise or services. Doctors often went to the sick person's home and made house visits. *How do these methods of delivery differ from those used today? Do you think the ones used today are better? Why or why not?*

The Concept of Customer Service

The concept or practice of customer service is not new. Over the years it has evolved from a meager beginning into a multibillion-dollar endeavor. In the past, when many people worked on farms, small artisans and business owners provided customer service to their neighbors. No multinational chain stores existed. Many small towns and villages had their own blacksmith, general store, boardinghouse, restaurant, tavern, barbershop, and similar service-oriented establishments owned and operated by people living in the town (often the place of business was also the residence of the owner). For people living in more rural areas, peddlers of kitchenware, medicine, and other goods made their way from one location to another to serve their customers and distribute various products. Further, to supplement their income, many people made and sold or bartered products from their homes in what came to be known as **cottage industries**. As trains, covered wagons, and stagecoaches began to cross the country, they carried vendors and supplies as well as provided transportation. During that whole era, customer service differed from what it is today by the fact that the owners and chief executive officers (CEOs) were also motivated frontline employees working face-to-face with their customers. They had a vested interest in providing good service and in succeeding.

When industry, manufacturing, and larger cities started to grow, the service industry really started to gain ground. In the late 1800s, as the mail services matured, companies such as Montgomery Ward and Sears Roebuck introduced the mail-order catalog to address the needs of customers. In rural areas, the population grew and expanded westward, and service providers followed.

Post–World War II Service

Following World War II, there was a continuing rise in the number of people in the United States in service occupations. According to an article published by the Bureau of Labor Statistics, "At the conclusion of the war in 1945, the service industry accounted for only 10 percent of nonfarm employment, compared to 38 percent for manufacturing. In 1982 services surpassed manufacturing as the largest employer among major industry groups. From 2000–2010 virtually all nonfarm wage and

LEADERSHIP INITIATIVE   1.1

To effectively manage the current and future service workforce, supervisors and managers will need to increase their knowledge of the world around them. This includes learning more about various cultures, technology, industry and organizational specifics, interpersonal skills, and all the areas covered in this text. This can be accomplished through ongoing training and educational activities (for example, classroom, e-learning, books and articles, benchmarking successful leaders and organizations, and secondary and postsecondary education).

FIGURE 1.1
Migration to the Service Industry

Typical Former Occupations	Typical Service Occupations
Farmer	Salesperson
Ranch worker	Insurance agent
Machinist	Food server
Engineer	Administrative assistant
Steelworker	Flight attendant
Homemaker	Call center representative
Factory worker	Repair person
Miner	Travel professional
Tradesperson (for example, watchmaker)	Child care provider
Railroad worker	Security guard

salary employment growth is expected to be in the service-producing sector, accounting for a net increase of 8.9 million jobs."[1]

Economically, employment based on consumer spending should grow from 83.2 million to 94.5 million dollars between 2000 and 2010. This is projected to add an additional 11.3 million net jobs by 2010.

The Shift to Service

Today, businesses have changed dramatically as the economy has shifted from a dependence on manufacturing to a focus on providing timely, quality service. The age of the **service economy** has been alive and strong for some time now. Tied to this trend has been the development of international quality standards by which effectiveness is measured in many multinational organizations.

To highlight the importance of customer service, in 1992, after lobbying by the International Customer Service Association (ICSA), the U.S. Congress proclaimed that the first full week of October each year would be celebrated as National Customer Service Week.

As shown in Figure 1.1, since the end of World War II, people have moved from other occupations to join the rapidly growing ranks of service professionals.

2   Growth of the Service Sector

Concept: Technology has affected jobs in the following ways: quantity of jobs created, distribution of jobs, and the quality of jobs. The service sector is projected to have the largest job growth.

[1]M. Toosi, "Consumer Spending: An Engine for U.S. Job Growth," *Monthly Labor Review,* U.S. Department of Labor, Bureau of Labor Statistics, Washington, D.C., November 2002, p. 12.

IMPROVING SERVICE QUALITY

Take a moment to list some of the changes you have personally witnessed in the business world during your lifetime. Are these changes for better or worse? With these changes in mind, what do you—or would you—do to improve service quality as a customer service professional in your chosen industry or position?

FIGURE 1.2 Fastest-Growing Occupations, 2000–2010

Source: U.S. Bureau of Labor Statistics, Office of Occupational Statistics and Employment Projections.

Occupation	Employment		Change		Most Significant Source of Education or Training
	2000	**2010**	**Number**	**Percent**	
Computer support specialists	506	996	490	97	Associate degree
Home health aides	615	907	291	47	Short-term on-the-job training
Computer software engineers, applications	380	760	380	100	Bachelor's degree
Computer systems analysts	431	689	258	60	Bachelor's degree
Personal and home care aides	414	672	258	62	Short-term on-the-job training
Computer software engineers, systems software	317	601	284	90	Bachelor's degree
Medical assistants	329	516	187	57	Moderate-term on-the-job training
Computer and information systems managers	313	463	150	48	Bachelor's and higher degree, plus work experience
Social and human service assistants	271	418	147	54	Moderate-term on-the-job training
Network and computer systems administrators	229	416	187	82	Bachelor's degree
Dental assistants	247	339	92	37	Moderate-term on-the-job training
Special education teachers, preschool, kindergarten, and elementary school	234	320	86	37	Bachelor's degree
Pharmacy technicians	190	259	69	36	Moderate-term on-the-job training
Fitness trainers and aerobics instructors	158	222	64	40	Postsecondary vocational award
Network systems and data communications analysts	119	211	92	77	Bachelor's degree

The Bureau of Labor Statistics has released labor figure projections covering the years 2000–2010 that estimate a rise in the supply of workers by over 17 million people, reaching 158 million people in 2010. During that period, the majority of the fastest employment growth in the top 15 occupations with the largest job growth are projected to be in the service sector.[2] See Figures 1.2 and 1.3.

In addition, as technology replaces many production line workers, increasing numbers of service jobs are created. This comes about because, as greater numbers and greater varieties of goods are produced, more service people, salespeople, managers, and other professionals are needed to design and market service delivery systems that support those products. Technology-related service jobs such as those of

[2]H. N. Fullerton, Jr., and M. Toosi, "Labor Force Projections to 2010: Steady Growth and Changing Composition," *Monthly Labor Review,* U.S. Department of Labor, Bureau of Labor Statistics, Washington D.C., November 2001, p. 21.

FIGURE 1.3 Occupations With the Largest Job Growth, 2000–2010

Source: U.S. Bureau of Labor Statistics, Office of Occupational Statistics and Employment Projections.

Occupation	Employment		Change		Most Significant Source of Education or Training
	2000	2010	Number	Percent	
Combined food preparation and serving workers, including fast food	2,206	2,879	673	30	Short-term on-the-job training
Customer service representatives	1,946	2,577	631	32	Moderate-term on-the-job training
Registered nurses	2,194	2,755	561	26	Associate degree
Retail salespersons	4,109	4,619	510	12	Short-term on-the-job training
Computer support specialists	506	996	490	97	Associate degree
Cashiers, except gaming	3,325	3,799	474	14	Short-term on-the-job training
Office clerks, general	2,705	3,125	430	16	Short-term on-the-job training
Security guards	1,106	1,497	391	35	Short-term on-the-job training
Computer software engineers, applications	380	760	380	100	Bachelor's degree
Waiters and waitresses	1,983	2,347	364	18	Short-term on-the-job training
General managers and operations managers	2,398	2,761	363	15	Bachelor's or higher degree, plus work experience
Truck drivers, heavy and tractor-trailer	1,749	2,095	346	20	Moderate on-the-job training
Nurses aides, orderlies, and attendants	1,373	1,697	323	24	Short-term on-the-job training
Janitors and cleaners, except maids and housekeeping cleaners	2,348	2,665	317	13	Short-term on-the-job training
Postsecondary teachers	1,344	1,659	315	23	Doctoral degree

database administrators, computer support specialists, computer scientists, computer engineers, and systems analysts are expected to continue to grow at a rapid pace.

Impact of the Economy

According to leading economists, today's economy is affecting jobs in three ways: (1) overall quantity of jobs created; (2) the distribution of jobs among industries, occupations, geographic areas, and organizations of different sizes; and (3) the quality of jobs, measured by wages, job security, and opportunities for development.

Quantity of Jobs Being Created

A variety of factors including prevailing interest rates and consumer demand typically cause companies to evaluate how many people they need and which jobs will be established or maintained. In addition, the advent of technology has brought with it the need for many new technical skills in the areas of computer hardware and software operation and maintenance. At the same time, technology has created an opportunity for organizations to transfer tasks previously performed by employees to machines, thus eliminating the need for staff and in many cases leading to **downsizing** (that is, the laying off or dismissal of employees).

Distribution of Jobs

Two parallel trends in job development are occurring. The first comes about from the need for employees to be able to have regular access to personal and professional networks and to engage in collaborative exchanges. This trend means that more jobs are likely to develop in major metropolitan areas, where ease of interaction with peers and suppliers, high customer density, and access to the most current business practices exist. Training and technology resources are also available in these areas. Access to technology resources helps ensure continued learning and growth of employees and also aids organizations in achieving their goals and objectives.

The second trend in job development arises from the ease of transmission and exchange of information by means of technology. It is called telecommuting. Employees can now work from their homes or satellite office location. Government agencies, technology-focused organizations, and many companies with large staffs in major metropolitan areas that experience traffic congestion (for example, Los Angeles, Boston, and Washington, D.C.) often use **telecommuting** to eliminate the need for employees to travel to work each day. The telephone and computer fax modem, make it possible to provide services from almost any remote location. For example, telephone sales and product support services can easily be handled from an employee's home if the right equipment is used. To do this, a customer calls a designated 800 number and a switching device at the company dispatches the call to an employee working at home. This is seamless to the customer, who receives the service needed and has no idea where it originated. You will learn more about technology in customer service in Chapter 9.

Today, many employees work from their homes all or part of the time. Telecommuting, as this is called, is used frequently by companies in large cities, such as Los Angeles, to decrease travel time. *Do you think you would need different skills or abilities to telecommute? Why or why not?*

Quality of Service Jobs

From an individual standpoint, anyone contemplating a move to a job, whether it is service or otherwise, should consider the quality of that position. Quality can be measured in a variety of ways, and each person values some things more than others do. However, some typical evaluating factors are level of compensation (pay), employee benefits, job security, opportunity for personal and professional growth, required amount of travel, quality of the work environment, structure of the job (that is, responsibilities, reporting hierarchy), and occupational safety. Safety is especially important when machinery and equipment are involved in daily task performance and in light of the rising trend of workplace violence.

Since the late 1990s there has been increasing economic growth, low interest rates, and new job opportunities. Unemployment rates reached a historic low then went up. However, as the social and workplace demographics continue to shift and people move around in our mobile society, job security has been affected and it is likely that competition for desired jobs will continue to become much more intense. This has become evident as the unemployment and interest rates have risen since the early years of the twenty-first century. Even so, a study done in 2001 by the International Customer Service Association (ICSA) on service employee and management salaries and bonuses showed an increase. In an ICSA white paper on

FIGURE 1.4
Average Annual Salary by Customer Service Position (excluding bonuses and benefits)

Source: N. Hallock, "Customer Service Industry Incentives, Bonuses and Employee Retention" (white paper), International Customer Service Association, Chicago, Ill., 2001.

Position	Study Year					
	2001		**1999**		**1997**	
	Mean	**Base**	**Mean**	**Base**	**Mean**	**Base**
Vice president	$122,528	68	$106,489	31	$104,418	59
Director	$87,854	161	$82,830	73	$75,386	157
Manager	$69,010	221	$59,207	157	$52,751	284
Asst. mgr./supervisor	$45,025	137	$45,359	114	$38,825	190
Order processing mgr./supervisor	$44,669	72	$42,598	37	$38,425	72
Senior rep./asst. supervisor	$37,473	184	$32,728	131	$31,380	234
Technical support person	$39,700	86	$34,850	64	$35,327	104
CS representative	$31,818	238	$28,876	178	$26,075	341
Order entry clerk	$24,990	94	$23,441	51	$21,088	108
CS clerk	$24,426	102	$23,572	59	$21,211	132
Other	$33,182	10	$42,926	16	—	—

the study[3] indicators of salary and bonus increases are shown to help increase retention (see Figure 1.4). Employees who obtain and maintain the better customer service jobs that provide good working conditions, security, and benefits will be better educated, trained, and prepared. They will also be the ones who understand and have tapped into the concept of professional networking. **Networking** is the active process of building relationships inside and outside the organization through meetings, interactions, and activities that lead to sound interpersonal relationships and sharing of resources. Practices such as joining and becoming actively involved in committees and boards of governors or directors will prove to be invaluable. Many good books have been published on the subject. The Internet (for example, Amazon.com, Barnes&Noble.com, and Border.com) can lead to such resources.

3   Addressing the Changes

Concept: All customer-based organizations must provide excellence in service and an environment in which customer needs are identified and satisfied.

Developing strategies for providing premium service that will capture and hold loyal customers has become a priority for most organizations. All customer-based organizations have one focus in common—they must provide service excellence and an environment in which customer needs are identified and satisfied—or perish.

To this end, organizations must become learning organizations, a term made popular by the author Peter Senge in his book *The Fifth Discipline.* Basically, a learning organization is one that uses knowledge as a basis for competitive advantage. This means providing ongoing training and development opportunities to employees so that they can gain and maintain cutting-edge skills and knowledge while projecting a positive can-do customer-focused attitude. A learning organization also ensures that there are systems that can adequately compensate and reward employees based on their performance. In such an organization, systems and processes are continuously examined and updated. Learning from mistakes, and adapting accordingly, is crucial. In the past, organizations took a reactive approach

[3]Nan Hallock, "Customer Service Industry Incentives, Bonuses and Employee Retention" (white paper), ICSA, Chicago, Ill., 2001.

FIGURE 1.5
United States:
Persons per Square
Mile, 2000

Source: U.S. Census, 2000.

to service by waiting for customers to ask for something or by trying to recover after a service breakdown. Often, a small customer service staff dealt with customer dissatisfaction or attempted to fix problems after they occurred. In today's economy, a proactive approach of anticipating customer needs is necessary and becoming common. To excel, organizations must train *all* employees to spot problems and deal with them before the customer becomes aware that they exist. If a service breakdown does occur, managers in truly customer-focused organizations should empower employees at all levels to do whatever is necessary to satisfy the customer. For this to happen, management must educate and train staff members on the techniques and policies available to help serve the customer. They must then give employees the authority to act without asking first for management intervention in order to resolve customer issues. This concept, known as **service recovery,** is described in detail in Part Four, "Enhancing Customer Relationships."

4   Societal Factors Affecting Customer Service

Concept: Many factors caused the economic shift from manufacturing to service. Increased technology, globalization of the economy, deregulation, and many government programs are a few factors. You will read about these and others in the following paragraphs.

You may wonder what, exactly, caused the economic shift from manufacturing to service. Some of the more important factors are discussed in the following sections.

Shifts in the Population Profile

The years between 1990 and 2000 saw the largest ever census-to-census growth in the population of the United States with 33 million people added (Figure 1.5). A major residual effect of this spurt is a larger customer base for organizations in all industries.

Other changes in the population that will affect the service economy include the following:

- In 1976, 36 percent of women had four or more children. That number dropped to 11 percent in 2000. The impact of this decline will be a smaller population under the age of 18 as customers, production workers, and service providers.

- 1.7 million people moved into the United States between March 1999 and 2000. Two-thirds of those people were not U.S. citizens and most (1.2 million) were located in the southern and western states. This creates many opportunities for service providers because many of these people are starting their lives over and need to purchase everything they need as they become acculturated into the U.S. way of life. This migration also presents challenges for service providers who encounter customers who speak English as a second language and have differing values, beliefs, needs, and expectations.

- Almost one in five people who moved within the United States, and one in ten who moved out of rental homes and into an owned one, did so because they wanted a new or better home. This movement creates a need for new products (for example, furniture and accessories), repairs and renovations, and a number of other services.

- Between 1974 and 2000, the proportion of married-couple families with children under the age of 18 dropped from 40 percent to 24 percent. This creates challenges to service providers in the form of a reduced need for services such as babysitting, home care, educational services, and a variety of products associated with families that have children (for example, family vacation packages).

- A majority of students (57 percent) had access to a computer both at home and in school. This opens a wide array of Internet product and service opportunities and helps prepare customers and service providers of the future for the use of technology.

Increased Efficiency in Technology

The development and increased sophistication of machines and computers have caused an increase in production and quality. Two side effects have been an increased need for service organizations to take care of the technology and a decrease in manufacturing and blue-collar jobs.

An advantage of this change is that machines can work 24 hours, seven-days-a-week with few lapses in quality, no need for breaks, and without increases in salary and benefits. This makes them extremely attractive to profit-minded business and corporate shareholders. Although technology can lead to the loss of some jobs, technological advances in the computer and telecommunications industry alone have created hundreds of service opportunities for people who monitor and run the machines and automated services. Everything from 800 numbers and telemarketing to shopping and service via the Internet, television, and telephone has evolved and continues to expand.

A major factor driving implementation of technology-based service is that, according to the 2000 U.S. Census figures, 50.5 percent of U.S. households have and use Internet access. This is up from 26.2 percent in 1998.

Globalization of the Economy

Beginning in the 1960s, when worldwide trade barriers started to come down, a variety of factors have contributed to expanded international cooperation and competition. This trend has been termed **globalization** with many companies focusing on **business-to-business (B2B)** initiatives, as well as, individual consumers. Since the 1960s, advances in technology, communication, and transportation have opened new markets and allowed decentralized worldwide access for production, sales, and service. To survive and hold onto current market share while opening new gateways, U.S. firms need to hone the service skills of their employees,

To help you recognize the impact this global trend has on you and your family as consumers, think about all the products you own (for example, car, microwave oven, television, computer, fax machine). List five major products along with their country of origin (you can find this on the warranty plate along with the product's serial number, usually on the back or bottom of the product).

strengthen their quality, and look for new ways of demonstrating that they cannot only deliver but exceed the expectations of customers. All of this means more competition and the evolution of new rules and procedures that they have not been able to obtain in the past. Sometimes the deciding factor for the customer, on whether to purchase a foreign or domestic product, will be the service you provide.

Deregulation of Many Industries

Over the years, we have witnessed the deregulation of a number of industries (airlines and the telephone and the utility industries in the later 1990s to the early 2000s). **Deregulation** is the removal of government restrictions on an industry. The continuing deregulation of major U.S. public services has caused competition to flourish. However, deregulation has also brought major industry shakeups, sometimes leading to breakdowns in service quality in many companies. These events have created opportunities for newly established companies to step in with improvements to close the gaps and better serve customers.

Geopolitical Changes

Events such as oil embargoes, political unrest, and conflicts and wars involving various countries have reduced U.S. business access and competition within some areas of the world (for example, Cuba, Vietnam, Iran, Iraq) while some countries have free access in those areas. These circumstances not only limit access to product, manufacturing, and distribution channels but also reduce the markets to which U.S. businesses can offer products and services. For example, every closed port or country border has a negative effect on travel industry professionals, such as reservationists, air transport and manufacturing employees, and tour guides.

Other positive and negative historical changes have occurred that—like it or not—have affected the way companies do business and will continue to do so into the twenty-first century. The passage of the **North American Free Trade Agreement (NAFTA)** made it possible for many U.S.-based companies to relocate and send jobs across borders in order to find less expensive labor forces, increase profits, and avoid unions. The demise of the Soviet Union and the political and economic chaos that ensued as companies jockeyed to establish business relationships with the Commonwealth of Independent States (CIS) has also had an impact. The unexpected resignation from office on the eve of the new millennium by Russian President Boris Yeltsin, and the successor he handpicked to finish his term, added political fuel that will no doubt have longstanding effects. Whether these effects will be positive or negative remains to be seen. Further events, such as trade agreements with China and the thawing of relations with Vietnam, have opened new political doors. The shift in relations with Iran and Iraq and several other nations as the result of human rights violations, violence, terrorism, and military-related actions have created obstacles to international trade and commerce.

Geopolitical events such as these will lead to more multinational mergers and a need for better understanding of diversity-related issues by employees and managers. With increased ease of transportation and communication, companies cannot afford to ignore international competitors. For years, American firms viewed Japan as their chief economic and business rival. Now other countries are challenging Japan (Taiwan, Korea, Vietnam, China) and are becoming firmly entrenched in the marketplace. An example of this was the introduction of the South Korea–made KIA car line into the U.S. market in the 1990s. Although many Pacific Rim countries experienced severe economic setbacks during the 1990s—from inflation and a variety of political factors—these countries have traditionally been strengthened through adversity.

Increase in the Number of White-Collar Workers

With the movement out of factories and mines, and off the farm, more people find themselves working at a traditional nine-to-five office job or providing service on a variety of work shifts (telephone and technical support centers). This trend has led to the creation of new types of service occupations: Office workers need to have someone clean their clothes, spruce up their homes (inside and out), care for their children, do their shopping, run their errands, and feed their families. In effect, the service phenomenon has spawned its own service trend.

Socioeconomic Programs

Two programs have begun in the United States that promise to have an impact on the labor force in general and on the service sector in particular. They are the Welfare to Work Partnership and Workforce Investment Act of 1998.

Welfare to Work Partnership

This program, the **Welfare to Work Partnership,** is a national, nonpartisan, not-for-profit organization created to encourage and assist businesses that hire individuals who are formerly on public assistance (welfare). The Welfare to Work Partnership was founded by United Airlines, United Parcel Service (UPS), Burger King, Monsanto, and Sprint and focuses on supporting small, medium, and large businesses that hire former welfare recipients.

According to the Welfare to Work Partnership, the impact on the labor force is potentially significant because there is a huge labor pool in the welfare ranks. One estimate is that over 4 million women, who are statistically the primary breadwinners on assistance, have on average over four years of experience. If these people can successfully gain access to the labor force, there will be a major effect on the service sector. This conclusion is substantiated in part by a 1998 Welfare to Work membership survey conducted by Wirthlin Worldwide. The study found that, in general, the positions offered to welfare recipients are most likely to be in the service arena—clerical (37 percent), custodial or janitorial (13 percent), service work (32 percent), and general labor (49 percent). And, as stated earlier, other service industries are spawned when more people enter the workplace. In the case of welfare recipients, 33 percent need transportation and 30 percent need child care.

Workforce Investment Act of 1998

The **Workforce Investment Act of 1998** was signed into law by President Bill Clinton and started a major initiative to streamline and improve public sector employment and training service. For the most part, the law replaced the old Job Training Partnership Act (JTPA) of 1982. The law required each state to establish a Workforce Investment Board to help develop a plan for implementing the law.

Basically, centers were established in each state to provide job seekers with a wide range of services, from skill assessment and counseling to training and job search assistance. The centers help people new to the job market develop work-readiness skills and find employment, and will also provide ongoing support. The impact of both the Welfare to Work Partnership and the Workforce Investment Act is that businesses have access to larger labor pools, training, and funding that can assist making them more competitive. They are also able to staff and maintain a workforce that is up to the task of facing a global challenge.

More Women Entering the Workforce

The fact that more women are in the workplace means that many of their traditional roles in society have shifted, out of necessity or convenience, to service providers such as cleaners, cooks, and child care providers. The tasks previously handled by the stay-at-home wife and mother are now being handled by the employees of various service companies. And, with these numbers continuing to grow each year, the need for more and better service providers will increase proportionately as workers search for someone to handle chores once delegated to the traditional homemaker.

As a matter of fact, the Department of Labor has published statistics showing that the number of women in the workplace, in all age groups, continues to grow more rapidly than the number of men. As a result, women's share of the workplace is projected to increase from about 47 percent in 2000 to approximately 48 percent in 2010.[4]

A More Diverse Population Is Entering the Workforce

As with the entrance of women into the workforce, the increase in numbers of people of color entering the workforce will have a profound impact on the business environment. Not only are the members of this expanded worker category bringing with them new ideas, values, expectations, needs, and levels of knowledge, experience, and ability, but as consumers themselves, they bring a better understanding of the needs of the various groups that they represent. By 2010, projections are that Hispanics will enter the workforce at a faster pace than in the past until their numbers will be larger than those of the African–American population. During the same period, white non-Hispanic workers will continue to make up two-thirds of the labor force.[5] (Figure 1.6)

A population made up of women, ethnically different, older people, and those with other diverse characteristics, make a better understanding of various groups essential for service success. *How can you improve your own knowledge of different groups so that you can better serve?*

You will explore these trends, and other diversity factors, further in Chapter 8.

[4]H. N. Fullerton, Jr., and M. Toosi, "Labor Force Projections to 2010: Steady Growth and Changing Composition," *Monthly Labor Review*, U.S. Department of Labor, Bureau of Labor Statistics, Washington D.C., November 2001, p. 21.
[5]Ibid.

FIGURE 1.6
Civilian Labor Force 1990–2000 and Projected 2010
(totals based on thousands of workers who stay in the workforce)

Source: U.S. Department of Labor, Bureau of Labor Statistics, Office of Occupational Statistics and Employment Projections.

Group	1990	1990–2000 Entrants	1990–2000 Stayers	2000	2000–2010 Entrants	2000–2010 Stayers	2010
Total	125,840	34,669	106,194	140,864	41,048	116,673	157,721
Men	69,011	17,783	57,464	75,247	20,379	61,842	82,221
Women	56,829	16,886	48,730	65,617	20,669	54,831	75,550
White non-Hispanic	97,818	21,363	81,599	192,962	24,873	84,245	109,118
Men	53,731	11,214	44,145	55,359	12,583	44,955	57,538
Women	44,087	10,149	37,455	47,604	12,290	39,290	51,580
Black non-Hispanic	13,566	4,694	11,435	16,129	5,627	13,286	18,913
Men	6,727	2,004	5,564	7,568	2,463	6,043	8,507
Women	6,839	2,689	5,872	8,561	3,164	7,243	10,407
Hispanic origin	10,720	5,667	9,700	15,368	7,331	13,617	20,947
Men	6,546	3,026	5,893	8,919	3,802	7,902	11,723
Women	4,174	2,641	3,807	6,449	3,511	5,713	9,224
Asian & other, non-Hispanic	3,735	2,946	3,459	6,404	3,218	5,526	8,743
Men	2,007	1,539	1,862	3,401	1,513	2,940	4,453
Women	1,728	1,406	1,597	3,003	1,705	2,586	4,290
Share (percent)	100%	100%	100%	100%	100%	100%	100%
Men	54.8	51.3	54.1	53.4	49.6	53.0	52.1
Women	45.2	48.7	45.9	46.6	50.4	47.0	47.9

More Older Workers Entering the Workforce

Think about the last time you went to a fast-food restaurant or a retail store like McDonald's, Wendy's, Burger King, Wal-Mart, Big Kmart, or Target. Did you notice the number of people serving and assisting you who seemed to be older than people you usually see in those roles? This relatively new phenomenon is the result of a variety of social factors. The most significant factor is that the median age of people in the United States is rising because of the aging of the "baby boom" generation (those born between 1946 and 1964).[6] For example, according to an *Orlando Sentinel* newspaper article of January 1, 2000, the average age of a resident in Orlando, Florida, was 36. And, from a workplace perspective, this means that more of the people in this age group will stay in the workplace or return once they leave. This may be caused by pure economic necessity, since many people may have not prepared adequately for retirement and cannot be certain that the Social Security system will support them. Some people return to the workplace for social reasons—they miss the work and/or the opportunity to interact with others and feel useful. Whatever the reason for the desire or willingness of older workers to reenter the workflow, many organizations have realized that they often have an admirable work ethic. Also, since there are not enough entry-level people in the traditional pool of younger workers (because of smaller birthrates during the 1970s), companies are actively recruiting older workers.

[6]According to U.S. Department of Labor Statistics, the baby boom generation (people born between 1946 and 1964) is one of the largest population groups in the country.

Desire for Better Use of Leisure Time

Nowadays, Americans and workers of other developed nations are enjoying increasing amounts of leisure time. In the United States, many workers now have more disposable income and as a whole are growing older. More Americans also have more money at their disposal. The 2000 Census shows that four in ten households earn in excess of $50,000 per year.

Americans and workers in other developed nations are enjoying increasing amounts of leisure time and purchasing products and services that aid their relaxation. *What can you do that will save time and effort for your customers and allow them more time to enjoy their leisure activities?*

Additionally, three in ten black households have achieved middle- and upper-income status. These factors have heightened a desire to relax, enjoy children and grandchildren, and do other things that they value—people want to use their free time in more personally satisfying ways. To accomplish this, they now rely more heavily on service organizations to maintain their desired lifestyle. Examples of some of the services tapped by the members of today's society are personal grocery shopping services, lawn services, dog walkers, laundry pickup and delivery, and executive book summaries that condense current business publications to a three- or four-page synopsis of key points.

Expectation of Quality Service

Most customers expect that if they pay a fair dollar, in return they will receive a quality product or service. If their expectations are not met, customers simply call or visit a competing company where they can receive what they think they paid for. Examples of the power of the consumer was the spending of billions of dollars by the U.S. government and businesses to ensure that the so-called **Y2K** bug did not debilitate computer systems at the stroke of midnight on December 31, 1999. Had preventive measures not been taken to fix a programming oversight made decades ago, there would have been a monumental consumer outcry as services shut down across the country and world. Another example of consumer clout was the initiatives to shore up the electrical grid system following the 2003 blackout because of public and political outrage.

The expectation of quality service that most consumers have also creates a need for better-trained and better-educated customer service professionals. Not only do these professionals need up-to-date product information, but they also need to be abreast of current organizational policies and procedures, what the competition offers, and the latest techniques in customer service and satisfaction.

Better-Educated Customers

Customers today are not only more highly educated than in the past, they are also well informed about the price, quality, and value of products and services. This has occurred in part through the advertising and publicity by companies competing for market share and by the activities of consumer information and advocacy groups that have surfaced. As Syms, a discount-clothing store, used to tout in its advertising, "An informed consumer is our best customer." That advertising campaign was based on the belief that if you shop around and compare quality and costs, you will come back to Syms. This type of strategy sends a message that "we have nothing to hide" and invites customer confidence.

Armed with knowledge about what they should receive for their money, consumers make it extremely difficult for less than reputable businesspeople to prosper or survive. With consumers now on the defensive and ready to fight back, all business owners find that they have to continually prove the worth of their products and services. They must provide customer satisfaction or face losing customers to competitors.

Increased Number of Small Businesses

The law defines a small business as "one that is independently owned and operated and is not dominant in its field of operation." In 2002, there were 22.9 million small businesses in the United States, which provide approximately 75 percent of the net new jobs added to the economy. Further, small businesses employ 50.1 percent of the private workforce and make 40.9 percent of private sales in the country while representing 97 percent of all U.S. exporters, according to the U.S. **Small Business Administration (SBA)**.[7]

Women and minorities play a major role in growth of small businesses. In 2000, women represented 38 percent of the self-employed and by 2001 owned over 9 million businesses in the United States. Minorities own 15 percent of American businesses, 99 percent of which are small businesses. These numbers show the power of women and minorities in shaping the economy of the United States and in providing products and services to millions of consumers.

Growth of E-Commerce

The last decade of the twentieth century was witness to unimagined use of the personal computer and the Internet by the average person. By 2003, e-commerce sales topped 12.5 billion dollars, which was a 27.8 percent increase from the previous year. Almost any product is available at the click of a mouse or keyboard, or voice command. Consumers regularly "surf the net" for values in products and services without ever leaving their homes or office. This new way of accessing goods and services through technology has been termed **e-commerce**.

Armed with a password, site addresses, and credit cards, shoppers use this virtual marketplace to satisfy needs that they likely did not know they had before logging onto their computer and connecting with the Internet. And, with so many options available for just a small investment of time, they can comparison shop simply by changing screens. No wonder the twentieth century saw the establishment of more millionaires and billionaires than any of its predecessors. The creators and owners of the most innovative sites and products can provide products and services worldwide without ever physically coming into contact with a customer, and yet can amass huge reserves of money. Examples of these success stories are eBay (an online auction service) and Amazon.com (an online book and product seller and auction line), which have become household names and are used by millions of shoppers yearly.

5 The Customer Service Environment

Concept: In this section the six components that make up a service environment and contribute to customer service delivery are discussed. Use these factors to ensure that a viable customer service environment is the responsibility of every employee of the organization—not just the customer service representatives.

---

[7]See <http://www.sba.gov/aboutba/sbastats.html>.

LEADERSHIP INITIATIVE   1.2

Stress the importance of service with employees for Customer Service Week in October of each year. Plan a number of service-oriented functions and celebrate your customers and service staff. Some possibilities include:

- Announce a jeans/casual day or week in which employees can come to work in less formal attire.
- Schedule a motivational speaker or humorist for an employee luncheon.
- Have a massage therapist come in to spend the day giving employees head and neck massages at their desks.
- Distribute gift bags with small presents (for example, hand lotion, scented candles, candy, or easy-listening music CDs).

- Pass out word search puzzles that contain service-related terms. As employees complete and turn them in throughout the day, give small prizes.
- Have a scavenger hunt by giving all employees a list of ten items to find. Reward the winner with prizes, give lapel buttons or T-shirts with customer service phrases on them, and celebrate the event with a pizza lunch.
- Decorate the work area with colorful streamers, balloons, customer service banners, and smiley face posters.
- Offer a stress management workshop for all employees.
- Start off Customer Service Week with a speech from a key executive, decorations, clowns, jugglers, and other fun activities.

FIGURE 1.7
Components of a Customer-Focused Environment

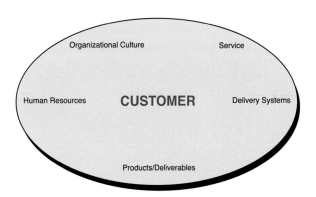

Let's take time to examine the six key components of a **customer service environment**, which will illustrate many factors that contribute to customer service delivery:

1. The customer
2. Organizational culture
3. Human resources
4. Products/deliverables
5. Delivery systems
6. Service

What goes into the making of quality customer service? This is discussed in the following sections.

The Customer

As shown in Figure 1.7, the key component in a customer-focused environment is the customer. All aspects of the service organization revolve around the customer. Without the customer, there is no reason for any organization to exist. And, since

Take a few minutes to think about your current organization or select any organization with which you have been associated and create two lists: one of your internal customers and another of your suppliers. Then compare your lists to see which customers also act as suppliers and help you better serve the external customers of your organization.

all employees have customers, either internal or external, there must be a continuing consciousness of the need to provide exceptional, enthusiastic customer service. As Karl Albrecht and Ron Zemke say in their book *Service America,* "If you're not serving the customer, you'd better be serving someone who is." This is true because if you aren't providing stellar support and service to internal customers, external customers usually suffer.

Internal Customers

Many people in the workplace will tell you that they do not have "customers." They are wrong. Anyone in an organization has customers. They may not be traditional customers who come to buy or use products or services. Instead, they are **internal customers** who are coworkers, employees of other departments or branches, and other people who work within the same organization. They also rely on others in their organization to provide services, information, and/or products that enable them to do their jobs.

Recognizing this formidable group of customers is important and crucial for on-the-job success. That is because, in the internal customer chain, an employee is sometimes a customer and at other times a supplier. At times, you may call a coworker in another department for information. Later that same day, this coworker may call you for a similar reason. For example, suppose you work in the service center of a company that sells automobile parts. The people in the accounting department might provide services to you in the form of a biweekly paycheck or information on customer accounts (supplier). At other times, they may call to request customer information related to an order so that they can ensure accuracy of an invoice (customer). Only when both parties are acutely aware of their role in this customer-supplier relationship can the organization effectively prosper and grow to full potential.

External Customers

External customers may be current or potential customers or clients. They are the ones who actively seek out, research, and buy, rent, or lease products or services offered by your organization. This group can involve business customers who purchase your product to include with its own for resale. It can also involve an organization that acts as a franchise or distributor. Such an organization buys your products to resell or uses them to represent your company in their geographic area.

Organizational Culture

Without the mechanisms and atmosphere to support frontline service, the other components of the business environment cannot succeed. Put simply, **organizational culture** is what the customer experiences. This culture is made up of a collection of subcomponents, each of which contributes to the overall service environment. The impact of culture on customer satisfaction is discussed further in Chapter 2.

Human Resources

To make the culture work, an organization must take great care in recruiting, selecting, and training qualified people—its **human resources**. That's why, when you apply (or applied) for a job as a customer service professional, a thorough screening process will be (or was) used to identify your skills, knowledge, and aptitudes. Without motivated, competent workers, planning, policy, and procedure change or systems adaptation will not make a difference in customer service. Many organizations go to great lengths to obtain and retain the "right" employees who possess the knowledge, skills, and competencies to professionally serve customers. Employees who are skilled, motivated, and enthusiastic about providing service excellence are hard to find and are appreciated by employers and customers. As noted earlier, organizations now rely on all employees to provide service excellence to customers; however, they also maintain specially trained "elite" groups of employees who perform specific customer-related functions. Depending on their organization's focus, these individuals have a variety of titles (for example, a customer service representative in a retail organization might be called a *member counselor* in an association, but these employees often perform similar functions). Some typical titles and functions performed by customer service personnel in organizations are described in the next sections.

Customer Service (CS)/Member Support Clerk

This is typically an entry-level position requiring strong organizational ability, an ability to follow instructions, listen, and manage time, and a desire to help. Key functions are clerical support, which includes filing, researching information, typing, and similar assignments.

Customer Service (CS) Representative/Member Counselor

This position is an entry-level position into the customer service field (although many people have years of experience in the job). Since these employees interact directly with customers and potential customers, they need strong interpersonal (communication, conflict management, listening) skills as well as a desire to help others, a fondness for working with people, a knowledge of organizational products and services, and thorough understanding of what a CS representative does. Key functions include interacting face-to-face or over the telephone with customers, receiving and processing orders or requests for information and services, responding to customer inquiries, handling complaints, and performing associated customer contact assignments.

Data Entry/Order Clerk

The data entry/order clerk is an entry-level position requiring knowledge of personal computers and software, ability to work on repetitive tasks for long periods of time, and an eye for accuracy. Key functions include verifying and batching

Work It Out 1.4   Types of Service

Take a minute to think about customer service. In what ways do organizations typically provide service to external customers?

Think about organizational strategies aimed at recruiting and training service employees. What are some things you have heard or read about that companies are doing to attract, hire, and keep qualified employees?

orders received from customer service representatives for input by computer personnel. In organizations that have personal computer systems connected by networks, data entry/order clerks enter data, and generate and maintain reports.

Senior Customer Service (CS) Representative/Member Counselor

This position is usually staffed by personnel with experience as CS representative. A position like this one requires a person with a sound understanding of basic supervisory skills, since job duties may include providing feedback, training, and support and administering performance appraisals to other representatives or counselors.

Service Technicians or Professionals

This group provides many different types of services and carries a variety of titles (for example, air-conditioning technologist, plumber, automotive specialist, office equipment technician, law enforcement officer, firefighter, sanitation worker). Each specialized area requires specific knowledge and skills.

Inbound/Outbound Telemarketing Specialist

Customer service representatives may perform some or all of the functions of this job, but often specially hired or trained employees fill the position. In many organizations these employees are full-time or part-time sales personnel whose job is to use the telephone to call customers or potential customers or receive orders or questions from customers. Employees in these positions need strong self-confidence because of the number of rejections to offers and irate calls they receive, sound verbal communication and listening skills, positive attitude, good knowledge of sales techniques, ability to handle people who are upset, and a desire to help others through identification and satisfaction of needs. Key functions include placing and/or receiving calls, responding to inquiries with product and service information, asking for and recording orders, and following up on leads and requests for information.

In addition to these positions, many organizations have supervisor, manager, director, and vice president positions in most of the job areas indicated or in the service area as a whole. The existence of higher-level positions provides opportunities for upward advancement and learning as experience is gained.

Products/Deliverables

The fourth component of a service environment is the product or **deliverable** offered by an organization. The product or deliverable may be a tangible item manufactured or distributed by the company, such as a piece of furniture, or a service available to the customer, such as a pest extermination service. In either case, there are two potential areas of customer satisfaction or dissatisfaction—quality and quantity. If your customers receive what they perceive as a quality product or service to the level that they expected, and in the time frame promised or viewed as acceptable, they will likely be happy. On the other hand, if customers believe that they were sold an inferior product or given an inferior service or one that does not match their expectations, they will likely be dissatisfied and could take their business elsewhere. They may also provide negative word-of-mouth advertising for the organization.

Delivery Systems

The fifth component of an effective service environment is the method(s) by which the product or service is delivered. In deciding on **delivery systems**, organizations examine the following factors.

> *Industry standards:* How is the competition currently delivering? Are current organizational delivery standards in line with those of competitors?
>
> *Customer expectations:* Do customers expect delivery to occur in a certain manner within a specified time frame? Are alternatives acceptable?
>
> *Capabilities:* Do existing or available systems within the organization and industry allow for a variety of delivery methods?
>
> *Costs:* Will providing a variety of techniques add real or perceived value at an acceptable cost? If there are additional costs, will consumers be willing to absorb them?
>
> *Current and projected requirements:* Are existing methods of delivery, such as mail, phone, and face-to-face service meeting the needs of the customer and will they continue to do so in the future?

Service

Stated simply, **service** is the manner in which you and other employees treat your customers and each other as you deliver your company's product(s) or other deliverables. Effective use of the techniques and strategies outlined later in this book is required in order to satisfy the needs of your customers.

6   Why Should Organizations Provide Good Service?

Concept: Without high-level customer service, companies lose business. The following chapters will build on the techniques and skills you need to develop and/or sharpen to keep this from happening.

Although the idea may seem almost too simple, the bottom line is that without high-level customer service, companies lose business. The remaining chapters will show you exactly what to do, and what skills to develop and sharpen, to stop this from happening. We'll look at why customers leave, and what can be done to prevent them from leaving.

Work It Out 1.6

The Customer Perspective

To get a better understanding of how your customers feel about service and their expectations, put yourself in the customer's place and answer the following question. As a customer, once you make a purchase or sign a lease, what do you expect of a product and the company selling or leasing it? Explain.

Once you have answered the question, your instructor will group students for an exchange of ideas and discussion.

Chapter Summary

As many organizations move toward a more quality-oriented, customer-focused environment, developing and fine-tuning policies, procedures, and systems to better identify customer needs and meet their expectations will be crucial. Through a concerted effort to perfect service delivery, organizations will be able to survive and compete in a global economy. More emphasis must be placed on finding out what the consumer expects and going beyond those expectations. Total customer satisfaction is not just a buzz phrase; it is a way of life that companies are adopting in order to gain and maintain market share. As a customer service professional, it will be your job to help foster a customer-oriented service environment.

SERVICE IN ACTION   AAA   CHAPTER 1

http://www.aaanewsroom.net

Formed in 1902, AAA is a not-for-profit federation that has grown to be the largest automobile club in the world with over 38,000 full-time employees in 1,100 offices (U.S. and Canada) serving over 45 million members. In addition to sponsoring the AAA Foundation for Traffic Safety, the School Safety Patrol Program throughout the United States, and many other safety initiatives over the years, AAA provides services to its member. Chief among the benefits to members are roadside assistance programs for stranded motorists. Members can visit one of the local AAA offices to purchase luggage and other travel prod-

ucts, make reservations for car rentals, hotels, and transportation, or book a cruise. AAA also offers many other services, including insurance (for example, travel, automobile, life, homeowners, and travelers), travel planning services, free maps and tour guides, car buying services, credit cards and financial services, and automobile-related services.

A key to AAA's success has been its focus on member responsiveness, quality service, and the trust that have been established through over a century of dedication to members, the community, and the United States and Canada.

Key Terms and Concepts

- business-to-business (B2B)
- cottage industry
- customer-focused organization
- customer relationship management (CRM)
- customer service
- customer service environment
- deliverables
- delivery systems
- deregulation
- downsizing
- e-commerce
- external customers
- globalization
- human resources
- internal customers
- learning organization
- networking
- North American Free Trade Agreement (NAFTA)
- organizational culture
- products
- service
- service economy
- service industry
- service recovery
- service sector
- Small Business Administration (SBA)
- telecommuting
- Welfare to Work Partnership
- Workforce Investment Act of 1998
- Y2K

Quick Preview Answers

1. T	5. F	9. T
2. F	6. T	10. T
3. T	7. F	11. T
4. T	8. T	12. T

Chapter Review Questions

Either on your own or in discussion with someone else, review what you have learned in this chapter by responding to the following questions:

1. What is service?
2. Describe some of the earliest forms of customer service.
3. What are some of the factors that have facilitated the shift to a service economy?
4. Why are more organizations developing specially trained customer service personnel?
5. What have been some of the causes of the changing business environment in recent decades?
6. What are the six key components of a customer service environment?
7. Describe the impact of a company's culture on its success in a customer-focused business environment.
8. What role does the human resources element of the customer service environment play in customer satisfaction?
9. What two factors related to an organization's products or deliverables can lead to customer satisfaction or dissatisfaction?
10. When organizations select a delivery method for products or services, where do they get information on the best approach to take?

Search It Out

Searching the Web for Salary and Related Information

To learn more about the history, background, and components of customer service occupations, select one of the topics below, log on to the Internet, and gather additional research data. One valuable site is the U.S. Department of Labor at <**http://stats.bls.gov**>.

Report your findings to your work team members, peers, or students depending on the setting in which you are using this book.

- Research the projected salaries and benefits for customer service providers in your industry or in one that interests you.
- Develop a bibliographic listing of books and other publications on topics introduced in this chapter. The resources should be less than five years old.

You can do this by going to sites such as:

<**http://www.Amazon.com**>
<**http://www.Borders.com**>
<**http://www.bn.com**>
<**http://www.glencoe.com/ps**>
<**http://www.books.mcgraw-hill.com**>

- Find the websites of at least three companies that you believe have adopted a positive customer service attitude and are benefiting as a result.
- Select any issue raised in this chapter and research it further.

Note: A listing of websites for additional research on specific URLs is provided on the Customer Service website at <**www.mhhe.com/lucas05**>.

Face to Face

Getting Ready for New Employee Orientation at PackAll

Background

PackAll is a packing and storage company headquartered in Minneapolis, Minnesota, with franchises located in 21 cities throughout the United States. Since opening its first franchise in Minneapolis in 1987, the company has shown great market potential, ending its first year with a profit and growing every year since.

The primary services of the organization are packaging and preparing nonperishable items for shipment and mailing via parcel post. Air-conditioned spaces for short-term storage of personal items and post office boxes are also available to customers.

To ensure consistency of service at all locations, specific standards for employee training and service delivery have been developed and implemented. Before owners or operators can hang up their PackAll sign, they must sign an agreement to comply with standards and must successfully complete a rigorous eight-week management-training program. The program focuses on the key management and business skills necessary to run a successful business and educates employees on corporate philosophy and culture. In addition management offers tips for guiding employee development. At intervals of three and six months after opening their operation, owners or operators are required to participate in a retreat during which they share best practices, receive additional management training, and have an opportunity to ask questions in a structured setting.

Your Role

Today, you joined a PackAll franchise in Orlando, Florida, as a customer service representative. New-employee orientation will be held tomorrow. At that time, you will learn about the service culture, policies and procedures, techniques for handling customers, and specific job skills and requirements.

Before being hired, you were told that your primary duties would be to service customers, provide information about services offered, write up customer orders, collect payments, and package and label orders.

Critical Thinking Questions

1. What interpersonal skills do you currently have that will allow you to be successful in your new position?
2. What general questions about handling customers do you have for your supervisor?
3. If a customer asks for a service that PackAll does not provide, how will you handle the situation? Exactly what will you say?

PLANNING TO SERVE

Working alone or with others, create a list of the major issues facing the service industry or your organization (if you are working) and which directly impact you. Also, list strategies that you can implement to personally address these issues.

To do this, draw a line down the center of a sheet of blank paper. On the left side write the word "Issues" and on the right side, the word "Strategies."

Here is an example of one issue with strategies to address it:

Issue	Strategies
Service industry is growing quickly.	Do Internet research to gather statistics on an occupation that I am currently in or in which I am interested. Identify geographic areas of opportunity, possible salary and benefits, and specific targeted employers.

Contributing to the Service Culture

From the Frontline Interview

David Littlehale has been in higher education publishing since 1979, when he started as a sales representative. Subsequent jobs have included serving as marketing manager, regional sales manager, and national sales manager, which have all had customer service (internal and external) as a primary focus.

1 What elements of an organization do you believe impact its service culture? Why?

Virtually all elements of the organization can have an impact on customers, but a service culture begins and ends with people. Leaders create the vision but frontline service providers provide the know-how to make it happen. Things like systems, bureaucracy/organizational structure, reward systems all play a role but committed, enthusiastic people solve lots of organizational problems, all the time.

2 What do you believe is the role of management in creating and maintaining a positive service culture? Why?

Management has the most important role in creating an organization and culture that cares passionately about great

DAVID LITTLEHALE, VP, National Sales Manager, McGraw-Hill/Irwin

customer service. It starts with hiring talented people and giving them the training and tools to do a great job, then holding them accountable. What are the priorities, what are the things that managers are paying attention to and measuring/rewarding? These choices drive employee behavior and need to be consistent with an unwavering focus on the customer. Finally, managers have the opportunity to be great role models of the kind and with the attitude and behavior that define a positive service culture. What we do matters much more than what we say.

3 What do you believe is the role of employees in creating and maintaining a positive service culture? Why?

In the most positive service cultures, employees are given the opportunity (are empowered) to take ownership of the customer experience and encouraged to be responsive and service-oriented in all their actions. The best employees love this opportunity and thrive in an organization that tells them to be proactive, to offer solutions and to resolve customer issues quickly. In fact, in my experience, almost every

"After you discover what your customers really want, you can turn to establishing your business goals and a strategy to achieve them. Whatever they are, they should be oriented toward the customer." Jan Carlzon, President, Scandinavian Airlines in his book Moments of Truth

Chapter Learning Objectives

After completing this chapter, you will be able to:

- Explain the elements of a service culture.
- Describe the job responsibilities of a typical service provider.
- Realize that service delivery is similar in large and small organizations.

- Recognize customer-friendly systems.
- Implement strategies for promoting a positive service culture.

employee *wants* to do the right thing and enjoys delivering great service and our job as managers sometimes is to just empower them, get out of the way, and support their instinctively great work.

4 In what way can an organization's culture negatively impact customer service?

Organizations can put up lots of barriers to great service, throw things in the way of people who want to do a great job for their customers. Big organizations are especially adept at complicating processes, and a more formal and bureaucratic approach to decision making. Dilbert rings true far too

often. Staying close to the customer is an exhausting effort at times and the culture has to reinforce the do or die nature of these relationships.

Critical Thinking

Based on David's responses, how well do you think customer service works in his organization? Why do you believe that? Do you agree or disagree with what he said? Why or why not?

Quick Preview

Before reviewing the chapter content, respond to the following questions by placing a "T" for true or an "F" for false on the rules. Use any questions you miss as a checklist of material to which you will pay particular attention as you read through the chapter. For those you get right, congratulate yourself, but review the sections they address in order to learn additional details about the topic.

_____ 1. Service cultures include such things as policies and procedures.

_____ 2. To remain competitive, organizations must continually monitor and evaluate their systems.

_____ 3. Advertising, service delivery, and complaint resolution are examples of customer-friendly systems.

_____ 4. To better face daily challenges and opportunities in the workplace, you should strive to increase your knowledge, build your skills, and improve your attitude.

_____ 5. Some of the tools used by organizations to measure service culture include employee focus groups, mystery shoppers, and customer lotteries.

_____ 6. By determining the added value and results for me (AVARFM), you can develop more personal commitment to service excellence.

_____ 7. Use of "they" language to refer to management when dealing with customers helps demonstrate your commitment to your organization and its culture.

_____ 8. Communicating openly and effectively is one technique for working more closely with customers.

_____ 9. Even though you depend on vendors and suppliers, they are not your customers.

_____ 10. Business etiquette dictates that you should return all telephone calls within four hours.

_____ 11. Your job of servicing a customer should end at the conclusion of a transaction so that you can switch your attention to new customers.

_____ 12. Customers want value for their money and effective, efficient service.

Answers to Quick Preview can be found at the end of the chapter.

1   Defining a Service Culture

Concept: Many elements contribute to a service culture.

What is a **service culture** in an organization? The answer is that it is different for each organization. No two organizations operate in the same manner, have the same focus, or provide management that accomplishes the same results. Among other things, a culture includes the values, beliefs, norms, rituals, and practices of a group or organization. Any policy, procedure, action, or inaction on the part of your organization contributes to the service culture. Figure 2.1 provides an overview of the typical elements of a service culture. Other elements may be specific to your organization or industry. You play a key role in communicating the culture to your customers. You may communicate through your appearance, your interaction with customers, and your knowledge, skill, and attitude. Culture also

FIGURE 2.1
Elements of a
Service Culture

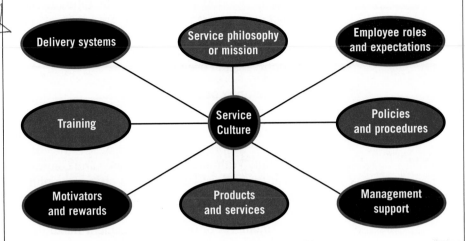

Many elements define a successful organization. Some of the more common are shown here.

Service philosophy or mission: The direction or vision of an organization that supports day-to-day interactions with the customer.

Employee roles and expectations: The specific communications or measures that indicate what is expected of employees in customer interactions and that define how employee service performance will be evaluated.

Delivery systems: The way an organization delivers its products and services.

Policies and procedures: The guidelines that establish how various situations or transactions will be handled.

Products and services: The materials, products, and services that are state of the art, competitively priced, and meet the needs of customers.

Management support: The availability of management to answer questions and assist front-line employees in customer interactions when necessary. Also, the level of management involvement and enthusiasm in coaching and mentoring professional development.

Motivators and rewards: Monetary rewards, material items, or feedback that prompts employees to continue to deliver service and perform at a high level of effectiveness and efficiency.

Training: Instruction or information provided through a variety of techniques that teach knowledge or skills, or attempt to influence employee attitude toward excellent service delivery.

encompasses your products and services, and the physical appearance of the organization's facility, equipment, or any other aspect of the organization with which the customer comes into contact. Unfortunately, many companies are product-centered and view customers from the standpoint of what company products or services they use. Successful organizations are customer-centered and focus on individual needs.

An organization's service culture is made up of many facets, each of which affects the customer and helps determine the success or failure of customer service initiatives. Too often, organizations overpromise and underdeliver because their cultural and internal systems (*infrastructure*) do not have the ability to support customer service initiatives. For example, suppose that management has the marketing department develop a slick piece of literature describing all the benefits of a new product or service provided by a new corporate partner. Then a special 800 number is set up to handle customer responses, but no additional staff is hired to handle the customer calls. The project is likely doomed to fail because adequate service support has not been planned.

Service Philosophy or Mission

Generally, an organization's approach to business, **mission** or its **service philosophy,** is driven from the top of the organization. Upper management, including members of the board of directors, when appropriate, sets the vision or tone and direction of the organization. Without a clearly planned and communicated vision, the service ethic ends at the highest levels. This is often a stumbling block where many organizations falter because of indecision or dissension at the upper echelons.

Leadership, real and perceived, is crucial to service success. In successful organizations, members of upper management make themselves clearly visible to frontline employees and are in tune with customer needs and expectations.

Although it is wonderful when organizations go to the trouble of developing and hanging a nicely framed formal mission or philosophy statement on the wall, if it is not a functional way of life for employees, it serves little purpose. (Figure 2.2 shows some typical philosophy or mission statements.)

Employee Roles and Expectations

In addition to some of the job responsibilities of service providers described in Chapter 1, many tasks and responsibilities are assigned to frontline service providers. Depending on your job, the size and type of your organization, and the industry involved, the **employee roles** and **expectations** may be similar from one organization to another, and yet they may be performed in a variety of different ways. Such roles and expectations are normally included in your job description and in your performance goals. They are updated as necessary during your tenure on the job. Where goals are concerned, you are typically measured against them during a performance period and subsequently rewarded or not rewarded, depending on your performance and your organization's policy.

RUMBA

For you and your organization to be successful in providing superior service to your external and internal customers, your roles and expectations must be clearly defined and communicated in terms of the following characteristics, sometimes referred to as **RUMBA** (realistic, understandable, measurable, believable, attainable).

Realistic Your behavior and responsibilities must be in line with the reality of your particular workplace and customer base. Although it is possible to transfer a standard of performance from one organization, and even industry, to another, modifications may be necessary to fit your specific situation. For example, is it realistic that all customer calls must be handled within a specified time period? Many managers set specific goals in terms of "talk time" for their customer service representatives. Can every angry customer be calmed and handled in a two- to three-minute time frame? If not, then a standard such as this sets up employees for failure.

After a performance goal has been set for you, evaluate it fairly and objectively for a period of time (possibly 30 days). This allows time for a variety of

Think about your own organization's service culture or, if you're not actively working as a customer service professional, the culture of an organization with which you are familiar.

1. What do you believe the service philosophy of this organization to be? Why?
2. Are there things that make the organization unique? If so, what are they?
3. What factors (positive or negative) about employee performance in this organization stand out in your mind?
4. Are there factors about the culture that detract from effectiveness? If so, what are they?

FIGURE 2.2
Sample Vision or Mission Statements

Organizations of all sizes and types have mission or vision statements, designed to communicate values and purpose to customers and employees.

A.B. Dick Company: "A.B. Dick will be the leading provider of broad-based, customer-driven solutions in an ever-changing graphic arts marketplace. To accomplish this, we will:
• Offer a broad range of efficient and reliable, traditional and digital solutions, supported by dedicated service, for the graphic arts market.
• Adapt to changing customer needs with an ongoing focus on stakeholder value.
• Foster a culture that drives employee commitment and ethical behavior."

Yamaha Motor Company: "We create 'Kando'—Touching People's Hearts. We at Yamaha Motor Company are committed to creating a higher level of customer satisfaction, using our ingenuity and enthusiasm to enrich people's lives."

Procter & Gamble: "We will provide products of superior quality and value that improve the lives of the world's consumers. As a result, consumers will reward us with leadership sales and profit growth, allowing our people, our shareholders, and the communities in which we live and work to prosper."

Creative Presentation Resources, Inc: "Our mission is to partner with clients in order to deliver timely, world-class human resource development interventions and products at a fair, competitive price."

Nissan Global: "Enriching people's lives."

Brunswick Hills Police Department: "It is the mission of the Brunswick Hills Police Department to enforce the laws of the United States of America, the State of Ohio, and the Resolutions of Brunswick Hills Township. Further, it is our mission to enforce the law with impartiality and courtesy, to respect the Constitutional Rights of all people, and to provide services to citizens of Brunswick Hills Township that will enhance their quality of life."

Juvenile Diabetes Foundation: "To find a cure for diabetes and its complications through the support of research."

Southwest Airlines: "The mission of Southwest Airlines is dedication to the highest quality of Customer Service delivered with a sense of warmth, friendliness, individual pride, and Company Spirit."

opportunities to apply it. At the end of the specified trial period, if you think the goal is unrealistic, go to your supervisor or team leader and discuss modifying it. In preparation for this discussion, think of at least two viable alternatives to the goals. Also, recognize that performance goals are often driven by organizational goals and those passed down from upper management. Although they might be modified, it may take some time for the change to come about, so be

LEADERSHIP INITIATIVE   2.1

Providing support to your service staff is an important role that supervisors and managers assume. To ensure that this responsibility is met, competent managers continually reevaluate policies and procedures to ensure that they do not conflict with mission and vision statements. They also set realistic performance goals and provide ongoing coaching and mentoring to those employees delivering direct service to internal and external customers. Although profit is the ultimate goal of many organizations, you can never lose sight of the fact that your customers must be your first priority in meeting profit and performance goals.

patient. Ultimately, if the goal cannot be modified, do your best to perform within the established standard so that your professional image does not suffer.

Understandable   You must have a sound understanding of your performance goals before you can act appropriately and effectively, just the way you need to understand how to do your job or how to communicate with others in the workplace. You should first try to participate in the establishment of your goals and those of your department or team. Once goals are in place, you and everyone else affected must have a clear understanding of them so that you can effectively reach the assigned goal.

As part of the understanding step, you should apply all the skills covered in Chapters 3 to 5 related to giving and receiving information effectively. If you do not understand your goals and responsibilities, ask for clarification.

Measurable   Can your performance be measured? Yes. Typically, factors such as time, productivity, quantifiable results, revenue, or manner of performance (how you accomplish your job tasks in terms of following an established step-by-step formula) are used to determine your accomplishment of goals. In a production environment, or in certain sales environments, performance can be measured by reviewing the number of products made or sales completed. In a purely customer-focused environment, **service measurement** can be in terms of factors such as talk time on the telephone, number of customers effectively served, customer feedback surveys and satisfaction cards, and letters or other written correspondence—or, on the negative side, by customer complaints.

Whatever the measure, it is your responsibility to be sure that you know the acceptable level and do your best to perform to that level. If something inhibits your performance, or if organizational obstacles such as conflicting priorities, overburdening multiple assignments, policies, procedures, equipment, or other employees stand in your way, you should immediately discuss the difficulties with the appropriate authority.

Believable   For any goal to be attained, it must be believable to the people who will strive to reach it and to the supervisors who will monitor it. The biggest issues in developing goals are to make them believable and to ensure that they make sense and tie in directly with the established overall departmental and organizational goals. Too often, employees are given assignments that are contrary to the ultimate purpose or mission of the organization. For example, suppose that your organizational philosophy states in part that your purpose is "to provide quality products at a competitive price in a low-pressure customer atmosphere." Your supervisor establishes a goal that requires you to have "x" number of sales per shift as an outbound sales representative. This number is two more than the typical average for a salesperson during a work shift. You recognize that to achieve this goal, you will have to be more "persuasive" than usual or than you feel comfortable.

The supervisor is putting you in the awkward position of either making your goals or facing punitive actions and losing rewards. Moreover, this practice can violate some basic principles of ethical behavior. This practice also defeats the part of the organizational philosophy that states, "in a low-pressure customer atmosphere." The topic of ethics will be discussed later in this chapter in the section "Twelve Strategies for Promoting a Positive Service Culture."

Attainable   Given the right training, management support, and organizational environment in which the tools, information, assistance, and rewards are provided, you can attain your goals. The determining factor, however, is you and your attitude toward achieving agreed-upon levels.

Managers should always attempt to set up win-win situations in which you, your organization, and ultimately, the customer benefit from any service encounter. However, you should be aware that in the "real world," this does not always happen—systems break down. In such cases, it is up to you to ensure that service continues to be delivered to customers in a seamless fashion. They should not hear about internal problems, and quite honestly, the customers probably do not care about these problems. They should be able to expect that products and services they paid for are delivered when promised, in the manner agreed upon, and without inconvenience to them. Anything less is unacceptable and is poor service.

Employee Roles in Larger Organizations

As customers have matured in their knowledge of service standards and what they expect of providers, they look for certain qualifications in those who serve. They gain knowledge from numerous sources that help them be more savvy in their dealings with businesses (for example, *Consumer Reports* magazine, Internet research, and television shows such as *20/20, Dateline,* and *60 Minutes*). Many times, these customers become sticklers about service and when they do not get the level of service they expect, they take their business elsewhere. In some cases, they might give the organization a second chance by complaining. This benevolent initiative, allowing organizations to "fix themselves," is often done as a test. If you or your peers fail, several things can occur. You may not only lose a customer, but you may also "gain" an onslaught of negative word-of-mouth publicity that can irreparably damage an organization's image as a whole and yours specifically.

Customers expect service employees to have the following qualifications and competencies in both large and small organizations.

- Broad general knowledge of products and service
- Interpersonal communication skills
- Technical expertise related to products sold and serviced
- Positive, customer-focused, "can-do" attitude
- Initiative
- Motivation
- Integrity
- Loyalty (to the organization, to products, and to customers)
- Team spirit

- Creativity
- Ethical behavior
- Time management skills
- Problem-solving capability
- Conflict resolution skills

Such skills and capabilities are crucial, whether you are operating a cash register, polishing a car, handling a returned item, repairing a sink, coaching an executive or technical manager (for example, a consultant who offers seminars on enhancing interpersonal skills), or dealing with a negative situation (for example, a shoplifter or disgruntled customer). If you fail to possess and/or exhibit any or all of these factors, the end result could be a breakdown in the relationship between you and your customer, with ultimately negative repercussions.

Employee Roles in Smaller Organizations

The growth of small businesses since the early 1990s has skyrocketed, especially women- and minority-owned businesses. Many small business entrepreneurs started out of necessity (because of layoffs or downsizing) or out of frustration caused by limitations within a larger structure (lack of promotion opportunity, low salaries, actual or perceived discrimination, poor management, or continual changes).

With this massive growth of sole proprietorships (one-owner businesses) and small businesses has come more choice for customers. This growth has also created problems for people making the transition from large to small organizations. This is because in addition to having to possess all the qualifications and characteristics listed earlier, employees in small businesses perform greatly varied tasks. Typically, the human resources and technical systems they might call upon for support are limited. If something goes wrong, they cannot "bump the problem upstairs," nor can they obtain immediate, on-site assistance. This often causes customer frustration or anger.

The types of jobs that fall into this struggling category run the gamut of industries. Some examples are:

- Accountant
- Consultant
- Automotive mechanic
- Computer technician
- Salesperson
- Caterer
- Tailor
- Personal shopper
- Office support staff
- Office equipment repairperson
- Office cleaning staff
- Child care provider
- Gardener
- Electrician and plumber
- Electronics repairperson
- Visiting nurse or nurse consultant
- Driver
- Temporary worker

To stave off failure and help ensure that customer needs are identified and satisfied, owners and employees in such establishments must continually strive to gain new knowledge and skills while working hard to deliver a level of service equal to that offered by the bigger organizations. The public is generally unforgiving and, like elephants, they have long memories—especially when service breaks down.

If you work in this type of environment, look for opportunities to provide stellar service and really go out of your way to practice your people skills. Get back to the basics that you will learn more about in Chapters 3 to 5—listen, ask questions, provide feedback, communicate well—and do not miss an opportunity to let your customers know that they are special and that you are there to serve their needs.

Owners and employees in sole proprietorships must work hard to deliver service equal to that given by larger organizations. *How can an owner make his or her organization special or different?*

Policies and Procedures

Although there are a lot of local, state, and federal regulations with which you and your organization must comply, many policies are flexible. If you go to your bank to deposit a fairly large check that exceeds the maximum amount that the bank will accept, the teller may inform you that there will be a seven-day hold put on the check until it clears the sender's bank. In this case, you might petition the branch manager and possibly get this period modified, since you are dealing with a "bank" policy.

Many customers negatively meet organizational culture directly when a service provider hides behind "company policy" to handle a problem. The goal should be to process customer requests and satisfy needs as quickly, efficiently, and cheerfully as possible. Anything less is an invitation for criticism, dissatisfaction, potential customer loss, and employee frustration.

Return policies are a case in point. Even though customers may not always be "right," they must be treated with respect and as if they are right to effectively provide service and generate future relationships. An effective return process is part of the overall service process. In addition to service received, the return policy of an organization is another gauge customers use to determine where they will spend their time and money. The return statements shown in Figure 2.3 send specific messages concerning the organizational culture of both organizations. Notice the tone or service culture that radiates from each example. Think about your "gut" reaction as a customer when you read both policies.

Organizations often hang up fancy posters and banners touting such claims as, "The customer is always right," "The customer is No. 1," or "We're here to serve YOU!" But at the moment of truth, when customers come into contact with employees, they frequently hear, "Please take a number so we can better serve you," "I can't do that," or (on the phone), "ABC Company, please hold—CLICK." Clearly, when these things occur, the culture is not customer-focused and a service has broken down. The important question for organizations is, "How do we fix our system?" The answer: make a commitment to the customer and establish an environment that will support that commitment. That's where you come in as a

POLICY 1

To err is human, to return is just fine . . .

Already read the book? Pages printed upside down? The package arrived bruised, battered, and otherwise weary from the trip? Actually, the only reason you need to return an item bought from us is this: You're not satisfied . . .

Having the chance to talk with our customer helps us learn and improve our service. It is also an opportunity to demonstrate the [organization's name] customer policy: YOU'RE RIGHT!

POLICY 2
Return Policy

Returns must meet the following criteria:

1. Books must be received within thirty (30) days of the invoice date. Please allow one week for shipping.
2. Books must be received in saleable condition. Damaged books will not be accepted for credit.
3. Refunds will not be made on videotapes and software unless they were defective at the time of purchase. Please notify [organization's name] of any such defects within ten (10) days of the invoice date.

Return Shipping Information

Returns must be shipped to [organization's name and full address].

Any returns not shipped to the above address will not be credited and FULL PAYMENT for shipping will be the responsibility of the shipper.

All charges incurred in returning materials, including customer's charges, if any, are the responsibility of the shipper.

Ensure that your returns are not lost or damaged.

Comments and Feedback

We value your opinion! If you need to return any of the enclosed material, please take a minute to let us know why. Your comments and suggestions will help us better meet your needs in the future.

customer service professional. Through conscientious and concerned assistance to customers, the organization can form a solid relationship with the consumer through its employees.

Products and Services

The type and quality of products and services also contribute to your organizational culture. If customers perceive that you offer reputable products and services in a professional manner and at a competitive price, your organization will likely reap the rewards of loyalty and positive "press." On the other hand, if products and services do not live up to expectations or promises, or if your ability to correct problems in products and services is deficient, you and the organization could suffer adversely.

Motivators and Rewards

In any employee environment, people work more effectively and productively when their performance is recognized and adequately rewarded. Whether the rewards are in the form of monetary or material items, or a simple verbal pat on the back by the manager, most employees expect and thrive on some form of recognition.

As a way of managing your own motivation level, it is important to remember that there will be many times when your only motivation and reward for accomplishing a goal or providing quality service will come from you. The reality is that every time you do something well or out of the ordinary, you may not receive a financial or any other kind of reward for it. On the other hand, many companies and supervisors go out of their way to recognize good performance. Many use public recognition, contests, games, employee activities (sporting or other events), financial rewards, incentives (gifts or trips), employee of the month or year awards, and a variety of other techniques to show appreciation for employee efforts. Whatever your organization does, there is always room for improvement and you should take time to make recommendations of your own.

Management Support

You cannot be expected to handle every customer-related situation that develops. In some instances, you will have to depend on the experience of a more experienced employee or your supervisor or manager and defer to his or her experience or authority.

A key role played by your manager, supervisor, and/or team leader is to provide effective, ongoing coaching, counseling, and training to you and your peers. By doing this, supervisors can pass on valuable information, guide, and aid your professional development. Also, it is their job to be alert to your performance and ensure that you receive appropriate rewards based on your ability to interact effectively with customers and fulfill the requirements of your job. Unfortunately, many supervisors have not had adequate training that would enable them to provide you with the support you need. They were probably good frontline service providers, with a high degree of motivation, initiative, and ability. As a result, their management promoted them, often without providing the necessary training, coaching, and guidance to develop their supervisory skills.

If you find that you are not receiving the support you need, there are some things you should consider doing in order to ensure that you have the information, skills, and support to provide quality service to your customers.

The key is to meet with your supervisor (or anyone else you feel could be helpful) to seek help as follows:

Ask Many Open-ended Questions

To get the information you need, you may have to take the initiative. Your customer does not want to hear you say, "Nobody showed me how," "I can't," "I don't know," or "It's not my job." Remember what you read earlier about seamless service. Here are some questions you might ask your supervisor:

- What are my exact duties? (Get a copy of your job description in writing if possible.)
- What are your expectations of me?
- How do I handle [name specific] situations?
- Who should I see about ————?
- Where are [materials, policies, equipment] located?
- Who is in charge when you are not available?
- What is my level of authority?

Strive for Improvement

Customer service can be frustrating, and in some instances, monotonous. You may need to create self-motivation strategies and continue to seek fulfillment or satisfaction. By remaining optimistic and projecting a can-do image that makes

FIGURE 2.4
Characteristics of an Effective Mentor

When searching for someone to mentor you, look for these characteristics:

- Willingness to be a mentor
- Experienced in the organization or industry and/or job you need help with
- Knowledgeable about the organization and industry
- Good communicator (verbal, nonverbal, and listening skills)
- Aware of the organizational culture
- Well connected inside and outside the organization
- Enthusiastic
- Good coaching skills and a good motivator
- Charismatic
- Trustworthy
- Patient
- Creative thinker
- Self-confident
- Good problem solver

FIGURE 2.5
Characteristics of a Successful Mentee

Since mentoring is a two-way process, you should make sure that you are ready to have a mentor. You should have the following characteristics:

- Willingness to participate, listen, and learn
- Desire to improve and grow
- Commitment to working with mentor
- Self-confidence
- Effective communication skills
- Enthusiasm
- Openness to feedback
- Adaptability
- Willingness to ask questions

customers enjoy dealing with you, you can influence yourself and others. Smile as an outward gesture of your "I care" philosophy. Many self-help publications and courses are available that can offer guidance in this area.

Look for ways to improve your skills and to raise the level of service you provide to your customer. Whether it is through formal training, mentoring, or simply observing positive service techniques used by others and mimicking them, work to improve your own skills. The more you know, the better you can assist customers and move your own career forward.

Look for a Strong Mentor in Your Organization

Mentors are people who are well acquainted with the organization, policies, politics, and processes well. They are well connected (inside and outside the organization), communicate well, have the ability and desire to assist you (the mentee), and are capable and experienced. Ask these people to provide support and help you grow personally and professionally. Many good books on the topic of mentoring are available. Figures 2.4 and 2.5 list some characteristics of a mentor and **mentee.**

Avoid Complacency

Anyone can go to work and just do what he or she is told. The people who excel are the ones who constantly strive for improvement and look for opportunities to grow professionally. They also take responsibility or ownership for service situations. Take the time to think about the systems, policies, and procedures in place in

Take a few minutes to respond to the following questions. Then your instructor will group you with others to discuss responses.

1. Have you ever witnessed or experienced a customer service situation in which a supervisor or manager became involved in an employee-customer encounter? If so, what occurred?
2. How do you feel the supervisor handled the situation?
3. Could the supervisor's approach have been improved? If so, how?

your organization. Can they be improved? How? Now take that information or awareness and make recommendations for improvements. Even though managers have a key role, the implementation and success of cultural initiatives (practices or actions taken by the organization) rest with you, the frontline employee. You are the one who interacts directly with a customer and often determines the outcome of the contact.

Some people might throw up their hands and say, "It wasn't my fault," "Nobody else cares, why should I," or "I give up." A special person looks for ways around roadblocks in order to provide quality service for customers. The fact that others are not doing their job does not excuse you from doing yours. You are being paid a salary to accomplish specific job tasks. Do them with gusto and with pride. Your customers expect no less. You and your customers will reap the rewards of your efforts and initiative.

Employee Empowerment 授权

Employee **empowerment** is one way for a supervisor to help ensure that service providers can respond quickly to customer needs or requests. The intent of empowerment is a delegation of authority where a frontline service provider can take action without having to call a supervisor or ask permission. Such authority allows on-the-spot responsiveness to the customer while making service representatives feel trusted, respected, and like an important part of the organization. Empowerment is also an intangible way that successful service organizations reward employees. Often someone who has decision-making authority feels better about himself or herself and their organization.

As a service provider, think of customer situations in which you have to get approval from a supervisor or manager before making a decision or taking action to serve your customers. If you feel having to do so is causing a delay in serving your customers, approach your supervisor and suggest having decision-making authority given to you.

Some examples of possible empowerment situations include the following:

- A cashier has to call a supervisor for approval of a customer's personal check.
- A cable television installer has to call the office for approval before adding an additional hookup for another room.
- A computer technician cannot comply with a customer's request that she make a backup CD-ROM of her hard drive before running a diagnostic test because policy prohibits it.
- A call center service representative does not have the authority to reverse late payment charges on the account of a customer who explained that he was in the hospital for three weeks with surgery complications.

Take a few minutes to think about and respond to these questions. Once you have responded, your instructor may form groups and have you share answers.

1. What type of skills training do you believe would be valuable for a customer service professional? Why?
2. What types of training have you had or do you need to qualify for a service position?

- A bank representative cannot waive returned check fees even though she acknowledges the bank created the error which resulted in bounced checks in the first place.
- An assistant cruise purser cannot correct a billing error until the purser returns from lunch.

Training

The importance of effective training cannot be overstated. To perform your job successfully and create a positive impression in the minds of customers, you and other frontline employees must be given the necessary tools. Depending on your position and your organization's focus, this training might address interpersonal skills, technical skills, organizational awareness, or job skills, again depending on your position. Most important, your training should help you know what is expected of you and how to fulfill those expectations. Training is a vehicle for accomplishing this and is an essential component of any organizational culture that supports customer service.

Take advantage of training programs. Check with your supervisor and/or training department, if there is one. If you work in a small company, have a limited budget for training, or do not have access to training through your organization, look for other resources. Many communities have lists of public seminars available through the public library, college business programs, high schools, chambers of commerce, professional organizations, and a variety of other organizations. Tap into these to gain the knowledge and skills you will need to move ahead. Also, your training and skill level will often determine whether you keep your job if your organization is forced to downsize and reduce staff.

2 Establishing a Service Strategy

Concept: A service provider helps determine approaches for service success.

The first step a company can take in creating or redefining its service environment is to do an inspection of its systems and practices to decide where the company is now and where it needs to be in order to be competitive in a global service economy. The manner in which internal and external customer needs are addressed should also be reviewed.

As a service provider, you should do your part in determining needed approaches for service success. From the perspective of a customer service professional, ask yourself the following questions to help clarify your role.

- Who is my customer?
- What am I currently doing, or what can I do, to help achieve organizational excellence?

The best way to create a service culture is to get everyone in the organization involved in planning and brainstorming. Everyone should be encouraged to share ideas about how and where internal changes need to be made to be more responsive to customer needs. *How do you think these ideas can be shared most effectively?*

- Do I focus all my efforts on total customer satisfaction?
- Am I empowered to make the decisions necessary to serve my customer? If not, what levels of authority should I discuss with my supervisor?
- Are there policies and procedures that inhibit my ability to serve the customer? If so, what recommendations about changing policies and procedures can I make?
- When was the last time I told my customers that I sincerely appreciated their business?
- In what areas of organizational skills and product and service knowledge do I need additional information?

3   Customer-Friendly Systems

Concept: System components are advertising, complaint resolution, and delivery systems.

A service culture starts at the top of an organization and filters down to the front-line employee. By demonstrating their commitment to quality service efforts, managers lead by example. It's not enough to authorize glitzy service promotional campaigns and send out directives informing employees of management's support for customer initiatives; managers must get involved. Further, employees must take initiative to solve problems and better serve the customer. They must be alert for opportunities and make recommendations for improvement whenever appropriate. Only in these situations can changes and improvements in the culture occur.

Typical System Components

Part of the effectiveness in serving customers can be accomplished through policies and practices that say, "We care" or "You're important to us." Some **customer-friendly systems** that can send positive messages are:

Advertising

Advertising campaigns should send a message that products and services are competitive in price and that the quality and quantity are at least comparable to those of competitors. Otherwise, customers will likely go elsewhere. An advertisement that appears to be deceptive can cost the organization customers and its reputation. For example, if an advertisement states that something is "free" (a cup of coffee, a buy-one, get-one-free item, tire rotation, or a consultation) but somewhere in the advertisement (in small print) there are restrictions ("with a purchase of $20 or more," "while supplies last," "if you buy two new tires," or "if you sign a one-year contract," then it may be viewed as deceptive. To prevent misunderstandings as a service provider, make sure that you point out such restrictions to customers when they call or ask questions. If you notice that an advertisement sounds a bit "tricky," inform your supervisor immediately. Possibly the ad was not proofread carefully enough before it was printed and/or aired. Remember, you have a vested interest in your organization's success. Take ownership.

Complaint Resolution

The manner in which complaints or problems are handled can signal the organization's concern for customer satisfaction. If an employee has to get approvals for the smallest decisions, the customer may have to wait for a supervisor to arrive (a supermarket cashier has to call for a manager to approve a check for $10, and when the supervisor arrives, he or she doesn't even look at the check before signing and walking away). This can lead to customer and employee frustration and irritation and makes the organization look inept.

As a service professional, you should make recommendations for improvement whenever you spot a roadblock or system that impedes provision of service excellence.

Service Delivery Systems

Your organization must determine the best way to deliver quality products and service and to provide effective follow-up support. Everything you do in customer service is crucial. This includes the way information is made available to customers, initial contacts and handling of customer issues, sales techniques (hard sell versus relationship selling), order collection and processing, price quotations, product and service delivery, invoicing, and follow-up. Customers should not have to deal with internal policies, practices, or politics. They should be able to contact you, get the information they need, make a buying decision, and have the product or service selected flawlessly delivered in a timely, professional manner. Anything less is poor service and may cost your organization in terms of lost business or customers.

Customers also expect value for their money. Part of this is professional, easy-to-access service. For example, if your organization does not have an 800, 877, or 888 number with online customer support, extended hours of operation, top-quality merchandise, and effective resolution of problems, your customers may rebel. They can do this by complaining, speaking negative word-of-mouth publicity, writing letters to consumer advocacy groups (television or radio stations, Better Business Bureaus, local, state, and federal government agencies), and/or going elsewhere for their needs.

Many ways are available for delivering service to customers. Two key factors involved in delivery are transportation modes (how products and services are physically delivered—by truck, train, plane, U.S. Postal Service, courier, and electronically) and location (facilities located centrally and easily accessible by customers). You will explore the use of technology in service delivery in detail when you read Chapter 9.

Direct Versus Indirect Systems

The type of delivery system used (direct or indirect contact) is important because it affects staffing numbers, costs, technology, scheduling, and many other factors. The major difference between the two types of systems is that in a direct contact environment, customers interact directly with people, whereas in an indirect system their needs are met primarily with self-service through technology (possibly integrated with the human factor).

There is a delicate balance in selecting a **service delivery system**. This is because each customer is unique and has personal preferences. While many prefer a hands-off self-service approach, others resent it and often view it as a loss of caring. Many banks discovered this fact in recent years. They saw technology as a cost-saving strategy to deliver service. Branches were closed as money was spent to upgrade automated phone systems and add automatic teller machines (ATMs). Many customers rebelled. The result is that companies like BankOne are now increasing their branch locations and retrofitting their branches and ATMs. Washington Mutual touts a high-touch customer environment complete with free checking, comfortable waiting areas, and play areas for children.

Figure 2.6 shows some ways by which organizations are providing service to customers and prospective customers.

Third-Party Delivery

In recent years, as companies strive to reduce costs, increase profit, and stay ahead of the competition, an interesting trend has occurred. Many companies are eliminating internal positions and hiring outside (third-party) organizations and individuals to assume eliminated and newly created roles (call center customer support functions, human resource benefits administration, accounting functions,

FIGURE 2.6
Service Delivery Systems

Many industries are using technology to provide service that has traditionally been obtained by a customer going to a supplier and meeting face-to-face with an organization's representative. The following lists compare the traditional (direct) and technological (indirect) approaches.

Direct Contact	Indirect Contact
Face-to-face	800, 877, 888 number
Bank tellers	Automated teller machines or online banking
Reservationists (airlines, hotels)	Online computer reservations
Front desk staff (hotels)	On-screen, in-room television checkout and bill viewing
Ticket takers (theme parks)	Ticket scanners
Customer service representatives	Online viewing to provide balance or billing information (credit card companies)
Lawyers	Telephone tip lines or e-mail
Photo developers	Self-service film kiosk or Internet transmission of digital images
Supermarket clerks	Online ordering and delivery
Towing dispatchers	In-car navigation and notification systems

and marketing). This practice of outsourcing provides multiple benefits while bringing with it some downsides. On the positive side, companies can save money by:

- Eliminating large ongoing salaries.
- Reducing health benefits, retirement, and 401(k) payments.
- Avoiding the need to purchase and update computers and equipment and a myriad of other equipment.
- Bringing in new, fresh expertise and perspectives from outside the organization.

    And, on the negative side:

- Long-term employee expertise is lost.
- Employee loyalty to the organization suffers.
- The morale of the "survivors" (employees whose jobs were not eliminated) is adversely affected.
- Managing becomes more complex.
- Customers must deal with "strangers" with whom they cannot build a long-term relationship because their provider may be gone the next time they call or stop by.

Many organizations have adopted the practice of redesignating job positions as either part-time or shared (by two employees who are both part-time and therefore do not qualify for all benefits because of the number of hours they work). Another common strategy is to fill positions with "temporary" employees contracted through a temporary staffing agency. All of this is done in an effort to reduce rising employee costs (especially benefits) while providing the necessary customer support.

Tools for Service Measurement

In a customer-oriented environment, it is important to constantly gauge service effectiveness. Organizations can use many ways to find out how well you and your peers are doing in servicing customers. Once the results of organizational self-assessments are obtained, they will likely be shared with you and other employees in an effort to determine ways to reduce shortcomings and enhance strengths. If your supervisor fails to share such results, simply ask. Again, you have a vested interest in improvement and if he or she forgets to include you in the improvement loop—or intentionally omits you, you should take initiative to demonstrate that you do care and are concerned with customer service delivery.

Here are some of the typical techniques or tools available for customer service data collection:

Employee focus groups. In such groups, you and others might be asked to comment or develop ideas on various topics related to customer service or employee and organizational issues. Although you will be providing interesting and valuable insights from your own perspective, remember that your views may differ significantly from those of your customers. For this reason, if your ideas are not implemented, do not be discouraged. Overriding organizational and customer issues to which you are not privy may be the reason.

Customer focus groups. Similar to the employee groups, these forums provide an opportunity to gather a group of customers (selected geographically, demographically by factors such as age, sex, race, income, or interests, or randomly

LEADERSHIP INITIATIVE

2.2

Measuring how well your organization is doing at meeting customer expectations and needs is crucial for profits and survival. Such measurements should be part of your ongoing strategic planning and not a periodic episode done only when you have time.

Once you measure service, create a report that details findings and is shared throughout the organization at all levels. Publicize successes and form focus groups made up of employees and customers to determine how to improve in deficit areas. You may also want to have a committee of employees in each department develop a set of customer service standards that are used to help ensure quality service. As an example, the following standards can be found on the U.S. Census Bureau's website (http://www.census.gov/mso/www/custstd.html).

- We will guarantee a quality product or service that meets or exceeds your expectations.
- We will provide you with realistic delivery times based on the nature of the request.
- We will respond promptly to all requests in accord with our resources and capabilities.
- We will provide you with choices for products, services, and the means of delivery.
- We will be courteous, respectful, responsible, and professional at all times.

The "Tools for Service Measurement" section briefly describes some of the tools available to you.

Among other responsibilities, customer service professionals make a point of communicating their company's commitment to service in face-to-face interactions with customers. *What skills does a customer service representative need to create a positive service culture when talking with customers?*

from lists). Customer focus groups are brought together to answer specific questions related to some aspect of product or service.

Mystery shoppers. These people may be internal employees or external consultants who pose as customers in on-site visits, over the telephone or online, to determine how well customers are being served.

Customer satisfaction surveys. This type of survey can be written or orally administered. It could be something as simple as an employee or manager chatting with customers at a restaurant and gathering their feedback, or it could be something more formal. Customers are sometimes asked to complete a brief questionnaire at the end of their service transaction. Some organizations do follow-up telephone satisfaction surveys; others put their surveys on their website and encourage feedback. Customers are often enticed to participate in a survey through the use of gifts, prizes, and discounts.

Customer comment cards. Many food service businesses use these simple cards to get immediate reactions and comments from customers following a visit.

Profit and loss statements or management reports. These reports are invaluable in spotting trends or dramatic changes in profits or losses that might indicate or lead to a service breakdown.

Employee exit interviews. These interviews are typically administered by the human resources or personnel department, or in smaller organizations, an officer or owner might informally ask questions of a departing employee. Such information can identify trends or concerns. Departing employees often feel that they have nothing to lose and will candidly provide valuable feedback about management practices, policies and procedures, and a multitude of other organizational issues.

Walk-through audits. Create a checklist of service factors (for example, responsiveness, friendliness, and so on) for supervisors or managers to use as they walk through a store or service facility to view the operations from a customer's perspective.

On-site management visits. These visits provide firsthand observation of service practice and allow interaction between managers, employees, and customers. They are especially helpful when there are off-site workers (at construction sites or branch offices), or operations consulting projects, or in-home services, such as plumbing). A side benefit of these types of visits is that they show that the organization is committed to fulfilling the customers' needs.

4 Twelve Strategies for Promoting a Positive Service Culture

Concept: To perform effectively as a customer service professional, you will need a plan.

Here are 12 strategies for service success.

1. *Explore your organization's vision.* By working to better understand the focus of the organization and asking yourself, "What's the Added Value And Results For Me? (AVARFM)," you can develop your own commitment to helping make the organization successful. An example of AVARFM might occur when a new policy is implemented that requires you to answer a phone by the third ring.

   A "mystery caller" system is in place as a means of monitoring compliance. Also, to each employee who meets the three-ring standard, rewards are given. You now have a reason or added value associated with compliance.

2. *Help communicate the culture and vision to customers—daily.* Customers have specific expectations. It does no good for the organization to have a vision if you do not help communicate and demonstrate it to the customer. Many companies place slogans and posters throughout the workplace or service area to communicate the vision. Although these approaches reinforce the message, a more effective means is for you to deliver quality customer service regularly. Through your attitude, language, appearance, knowledge of products and services, body language, and the way you communicate with your customers,

As a frontline contact with customers, you will be asked a variety of questions about the company and its products. *What skills will you need and what information should you give customers in this situation?*

they will feel your commitment to serve them. You will read more about techniques for presenting yourself professionally in later chapters.

3. *Demonstrate ethical behavior.* Ethical behavior is based on values—those of the society, organization, and employees. These values are a combination of beliefs, ideologies, perceptions, experiences, and a sense of what is right (appropriate) and wrong (inappropriate). Successful demonstration of ethical behavior is often determined by the values of the customer and how they perceive your behavior, and the customer often holds you and your organization to high standards. Thus, it is crucial for you to be aware of your words and actions so that you do not inadvertently send a negative ethical message to your customers.

How do you know which values your organization holds as important? Many times, they are communicated in an employee manual distributed during new hire orientation. Sometimes they are emblazoned on a plaque on the wall, possibly as part of the mission or philosophy statement or next to it. However, the reality test or "where the rubber meets the road" related to your organization's values comes in the day-to-day operational actions of you and your organization.

From an ethical standpoint, it is often up to you and your frontline peers to assess the situation, listen to your customers' requests, scrutinize your organizational policies and procedures, consider all options, and then make the "right" decision. This decision is fair—to your customer and your organization—and it is morally and legally right. A 1999 movie (*The Insider* with Al Pacino and Russell Crowe) epitomized the issues of ethical behavior. The movie is based on a true story of a tobacco industry insider who blew the whistle on his company, which publicly denied the harmful side effects of smoking. Even though the man stood to lose everything, possibly even his life, he acted out of conscience in an effort to help others.

The key to ongoing customer relations is trust. Without it, you have no relationship and cannot win customer loyalty.

4. *Identify and improve your service skills.* Take an inventory of your interpersonal and customer service skills; use the strengths, and improve the weaker areas. By continually upgrading your knowledge and skills related to people, customer service, and products and services offered, you position yourself as a resource to the customer and an asset to the organization.

5. *Become an expert on your organization.* As the frontline contact person with customers, you are likely to receive a variety of questions related to the organization.

Typical questions involve organizational history, structure, policies and procedures systems, products, or services. By being well versed in the many facets of the organization and its operation, related industry topics, and your competition, you can project a more knowledgeable, helpful, and confident image that contributes to total customer satisfaction.

6. *Demonstrate commitment.* As an employee with customer contact opportunities and responsibilities, you are the organization's representative. One mistake that many frontline employees (and many supervisors) make in communications with customers is to intentionally or unintentionally demonstrate a lack of commitment or support for their company and a sense of powerlessness. A common way in which this occurs is with the use of "they" language when dealing with customers. This can be in reference to management or policies or procedures, for example, "Mrs. Howard, I'd like to help but our policy says . . ." or "Mrs. Howard, I've checked on your request, but my manager (they) said we can't . . ."

An alternative to using "they" language is to take ownership or responsibility for a situation by telling the customer what you can do, not what you cannot do. Customers are not interested in internal strife or procedures; they want to have their needs satisfied. To try to involve customers in situations that are out of their control and that do not concern them is unfair and unwise. Positive language and effort on your part can reduce or eliminate unnecessarily dragging the customer in. Here's one approach: "Mrs. Howard, I'm terribly sorry that you were inconvenienced by our mistake (policy or omission). What I can do to help resolve this situation is . . ."

7. *Partner with customers.* Customers are the reason you have a job and the reason your organization continues to exist. With that in mind, you should do whatever you can to promote a positive, healthy customer-provider relationship. This can be done in a number of ways, many of which will be addressed in detail in later chapters. Here are some simple techniques:

- Communicate openly and effectively.
- Smile—project a positive image.
- Listen intently, and then respond appropriately.
- Facilitate situations in which customer needs are met and you succeed in win-win situations helping accomplish organizational goals.
- Focus on developing an ongoing relationship with customers instead of taking a one-time service or sales opportunity approach.

8. *Work with your customer's interest in mind.* Think to yourself, "If I were my customer, what type of service would I expect?" Then, set out to provide that service.

9. *Treat vendors and suppliers as customers.* Some customer service employees view vendors and suppliers as salespeople whose only purpose is to serve them. In fact, each contact with a vendor or a supplier offers a golden opportunity to tap into a pre-established network and potentially expand your own customer service base while providing better service to existing customers. People remember how they are treated and often act in kind.

(Here's a hint: Even if your organization does not have a formal policy regarding returning calls, business etiquette dictates that you return all calls and do so within 24 hours or by the next business day. Even better, do so by the close of the business day if possible. Telephone skills will be discussed in more detail in Chapter 9.)

10. *Share resources.* By building strong interpersonal relationships with coworkers and peers throughout the industry, you can develop a support system of resources. Sometimes customers will request information, products, or services that are not available through your organization. By being able to refer customers to such sources, you will have provided a service, and they are likely to remember that you helped them indirectly.

11. *Work with, not against, your customers.* Customers are in the enviable position of being in control. At no time in recent history has the cliché "it's a buyers market" been more true, and many consumers know it. To capitalize on this situation, many organizations have become very creative and proactive in their efforts to grab and hold customers. One large Colorado-based national supermarket, Albertson's, developed a series of commercials touting, "Albertson's—it's your store" and stressing that corporate efforts were focused on customer satisfaction. Your efforts should similarly convey the idea that you are working with customers to better serve them.

12. *Provide service follow-up.* Providing follow-up is probably one of the most important service components. Service does not end when the service encounter or sale concludes. There are numerous follow-up opportunities to ensure that customer satisfaction was attained. This can be through a formal customer satisfaction survey or telephone callback system or through an informal process of sending thank-you cards, birthday cards, special sale mailings, and similar initiatives that are inexpensive and take little effort. Think of creative ways to follow up, and then speak to your supervisor about implementing them. These types of efforts reinforce service commitment to customers and let them know that you want to keep them as your customers.

5   Separating Average Companies From Excellent Companies

Concept: Ask questions to determine the service environment in a company in which you need employment.

Whether you are currently a service provider in an organization or seeking employment as a service provider, it is important to recognize what makes organizations successful in serving customers. If you are seeking employment, these factors can be used as a basis for questions you might ask interviewers in order to determine what type of service environment exists:

- Executives spend time with the customers.
- Executives spend time talking to frontline service providers.
- Customer feedback is regularly asked for and acted upon.
- Innovation and creativity are encouraged and rewarded.
- Benchmarking (identifying successful practices of others) is done with similar organizations.
- Technology is widespread, frequently updated, and used effectively.
- Training is provided to keep employees current of industry trends, organizational issues, skills, and technology.
- Open communication exists between frontline employees and all levels of management.

- Employees are provided with guidelines and empowered (in certain instances, authorized to act without management intervention) to do whatever is necessary to satisfy the customer.
- Partnerships with customers and suppliers are common.
- The status quo is not acceptable.

6   What Customers Want

Concept: Customers expect effective, efficient service and value for their money. Customers also expect certain common things that service providers can furnish.

Most customers are like you. And **what customers want** is value for their money and effective, efficient service. They also expect certain intangible things during a service encounter. Here are seven common things that customers want and expect if they are to keep doing business with you and your organization:

1. *Personal recognition.* This can be demonstrated in a number of ways (sending thank-you cards or notes, or birthday cards, returning calls in a timely fashion, taking the time to look up information that might be helpful even if the customer did not ask for it). A simple way to show recognition to a customer who enters your work area, even if you cannot immediately stop what you are doing to serve him or her, is to smile and acknowledge the person's presence. If possible, you might also offer the customer the option of waiting, having a seat, and so on.

2. *Courtesy.* Basic courtesy involves pleasantries such as "please" and "thank you" as there is no place or excuse for rude behavior in a customer service environment. Even though customers may not always be right, you must treat them with respect. If a situation becomes too intense and you find yourself "losing it," call upon someone else to serve that customer.

3. *Timely service.* Most people don't mind waiting briefly for service if there is a legitimate reason (as when you are waiting on another customer or obviously serving another customer on the phone), but they do not like to spend what they believe is undue amounts of time waiting to be served. Your challenge as a customer service professional is to provide prompt yet effective service.

4. *Professionalism.* Customers expect and should receive knowledgeable answers to their questions, service that satisfies their needs and lessens effort on their part, and service personnel who take pride in their work. You can demonstrate these characteristics by exemplifying the ethics talked about earlier, and the communication behaviors outlined in later chapters of this book.

5. *Enthusiastic service.* Customers come to your organization for one purpose—to satisfy a need. This need may be nothing more than to "look around." Even so, they should find a dedicated team of service professionals standing by to assist them in whatever way possible. By delivering service with a smile, offering additional services and information, and taking the time to give extra effort in every service encounter, you can help guarantee a positive service experience for your customer.

6. *Empathy.* Customers also want to be understood. Your job as a service provider is to make every effort to be understanding, and to provide appropriate service. To succeed, you must be able to put yourself in the customer's position or look

Now that you know what goes into making a customer environment "customer-friendly," think about your own expectations when you patronize a company. Share your answers with others in the class.

Based on your own experiences, list four or five expectations that you feel are typical of most customers.

at the need from the customer's perspective as much as possible. This is especially true when customers do not speak English well or have some type of disability that reduces their communication effectiveness. When a customer has a complaint or believes that he or she did not receive appropriate service, it is your job to calm or appease in a nonthreatening, helpful manner and show understanding.

A common strategy for showing empathy is the **feel, felt, found technique.** When used, a service provider is demonstrating a compassionate understanding of the customer's issue or situation. For example, a customer is upset because the product desired is not in stock. A service provider might respond by saying: "Mr. Philips, I know how you *feel*. I've *felt* the same way when I had my heart set on a specific item. I've actually *found* that the alternative product I described to you has the same features and performs several other functions as well."

In using such a technique you are trying to psychologically bond with the customer while pointing out that he or she is not alone in his or her emotional response. You have also introduced an alternative solution for consideration.

7. *Patience.* Customers should not have to deal with your frustrations or pressures. Your efficiency and effectiveness should seem effortless. If you are angry because of a policy, procedure, management, or the customer, you must strive to mask that feeling. This may be difficult to do when you believe that the customer is being unfair or unrealistic, however. By suppressing your desire to speak out or react emotionally, you can remain in control, serve the customer professionally, and end the contact sooner. Some tips on managing difficult customers and your own stress levels will be addressed in Chapters 7 and 10.

Chapter Summary

Professional customer service helps highlight and define service culture. Everything customers experience from the time they contact an organization in person, on the phone, or through other means, affects their perception of the organization and its employees. To positively influence their opinion, you must constantly be alert for opportunities to provide excellent service. Taking the time to provide a little extra effort can often mean the difference between total customer satisfaction and service breakdown.

SERVICE IN ACTION   Circuit City Stores, Inc.   **CHAPTER 2**

http://www.circuitcity.com

Circuit City is headquartered in Richmond, Virginia, and is the second-largest electronics superstore chain in the United States. Opened in the middle of the twentieth century, the store has made tremendous strides in growth. Circuit City now has over 600 stores, 40,000+ associates, over 3,500 products, and a formidable website presence. At the end of the fiscal year in 2002, sales were up 5 percent to $9.95 billion.

The company's stated goal is to offer low, competitive prices, high service standards, and a wide selection of products to meet all consumer needs. A current advertising promotion focuses on "we're with you." Advertisements stress that Circuit City puts customers first and promises to deliver superior electronics solutions to America's families. Obviously, their focus is to capture the hearts and minds of electronics shoppers by stressing the value of shopping with Circuit City. Looking at the sales revenue, the strategy seems to be paying off.

Some of the product offerings online and in a Circuit City store include cameras, printers, accessories, software, office furniture, audio equipment, car stereos systems, televisions and entertainment units, music CDs, wireless phones, phones and office equipment. To stay competitive, Circuit City is partnering with product manufacturers to offer items not available to competitors. For example, in 2002 the company formed an alliance with Sharper Image to showcase "the best of Sharper Image" in Circuit City stores.

To further appeal to consumers, the organization offers such policies as no-hassle returns of items, a 110 percent price-match guarantee, and online real-time inventory where customers can find out which stores in the area has products they want to purchase. Additionally, on the Circuit City Internet site, customers can view articles and information about products and see how other customers have rated the company for service.

Key Terms and Concepts

customer friendly systems	feel, felt, found technique	RUMBA
employee expectations	mentee	service culture
employee roles	mentor	service delivery systems
empowerment	mission	service measurement
		service philosophy
		what customers want

Quick Preview Answers

1. T	5. F	9. F
2. T	6. T	10. F
3. T	7. F	11. F
4. T	8. T	12. T

Chapter Review Questions

1. What are some of the key elements that make up a service culture?
2. How does management's service philosophy affect the culture of an organization?
3. How does RUMBA help clearly define employee roles and expectations? Why is each component important?
4. How can policies and procedures affect the customer's impression of customer service?
5. What questions should you ask yourself about your role as a service provider?
6. What are some indicators that a company has customer-friendly systems in place?

7. What are some of the tools used by organizations to measure their service culture?

8. What are some strategies for helping promote a positive customer culture?

9. What separates average organizations from excellent ones?

10. What are some typical things that customers want?

Search It Out

Customer Service and Corporate Culture

Log on to the Internet and research the mission statements of at least five organizations. Look for common values shared by the companies. You can locate information by going to available search engines (Yahoo.com, Infoseek.com, google.com, AltaVista.com, Excite.com, or AskJeeves.com) and typing in the name of a company, then searching its site for "mission statement." Be prepared to share your findings at the next scheduled meeting.

Note: A listing for additional research on specific URLs is provided on the Customer Service website at <**www.mhhe.com/Lucas05**>.

Collaborative Learning Activity

Service Culture

Along with assigned group members, go on a field trip to several local organizations before your next class meeting. Use Figure 2.1, Elements of a Service Culture, as a guideline to determine the level and quality of the service culture of each organization visited. Take notes and be prepared to share your observations with other groups when you return to class. As part of your note-taking, answer the following questions about each organization:

1. Did you notice any overt signs that indicated the organizations' cultural philosophy (mission or philosophy statements on walls)? If yes, what were they?

2. In what way was service delivered and how did the delivery indicate the organization's philosophy related to customer service?

3. What did the organization's products and services say about its approach to service (quality and quantity, availability, and service support)?

4. What evidence did you see of management support for the service initiatives being used by employees?

5. What indicators of motivators and rewards did you notice (employee of the month or year plaques, parking space for employee of the month, visible indicators of rewards on employees' clothes or uniforms, for example items such as pins or buttons)?

6. Were there any indications that training of employees is occurring (employees have a consistent greeting or closing "Thanks for shopping at ———")?

Face to Face

You and Your New Job in Customer Service

In the following case study, you are a new employee and are excited and happy to begin your position in customer service with United Booksellers. Read about the company and your role in customer service; then answer the questions at the end of the case study.

Background

United Booksellers is the fifth-largest retailer of publications on the West Coast of the United States. It started 15 years ago as a family-owned bookstore in Seattle, Washington, and has grown to over 125 stores in seven states. The organization currently employs 3,000 employees, each of whom receives extensive customer service training prior to being allowed to interact with customers.

Recent issues of *Booksellers Journal* and *Publishers Select* magazine have heralded the quality service and friendly atmosphere of the organization. United Booksellers has been praised for the appearance of the facilities, helpfulness and efficiency of employees, wide selection of publications, and intimate coffee shops where patrons can relax and read their purchases over a hot cup of fresh cappuccino.

Your Role

As a new customer service professional with United Booksellers, you are excited about starting your job, which will require continual customer contact. As a child, you watched your siblings perform customer service functions at the local Burger Mania Restaurant and always thought you'd like to follow their lead. Since you like people, enjoy a challenge, don't get stressed out easily, and have hopes of moving into management, you anticipate that this job should be just right for you. In this position, you'll be expected to receive new publications from publishers log in receipts, stock shelves, assist customers, and occasionally work as backup cashier.

Critical Thinking Questions

1. Are there indicators of United Booksellers' service culture? If so, what are they?
2. If you were an employee, in what ways would you feel that you could contribute to the organizational culture?
3. If you were a customer, what kind of service would you expect to receive at United Booksellers? Why?

PLANNING TO SERVE

To better understand the role of service providers in helping establish and maintain a positive service culture, think about what you read in this chapter. Also, think about factors related to service cultures in organizations with which you are familiar.

Make a list of five to ten key culture elements. Beside these elements, create a list of strategies that you can/could take as a service provider to improve them if you worked in such an organization.

Share your list with others in the class.

Customer Service Skills Assessment

RATE YOUR COMMUNICATION BEHAVIOR:
We all have an image of how well we relate to others in various areas of our life—with family, in the workplace, or at social functions. To be successful in dealing with customers, you must know your skill levels for communicating and interacting with others. To help you get a better idea of how well you are currently performing in these areas, take a few minutes before beginning Part II, "Skills for Success," to rate the following statements using the key. This information is for your personal benefit and will help you focus on specific information as you read this book. The statements describe behavior commonly exhibited by people who are successful in customer relationships. Rate yourself honestly, as you feel others would.

NOTE: Since your self-image often differs from the image others have of you, make copies of this survey before you rate yourself. Once you have completed the survey, distribute the copies to people familiar with your behavior in dealing with others. Ask them to rate your general ability to relate. Even if you have not had customer service experience, their feedback will be helpful, for your interpersonal habits often carry over to customer encounters. Compare all the results and develop an action plan to improve your skills after you have read this book.

DIRECTIONS: Select the number that best describes your behavior when you work with internal customers (peers, coworkers, bosses, subordinates, external customers).

KEY: 1 = Rarely 2 = Sometimes 3 = Frequently 4 = Usually 5 = Always

_____ 1. I smile when interacting with others.

_____ 2. I attempt to set up relationship situations from which I and the other party gain.

_____ 3. I strive to meet the needs and expectations of others.

_____ 4. I provide prompt, specific feedback to inquiries I receive.

_____ 5. I try to imagine how I would feel when dealing with irate people and then work actively toward calming them.

_____ 6. I actively solicit, listen to, and follow up on questions, suggestions, and complaints.

_____ 7. I offer alternatives when someone's original request of me cannot be fulfilled.

_____ 8. I encourage continued association by demonstrating the benefits of future interactions.

_____ 9. I answer the telephone promptly and in a professional manner.

_____ 10. I am proactive (actively look for opportunities to improve) in finding ways to better deal with people.

SCORING:

45–50	Excellent people-oriented skills/attitude.
40–44	Good job; keep it up.
30–39	Fair effort; stay focused on improving relationships and work toward improvement.
20–29	Room for improvement; get some personal coaching from experts (counselors/professors/supervisors) to help you improve.
Below 20	Evaluate your approach to dealing with people; focus on Chapters 3–12.

CHAPTER THREE

Positive Verbal Communication

From the Frontline Interview

For the past three years, Ginger Simpson has been a Region HR Director for FedEx Ground. Prior to that she was a Senior HR Representative for Federal Express Services. The HR staff at FedEx provides service to over 1,800 employees (internal customers) in the southern part of Florida, Georgia, and Alabama and in Puerto Rico. The job requires extensive contact with, and service to, internal and external customers on matters relating to staffing, compensation, training and development, and labor/employee relations. In addition to her FedEx role, Ginger is an adjunct college instructor and teaches interviewing skills classes. Prior to coming to FedEx, she served as the first female director of the Navy's Senior Enlisted Academy, was appointed to the Partnership for Peace Program, and following her retirement was appointed to serve on the Defense Advisory Committee for Women in the Services and also served on the Kassaumbaum-Baker committee for Integrated Training.

GINGER SIMPSON,
Region Human Resources
Manager,
FedEx Ground

1 **In what ways have you seen a service provider's ability to communicate verbally positively influence customer service? Please explain/provide example(s).**

Customers have expectations of service providers. To satisfy customer needs, you need to focus on several key elements related to communication. Crucial are identifying who people are and what they need, and having personal knowledge of the business in order to build partnerships with customers. To do this you must understand people and the organization.

An example of the power of these elements can be seen at FedEx, which is a continuous improvement environment. As such, members of the human resource staff must continually help internal customers (employees) recognize how they should act in a changing environment. Additionally, they must spend time and energy helping to implement change by communicating it positively and getting people to see the positive nature of change.

2 **In what ways have you seen a service provider's ability to communicate verbally negatively influence customer service? Please explain/provide example(s).**

Virtually every hour of every day, managers call upon their communication skills and they inadvertently fail to attend to the information needs of our people. Personality style of the managers and the employees play an important role in communication with customers. People communicate what they believe. What service providers know and how well they do their jobs are often reflected in their interactions with customers. When they cannot articulate information and ideas well, distrust can occur between them and customers. This often occurs.

Chapter Learning Objectives

After completing this chapter, you will be able to:

- Help ensure positive customer interactions in your workplace.
- Recognize the elements of effective two-way interpersonal communication.
- Project a professional customer service image.
- Avoid language that could send a negative message and harm the customer relationship.
- Provide feedback effectively.
- Deal assertively with others.

Attainment of knowledge and skills are prime tools to assist staff at FedEx and in other organizations. Training employees to assume a "learning" mentality and to take personal responsibility for that learning is crucial in today's service environment. They must continually seek new knowledge and skills toward self-improvement. In addition to gaining the knowledge, service employees need to be able to know where and how to effectively access information. For example, at FedEx, we have a wonderful Intranet system on which employees can access online technical training programs to learn new skills. Convincing people of the value of getting onto the system and taking advantage of the resource is sometimes a challenge, but those who do try it gain immensely.

3 What are some of the biggest challenges you see being faced by service providers when communicating verbally with a customer? Please explain/give example(s).

Listening to understand what is being communicated. When dealing with customers, the HR staff at FedEx must get past any emotion and get to the facts. Service providers have to show how they can contribute value to the customer. Some specific techniques:

Effective questioning (open-ended).

Paying individual attention to our customers (one-on-one).

Planning communication (for example, who we need to talk with at a customer site).

Providing added value by giving one piece of information that they do not already know.

Earning trust and respect by allowing customers to get to know their service providers.

Mediating any differences via conference calls.

Being uplifting and optimistic.

4 What advice can you provide to new service providers related to effective verbal communication?

Schedule communication for success. Give communication the priority it deserves by planning and implementing team meetings on a regularly scheduled basis. Being disciplined about conducting meetings and attending forums within workgroups sends a tremendous signal to your customers that communicating and keeping in touch are some of the most important things you can do.

One of the best ways for service providers to be successful is to adopt a positive attitude. You have to believe that everyone is doing his or her best and trying hard in any given situation. Generally, people are hungry for information that they can attain in a quick fashion. By providing ways to expedite a customer's learning curve and helping the customer better understand service providers can be very successful. Make yourself available to customers whenever possible, learn to hear them, consider them, and value their viewpoints.

Critical Thinking

Based on Ginger's responses, how important is communication to effective customer service? How successful do you think FedEx Ground is in achieving effective communication with its customers? Why or why not?

Quick Preview

Before reviewing the chapter content, respond to the following questions by placing a "T" for true or an "F" for false on the rules. Use any questions you miss as a checklist of material to which you will pay particular attention as you read through the chapter. For those you get right, congratulate yourself, but review the sections they address in order to learn additional details about the topic.

_____ 1. Feedback is not an important element in the two-way communication model.

_____ 2. Customers appreciate your integrity, and they trust you more when you use language such as "I'm sorry" or "I was wrong" when you make a mistake.

_____ 3. Phrases such as "I'll try" or "I'm not sure" send a reassuring message that you're going to help solve a customer's problem.

_____ 4. When you use agreement or acknowledgment statements, customers can vent without their emotions escalating.

_____ 5. You should attempt to make a positive impression by focusing on the customer and his or her needs during your initial and subsequent contacts.

_____ 6. Having one prepared greeting and closing statement to use with all customers is a good practice.

_____ 7. When you are not certain of an answer, it is a good idea to express an opinion or speculate when something will occur if a customer asks.

_____ 8. An acceptable response to a customer's question about why something cannot be done is "Our policy does not allow . . ."

_____ 9. You should delay feedback whenever possible unless you're communicating in writing.

_____ 10. The appearance of your workplace has little impact on customer satisfaction as long as you are professional and help solve problems.

_____ 11. Assertive communication means expressing your opinions positively and in a manner that helps the customers recognize that you are confident and have the authority to assist them.

_____ 12. Assertiveness is another word for "aggressiveness."

Answers to Quick Preview can be found at the end of the chapter.

1   The Importance of Effective Communication

Concept: You represent your organization, and customers will respond according to you and your actions.

As a customer service professional, you have the power to make or break the organization. You are the front line in delivering quality service to your customers. Your appearance, actions or inactions, and ability to communicate say volumes about the organization and its focus on customer satisfaction. For all these reasons, you should continually strive to project a polished, professional image and go out of your way to make a customer's visit or conversation with you a pleasant and successful one.

A key element in making your interactions with customers successful is to recognize how you tend to communicate. The easiest way to find out how you

Two-way communication is the foundation of effective customer service. *How can you be sure that you are listening to the customer?*

communicate is to ask those who know you best. Unfortunately, many people are leery about requesting feedback because of what they might hear. Conversely, most people have difficulty giving useful feedback because they either never learned how to do it or are uncomfortable doing it. In any event, try it. Ask a variety of people for their feedback because each person will likely have a different perspective. In addition to any specifics you would like to learn for yourself, ask the following questions of those with whom you interact regularly:

Do I tend to smile when I speak?

What other body cues (nonverbal signals) do I use regularly when I speak?

What mannerisms do I typically use when speaking?

How would you categorize my overall presence when I speak (confident, uncertain, timid, relaxed)? Why do you perceive that?

What "pet" words or phrases do I use regularly?

When I speak, how does my tone sound (assertive, attacking, calming, friendly, persuasive)? What examples of this can you provide?

When I am frustrated or irritated how do you know it?

2 Ensuring Two-Way Communication

Concept: Two-way communication involves the sender and the receiver who each contribute to the communication process. Part of the process is deciding which is the best channel to ensure clear message delivery.

As a customer service professional, you are responsible for ensuring that a meaningful exchange of information takes place. By accepting this responsibility, you can perform your job more efficiently, generate goodwill and customer loyalty for the organization, and provide service excellence. To facilitate this, you should be aware of all the elements of **two-way communication** and the importance of each. Figure 3.1 shows a communication model that clarifies the process.

Interpersonal Communication Model

Environment. The environment (office, store, and group or individual setting) in which you send or receive messages affects the effectiveness of your message.

Sender. You take on the role of **sender** as you initiate a message with your customer. Conversely, when customers respond, they assume that role.

FIGURE 3.1
Interpersonal
Communication
Model

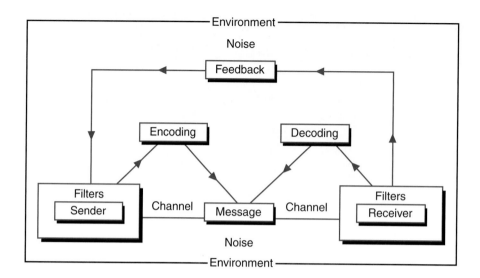

Receiver. Initially, you may be the **receiver** of your customer's message; however, once you offer feedback, you switch to the sender role.

Message. The **message** is the idea or concept that you or your customer wish to convey.

Channel. The method you choose to transmit your message (over the phone, in person, by fax, by modem, or by other means) is the **channel**.

Encoding. **Encoding** occurs as you evaluate what must be done to effectively put your message into a format that your customer will understand (language, symbols, and gestures are a few options). Failing to correctly determine your customer's ability to decode your message could lead to confusion and misunderstanding.

Decoding. **Decoding** occurs as you or your customer converts messages received into familiar ideas by interpreting or assigning meaning. Depending on how well the message was encoded or whether filters interfere, the received message may not be the one originally sent.

Feedback. Unless a response is given to messages received, there is no way to determine whether the intended message was received. **Feedback** is one of the most crucial elements of the two-way communication process. Without it, you have a monologue.

Filters. **Filters** are factors that distort or affect the messages you receive. They include, among other things, your attitude, interests, biases, expectations, education, beliefs, and values.

Noise. **Noise** consists of physiological or psychological factors (your physical characteristics, level of attention, message clarity, loudness of message, or environmental factors) that interfere with the accurate reception of information.

3   Avoiding Negative Communication

Concept: Use positive words or phrases, rather than emphasize the negative.

You can squelch customer loyalty and raise customer frustration in a number of ways when communicating. Your choice of words or phrasing can often lead to

LEADERSHIP INITIATIVE

3.1

One of the easiest ways for supervisors and managers to help ensure that effective interpersonal communication occurs in the workplace is to be certain that all employees are trained in the skill. Sessions on effective listening, giving and receiving feedback, questioning, and verbal and non-verbal communication can increase employee effectiveness and efficiency. This occurs by using learned skills to reduce potential misunderstandings and conflict, helping eliminate errors related to listening, and enhancing customer service.

FIGURE 3.2
Words and Phrases That Damage Customer Relationships

Here are some words and phrases that can lead to trouble with your customers. Avoid or limit their use.

You don't understand.	You're wrong or mistaken.
You'll have to . . .	You aren't listening to me.
You don't see my point.	Listen to me.
Hold on (or hang on) a second.	I never said . . .
I (we, you) can't . . .	In my opinion . . .
Our policy says (or prohibits) . . .	What's your problem?
That's not my job (or responsibility).	The word *problem.*
You're not being reasonable.	Do you understand?
You must . . .	Are you aware . . .
You should . . .	The word *but.*
What you need to do is . . .	Global terms (always, never, nobody).
You'll have to . . .	The word *no.*
Why don't you . . . ?	Endearment terms (honey, sweetie, sugar, baby).
I don't know.	Profanity or vulgarity.

either satisfaction or confrontation or it can destroy a customer-provider relationship. Customers do not want to hear what you can't do; they want to hear how you're going to help satisfy their needs or expectations. Focus your message on how you can work with the customer to accomplish needs satisfaction. Don't use vague or weak terminology. Instead of "I'm not sure . . ." or "I'll try . . ." say, "Let me get that answer for you . . ." or "I can do . . ."

Another pitfall to watch out for is the use of **global terms** (inclusive expressions such as *always, never, everyone, all*). If your customer can give just one example for which your statement is not true, your credibility comes into question and you might go on the defensive. Suppose you say, "We always return calls in four hours," yet the customer has personally experienced a situation when that did not happen. Your statement is now false. Instead, phrase statements to indicate possible variances such as, "We attempt to return all calls within four hours" or "Our objectives is to return calls within four hours." Be careful, too, about "verbal finger pointing," especially if your customer is already upset. This tactic involves the use of the word *you*, as in "You were supposed to have called back to remind me" or "You didn't follow the directions I gave you." This is like pointing your finger at someone or using a patronizing tone to belittle them. People are likely to react powerfully and negatively to this type of treatment. See Figure 3.2.

To help you determine how you sound to others, try a bit of objective self-analysis. To do this, place a cassette recorder nearby, either at home or in the office, and leave it on for about 45 minutes to an hour while you interact with other people. Then play the cassette to hear what your voice sounds like when you communicate verbally with others. Be especially alert for verbal cues that send a negative message or seem to be misinterpreted by the other people involved. Also, listen carefully to the manner in which others respond to you. Do their words or voice tone seem different from what you expected? Did they seem to respond to your comments in a way that shows confusion, frustration, or irritation because of what you said or how you said it? If you answer yes to these questions, and this occurs several times on the tape, go back to the people involved in the conversation and ask them to help you interpret what's on the tape. You may find that your communication style is doing more to hurt than help in gathering information and building relationships with others.

FIGURE 3.3

Words and Phrases That Build Customer Relationships

Some phrases can assist you in strengthening relationships with your customers. Such language reinforces your integrity and encourages customers to trust you. How do you or could you use these words? Which ones do you use the most?

Please.
Thank you.
I can or will . . .
How may I help?
I was wrong.
I understand (appreciate) how you feel.
Situation, issue, concern (instead of *problem*).
Often, many times, some (instead of *global terms*).

You're right.
May I . . . ?
Have you considered . . .
I'm sorry (I apologize) for . . .
However, and or *yet* (instead of *but*).
It's my (our) fault.
Would you mind . . .
What do you think?
I appreciate . . .
Use of customer's name.

4 Communicating Positively

Concept: A positive approach can produce positive results.

Just as you can turn customers off with your word choice, you can also win them over. Figure 3.3 contains some tips.

Plan Your Messages

You should think out everything from your greeting to your closing statements before you come into contact with a customer. Know what you want and need to say, avoid unnecessary details or discussion, and be prepared to answer questions about the organization, its products and services, and the customer's order.

Greet Customers Warmly and Sincerely

If appropriate, shake hands, smile often, and offer a sincere welcome, not the canned "Welcome to . . ." Instead, use whatever your organizational policy dictates, such as, "Good morning/afternoon, welcome to . . . , my name is . . . , how may I assist or help you?"

Even on the telephone you should smile and verbally shake your customer's hand, because your smile can definitely be heard in your voice. You will learn more about customer service and telephone etiquette in Chapter 9.

Use Customer-Focused Language

A mistake by many service providers is to communicate as if they are the important element of a transaction. In reality, it is the customer upon whom a message should be focused. The following examples show the difference in focus:

Provider-Centered

- I'll send out a form that we need you to complete and sign.
- Let me explain the benefits of this product.

Customer-Centered

- To make sure that we have all the information needed to ensure you the best service . . .
- As a savvy consumer, you'll appreciate the benefits of this product.

Use Eye Contact Effectively

In addition to greeting the customer, make regular eye contact (no longer than three to five seconds at a time) and assume a positive approachable posture throughout your interaction with a customer. More discussion on the topics of eye contact and nonverbal communication appears in Chapter 4.

Listen Carefully and Respond Appropriately

Listening is the key element of two-way verbal communication. The manner in which you listen and respond often determines the direction of the conversation. When customers feel that they are not being listened to, their attitude and emotions can quickly change from amiable to confrontational. If necessary, review Chapter 5 for specific suggestions on effective listening.

Be Specific

Whenever you have to answer questions, especially details relating to costs, delivery dates, warranties, and other important areas of customer interest, give complete and accurate details. If you leave something out, possibly because you believe that it isn't important, you can bet that the customer will feel it was important, and will be upset.

Examples:

If deliveries are free, but only within a 50-mile radius, make sure that you tell the customer about the mileage policy. (The customer may live 51 miles away!) If a customer calls to ask for the price of an item and your quote does not include tax, shipping and handling, say so. Give the total cost, so that there are no surprises when they drive to the store to make the purchase or order from your website and end up paying more.

Use Positive "I" or "We" Messages

In addition to avoiding the "you" statements mentioned earlier, focus on what "I" or "we" can do for or with the customer. In addressing the customer, state the specific service approaches you will take, for example, "I'll handle this personally," as

opposed to "I'll do my best" or "I'll try." Expressions like "I'll handle this personally" sound proactive and positive. **I or we messages** go a long way in subtly letting the customer know that you have the knowledge, confidence, and authority to help out.

Use "Small Talk"

Look for opportunities to communicate on a personal level or to compliment your customer. If you establish quickly a relationship with your customers, they are less likely to attack you verbally or complain. Listen to what they say. Look for things specific that you have in common. For example, suppose your customer mentions that she has just returned form Altoona, Pennsylvania, where she visited relatives. If you grew up in or near Altoona, comment about this and ask questions. By bonding with the customer, you show that you recognize the customer as more than a nameless face.

One thing to keep in mind about **small talk** is that you must listen to your customer's words and tone. If it is obvious he or she is impatient or in a hurry, skip the small talk and focus on efficiently providing service.

Use Simple Language

Many interpersonal impartation decompositions can be ascribed to one singular customer service professional fallacy—that all customers can discern the significance of the employee's vernacular. Simply stated: *Many customer service professionals fail to use language their customers can understand.*

When dealing with customers, especially if you are selling or servicing in a technical field, use terms and explanations that are easily understood. Watch the customer's nonverbal body language for signs of confusion or frustration as you speak, and frequently ask for feedback and questions.

If you are on the telephone, listen for sounds of confusion or pauses that may indicate that the customer either did not understand something you said or has a question.

Paraphrase 释义

To ensure that you get the message the customer intended to communicate, take time to ask for feedback. Do this by repeating to the customer the message you heard, but in your own words—**paraphrase.** An example would be, "If I understand the problem, Mrs. Hawthorne, you bought this item on June 28 as a present for your son. When he tried to assemble it, two parts were missing. Is that correct?"

Ask Positively Phrased Questions

Sometimes the simplest things can cause problems, especially if someone is already irritated. To avoid creating a negative situation or escalating customer emotions, choose the wording of your questions carefully. Consider these two specific techniques. The first is to find a way to rephrase any question that you would normally start with "Why?" The reason is that this word cannot be inflected in a way that doesn't come across as potentially abrasive, intrusive, or meddlesome. As with many experiences you have, the origin of negative feelings toward the word likely stem from childhood. Remember when you used to want to do something as a child and were told no? The word that probably came out of your mouth (in a whiney voice) was "Why?" This was a verbal challenge to the person who was telling you that you couldn't do something. And the response you probably heard was "Because I said so" or "Because I'm the mommy (or daddy), that's why." Most likely, you didn't like that type of response then, and neither did your customers when they were children. The result of this early experience is that when we hear the word *why*, it can sound like a challenge and can prompt a negative emotional reaction. To prevent this from occurring, try rewording your "Why" questions.

Examples:

Instead of	Try
Why do you feel that way?	What makes you feel that way?
Why don't you like . . . ?	What is it that you don't like about . . . ?
Why do you need that feature?	How is that feature going to be beneficial to you?
Why do you want that color?	What other colors have you considered?

The second technique to consider regarding question phrasing is to ask questions that do not create or add to a negative impression. This is especially important if you have a customer who is already saying negative things about you, your product or service, or the company. By asking questions that start with a negative word and trying to lead customers to an answer, you can be subtly adding fuel to a fire. For example, suppose your customer is upset because he ordered window blinds through the mail and did not get the color he wanted. He has called you to complain. You have asked a few questions to determine the color scheme of the room in which the blinds will be installed. You say, "Based on what you have told me, don't you think the color you received would work just as well?" Your customer now launches into a tirade. He probably thinks that you were not listening to him, were not concerned about his needs, and presumed you could lead him to another decision.

Here are some more examples of questions that could cause communication breakdowns, along with some suggested alternatives.

Examples:

Instead of	Try
Don't you think . . . ?	What do you think . . . ?
Wouldn't this work as well?	How do you think this would work?
Couldn't we do . . . instead?	Could we try . . . instead?
Aren't you going to make a deposit?	What amount would you like to deposit?
Don't you have two pennies?	Do you have two pennies?
Shouldn't you try this for a week before we replace the part again?	How do you feel about trying it for a week to see how it works before we replace the part again?

Communicate to Your Customer's Learning Style

People process information in one of three ways—visually (seeing), aurally (hearing), or kinesthetically (touching). (Figure 3.4 gives examples of people's **learning styles** and how they express their preferences.) To increase the likelihood that the messages you send are received in the most positive and successful manner, you should strive to encode them based on your customers' preferred style of learning. By being aware of their verbal and physical reactions and mannerisms, you can often determine the best way to send messages.

FIGURE 3.4
Personal Learning Orientations

Message Preference	Orientation	Environmental Influences	Verbal Clues
Visual (seeing)	Images or pictures	Amount of stimulus Lighting Colors Design patterns	• I see what you mean. • I think I get the picture. • Some people can't see the forest for the trees. • Look at it this way. • Help me visualize what you're saying. • That gives me the big picture. • The way I see it . . . • It appears to me.
Aural (hearing)	Words or language	Noise levels Sound pitch (high or low) Speed of message Diversity of sounds	• That sounds okay. • That's music to my ears. • Let me hear more about that. • If I'm hearing you correctly. • It sounds like you're saying . . . • As I hear it. • We'd better keep our ear to the ground. • In one ear and out the other. • Sounds a little strange to me. • I hear exactly what you're saying. • Talk is cheap. • Something doesn't sound right.
Kinesthetic (hands-on)	Experience or practical application	Proxemics (space) Touch Room temperature Room arrangement	• I think I've got a grip on what you're saying. • It feels to me . . . • That's a little too close for comfort. • How do you feel about this? • I'm not sure I'm comfortable with . . . • Things are really heating up. • Let's roll up our sleeves and get started. • I'm not sure I can go for that. • How do you feel about. . . ? • Let's analyze this. • I can't quite grasp your meaning. • If the shoe fits.

Ask Permission

Get customer approval before taking action that was not previously approved or discussed, such as putting a telephone caller on hold or interrupting. By doing so, you can raise the customers to a position of authority, boost their self-esteem, and empower them (to say yes or no). They'll likely appreciate all three. You'll learn more about telephone etiquette and effective usage in Chapter 9.

Agree With Customers

Like most other people, customers like to hear that they are right. This is especially true when a mistake has been made or something goes wrong. When a customer has a complaint or is upset because a product and/or service does not live up to expectations, acknowledge the emotion he or she is feeling and then move on and help resolve the issue. Defusing by acknowledgment is a powerful tool. However, listen carefully for the level of emotion. If the customer is very angry, you may want to choose your words carefully. For example, suppose you have a customer who has called or returned to your store on four occasions to address a single problem with a product. She has been inconvenienced, has not gotten satisfaction in the previous encounters, and has spent extra time in an effort to correct the problem. When she calls or arrives, her voice tone and volume are elevated and she is demanding that you get a supervisor. In this situation, your best approach probably is to let her vent and describe the problem without interrupting, apologize as often as appropriate, and do everything you can to resolve the issue fairly (assuming that she has a legitimate complaint). You would not want to use a statement that could further enflame her. Although phrases such as, "You sound upset Ms. O'Malley," or "I can understand how you feel" can help diffuse some tense situations, they can come across as patronizing and insincere when someone is really angry. Instead of using such terminology, try looking for something she is saying that you can agree with. Also, remember that when customers get angry, raise their voices, and say certain things, they are not typically angry with you—they are frustrated and angry with the organization and/or system. For example, suppose Ms. O'Malley says something like, "You people are a bunch of idiots. I've been coming in here for years and I always have problems. Why don't you hire someone with brains to serve your customers?" The normal human response would be to retaliate. However, think back on what happened when you were a child at the playground. When someone pushed you or called you a name and you responded with name-calling or pushed back, emotions escalated until someone either struck out or ran away crying. No one won. The relationship was damaged, possibly irreparably. In the case of Ms. O'Malley, if you strike back with similar comments, neither of you will win. Moreover, you will likely lose a valued customer who will tell her story to many friends—and you will have to explain to your boss why you acted the way you did. Instead, try a defusing technique in which you seek something to agree upon. For example, you might reply, "I know this is frustrating, especially when it seems we haven't done a good job solving your problem." After this, assuming she doesn't launch back in with another tirade, you might then offer, "Let me help you take care of this right now." If she does verbally attack again, let her vent and then try another calm agreement response, followed by a second offer to assist. The value in this approach is that in letting Ms. O'Malley vent, you are discovering her emotions and possibly the history of the problem by listening actively. If you need more information, you can ask questions once

LEADERSHIP INITIATIVE

3.2

Leaders should take the time to regularly gather customer and employee ideas, perspectives, and comments. This can be accomplished by supervisors and managers walking around the service environment to observe and talk to people. If your organization provides service primarily via technology, use other communication survey techniques, such as e-mail, telephone, written questionnaires, customer and employee feedback forms, or focus groups. The key is to ask the right questions, objectively listen to the responses and to take appropriate action on information received. If information-gathering becomes part of the organizational culture, trust and service levels will likely increase.

you have defused her emotions and she calms down a bit. Typically, if you remain calm and objective and look for minor things with which you can agree, the customer will back off. Also, the customer will likely start to see that she is the one out of control and that you are being professional while trying to help her. If the customer truly wants the problem to be solved, she soon realizes that cooperation with you is necessary.

In many cases, if you resolve the customer's problem professionally, the customer will often apologize for his or her actions and words.

Elicit Customer Feedback and Participation

Make customers feel as if they are a part of the conversation by asking questions. Ask opinions, find out how they feel about what you're doing or saying, and get them involved by building **rapport** through ongoing dialogue. Acknowledge their ideas, suggestions, or information with statements such as, "That's a good idea (or suggestion or decision)." This will foster a feeling that the two of you are working together to solve a problem. The beauty of such an approach is that if the customer comes up with an idea and you follow through on it, he or she feels a sense of ownership and is less likely to complain later or feel bad if things don't work out as planned.

Close the Transaction Professionally

Instead of some parroted response used for each customer like, "Have a nice day," offer a sincere "thank-you" and encourage the customer to return in the future. Remember that part of a service culture is building customer loyalty. You will have an opportunity to examine that subject in depth in Chapter 12.

Address Pet Peeves

Most people have something that bothers them about how others communicate or behave. These hot buttons or **pet peeves** can lead to customer relationship breakdowns if you are not aware of what your pet peeves are and how you come across to others. By identifying and acknowledging your potential irritants, you can begin to modify your behavior in order to prevent problems with customers. You may also be able to avoid situations in which such behaviors are present or might manifest themselves and cause problems for you.

Your customers also likely have a list of things that they dislike about service providers. If you exhibit one of their pet peeves while serving them, you could find yourself opposite a disgruntled person who is not afraid to voice his or her displeasure. They may even escalate their complaint to your supervisor or elsewhere.

To help identify possible behaviors that might cause customer relationship problems, create a list of pet peeves that you have related to service providers. Next, create a list of things that you can do to avoid or correct the items on the list. After about 15 minutes, share your list with others in the class.

An alternative is for your instructor to form groups of four to five students and do this as a group activity.

Some typical behaviors that service providers exhibit, and that might bother customers, include:

Disinterest in serving.

Excessive wait times.

Unprofessional service provider appearance.

Lack of cleanliness (environment or service provider).

Abruptly putting someone on telephone hold without their permission.

Failing to answer telephone within four rings.

Eating or chewing while dealing with a customer.

Lack of knowledge or authority.

Poor quality of service.

Condescension (taking an air of superiority to the customer).

Rudeness or overfamiliarity.

5 Projecting a Positive Image

Concept: Make the customer feel special and important. Take responsibility for what you say and do.

Knowing what to say and when to say it in a customer service environment can often determine the outcome of a customer encounter. As mentioned before, it is not only what you say but how you say it that makes an impression on your customers. As a customer service professional, you should always attempt to make a positive impression by focusing on the customer and his or her needs during your initial contact and all subsequent ones. This effort benefits you and the customer immediately and the organization in the long term. Here are some tips for projecting a positive image and communicating professionally.

Make Customers Feel Welcome

Most people like to feel as if they belong, to be recognized as special, and to be seen as individuals. Know the customer's name, use it in greeting him or her, several times throughout the conversation, and when closing the encounter. Try to avoid using negative-sounding "you" messages as a primary means of addressing your customer. For example, instead of "You'll need to fill out this form before I can process your refund," try "Mr. Renaldi, if you could please provide some information on this form while I start processing your refund, we'll have you out of here in a minute." The latter approach makes it sound as if you recognize customers as being important, respect their time, and are not dictating to them. This can often mean the difference between a smile from your customer and a confrontation and demand to speak to a supervisor.

73

Many companies go out of their way to send the message of "family." For example, the Saturn automobile company advertisements tout that customers become part of the "Saturn family" once they buy a car from the company. Similarly, CarMax and several other national automobile chains go to great lengths to make the customer feel welcome and special. For example, they drape a huge ribbon over a newly purchased vehicle in a well-lighted garage, available sales representatives gather round with the customer to congratulate him or her on being part of the "family," and photographs are taken of this "special moment."

Focus on the Customer as a Person

Strive to let customers know that you recognize them as persons and appreciate their time, effort, patience, trust, and business. This is important. To deliver quality service effectively, you must deal with the human being before you deal with his or her needs or business concerns. For example, if someone has waited in a line or on hold for service, as soon as this person steps up or you come back on the line, smile warmly (yes, even on the phone, since a smile can be heard in your voice), thank him or her for being patient, apologize for the wait, and ask what you can do to assist him or her. Often in such situations the service provider says something like, "Next," (sounds canned and not customer-focused) or "Can I help the next person?" (better, but still goes straight to business without an apology or without recognizing the customer's inconvenience or wait). On the phone the service provider goes straight to, "This is Jean, how may I help you?" (with no recognition of the customer's inconvenience).

Another opportunity to focus on the customer occurs at the end of a transaction or call. If your organization does not have a standard parting comment to use with customers, simply smile and say something like, "Mr. Rinaldi, thank you for coming to (or calling) ABC Corporation. Please come back (or call) again." The key is that you must sound sincere. You may even want to modify your parting statement for subsequent customers so that it sounds more personal—and so the next person in line doesn't hear you parrot the same words with each customer.

Offer assistance. Even if a problem or question is not in your area of responsibility, offer to help get answers, information, or assistance. Your customer will likely appreciate the fact that you went out of your way to help.

Be prepared. Know as much as possible about the organization, its products and services, your job, and as appropriate, the customer. Also, make sure that you have all the tools necessary to serve the customer, take notes, and do your job in a professional manner. This allows you to deliver quality information and service while better satisfying customer needs and expectations.

Provide factual information. Don't express opinions or speculate why something did or didn't, or will or will not, occur. State only what you are sure of or can substantiate. For example, if you are not sure when a delivery will take place or when a coworker who handles certain functions will return, say so, but offer to find the answer or handle the situation yourself. Don't raise customer expectations by saying, "This should be delivered by 7:30 tomorrow morning," or "Sue should be back from lunch in 10 minutes." If neither event occurs, the customer is likely to be irritated.

Be helpful. If you cannot do something or don't have a product or service, admit it but be prepared to offer an alternative. Do not try to "dance around" an issue in an effort to respond in a manner that you feel the customer expects.

Think of times when you have been put on hold or stood in a line.

1. How did the service provider address you when it was your turn for service?
2. Did you feel special or did you feel like the next in a long line of bodies being processed? Why?
3. When the service provider simply picked up the phone and offered to assist you or shouted "Next" while you waited in line, what thoughts went through your mind about the provider and the organization?
4. What could service providers do or say to eliminate negative customer feelings in such situations?

Most people will spot this tentative behavior, and your credibility will suffer as a result. Do not insult your customer's intelligence by taking this approach. You and the organization will lose in the long run.

Accept responsibility. Take responsibility for what you do or say and, if necessary, for actions taken by someone else that failed to satisfy the customer. Don't blame others or hide behind "they said" or "policy says" excuses. When something goes wrong, take responsibility and work to resolve the problem positively and quickly. If you don't have the authority needed, get someone who does, rather than referring the customer to someone else.

Take appropriate action. You should take whatever action is necessary to satisfy the customer. Sometimes this may mean bending the rules a bit. In such cases, it may be easier to ask forgiveness from your supervisor than to explain why you lost the organization a good customer. If a request really cannot be honored because it is too extreme (a customer demands a free $100 item because he or she had to return one that did not work properly), explain why and then negotiate and offer alternatives. In Chapter 13 you will find some suggestions for appropriate service recovery strategies.

6 Providing Feedback

Concept: Your feedback could affect the relationship you have or are building with your customers. The effect may be positive or negative, depending on the content and delivery.

Feedback is a response to messages a listener receives. This response may be transmitted verbally (with words) or nonverbally (through actions or inaction). Depending on the content and delivery, your feedback could positively or negatively influence your relationships with your customers. Figure 3.5 offers some tips on providing feedback effectively, and the two types of feedback are discussed in the following sections.

Verbal Feedback

The words you choose in providing feedback to your customers are crucial to interpretation and understanding. Before providing feedback, you should take into consideration the knowledge and skill level of your customer(s). This is part of the "encoding" discussed earlier in the section "Interpersonal Communication Model" earlier in this chapter. Failure to consider the customer could result in breakdowns in understanding. For example, if you choose words that are not likely

FIGURE 3.5
Guidelines for Providing Positive Feedback

Here are 10 tips for effectively providing feedback:

1. When appropriate, give feedback immediately when communicating face-to-face or over the telephone.
2. Communicate in a clear, concise manner.
3. Remain objective and unemotional when providing feedback.
4. Make sure that your feedback is accurate before you provide it.
5. Use verbal and nonverbal messages that are in congruence (agree with each other).
6. Verify the customer's meaning before providing feedback.
7. Make sure that your feedback is appropriate to the customer's original message (active listening helps in getting the original message).
8. Strive to clarify feedback when the customer seems unclear of your intention.
9. Avoid overly critical feedback or negative language (as described in this chapter).
10. Do not provide feedback if it could damage the customer-provider relationship.

to be part of your customer's vocabulary, because of the customer's education and/or experience, your message may be confusing. Also, if you use acronyms or technical terms (jargon or unfamiliar to the customer), the meaning of the message could get lost. When providing **verbal feedback**, you should also be conscious of how your customer is receiving your information. If the customer's body language or nonverbal cues (gestures, facial expressions) or words indicate misunderstanding, you should pause, and take any corrective action necessary to clear up the misunderstanding.

To check your perception of nonverbal cues, use the following process:

1. Identify the behavior observed.
   Example: "Mr. Warlinkowski, when I said that it would be seven to ten days before we could get your new sofa delivered to your home, your facial expression changed to what appeared to be one of concern."
2. Offer one or two interpretations.
   Example: "I wasn't sure whether you were indicating that the time frame doesn't work for you, or whether something else went through your mind."
3. Ask for clarification.
   Example: "Which was it?"

By asking for clarification, you reduce the chance of having a dissatisfied customer. You also send a message that you are paying attention to the customer.

非言语交际 Nonverbal Feedback

Nonverbal feedback will be explored in depth in Chapter 4. Here are a few ways in which feedback can be given nonverbally.

Body Language

The ways in which you sit, stand, gesture, position your body (face to face or at an angle), or use facial expressions can all send positive or negative messages.

Actions

By responding to the request of a coworker or external customer in a timely, correct manner, you can send a message of "I care" or "You're important." On the negative side, failure to act or a delay could be perceived as a lack of concern. Moreover, it is important to recognize that the amount of time you allocate to individuals can send a powerful message. For example, suppose a coworker comes into your work area and says that she needs to speak with you about information that you have which is needed for a project deadline she has. You invite her to have a seat and then tell her you have only a few minutes to talk because you're expecting an important call. Two minutes later, the phone rings and you ask to be excused while you take the call. She leaves, and from her cubicle, which is next to yours, she can overhear your conversation. From your laughter, comments, and tone of voice, she concludes that you are on a personal call. She waits patiently for almost 20 minutes and then has to go to another meeting.

The messages that you have sent nonverbally are that you are not a team player, for you do not appear to be supporting her in the project, and that you value personal calls over important business issues with an internal customer. Such actions could haunt you when your coworker relates the incident to others or possibly to a supervisor. Also, if you need her support in the future, you may find that she is reluctant to help you out.

Appearances 外观.

The way you look physically (hygiene and grooming), dress, and how you maintain your work area sends a message of either professionalism or indifference.

A workplace that is unkempt and untidy may give the impression that the person is also untidy and disorganized. *What do you think of a person who has a messy workplace? Do you think the company is responsible for getting an employee to clean up?*

Even though you provide attentive, quality service, the customer will typically form an opinion of you and your organization within 30 seconds based on your appearance and that of your work space. This opinion may make the difference in whether the customer will continue to patronize your organization or go to a competitor. For example, a disorganized desk with piles of papers scattered over it may seem functional to you, but many people think of a person with such a work space as disorganized, unmotivated, and unprofessional. Likewise, your clothing, grooming, and choice of jewelry or other accessories could send a negative message to some people. It is crucial to be able to distinguish between what is appropriate for the workplace and what is appropriate for a night out. We'll cover nonverbal cues more thoroughly in Chapter 4.

坚定自信.

7   Dealing Assertively With Customers

Concept: Express ideas simply without weakening your position.

Your level of assertiveness is directly tied to your style of behavior. Some people are direct and to the point; others are calm and laid back. Neither style is better or worse than the other. What is important is to be able to recognize which style to call upon in various situations. You will explore behavioral styles in detail in Chapter 6.

To emphasize that different people often have different perceptions of what they see, and the importance of appearance, look at the photographs of the people below. Describe your reactions to and perceptions of each as asked below. Once finished, compare your responses to those of fellow students.

Photo 1

Photo 2

Photo 3

Photo 4

Photo 5

Photo 6

Photo 7

Photo 8

Photo 1
1. What are your perceptions?_____
2. Explain why you have these perceptions._____
3. How might your perception affect your ability to effectively serve this person?_____

Photo 2
1. What are your perceptions?_____
2. Explain why you have these perceptions._____
3. How might your perception affect your ability to effectively serve this person?_____

Photo 3
1. What are your perceptions?_____
2. Explain why you have these perceptions._____
3. How might your perception affect your ability to effectively serve this person?_____

Photo 4

1. What are your perceptions?_____

2. Explain why you have these perceptions._____

3. How might your perception affect your ability to effectively serve this person?_____

Photo 5

1. What are your perceptions?_____

2. Explain why you have these perceptions._____

3. How might your perception affect your ability to effectively serve this person?_____

Photo 6

1. What are your perceptions?_____

2. Explain why you have these perceptions._____

3. How might your perception affect your ability to effectively serve this person?_____

Photo 7

1. What are your perceptions?_____

2. Explain why you have these perceptions._____

3. How might your perception affect your ability to effectively serve this person?_____

Photo 8

1. What are your perceptions?_____

2. Explain why you have these perceptions._____

3. How might your perception affect your ability to effectively serve this person?_____

FIGURE 3.6
Nonassertive and
Assertive Behaviors

The following list contains examples of nonassertive and assertive language and behaviors, along with tips for increasing your assertiveness.

Nonassertive	Assertive
• Poor eye contact while speaking.	• Look customer in the eye as you speak.
• Weak ("limp fish") handshake.	• Grasp firmly without crushing (web of your hand against web of the other person's hand).
• Rambling speech, not really stating.	• Think, Plan, Speak a specific question or information.
• Use of verbal paralanguage (ah, um, you know).	• Stop, gather thoughts, speak.
• Apologetic in words and tone.	• Apologize if you make a mistake; (I'm sorry, please forgive me) then take control and move on with the conversation.
• Soft, subdued tone.	• Increase volume, sound firm and convincing.
• Finger pointing; blaming others.	• Take responsibility; resolve the problem.
• Nervous gestures, fidgeting.	• Hold something; grasp a table or chair; fold your hands as you talk.

Generally, assertive communication deals with expressing ideas positively and with confidence. An example would be to stand or sit erect, make direct eye contact, smile, listen empathetically, and then calmly and firmly nod and explain what you can do to assist the customer.

Figure 3.6 lists several examples of nonassertive and assertive language and behaviors. Additional resources are listed in the Bibliography.

To strengthen your ability to provide feedback, work with two other people (one partner and one observer) to practice your skill in delivering feedback.

Select a topic for discussion.

Spend 10 minutes talking about your selected topic with your partner.

During the conversation, you and your partner should use verbal and nonverbal feedback.

At the end of the 10 minutes, ask your partner, and then the observer, the following questions.

1. How did I do in providing appropriate verbal feedback? Give examples.
2. How did I do in providing appropriate nonverbal feedback? Give examples.
3. How well did I interpret verbal and nonverbal messages? Give examples.
4. What questions did I ask to clarify comments or feedback provided? Give examples.
5. What could I have done to improve my feedback?

8 Assertive Versus Aggressive Service

Concept: Assertive service is good for solving problems; aggressive service may escalate them.

Do not confuse assertive with aggressive service. Why is the distinction so important in customer service? What's the difference? The answer: **Assertiveness** can assist in solving problems; aggression can escalate and cause relationship breakdowns. Asserting yourself means that you project an image of confidence, are self-assured, and state what you believe to be true in a self-confident manner. Aggression involves hostile or offensive behavior, often in the form of a verbal or even physical attack. Aggressive people send messages verbally and nonverbally that imply that they are superior, or in charge. They often do this through behavior and language that is manipulative, judgmental, or domineering. An assertive person states (verbally and nonverbally), "Here's my position. What's your reaction to that?" An aggressive person sends the message, "Here is my position. Take it or leave it." Obviously, the two modes of dealing with customers create very different service experiences. The manner in which you nonverbally or verbally approach, address, and interact with customers may label you as either assertive or aggressive. Consider the following interactions between a customer and a service provider:

Assertive Behavior Example

Customer (returning an item of merchandise):	Excuse me, I received this sweater as a present and I'd like to return it.
Service Provider (smiling):	Is there something wrong with it?
Customer (still smiling):	Oh no. I just don't need another sweater.
Service Provider (still smiling):	Do you have a receipt?
Customer (not smiling):	No. As I said, it was a gift.
Service Provider (handing over a form):	That's all right. But I will need you to fill out the top portion of this form with your name, phone number, and reason for return. And please sign at the bottom.

Aggressive behavior can lead to relationship failure. When someone verbally attacks another, the chances of emotions escalating and relationships failing increase significantly. *How can you avoid aggressive behavior in a relationship?*

Customer (not smiling):	Does this mean I have to get out of line and then wait again? I've already been in line for ten minutes.
Service Provider (smiling):	Well, rather than delay the line, if you could step over to that table to fill out the form, and then bring it back to me, I'll take care of you.
Customer (smiling):	Okay, thanks.

In this example, the service provider is trying to assure the customer, through words and body language, that he or she is there to assist the customer.

Aggressive Service Example

Customer (returning an item of merchandise):	Excuse me, I received this sweater as a present and I'd like to return it.
Service Provider (not smiling):	What's wrong with it?
Customer (smiling):	Oh nothing, I just don't need another sweater.
Service Provider (still not smiling):	Do you have a receipt?
Customer (not smiling):	No. As I said, it was a gift.

Service Provider (handing over a form):	Well, our policy requires that you'll have to fill out this form since you don't have a receipt.
Customer (not smiling):	Does that mean I have to get out of line and then wait again? I've already been in line for 10 minutes.
Service Provider (not smiling):	The line's getting shorter. It shouldn't take long. Next . . .

In this example, the service provider is not doing well on service delivery, nor is he or she projecting a positive image. The nonverbal and verbal messages convey an almost hostile attitude. This type of behavior can easily escalate into an unnecessary confrontation.

Providing Assertive Service

You will find that it is important to recognize your own level of knowledge, ability, and authority in any situation. If you do not send a message of confidence and competence through your personal demeanor while showing respect for your customer, the customer-provider relationship can quickly be spoiled. To project an assertive image as opposed to an aggressive one try focusing in the following areas:

Facial expressions. Smile and demonstrate warmth and a willingness to help.

Voice. Remain calm, steady, and self-assured. Use inflection without raising volume to emphasize your speech. State your issues, ideas, or concerns in a manner that does not project an assumptive or threatening tone. Remember to smile and maintain a delivery pace that shows you are not rushed or stressed.

Posture. Stand or sit erect, but not rigid. Occasionally lean forward to emphasize key points.

Gestures. Use open gestures with arms and hands. Gesture with open palms as opposed to pointing.

Eye contact. Maintain intermittent eye contact as you smile. Avoid squinting or glaring.

Win-win solutions. Work toward mutual understanding and the attainment of resolutions that allow the organization and the customer to succeed.

Responding to Conflict

Conflict should be viewed as neither positive nor negative. Instead, it is an opportunity to identify differences that may need to be addressed when dealing with your internal and external customers. It is not unusual for you to experience conflict when dealing with someone else. In fact it is normal and beneficial as long as you stay focused on the issue rather than personalizing and internalizing the conflict. When you focus on the individual, or vice versa, conflict can escalate and can ultimately do irreparable damage to the relationship.

Conflict typically results when you and someone else disagree about something. The following are examples of five forms of conflict that might occur in your organization.

Between individuals. You and your supervisor or another employee disagrees on the way a customer situation should be handled.

Between an individual and a group. You disagree about a new customer procedure created by your work team.

Between an individual and an organization. A dissatisfied customer feels that your organization is not providing quality products or services.

Between organizational groups. Your department has goals (for example, the way customer orders or call handling procedures are processed) that create additional requirements or responsibilities for members of another department.

Between organizations. Your organization is targeting the same customers to sell a new product similar to one that an affiliate organization markets to that group.

Causes of Conflict

There are many causes of conflict. The following are some common ones.

Conflicting values and beliefs. These sometime create situations in which the perceptions of an issue or its impact vary. Since values and beliefs have been learned over long periods of time and are often taken personally at face value, individuals get very defensive when their foundations are challenged. For example, you might have been taught that it is ethically and morally wrong to lie to a customer, yet your supervisor tells you that it is ethically and morally wrong to lie to a customer, yet your supervisor tells you that it's okay to tell *a little white lie* (slight exaggeration) to explain a missed delivery.

Personal style differences. As you will read in Chapter 6, each person is different and requires special consideration and a unique approach in interactions. For example, your supervisor has a high D style, is much focused, and typically wants to know only the bottom line in any conversation. You have a high E style and find it difficult to share information without providing a lot of details in a highly emotional fashion. When the two of you speak, this can lead to conflict unless one or both of you is willing to adapt your communication style.

Differing perceptions. People often witness or view an incident or issue differently. This can cause disagreement, frustration, and a multitude of other emotional feelings. For example, an employee (Sue) tells you that she is upset because a deadline was missed because another employee (Fred) did not effectively manage his time. Fred later commented to you that your supervisor pulled him off the project in question in order to work on another assignment. This resulted in his missing the original assignment deadline and a perception by Sue that he could not manage time.

Inadequate or poor communication. Any time there is inadequate communication, the chance for conflict escalates. For example, an angry coworker (Leonard) confides to you that he forgot to tell a customer about limitations on your organizations return policy. As a result, when the customer brought a product back, another coworker had to deal with a frustrated and angry customer.

Contrary expectations. When one party expects something not provided by another, conflict will likely result. For example, your company offers a 90-day parts-only warranty on equipment that you sell; however, when it breaks down within that period, the customer expects free service also. If that expectation is not met, you have to deal with conflict and the customer is potentially dissatisfied.

Inadequate communication. People generally like to know what to expect and do not want a lot of surprises from their supervisor. When they get mixed signals because of inconsistency, frustration and conflict could result. For example, your supervisor told the entire service staff that in the future, each employee would have an opportunity to earn bonuses based on how many customers they could convince to upgrade their membership in the organization. You believe that you have sold the most for the month, yet when you point this out to your supervisor, he tells you that the bonus only applies if you have high sales for two months in a row.

Goals that are out of sync. Frustration and resentment can result from misaligned efforts. For example, you have been working as a service technician for over a year and have learned that, on average, it takes about 1½ hours to install a new telephone line. Your supervisor regularly counsels you because you do not accomplish the feat within the goal of 1 hour.

Opposition over shared resources. When two people or groups vie for the same resources, conflict usually results. For example, all monies for employee training are lumped into a central training budget in your organization. You have been requesting to go to a customer service training skills program for the past six months, however, you are told that there is only enough money to train people from the technical staff to learn new computer software.

Outcomes dependent on others. Whenever you have two or more people, departments, or organizations working jointly toward goal attainment, the potential for conflict exists. For example, your department receives customer orders over the telephone, and then forwards them to the fulfillment department for processing and order shipment. If the fulfillment process breaks down, a customer has your name and number, and he or she typically contacts you. If the customer is unhappy, it is you who has to placate him or her and spend time resolving the conflict.

Misuse of power. Resentment, frustration, and retaliation often result when employees believe that their supervisor is abusing their authority or power. For example, you overhear your supervisor telling an attractive employee that unless certain sexual favors are granted, she will not receive a desired promotion.

Guidelines for Effective Conflict Management

Even though each situation and person you deal with will differ, there are some basic approaches that may help in resolution of disagreement(s). Try the following strategies.

- *Remain calm.* You cannot be part of the solution if you become part of the problem. If you are one of the factors contributing to the conflict, consider getting an objective third party to arbitrate; possibly a coworker or your supervisor.
- *Be proactive in avoiding conflict.* As a customer service representative for your organization, you must try to recognize the personalities of those with whom you come into contact daily. If you are dealing with coworkers or peers, try to identify their capabilities and the environments most conducive to their effectiveness. If you are interacting with a customer, use verbal and nonverbal techniques discussed in Chapters 3 and 4 to help determine the customer's needs. Approach each person in a fashion that can lead to win-win situations; do not set yourself and others up for conflict or failure.
- *Keep an open mind.* Be cautious in order to avoid letting your own values or beliefs influence your objectivity when working toward conflict identification and resolution. As you will read later, this can cause damage to your long-term relationship(s).

- *Identify and confront underlying issues immediately.* Because of the emotional issues often involved in dealing with problem situations, few people enjoy dealing with conflict; however, if you fail to acknowledge and confront issues as soon as they become known, tensions may escalate.
- *Clarify communication.* Ensure that you elicit information on the causes of the conflict and provide the clear, detailed feedback necessary to resolve the issue. This effort can sometimes test your patients and communication skills, but is a necessary step in the resolution process.
- *Stress cooperation rather than competition.* One of your roles as a service provider is to ensure that you work toward common goals with your coworkers, supervisor, and customers. When one person succeeds at the expense of another's failure, you have not done your job. Encourage and develop teamwork and cooperation when dealing with others.
- *Focus resolution efforts on the issues.* Do not get caught up in or allow finger-pointing, name-calling, or accusations. Keep all efforts and discussions directed toward identifying and resolving the real issue(s). Stay away from criticizing or blaming others.
- *Follow established procedures for handling conflict.* It is easier to implement a process already in place than to have to quickly come up with one. That is why most customer service organizations have set customer complaint handling procedures.

Salvaging Relationships Following Conflict

Managing conflict involves more than just resolving the disagreement. If you fail to address the emotional and psychological needs of those involved, you may find the conflict returning and/or severe damage to the relationship may occur.

Depending on the severity of the conflict and how it was handled at each step of the resolution process, it may be impossible to go back to the point in the relationship that you were in before the disagreement. The key to reducing this possibility is to identify and address conflicting issues as early as possible. The longer an issue remains unresolved, the more damage it can cause. Whenever possible, apply one or more of the following strategies to help protect and salvage the relationship(s) between you and your coworkers, supervisor, and customers.

- *Reaffirm the value of the relationship.* You cannot assume that others feel the same as you or understand your intent unless you communicate it. Tell them how much you value your relationship. This is especially important when dealing with customers. Recall the statistics from Chapter 1 about how many people a dissatisfied customer might tell about the experience and the damage it can do to the organization.
- *Demonstrate commitment.* You must verbalize and demonstrate your desire to continue or strengthen your relationship. The way to do this with customers is through **service recovery,** which will be addressed in detail in Chapter 13.
- *Be realistic.* Because of behavioral styles, it is difficult for some people to "forgive and forget." You have to systematically help restore their trust. It can take a while to accomplish this, but the effort is well worth it.
- *Remain flexible.* A solid relationship involve the ability to give and take. It is especially crucial that you and the other people involved make concessions following conflict.
- *Keep communication open.* One of the biggest causes of conflict and destroyed relationships is poor communication.

FIGURE 3.7
Conflict Resolution
Styles

Among other things, the way in which you and your customers deal with conflict is influenced by their behavioral style preference (temperament), cultural values and beliefs, and what they have been taught (learned behavior). The following are five typical approaches to handling conflict that were developed by Kenneth Thomas.[1]

Avoidance is a totally uncooperative and unassertive way of dealing with conflict. When using this approach, you ignore the conflict; often in the hope that it will simply go away. Generally, this does not work and the issue may resurface again, only with more emotion attached. There are times when this strategy might be appropriate, such as the timing for a discussion is not appropriate or emotions have escalated to a point where physical danger is imminent. In either situation it might be prudent to postpone dealing with a person or issue. Generally, the avoidance approach has a lose-lose outcome in which no one gets what they need or want.

Compromise is a partial resolution and is between assertiveness and cooperativeness. When compromising occurs, both parties give and take in order to resolve a situation. You might consider such a strategy when power or controlling a situation is not important to either party, when trying to just get past an issue, or when it is in the best interest of both parties to maintain the relationship. Typically, compromise ends up with a win/lose-win/lose result.

Competition focuses on a dominance mind-set in which someone comes out the winner. High D personality style people often take this approach to resolving conflict situations. If you choose this approach to dealing with someone who disagrees with you, you likely focus on your success above that of the customer and the organization. This approach is a win-lose strategy in which you win at the expense of your customer's loss and can lead to escalated emotions and ultimately a lost customer.

Accommodation happens when you and your organization take an approach to dealing with customer conflict that allows the customer to win the outcome. This might be appropriate if you value the relationship (for example, a longtime customer who spends a lot of money with your organization) or if what the customer wants is really inconsequential compared to what might happen if you do not grant the customer's wish (for example, the customer wants you to pay overnight shipping for an item because it was out of stock when ordered and it is needed for a special event). This can create challenges if not done correctly because some customers might come to expect similar concessions each time something goes wrong in the future. In the extreme, this approach is a lose-win strategy and ends up with you and your organization giving in and "losing" while the customer gains everything desired.

Collaboration results in the only true win-win outcome for both parties. When collaborating, you and your customer actively try to see the other person's perspective and come to a mutual agreement. For this option to work, trust is crucial. It is a good strategy to try to bring out and resolve lingering issues and to creatively solve a problem. Collaboration is both cooperative and assertive in its approach.

[1]K. Thomas, *The Handbook of Industrial and Organizational Psychology,* edited by Marvin Dunnette, Rand McNally, Chicago, Ill., 1976.

- *Gain commitment.* You cannot do it all by yourself. Get a commitment to work toward reconciliation from any other person(s) involded in the conflict.
- *Monitor progress.* Do not assume because the conflict was resolved that it will remain that way. Deep-seated issues often resurface, especially when commitment was not obtained. With customers, be sure to do the follow-up that you have read about in earlier chapters.

Chapter Summary

Providing service that makes a customer feel special can lead to customer satisfaction and loyalty to you and your organization. By responding appropriately and in a positive manner (verbally and nonverbally), you will increase your likelihood of success. When additional information is needed, it is up to you to ask questions that will elicit useful customer feedback. You must then interpret and respond in kind with feedback that lets the customer know you received the intended message. You must also let your customers know that you'll take action on their needs or requests.

SERVICE IN ACTION   FedEx   CHAPTER 3

http://www.fedex.com

FedEx is headquartered in Memphis, Tennessee, and began with the founding of Federal Express in 1971 and has long been a leader in the global economy. In 1998 the corporation FDX Corp. was established and in January 2000, FedEx Corp. The company began building its international network early on with FedEx Express and today that network covers more than 215 countries with on-time, reliable transportation solutions. Through a series of mergers, acquisitions, and partnerships (for example, in 2002 with the U.S. Postal service), FedEx has become a powerhouse in the freight delivery business worldwide. As stated on the FedEx website, "Our goal is to deliver the perfect customer experience every time—one that's seamless, convenient and efficient."

Today, FedEx has revenues of over $22 billion dollars, handles 5.3 million shipments a year, employs approximately 219,000 employees and contractors worldwide, and has 638 aircraft and approximately 70,000 motorized vehicles for ground delivery.

To handle the average daily transactions of more than 2 million tracking requests and 500,000 shipping transactions, the company is continually updating its technology. FedEx was the first freight company to use bar-code labeling and the first to use time-definite freight service.

Key Terms and Concepts

assertiveness	I or we messages	rapport
channel	learning style	receiver
decoding	message	sender
encoding	noise	service recovery
feedback	nonverbal feedback	small talk
filters	paraphrase	two-way communication
global terms	pet peeves	verbal feedback

Quick Preview Answers

1. F	5. T	9. F
2. T	6. F	10. F
3. F	7. F	11. T
4. T	8. F	12. F

Chapter Review Questions

1. What are some things you can do as a customer service professional to project a positive image to the customer?

2. What element(s) of the Interpersonal Communication Model do you believe are the most important in a customer service environment? Explain.

3. What are some strategies to use in order to avoid words or phrases that will negatively affect your relationship with your customer?

4. What are some of the tips outlined in this chapter for ensuring effective customer interactions?

5. What is feedback?

6. How can verbal feedback affect customer encounters?

7. Give some examples of nonverbal feedback and explain how they can affect customer interactions.

8. List at least five tips for providing positive feedback.

Search It Out

Search the Web for Information on Verbal Communication

Log on to the Internet to research topics related to verbal communication, such as those presented in this chapter. Use various search engines (Yahoo.com, AltaVista.com, and Excite.com); your results will be different with each. Look for one or more of the following, print out pages you feel are helpful, and be prepared to share your findings with your peers in class. Some possible topics are:

Interpersonal communication
Two-way communication
Questioning
Learning styles
Positive image
Verbal feedback
Nonverbal feedback
Assertiveness

Note: A listing for additional research on specific URLs is provided on the Customer Service website at **<www.mhhe.com/lucas05>**.

Collaborative Learning Activity

Role-Playing to Improve Verbal Communication

Find a partner and use the following role-plays to improve your verbal communication skills. After reading the scenarios, pick the two for which you want the most feedback. Next, take a moment to think about how each of you will play your part and then have a two- or three-minute dialogue centering on the situation.

For the four scenarios, alternate roles with your partner: each of you should role-play twice, and each of you will be the debriefer twice. If possible, videotape or audiotape the conversation. This will allow each of you to see or hear how you seem when you interact with others. After the role-play, discuss how each of you felt about the way the other person handled the situation. Each of you should ask the other these questions about your own performance:

What did I do well?
What did I not do so well?
What can I do to improve in the future?

Scenario 1

You are a customer service professional in a dry cleaner's shop. A customer who has been coming in for years stops by with a silk shirt that has a stain that, according to him, was not there before the most recent dry cleaning. He is upset because the garment is expensive and was to have been worn to a class reunion yesterday.

Scenario 2

You are a member services representative in an automobile club that provides maps, trip information, towing and travel services, and a variety of travel-related products. A member has stopped by to find out whether she can get a replacement membership card and assistance in planning an upcoming vacation.

Scenario 3

You are a counter clerk in a fast-food restaurant. It is lunchtime, and the restaurant is full of patrons. As you are taking an order from a customer, a second customer steps to the front of the line, interrupts the first customer, and demands a replacement sandwich because the one she received is not what she ordered.

Scenario 4

As a clerk in a local video rental store, you see many of the same patrons regularly and have a fairly good relationship with many of them. One of the regular customers has just come in to rent a video but is not sure what he wants. You must determine his needs and properly assist him. Be sure to ask probing, open-ended questions, phrased positively, to help you get the information you need.

Face to Face

Seeking Information From a Client

Background

LKM Graphics has been in business in Norfolk, Virginia, for almost five years. The company employs 17 full-time graphic employees, a part-time administrative assistant, and three interns from Old Dominion University's graphic arts program. During a typical week, LKM prints 300,000 to 400,000 documents for businesses in the surrounding Tidewater metropolitan area. Most clients have 15 or fewer employees, although there are two active and ongoing government contracts with the Naval Operations Base, which is nearby. The owner of LKM, Linda McLaroy, hired you three years ago when you graduated from the graphic arts program. You are now one of the senior graphics account managers with the company and supervise four other team members.

Your Role

As a quality control measure, each month you are required to visit the clients assigned to your region. During those visits, you are to answer questions, deliver completed orders, verify customer satisfaction, collect feedback data, and look for new orders. On a recent visit to Brickman Bakery, you met the new office manager, Sylvia Greco. You had been told by a friend who works at Rickman's that

Sylvia is considering closing her account with LKM Graphics and moving it to a competitor. Prior to joining Brickman's last month, she had been employed by another organization in the area and had developed a strong relationship with your competitor. Since she is comfortable with the competitor's operation and has friends there, she wants to maintain the relationship. You've also heard through the grapevine that Sylvia prefers to work with your competitor's account representative.

Critical Thinking Questions

1. Since you don't have a relationship with Sylvia, what will you do to get off to a solid start during your visit?
2. How should you approach Sylvia verbally and nonverbally?
3. What strategies among the ones discussed in this chapter can you use to find out where you and LKM stand in Sylvia's mind?

PLANNING TO SERVE   CHAPTER 3

Based on the content of this chapter, create a Personal Action Plan focused on improving your verbal communication skills when providing service to your customers. Begin by taking an objective assessment of your current verbal communication strengths and areas for improvement. Once you have identified deficit areas, set goals for improvement.

Start your assessment by listing as many strengths and areas for improvement as you are aware of. Share your list with other people who know you well to see if they agree or can add additional items. Keep in mind that you will likely be more critical of yourself than other people will. Additionally, you may be sending messages that you are not aware of because

of the way you currently communicate. For those reasons, keep an open mind when considering their comments.

Once you have a list, choose two or three items that you think need the most work and can add the most value when interacting with others. List these items on a sheet of paper along with specific courses of action you will take for improvement, the name of someone you will enlist to provide feedback on your behavior, and a specific date by which you want to see improvement. Related to the latter, keep in mind that research shows that it takes on average 21 to 30 days to see behavioral change; therefore, set a date that is at least in this range.

Verbal Communication Strengths	Areas for Improvement

Top Three Items	Who Will Help	Date for Change
1.		
2.		
3.		

Nonverbal Communication in Customer Service

From the Frontline Interview

Frank Ross was a police officer for 37 years; serving as a police chief for 23 of those years. Since retiring as police chief from his last agency, Frank has been appointed Executive Director of Support Services for the City of Titusville, Florida.

1 Throughout your career, what role has nonverbal communication played in your ability to do your job?

As a police chief, I often noticed that customer body language was not consistent with their spoken communication because of the position of my office. Problem resolution becomes difficult if verbal communications are inconsistent with nonverbal communications. The police environment requires sensitivity to customer interactions for survival. Much of this depends upon your ability to effectively identify nonverbal communications.

My current job involves human resources, finance, management information systems, purchasing and contracting, and utility billing. As with the police job, this position requires extensive interaction with internal and external customers. Customer interaction is a major part of my Support Services role. When nonverbal cues break down in difficult situations, such as, union contract negotiations, health insurance issues, and employee benefits, challenges occur.

**FRANK ROSS,
Executive Director of
Support Services, *City of
Titusville, Florida***

2 What do you believe to be the role of nonverbal communication in effectively dealing with customers? Why?

People have difficulty with confrontational type issues. This could involve the absence of assertiveness or not wanting to offend. Therefore, one must rely heavily on nonverbal communications to identify the problem. Otherwise, you may expend resources providing inappropriate solutions. Communications are best when verbal communications are consistent with nonverbal ones. Nonverbal communications can often signal anger, frustrations, and other communications roadblocks, which must be addressed first to begin effectively communicating. Nonverbal language also suggests whether or not someone is receptive to your proposals or suggestions. This is useful in labor negotiations and pending sales.

3 How have you seen effective nonverbal communication skills used to help improve customer relationships?

To be successful in dealing with people, you must first be able to read the body language to determine the depth and scope of an issue. Is the customer receptive to offers and suggestions or in denial? We see the need for this skill in both hostage and labor negotiations.

Effective communications also begin with first impressions. In a positive service environment, proper introductions,

Chapter Learning Objectives

After completing this chapter, you will be able to:

- Define nonverbal communication.

- Recognize the potential impact on customers of nonverbal communication.

- Effectively use nonverbal cues to achieve and improve customer satisfaction.

- Explain the effect that gender and culture have on communication.

- Describe the advantages of customer-focused behavior.

- Project a customer-focused image through the effective use of nonverbal cues.

---

friendly gestures, and openness to discussions will foster effective communications. Is our hand extended in friendship, or are our arms folded and closed to discourage further communications? Certainly, a smile can set the stage for further discussions. You can see anger, anticipation, anxiety, joy, and other traits by watching and paying attention to the body language. You can build on the positive or address the negative to open channels of communications with the customer. For example, when negotiating with a hostage taker who has a knife to a victim's throat, you move closer to engage the suspect and at some point, he or she will tell you not to take another step through body language. If you have violated personal space, you pose a threat to the victim. This applies in the business world to a lesser degree of severity.

4 In what ways have you seen a service provider's negative nonverbal cues cause problems with customers?

When going into a store to make a purchase, if a clerk sees you, but fails to make or maintain further eye contact, a negative message is sent. At that point she or he has closed you out, indicating a lack of desire to provide you good service. The result is that you become frustrated and either leave the store or confront the clerk. Either way, effective communications have been minimized. In law enforcement, a police officer needs to talk to individuals involved in a dispute to resolve a conflict. One party may turn or walk away while the officer is investigating. This can lead to a negative reaction by the officer and a confrontation can occur. This happens because by turning away a person sends all types of negative signals to the investigating officer.

5 What advice can you give representatives regarding the importance of using positive nonverbal communication skills when interacting with customers face-to-face or over the telephone?

The job must be fun. A service representative must have a positive attitude and enjoy what he or she does. Consider any customer engagement a challenge while developing a warm, friendly, and winning attitude. Encourage interaction. Be flexible and willing to negotiate a solution by demonstrating a willingness to listen to alternatives. Additionally, develop service talents and skills necessary to be successful. For example, it is difficult to make a quarterback into a wide receiver because they have different interests, talents, and skills. Both positions require good athletes who have the abilities for their individual positions. Similarly, just because someone is talented in one area of his or her life does not mean instant success in a service occupation. You can improve your technical skills to become a great sales or service representative, but you will not be successful without the appropriate talents. Learn what you are good at and do that.

Critical Thinking

What value do you think a customer service provider might gain by following some of the advice that Frank has provided? How does what he said apply to customer service environments with which you are familiar?

Quick Preview

Before reviewing the chapter content, respond to the following questions by placing a "T" for true or an "F" for false on the rules. Use any questions you miss as a checklist of material to which you will pay particular attention as you read through the chapter. For those you get right, congratulate yourself, but review the sections they address in order to learn additional details about the topic.

_____ 1. It is possible for you to not send nonverbal messages.

_____ 2. By becoming knowledgeable about body language, you can use the cues you observe to accurately predict the meaning of someone's message.

_____ 3. By leaning toward or away from people as they speak, you can communicate your level of interest in what they are saying.

_____ 4. Smiling may mean that someone agrees with what you say. Smiling may also mean that the person is listening.

_____ 5. The use of open, flowing gestures could encourage listening and help illustrate key points.

_____ 6. Taking the time to polish your shoes and clean and press your clothing can help in presenting a positive personal image.

_____ 7. Vocal qualities have little impact on the way others perceive you.

_____ 8. Pauses in your oral message delivery can nonverbally say, "Think about what I just said" or "It's your turn to speak."

_____ 9. The words you use can distort message meaning.

_____ 10. Spatial preferences are the same throughout the world.

_____ 11. People often draw inferences about you based on the appearance of your office.

_____ 12. The amount of time you allocate for meetings with people could nonverbally communicate your feelings about the importance of those people.

Answers to Quick Preview can be found at the end of the chapter.

1   What Is Nonverbal Communication?

Concept: Nonverbal messages can contradict or override verbal messages. When in doubt, people tend to believe nonverbal messages.

The phenomenon of messages sent via nonverbal means has fascinated people for decades. The general public became aware of this subject when the book *Body Language*[1] and several others were published over four decades ago. In *Body Language*, Julius Fast defined various postures, movements, and gestures by ascribing to them the unspoken messages that they might send to someone observing them (for example, defensiveness or accessibility). Since then, hundreds of articles, books, and research studies have explored the topic and expanded the knowledge on the subject.

By being aware that you constantly send **nonverbal messages** to others and that it is impossible for you to *not* communicate, you can increase your effectiveness in

---

[1]Julius Fast, *Body Language,* Pocket Books, New York, 1960.

LEADERSHIP INITIATIVE

4.1

Since nonverbal cues play such an important role in successful service environments, it is crucial that supervisors be skilled in the area themselves. To accomplish this, attend classes on effective nonverbal communication. Once you have gained the knowledge, be conscious of the cues you send to others. Additionally, provide your employees with nonverbal communication skills training, coach them, and provide ongoing feedback on their communication behavior so that they can improve.

FIGURE 4.1
Communication of Feelings

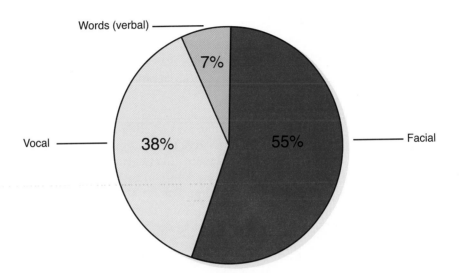

customer encounters or anywhere you come into contact with another person. A significant fact to remember is that, according to a classic research study on how feelings are transmitted between two people during communication, nonverbal signals can contradict or override verbal messages.[2] This is especially true when emotions are high. In Mehrabian's study, it was found that in communication between two people, 55 percent of message meaning (feelings) is extracted from facial and other body cues, 38 percent is taken from vocal cues, and 7 percent is received from the actual words used. (The various cues will be discussed in more detail later in this chapter.) This should not be construed to mean that your words are not important; they are just typically overridden by facial and vocal cues. When in doubt about your message meaning, people tend to believe the nonverbal (facial and vocal) parts. Figure 4.1 illustrates the importance of the different types of cues.

Although nonverbal cues carry powerful messages, it is important to understand that there is considerable room for misinterpretation of the cues used by different people. The skill of recognizing, assigning meaning, and responding appropriately to nonverbal messages is not exact. Human behavior is too unpredictable and the interpretation of nonverbal cues is too subjective for accuracy of interpretation to occur with consistency. This is because different cues have different meanings depending on where they were learned, who is interpreting them, and so on.

[2]Albert Mehrabian, *Silent Messages: Implicit Communication of Emotions and Attitudes*, 2nd ed., Wadsworth Publishing, Belmont, Calif., 1981, pp. 75–80.

2   The Scope of Nonverbal Behavior

Concept: Background, culture, physical conditions, communication ability, and many other factors influence whether and how well people use body cues.

In addition to verbal and written messages, you continually provide nonverbal cues that tell a lot about your personality, attitude, and willingness and ability to assist customers. Customers receive and interpret the messages you send, just as you receive and interpret their messages. The following categories of nonverbal cues are discussed in this chapter.

Body language	Spatial cues (proxemics)
Vocal cues	Environmental cues
Appearance or grooming	Miscellaneous cues (habits, time usage, follow-through)

Body Language

Recognizing, understanding, and reacting appropriately to the body language of others, as well as using positive body language yourself, allow you to communicate with your customers more effectively. The key to "reading" **body language** is to realize that your interpretations should be used only as an indicator of the customer's true message meaning. This is because background, culture, physical con-

Nonverbal cues such as eye contact, proximity, smiling, and gesturing send powerful messages. *What cues do you regularly send that impact the way customers perceive you and your organization?*

dition, communication ability, and many other factors influence whether and how well people use body cues. Remember that not everyone uses nonverbal cues in the same manner that you do. Placing too much importance on nonverbal cues could lead to miscommunication and possibly a service breakdown. Some typical forms of body language are discussed in the following sections.

Eye Contact

It has been said that the eyes are "the windows to the soul." Eye contact is very powerful. Criminal investigators are often taught to observe eye movement in order to determine whether a suspect is being truthful or not. In most Western cultures, the typical period of time that is comfortable for holding eye contact is five to ten seconds; then an occasional glance away is normal. Looking away more often can send a message of disinterest or dishonesty. If either the length or the frequency of eye contact differs from the "norm," many people might think that you are being rude or offensive. They might also interpret your behavior as an attempt to exert power or as flirting. In any case, your customer might become uncomfortable and may react in an undesirable manner (for example, become upset or end the contact). Also, looking down before answering questions, glancing away continually as your customer talks, blinking excessively, and other such eye movements can create a negative impression. The customer's eye contact can also send meaningful messages to you. A customer's lack of direct eye contact with you could send a variety of messages, such as lack of interest, confidence or trust, or honesty. For example, if you are watching a customer shop and notice a quick loss of eye contact, the customer might be nervous because he or she is shoplifting, or the customer simply might not want your attention and assistance. Eye contact accomplishes a number of purposes; for example, it can

- Indicate degrees of attentiveness or interest.
- Help indicate and sustain intimate relationships.
- Influence attitude change and persuasion.
- Regulate interaction.
- Communicate emotions.
- Define power and status relationships.
- Assume a central role in the management of impressions.[3]

Another aspect of nonverbal communication has to do with the size of the pupils. Much research has been done on the correlation between a person's interest in an item or object being viewed and the size of the person's pupils. Typically, when a customer is interested in an item, his or her pupils will *dilate* (grow larger). This fact can be parlayed into increased sales and customer satisfaction because an astute and experienced salesperson can watch for dilation as a customer looks over merchandise. For example, even if a customer displays only mild interest in an item after asking the price, and then moves on to another, the salesperson who has observed the customer's interest as revealed by dilation of the pupils might be able to influence the customer's buying decision. But, as with all nonverbal communication, if you are using this technique, remember that there is room for misinterpreting a cue. To avoid this kind of mistake, listen carefully to voice tone and observe other signals so that you do not appear to be pushy.

Posture

Basically, **posture** (or stance) involves the way you position your body. Various terms describe posture (for example, formal, rigid, relaxed, slouched, awkward, sensual, defensive). By sitting or standing in an erect manner, or leaning forward or away as you speak with customers, you can send a variety of messages. By standing or sitting with an erect posture, walking confidently, or assuming a relaxed, open posture, you might appear to be attentive, confident, assertive, and ready to assist your customer. On the other hand, slouching in your seat, standing with slumped shoulders, keeping your arms crossed while speaking to someone, shuffling or not picking up your feet when walking, or averting eye contact can say that you are unsure of yourself, are being deceitful, or just have a poor customer service attitude.

In addition, your behavior when listening to a customer speak can affect his or her feedback and reaction to you. For example, if you lean forward and smile as the customer speaks, you signal that you are interested in what is being said and that you are listening intently. Leaning away could send the opposite message.

Facial Expressions

The face is capable of making many expressions. Your face can signal excitement, happiness, sadness, boredom, concern, dismay, and dozens of other emotions. By being aware of the power of your expressions and using positive ones, such as

[3]Leathers, D. G., *Successful Nonverbal Communication*, 3rd ed. Allyn and Bacon, Boston, 1997, p. 54.

Take a few minutes to look at each of the faces shown below. Write the emotion that you believe each image portrays on the rules.

smiling, you can initiate and sustain relationships with others. In fact, smiling seems to be one of the few nonverbal cues that has a universal meaning of friendship or acceptance. Smiling typically expresses a mood of friendship, cheerfulness, pleasure, relaxation, and comfort with a situation. On the other hand, some people smile to mask nervousness, embarrassment, or deceit. In some situations, smiling (yours and a customer's) may even lead to problems. For example, suppose that you are a male service representative working at a customer service desk in an electronics store. A male customer from the Middle East and his wife step up to your counter. You smile and greet the husband, and then turn your attention to the wife and do likewise, possibly adding, "How are you today?" She smiles and giggles as she looks away in an embarrassed effort to avoid eye contact. At this point, you notice that the husband looks displeased. A cultural factor may be involved. Although your intention was to express friendliness and openness, because of his cultural attitudes the husband may interpret your words and smiling as flirtatious and insulting.

Don't think that you should ignore the wives of your customers. Rather, be cognizant of cultural and personal differences that people may have, and take your cue from the customer. As the world grows smaller, it is more crucial than ever that you expand your knowledge of different cultural attitudes and recognize that your ways are not the ways of everyone.

Nodding of the Head

Nodding of the head is often used (and overused) by many people to signal agreement or to indicate that they are listening to a speaker during a conversation.

You must be careful when you are using this technique, and when you are watching others who are doing so, to occasionally pause to ask a question for clarification. Stop and ask for or provide feedback through a paraphrased message. A question such as, "So what do you think of what I just said?" will quickly tell you whether the other person is listening and understands your meaning. The answer will also make it clear if the other person is simply politely smiling and nodding—but not understanding.

If you are a woman, be careful not to overuse the nodding technique. Research has shown that women often nod and smile more than men do during a conversation. Doing so excessively might damage your credibility or effectiveness, especially when you are speaking to a man. The interpretation may be that you agree or that you have no opinion, whether you do or not.

Although nodding your head generally signals agreement, if you nod without a verbal acknowledgment or **paralanguage** (a vocal effect such as "uh huh, I see, hmmm") a missed or misinterpreted cue could result. For example, suppose that you want to signal to a customer that you are listening to and understand her request. You may nod slowly, vocalize an occasional "I see" or "Uh-huh," and smile as she speaks. She might interpret this to mean that you are following her meaning and are nonverbally signaling acceptance of it. But if she is stating something contrary to your organization's policy or outside your level of authority, she might misinterpret your signals thinking that you *agree* with her, not that you are merely signaling *understanding*. Later, she might be upset, saying something like, "Well, earlier you nodded agreement when I said I wanted a replacement."

Gestures

The use of the head, hands, arms, and shoulders to accentuate verbal messages adds color, excitement, and enthusiasm to your communication. Using physical movements naturally during a conversation with a customer may help make a point or result in added credibility.

Typically, such movements are designed to gain and hold attention (for example, waving a hand to attract the attention of someone), clarify or describe further (for example, holding up one finger to indicate the number 1), or emphasize a point (for example, pointing a finger while angrily making a point verbally).

Open, flowing gestures encourage listening and help explain messages to customers (gesturing with arms, palms open and upward, out and away from the body). On the other hand, closed, restrained movements could send a message of coolness, insecurity, or disinterest (tightly crossed arms, clinched fists, hands in pockets, hands or fingers intertwined and held below waist level or behind the back).

The key is to make gestures seem natural. If you do not normally use gestures when communicating, you may want to practice in front of a mirror until you feel relaxed and the gestures complement your verbal messages without distracting.

Figure 4.2 summarizes positive and negative communication behaviors discussed in this chapter.

FIGURE 4.2
Positive and Negative Nonverbal Communication Behaviors

Positive	Negative
Brief eye contact (3 to 5 seconds)	Yawning
Eyes wide open	Frowning or sneering
Smiling	Attending to matters other than the customer
Facing the customer	Manipulating items impatiently
Nodding affirmatively	Leaning away from customer as he or she speaks
Expressive hand gestures	Subdued or minimal hand gestures
Open body stance	Crossed arms
Listening actively	Staring blankly or coolly at customer
Remaining silent as customer speaks	Interrupting
Gesturing with open hand	Pointing finger or object at customer
Maintaining professional appearance	Casual unkempt appearance
Clean, organized work area	Disorganized, cluttered work space

Simple nonverbal cues like smiling at a customer send powerful messages that a service provider is customer-focused. *How do you feel when a service provider smiles at you?*

Vocal Cues

Vocal cues, that is, pitch, volume (loudness), rate, quality, and articulation and other attributes of verbal communication, can send nonverbal messages to customers.

Pitch

Changes in voice tone (either higher or lower) add vocal variety to messages and can dramatically affect interpretation of meaning. These changes are referred to as **inflection** or **pitch** of the voice or tone. Inflection is the "vocal punctuation" in oral message delivery. For example, a raised inflection occurs at the end of a question and indicates a vocal "question mark." Some people have a bad habit of raising

To see what you look like when you gesture and communicate nonverbally, stand in front of a mirror or videotape yourself as you practice expressing nonverbal cues that demonstrate the following emotions:

1. Sadness
2. Frustration
3. Disgust
4. Happiness
5. Love
6. Fear
7. Anger
8. Excitement
9. Concern
10. Boredom
11. Skepticism
12. Complacency
13. Frustration
14. Optimism

inflection inappropriately at the end of a statement. This practice can confuse listeners for they hear the vocal question mark, but they realize that the words were actually a statement. To rectify this communication error, be sure that your inflection normally falls at the end of sentence statements. Another technique is to use a vocal "comma" in the form of a brief pause as you speak.

Volume

The range in which vocal messages are delivered is referred to as the degree of loudness or **volume**. Depending on surrounding noise or your customers' ability to hear properly, you may have to raise or lower your volume as you speak. Be careful to listen to customer comments, especially on the telephone. If the customer keeps asking you to speak up, check the position of the mouthpiece in relation to your mouth, adjust outgoing volume (if your equipment allows this), try to eliminate background noise, or simply speak up. On the other hand, if he or she is saying, "You don't have to shout," adjust your voice volume or the positioning of the mouthpiece accordingly.

Also, be aware of the volume of your voice, for changes in volume can indicate emotion and may send a negative message to your customer. For example, if a communication exchange with a customer becomes emotionally charged, your voice might rise, indicating that you are angry or upset. This may escalate emotions and possibly lead to a relationship breakdown.

Rate of Speech

Rate of speech varies for many people. This is often a result of the person's communication abilities, the region of the United States in which he or she was reared, or his or her country of origin. An average rate of speech for most adults in Western cultures is 125 to 150 words per minute (wpm). You should recognize this because, as we discussed in Chapter 3, speed of delivery can affect whether your message is received and interpreted correctly. Speech that is either too fast or too slow can be distracting and cause loss of message effectiveness.

Voice Quality

Message interpretation is often affected by the sound or quality of your voice.

The variations in your **voice quality** can help encourage customers to listen (for example, if your voice sounds pleasant and is accompanied by a smile) or discourage

To practice how changes in your vocal quality affect the meaning of your message, try this activity. Pair up with someone. Take turns verbally delivering the following sentences. Each time, place the vocal emphasis on the word in boldface type.

I said I'd do it.   I said I'd **do** it.

I **said** I'd do it.   I said I'd do **it**.

I said **I'd** do it.

them (for example, if it is harsh-sounding), based on their perception of how your voice sounds. Some terms that describe unpleasant voice quality are *raspy, nasal, hoarse,* and *gravelly.* Such qualities can be a problem because others are less likely to listen to, want to listen to, or interact with you if your voice quality is irritating. If you have been told, or you recognize, that your voice exhibits one or more of these characteristics, you may want to meet with a speech coach who specializes in helping improve vocal presentation of messages. Most local colleges and universities can supply the name of an expert, possibly someone on their staff. By taking the initiative to improve your voice quality, you can enhance your customer service image.

Articulation

Also known as **enunciation** or **pronunciation** of words, **articulation** refers to the clarity of your word usage. If you tend to slur words ("Whadju say?" "I hafta go whitja") or cut off endings (goin', doin', gettin', bein'), you can distort meaning or frustrate listeners. This is especially true when communicating with customers who do not speak English well and with customers who view speech ability as indicative of educational achievement or your ability to assist them effectively. If you have a problem articulating well, practice by gripping a pencil horizontally between your teeth, reading sentences aloud, and forcing yourself to enunciate each word clearly. Over time, you will find that you slow down and form words more precisely.

Pauses

Pauses in communication can be either positive or negative depending on how you use them. From a positive standpoint, they can be used to allow a customer to reflect on what you just said, to verbally punctuate a point made or a sentence (through intonation and inflection in the voice), or to indicate that you are waiting for a response. On the negative side, you can irritate someone through the use of too many vocal pauses or **interferences.** The latter can be audible sounds ("uh," "er," "um," "uh-huh") and are often used when you have doubts or are unsure of what you are saying, not being truthful, or nervous. They are sometimes called **verbal fillers.**

Silence

Silence is a form of tacit communication that can be used in a number of ways, some more productive than others. Many people have trouble dealing with silence in a conversation. This is unfortunate, because silence is a good way to show respect or show that you are listening to the customer while he or she speaks. It is also a simple way to indicate that the other person should say something or contribute some information after you have asked a question. You can also indicate agreement or comprehension by using body language and paralanguage, as discussed earlier. On the negative side, you can indicate defiance or indifference by coupling your silence with some of the nonverbal behaviors listed in Figure 4.2. Obviously, this can damage the customer-provider relationship.

Semantics

Semantics has to do with choice of words. Although not nonverbal in nature, **semantics** is a crucial element of message delivery and interpretation. You can aid or detract from effective communication depending on the words you use and how you use them. Keep in mind what you read earlier about the Mehrabian study and the fact that 7 percent of message meaning comes from the words you choose to use.

If you use a lot of jargon (technical or industry-related terms) or complex words that customers may not understand because of their background, education, culture, or experience, you run the risk of irritating, frustrating, or dissatisfying them and thus damaging the customer-provider relationship.

Appearance and Grooming

Through your **appearance and grooming** habits, you project an image of yourself and the organization. Good personal hygiene and attention to your appearance are crucial in a customer environment. Remember, customers do not have to return if they find you or your peers offensive in any manner. And, without customers, you do not have a job.

Hygiene

Effective **hygiene** (regular washing and combing of hair, bathing, brushing teeth, use of mouthwash and deodorant, and washing hands and cleaning fingernails) is basic to successful customer service. This is true, even when you work with tools and equipment, or in other skilled trades in which you get dirty easily. Most customers accept that some jobs are going to result in more dirt and grime than others. However, they often have a negative feeling about someone who does not take pride in his or her personal appearance and/or hygiene. Such people are often perceived as inconsiderate, lazy, or simply dirty. For example, if you failed to wash prior to reporting to work, you could be offensive in appearance to customers and coworkers (you might even have an unpleasant odor). This could result in people avoiding you or complaining about you. Naturally, this would reduce your effectiveness on the job and lower customer satisfaction.

A number of grooming trends have been prompted by many Hollywood actors. One is for men to appear with a one- or two-day beard stubble. While this may look sexy in movies, it has little place in a professional work environment. Likewise, prominent tattoos and visible piercings not only raise some eyebrows, but also can cause a negative customer reaction based on stereotypes of people who have such things. In many cases, these reactions are from older customers (for example, baby boomers). Since this group is one of the largest market forces, their views should be considered if you want to be a successful service provider.

Although good hygiene and grooming are important, going to an extreme through excessive use of makeup, cologne, or perfume can create a negative impression and may even cause people to avoid you. This is especially true of people who have allergies or respiratory problems, or people with whom you work in confined spaces.

Clothing and Accessories

Cleaned and pressed clothing, as well as polished shoes, helps project a positive, professional image. Certain types of clothing and accessories are acceptable in the work environment, but others are inappropriate. If your organization does not have a policy outlining dress standards, always check with your supervisor before wearing something that might deviate from the standards observed by other employees or might create an unfavorable image to the public. For example, spike heels and miniskirts, or jeans, bare midriffs, T-shirts, and tennis shoes, might be appropriate for a date or social outing, but they may not be appropriate on the job. They could actually cause customer disapproval and/or complaints and lost business to your organization.

If you are in doubt about appropriate attire, many publications and videos are available on the subject of selecting the right clothing, jewelry, eyeglasses, and accessories. Check with your corporate and/or local public library or the Internet.

Spatial Cues

Each culture has its own **proxemics** (zones in which interpersonal interactions take place) or **spatial cues** for various situations. When you violate this distance, the comfort level of other people is likely to decrease, and they may become visibly anxious, move away, and/or become defensive or offended. For example, suppose that you have an intimate or friendly spatial relationship with a coworker or with someone who regularly comes into your place of business. Outside the workplace, you and this person typically engage in interactions from zero to four feet (joking around, touching, kissing, and holding hands). But if you exhibited similar behavior in the workplace, you could create a feeling of discomfort in others, especially customers or other people who do not know you. Even if they are aware of your relationship with this person, the workplace is not the appropriate place for such behavior. Any touching should be restricted to standard business practices (for example, shaking hands palm to palm). In fact, touching other than this can lead to claims of a hostile work environment and could lead to a lawsuit according to numerous federal and state laws.

In the United States and many Western cultures, studies have resulted in definitions of approximate comfort zones. These may vary, for example, when someone has immigrated to a Western environment and still retains some of his or her own culture's practices related to space.

Intimate distance (0 to 18 inches). Typically this distance is reserved for your family and intimate relationships. Most people will feel uncomfortable when a service provider intrudes into this space uninvited.

Personal distance (18 inches to 4 feet). This distance is used when close friends or business colleagues, with whom you have established a level of comfort and trust, are together. It might also occur if you have established a long-term customer relationship that has blossomed into a semifriendship. In such a situation, you and the customer may sometimes exchange personal information (vacation plans, children, and so forth) and feel comfortable standing or sitting closer to one another than would normally be the case.

Pair up with someone and stand facing him or her from across the room. Start a conversation about any topic (for example, how you feel about the concepts addressed in this chapter or how you feel about the activity in which you are participating) and slowly begin to move toward one another. As you do so, think about your feelings related to the distance at which you are communicating. Keep moving until you are approximately one inch from your partner. At that point, start slowly backing away, again thinking about your feelings. When you get back to your side of the room, have a seat and answer these questions:

1. How did you feel when you were communicating from the opposite side of the room (what were your thoughts)?
2. At what distance (moving forward or back) did you feel most comfortable? Why?
3. Did you feel uncomfortable at any point? Why or why not?
4. How can you use the information learned from this activity in the customer service environment?

Being aware of how people may react to violations of their space is necessary for those in customer service. Depending on circumstances, there might be misperceptions of intentions and harassment claims. *How do you feel when someone gets too close to you during a conversation? What is "too close" for you?*

Social and work distance (4 to 12 feet). This is usually the distance range in the customer service setting. It is typically maintained at casual business events and during business transactions.

Public distance (12 or more feet). This distance range is likely to be maintained at large gatherings, activities, or presentations where most people do not know one another, or where the interactions are formal in nature.

Environmental Cues

The **environment cues** of the surroundings in which you work or service customers also send messages. For example, if your work area looks dirty or disorganized, with pencils, files, and papers scattered about, or if there are stacks of boxes, papers stapled or taped to walls, and trash or clutter visible, customers may perceive that you and the organization have a lackadaisical attitude or approach to business. This perception may cause customers to question your ability and commitment to serve.

Granted, in some professions keeping a work area clean all the time is difficult (service station, construction site office, manufacturing environment). However, that is no excuse for giving up on cleanliness and organization of your area. If each employee takes responsibility for cleaning his or her area, cleaning becomes a routine event during a work shift and no one has to get stuck with the job of doing cleaning tasks at a specific time. Also, the chance that a customer may react negatively to the work area is reduced or eliminated.

To help reduce negative perceptions, organize and clean your area regularly, put things away and out of sight once you have used them (calculators, extra pencils, order forms, extra paper for the printer or copier, tools and equipment, supplies). Also, clean your equipment and desk area regularly (telephone mouthpiece, computer monitor and keyboard, cash register and/or calculator key surface, tools).

It is also important to remove any potentially offensive items (photos of or calendars displaying scantily clad men or women; cartoons that have ethnic, racial, sexual, or otherwise offensive messages or that target a particular group; literature, posters, or objects that support specific political or religious views; or any item that could be unpleasant or offensive to view). Failure to remove such material might result in legal liability for you and your organization and create a hostile work environment.

Miscellaneous Cues

Other factors, such as the **miscellaneous cues** discussed in the following sections, can affect customer perception or feelings about you or your organization.

Personal Habits

If you have annoying or distracting habits, you could send negative messages to your customer. For example, eating, smoking, drinking, or chewing food or gum while servicing customers can lead to negative impressions about you and your organization. Any of the following nonverbal and verbal habits can lead to relationship breakdowns:

Touching the customer.

Scratching or touching parts of your body.

Using pet phrases or speech patterns excessively ("Cool," "You know," "Groovy," "Am I right?" "Awesome," "Solid").

Talking endlessly without letting the customer speak.

Talking about personal problems.

Complaining about your job, employer, coworkers, or other customers.

Time Allocation and Attention

Some organizations have standards for servicing customers within a specific time frame (for example, returning phone calls within four hours), but these **time allocations** are ranges because customer transactions cannot all be resolved in a specified period of time. The key is to be efficient and also effective in your efforts. Continually reevaluate your work habits and patterns to see whether you can accomplish tasks in a more timely fashion. The amount of time you spend with customers often sends subliminal messages of how you perceive their importance. For example, suppose that you are a salesperson in an exclusive clothing store. A teenage male customer (cutoff jeans, sandals, and T-shirt) enters and encounters one of your coworkers who says courteously "May I help you?" without smiling. As she meanders near the customer, she gives a disapproving look as she searches for other customers to serve. At some point, a well-dressed older woman wearing a suit arrives. The salesperson greets her warmly with a smile and proceeds to follow her around, assisting attentively, for the next 10 minutes, while the original customer waits to have a question answered. This certainly could tell the first customer that he is not welcome or respected.

Follow-Through

Follow-through, or lack of it, sends a very powerful nonverbal message to customers. If you tell a customer you will do something, it is critical to your relationship that you do so. If you can't meet agreed-upon terms or time frames, get back to the customer and renegotiate. Otherwise, you may lose the customer's trust. For example, suppose you assure a customer that an item that is out of stock will arrive by Wednesday. On Tuesday, you find out that the shipment is delayed. If you fail to inform the customer, you may lose that sale and the customer.

Proper Etiquette and Manners

People appreciate receiving appropriate respect and like to deal with others who have good **manners** and practice **etiquette**. Many books and seminars address the dos and don'ts of servicing and working with customers. From a nonverbal message standpoint, the polite things you do (saying "please," "thank you," asking permission, or acknowledging contributions) go far in establishing and building relationships. Such language says, "I care" or "I respect you." In addition, behavior that affects your customer's perception of you can also affect your interaction and ability to provide service (interrupting others as they speak, talking with food in your mouth, pointing with your finger or other items such as a fork while eating). Many good books are available on manners and dining etiquette if you are unsure of yourself.

Color

Although color is not as important as some other factors related to nonverbal communication in the customer service environment, the way in which you use various colors in decorating a work space and in your clothing can have an emotional impact. You should at least consider the colors you choose when dressing for work. Much research has been done by marketing and communication experts to determine which colors evoke the most positive reactions from customers. In various studies involving the reaction people had to colors, some clear patterns evolved. Figure 4.3 lists various **colors** and the **emotional messages** they can send.

3   The Role of Gender in Nonverbal Communication

Concept: Research indicates that boys and girls and men and women behave differently. Young children are sometimes treated differently by their parents because of their gender preference (either female or male child may be preferred).

FIGURE 4.3
The Emotional
Messages of Color

Color	Emotion or Message
Red	Stimulates and evokes excitement, passion, power, energy, anger, intensity. Can also indicate "stop," negativity, financial trouble, or shortage.
Yellow	Indicates caution, warmth, mellowness, positive meaning, optimism, and cheerfulness. Yellow can also stimulate thinking and visualizing.
Dark blue	Depending on shade, can relax, soothe, indicate maturity, and evoke trust and tranquillity or peace.
Light blue	Projects a cool, youthful, or masculine image.
Purple	Projects assertiveness or boldness and youthfulness. Has a contemporary "feel." Often used as a sign of royalty, richness, spirituality, or power.
Orange	Can indicate high energy or enthusiasm. Is an emotional color and sometimes stimulates positive thinking.
Brown	An earth tone that creates a feeling of security, wholesomeness, strength, support, and lack of pretentiousness.
Green	Can bring to mind nature, productivity, positive image, moving forward or "go," comforting, growth, or financial success or prosperity. Also, can give a feeling of balance.
Gold and silver	Signals prestige, status, wealth, elegance, or conservatism.
Pink	Projects a youthful, feminine, or warm image.
White	Not really a color (actually, an absence of it). Typically used to indicate purity, cleanliness, honesty, and wholesomeness. Is visually relaxing.
Black	Lack of color. Creates sense of independence, completeness, and solidarity. Often used to indicate financial success, death, or seriousness of situation.

Much has been discovered and written about differences in **gender communication** and interactions with others. For example, some researchers have found that females are more comfortable being in close physical proximity with other females than males are being close to other males. Although similarities exist between the ways in which males and females relate to one another, there are distinct differences in behavior, beginning in childhood and carrying through into adulthood.

In the book *The Difference,* Judy Mann hypothesizes that boys and girls are different in many ways, are acculturated to act and behave differently, and have some real biological differences that account for their actions (and inactions), which are examined from a number of perspectives. The book discusses various studies that have found that boys and girls typically learn to interact with each other, and with members of their own gender, in different ways. Girls tend to learn more nurturing and relationship skills early, whereas boys approach life from a more aggressive, competitive stance. Girls often search for more "relationship" messages during an interaction and strive to develop a collaborative approach; boys typically focus on competitiveness or "bottom-line" responses in which there is a distinct winner. Obviously, these differences in approaches to relationship building can have an impact in the customer service environment, where people of all walks of life come together.

The lessons learned early in life usually carry over into the workplace and affect customer interactions. If you fail to recognize the differences between the sexes and do not develop the skills necessary to interact with both men and women, you could experience some breakdowns in communication and ultimately in the customer-provider relationship.

The basis for gender differences is the fact that the brains of males and females develop at different rates and focus on different priorities throughout life. For example, women often tend to be more bilateral in the use of their brain (they can

FIGURE 4.4

Men and women differ in their approach to relationships. Here are some general behavioral differences that are seen in many men and women.

	Females	Males
Body	Claim small areas of personal space (e.g., cross legs at knees or ankles).	Claim large areas of personal space (e.g., use figure-four leg cross, or armrests on airplanes).
	Cross arms and legs frequently.	Use relaxed arm and leg posture (e.g., over arm of a chair).
	Sit or stand close to same sex.	Sit or stand away from same sex but closer to females.
	Use subdued gestures.	Use dramatic gestures.
	Touch more (both sexes).	Touch males less, females more.
	Nod frequently to indicates receptiveness.	Nod occasionally to indicate agreement.
	Lean forward toward speaker.	Lean away from speaker.
	Glance casually at watch.	Glance dramatically at watch (e.g., with arm fully extended and retracted to raise sleeve).
	Hug and possibly kiss both sexes upon greeting.	Hug and possibly kiss females upon greeting.
Vocal	Use high inflection at end of statements inflection (sounds like a question).	Use subdued vocal inflection
	Use high pitch.	Use low pitch.
	Speak at faster rate.	Speak at slower rate.
	Use paralanguage frequently.	Use paralanguage occasionally.
	Express more emotion.	Express less emotion.
	Use more polite "requesting" language (e.g., "Would you please?")	Use more "command" language (e.g., "Get me the . . .)
	Focus on relationship messages.	Focus on business messages.
	Use vocal variety.	Often use monotone.
	Interrupt less, more tolerant of interruptions.	Interrupt more, but tolerate interruptions less.
	Use more precise articulation.	Use less precision in word endings and enunciation (e.g., drop the "g" in –ing endings).
Facial	Maintain eye contact.	Glance away frequently.
	Smile frequently.	Smile infrequently (with strangers).
	Use expressive facial movements.	Show little variation in facial expression.
Behavior	Focus more on details.	Focus less on details.
	Are more emotional in problem solving	Are analytical in problem solving, (e.g., try to find cause and fix problem).
	View verbal rejection as personal.	Do not dwell on verbal rejection.
	Apologize after disagreements.	Apologize less after disagreements.
	Hold grudges longer.	Do not hold grudges.
Environmental	Commonly display personal objects in the workplace.	Commonly display items symbolizing achievement in the workplace.
	Use bright colors in clothing and decorations.	Use more subdued colors in clothing and decorations.
	Use patterns in clothing and decoration.	Use few patterns in clothing.

switch readily between the left and right brain hemispheres in various situations). Men, on the other hand, tend to be more lateral in their thinking. This means that they favor either the left hemisphere (analytical, logical, factual, facts-and figures-oriented) or the right hemisphere (emotional, creative, artistic, romantic, expressive of feelings). This results in a difference in the way each gender communicates, relates to others, and deals with various situations. Figure 4.4 lists some basic behavioral differences between females and males.

To get a better idea of how males and females communicate and interact differently, go to a library or to the Internet and gather information on the topic. Look specifically for information on the following topics:

Brain differences between men and women and the impact of these differences on communication and relationships.

Differences in nonverbal cues used by men and women.

Base for the communication differences in the workplace or business world between men and women.

4 The Impact of Culture on Nonverbal Communication

Concept: To be successful in a global economy, you need to be familiar with the many cultures, habits, values, and beliefs of a wide variety of people.

As you read in Chapter 1, and will again in Chapter 8, cultural diversity is having a significant impact on the customer service environment. The number of service providers and customers with varied backgrounds is growing at a rapid pace. This trend provides a tremendous opportunity for personal knowledge growth and interaction with people from cultures you might not otherwise encounter. However, with this opportunity comes challenge. If you are to understand and serve people who might be different from you, you must first become aware that they are also very similar to you. In addition, if you are to be successful in interacting with a wide variety of people, you will need to understand the **impact of culture** by learning about many <u>cultures, habits, values, and beliefs</u> from around the world. The Internet is a fertile source for such information. Take advantage of it, or visit your local library to check out books on different countries and their people. Join the National Geographic Society, and you will receive its monthly magazine, which highlights different cultures and people from around the globe.[4]

To become more skilled at dealing with people from other cultures, develop an action plan of things to learn and explore. At a minimum, familiarize yourself with common nonverbal cues that differ dramatically from one culture to another. Specifically, look for cues that might be perceived as negative in some cultures so that you can avoid them. Learn to recognize the different views and approaches to matters such as time, distance, touching, eye contact, and use of colors so that you will not inadvertently violate someone's personal space or cause offense.

5 Unproductive Behaviors

Concept: You should be aware of habits or mannerisms that can send annoying or negative messages to customers.

Many people develop unproductive nonverbal behaviors without even realizing it. These may be nervous habits or some mannerism carried to excess (scratching,

---

[4]National Geographic Society, <http://www.nationalgeographic.com>.

LEADERSHIP INITIATIVE

4.2

Supervisors should take responsibility for coaching and training their employees, even if the organization does not have a formal training initiative. To accomplish this task, look at the various cultural groups in your employee ranks and customer base. Gather specific tips related to effective nonverbal communication within these cultures. Share what you find with employees so that they can more effectively interact with a variety of people.

pulling an ear, or playing with hair). In a customer environment, you should try to minimize such actions because they might send a negative or annoying message to your customers. An easy way to discover whether you have such behaviors is to ask people who know you well to observe you for a period of time and tell you about anything they observe that could be a problem. Here are some more common behaviors that can annoy people and cause relationship breakdowns or comments about you and your organization.

Unprofessional Handshake

Hundreds of years ago, a handshake was used to determine whether a person was holding a weapon. Later, a firm handshake became a show of commitment, of one's word, or of "manhood." Today, in Western cultures and many others in which the Western way of doing business has been adopted, both men and women in the workplace are expected to convey greeting and/or commitment with a firm handshake. Failure to shake hands appropriately (palm to palm), with a couple of firm pumps up and down, can lead to an impression that you are weak or lack confidence. The grip should not be overly loose or overly firm.

Fidgeting

Using nervous mannerisms can indicate to a customer that you are anxious, annoyed, or distracted, and should therefore be avoided, if possible. Such signals can also indicate that you are nervous or lack confidence. Cues such as playing with or putting hair in your mouth, tugging at clothing, hand-wringing, throat-clearing, playing with items as you speak (pencil, pen, or other object), biting or licking your lips, or drumming your fingers or tapping on a surface with a pencil or other object can all send a potentially annoying and/or negative message.

Pointing a Finger or Other Object

This is a very accusatory mannerism and can lead to anger or violence on the part of your customer. If you must gesture toward a customer, do so with an open flat hand (palm up) in a casual manner. The result is a less threatening gesture that almost invites comment or feedback, because it looks as if you are offering the customer an opportunity to speak.

Raising Eyebrow

This mannerism is sometimes called the *editorial eyebrow* because some television broadcasters raise their eyebrow. With the editorial eyebrow, only one eyebrow is arched, usually in response to something that the person has heard. This mannerism often signals skepticism or doubt about what you have heard. It can be viewed as questioning the customer's honesty.

Peering Over Glasses

This gesture might be associated with a professor or someone who is in a position of authority looking down on a student or subordinate. For that reason, a customer may not react positively if you peer over your glasses. Typical nonverbal messages that this cue might send are displeasure, condescension, or disbelief.

Crossing Arms

Typically viewed as a closed or defiant posture, crossing your arms may send a negative message to your customer and cause a confrontation. People often view this gesture as demonstrating a closed mind, resistance, or opposition.

Holding Hands Near Mouth

By holding your hands near your mouth, you will muffle your voice or distort your message. If someone is hearing impaired or speaks English as a second language and relies partly on reading your lips, this person will be unable to understand your message. Also, placing your hands over or in front of your mouth can send messages of doubt or uncertainty, or can suggest that you are hiding something.

6   Strategies for Improving Nonverbal Communication

Concept: Nonverbal cues are all around us. Vocal and visual cues related to customers' feelings or needs are important and may mean the difference between a successful or unsuccessful customer service experience.

The four strategies discussed in this section will help you improve your nonverbal communication skills if you practice them and try to understand the behavior of others.

Seek Out Nonverbal Cues

Too often, service providers miss important vocal and visual clues related to customer feelings or needs because they are distracted doing other things or not being attentive. These missed opportunities can often mean the difference between a successful and an unsuccessful customer experience. Train yourself to look for nonverbal cues by becoming a "student of human nature." Nonverbal cues are all around you, if you simply open your eyes and mind to them. Start spending time watching people in public places (at supermarkets, malls, airports, bus stops, school, or wherever you have the chance). Watch the behavior of others you see, and the behavior of the people with whom they are interacting. Try to interpret the results of each behavior. However, keep in mind that human nature is not exact and that many factors affect the nonverbal cues used by yourself and others (culture, gender, environment, and many more). Be aware that you may be viewing through your own filters or biases, so evaluate carefully. Also, look at **clusters,** or groups **of nonverbal behaviors,** and the language accompanying them instead of interpreting individual signals. These clusters might be positive (smiling, open body posture, friendly touching) or negative (crossed arms, looking away as someone talks, or angry facial expressions or gestures). Evaluating clusters can help you gain an accurate view of what is going on in a communication exchange.

From your observations, objectively evaluate what works and what doesn't, and then modify your behavior accordingly to mimic the positive things you learn.

Confirm Your Perceptions

Let others know that you have received and interpreted their nonverbal cues. Ask for clarification by **perception checking,** if necessary. This involves stating the behavior observed, giving one or two possible interpretations, and then asking for clarification of message meaning. For example, suppose that you are explaining the features of a piece of office equipment to a customer and he reacts with a quizzical look. You might respond with a statement such as, "You seem surprised by what I just said. I'm not sure whether you were surprised by something I said or whether I was unclear in my explanation. What questions do you have?" By doing this, you focus on his behavior and also provide an opportunity for him to gain additional necessary information.

Seek Clarifying Feedback

In many instances you need feedback in order to adjust your behavior. You may be sending cues you do not mean to send or to which others may react negatively. For example, assume that you are on a cross-functional work team with members of various departments in your organization and have been in a meeting to discuss ideas for creating a new work process. During a heated discussion of ideas, you excuse yourself briefly to get a drink of water in order to take a pill. Later, a teammate mentions that others commented about your frustration level and the fact that you bolted out of the room. To determine what behaviors led to the team's reaction, you might ask something like, "What did I do that made people perceive that I was upset?" If you find out why people viewed your behavior the way they did, you offer an explanation in your next team meeting and avoid exhibiting similar behaviors in the future.

Another example might be to ask a coworker whether the clothing you have on seems too formal for a presentation you will give later in the day. Keep in mind, though, that some people will not give you honest, open feedback. Instead, they tell you what they think you want to hear or what they think will not hurt your feelings. It is usually best to elicit information from a variety of sources before making any behavioral changes, or deciding not to make them.

Analyze Your Interpretations of Nonverbal Cues

One way to ensure that you are accurately evaluating nonverbal cues given by a variety of people is to analyze your own perceptions, stereotypes, and biases. The way you view certain situations or groups of people might negatively affect your ability to provide professional and effective customer service to all your customers. This is especially true of customers in the groups toward which you feel a bias. Without realizing it you may send negative nonverbal cues that could cause a relationship breakdown and lead to a dissatisfied customer.

You will explore interactions with various groups and relationship-building strategies in more detail in Chapter 8.

To help you understand the importance that nonverbal cues play in effective interpersonal communication, select any section from this chapter and review the information in it. Once you are familiar with the section you have chosen, meet with a partner (preferably someone you know well) and have a 5- to 10-minute conversation about any topic of your choice. Do not inform your partner of what you're doing, but as you talk, intentionally send negative signals. For example, you might use any of the following nonverbal cues as you talk: stare blankly, do not smile, do not nod or use paralanguage when he or she speaks, look distracted, cross your arms, lean away, look at your watch frequently, play with a pencil or pen, or fidget.

As the conversation progresses, mentally note your partner's reaction to your cues. After 5 to 10 minutes, stop and explain what you've been doing. Ask what he or she noted about your behavior as you were talking. Chances are that he or she will be able to list several of your behaviors. Next, ask how your behaviors made him or her feel. Finally, ask what you might have done to seem more positive during the conversation.

Be prepared to discuss your experiences in class.

7 Customer-Focused Behavior

Concept: Being customer-focused in your behavior may help you solve a customer's problem or eliminate the opportunity for a problem to develop. The nonverbal cues discussed in this section can help you stay customer-focused.

The nonverbal behavior you exhibit in the presence of a customer can send powerful messages. You should constantly remind yourself of advice you may have heard often: "Be nice to people." One way you can indicate that you intend to be nice is to send customer-focused messages regularly and enthusiastically through your nonverbal cues. Here are some simple ways to accomplish this when you are dealing with internal and external customers:

Stand Up, If Appropriate If you are seated when a customer arrives or approaches you, stand up and greet him or her. This shows that you respect the person as an equal and are eager to assist her or him.

Act Promptly The speed with which you assist customers, gather information, or respond to customers tells them what you think of their importance. If your service to the customer will take longer than planned or will be delayed, notify the customer, tell him or her the reason, and offer service alternatives if they are appropriate and available.

Guide Rather Than Direct If customers must go to another person or area of the organization, or if they ask directions, personally guide them or have someone else do so, if possible. Do not simply point or direct. If you are on the telephone and you need to transfer a customer, give the extension of the person you're connecting to (in case of disconnection), transfer the call, and stay on the line to introduce the customer to the other service provider. Once the connection is made, excuse yourself and thank the customer for calling; then disconnect quietly.

Be Patient With Customers Provide whatever assistance is necessary without appearing to push customers away. Patiently take the time to determine whether a customer has additional needs. It is fine to ask questions such as, "Will there be anything else I can assist you with?" to signal the end of your interaction with a customer. Just be sure that you do it with a smile and pleasant tone so that the customer does not feel "dumped" or abandoned.

Offer Assistance   Offer to assist with packages, especially if a customer is elderly, has a disability, has numerous packages, or appears to need help. Similarly, if someone needs assistance with a door or in getting from one place to another, offer to help. If the person says, "No, thank you," smile and go on your way. Do not assume that someone needs help, grab an arm to guide him or her, or push open a door. Such actions could surprise a person and throw him or her off balance. This is especially true of someone with a mobility or sight impairment who has learned to navigate using canes or other assistance. Upsetting a person's momentum or "system" could cause a fall or injury, which in turn could result in embarrassment and/or a liability situation for you or your organization.

Reduce Customer Wait Times   Nobody likes waiting, so keep waits to a minimum. If long delays are anticipated, inform the customer, offer alternatives, and work to reduce wait time.

Allow Customers to Go First   As a show of respect, encourage and allow customers to precede you through cafeteria lines, through doors, onto escalators or elevators, into vehicles, and so on. This projects an air of respect and courtesy. If he or she declines, do not make a scene and insist; simply go first yourself.

Offer Refreshments, if Appropriate   Take care of your "guests" the same way you would at home. Offer to get them something to drink if they come to your office or if they are attending lengthy meetings. You may also want to offer reading materials if they are in a waiting area. Be sure that reading materials are current and professional-looking. Discard old or worn materials.

Be Professional   Avoid smirking, making faces, or commenting to other customers after a customer leaves or turns his or her back. Such activity is unprofessional and will probably make the second customer wonder what you'll do when he or she leaves.

8   Advantages of Customer-Focused Behavior

Concept: As you have learned in this chapter, many different factors affect behavior and influence how a customer perceives your ability to provide good customer service. By treating customers with respect, communication improves. This applies to both internal and external customers.

Because of the competitive nature of business, organizations and customer service professionals should strive to pull ahead of the competition in any positive way possible. Simple courteous nonverbal behavior can be one way to beat the service quality levels of other companies. Why should you be courteous?

Image Is Enhanced   First impressions are often lasting impressions. A more professional impression is created when you and the organizational culture are customer-focused. When your customers feel comfortable about you and the image projected, they are more likely to develop a higher level of trust and willingness to be more tolerant when things do go wrong occasionally.

Customer Loyalty Increases   People often return to organizations where they feel welcome, serviced properly, and respected. In Chapter 12, you will explore specific strategies for increasing customer loyalty.

Word-of-Mouth Advertising Increases   Sending regular positive nonverbal messages can help create a feeling of satisfaction and rapport. When customers are satisfied, and feel comfortable with you and your organization, they typically tell three to five other people. This increases your customer base while holding down formal advertising costs (newspapers and other publications, television, and radio).

Complaints Are Reduced   When people are treated fairly and courteously, they are less likely to complain. If they do complain, their complaints are generally directed to a lower level (below supervisory level) and are generally expressed with low levels of anger. Simple things like smiling or attentive actions can help customers relax and feel appreciated.

Employee morale and esteem increase. If employees feel that they are doing a good job and get positive customer and management feedback, they will probably feel better about themselves. This increased level of self-esteem affects the quality of service delivered.

Keep in mind your role in helping peers feel appreciated. They are often your internal customers and expect the same consideration and treatment as your external customers expect.

Financial Losses Decrease   When customers are satisfied, they are less likely to file lawsuits, steal, be abusive toward employees (who might ultimately resign), and spread negative stories about employees and the organization. Building good rapport through communication can help in this area.

Employee-Customer Communication Improves   By treating customers in a professional, courteous manner, you encourage them to freely approach and talk to you. Needs, expectations, and satisfaction levels can then be more easily determined.

Chapter Summary

Once you become aware of the potential and scope of nonverbal communication, it can be one of the most important ways you have of sharing information and messages with customers. Limitless messages can be conveyed through a look, a gesture, a posture, or a vocal intonation. To be sure that the messages received are the ones you intended to send, be vigilant about what you say and do and how you communicate. Also, watch carefully the responses of your customers. Keep in mind that gender, culture, and a host of other factors affect the way you and your customers interpret received nonverbal cues.

To avoid distorting customer messages, or sending inappropriate messages yourself, keep theses two points in mind: (1) Use a nonverbal cue you receive from others as an indicator and not as an absolute message. Analyze the cue in conjunction with the verbal message to more accurately assess the meaning of the message. (2) Continually seek to improve your understanding of nonverbal signals.

One final point: Remember that you are constantly sending nonverbal messages. Be certain that they complement your verbal communication and say to the customer, "I'm here to serve you."

SERVICE IN ACTION   Starbucks Corporation   CHAPTER 4

http://www.starbucks.com

According to Starbucks 2002 Annual Report to shareholders, its goal is "to become the leading retailer and brand of coffee in each of its target markets by selling the finest quality coffee and related products and by providing superior customer service, thereby building a high degree of customer loyalty." These stated objectives help explain why Starbucks has quickly become a household name throughout many parts of the world with nearly 3,900 outlets.

Founded in 1971 in Seattle, Washington, Starbucks continues to flourish. A secret to Starbucks success and expansion is the way the company addresses the needs of its customer markets. The format of the Starbucks stores can be varied from a full-size coffee shop to a small kiosk with the differences being the array and amount of products stocked and offered. In addition, Starbucks continues to think outside the box and has signed licensing agreements with hotel chains, airports, food service companies, warehouse clubs, supermarkets, and a number of other venues that carry its products. 1996 Starbucks and Dreyer's Grand Ice Cream, Inc., formed a partnership to introduce Starbucks® Ice Cream and Starbucks Ice Cream bars. Starbucks Ice Cream quickly became the number one brand of coffee ice cream in the United States.

Overall, customers have responded favorably and the company's revenues reflect its success with revenues for 2002 up nearly two and a half times those of 1998.

Service and treatment of employees are two cornerstones of any successful company. The Starbucks guiding principles from its mission statement, relating to creating a great work environment where people are treated with respect and dignity and developing enthusiastically satisfied customer, have helped form a culture that is prospering. It has also led to an environment that earned Starbucks a ranking on *Forbes* magazine's 100 Best Companies to work for in 2003.

Key Terms and Concepts

appearance or grooming
articulation, enunciation, or pronunciation
body language
clusters of nonverbal behavior
emotional messages of color
environmental cues
etiquette and manners
gender communication

hygiene
impact of culture
inflection
interferences
miscellaneous cues
nonverbal messages
paralanguage
pauses
perception checking
pitch

posture
proxemics or spatial cues
rate of speech
semantics
silence
time allocation
verbal fillers
vocal cues
voice quality
volume

Quick Preview Answers

1. F
2. F
3. T
4. T

5. T
6. T
7. F
8. T

9. T
10. F
11. T
12. T

Chapter Review Questions

1. What are six categories of nonverbal cues?
2. What are some of the voice qualities that can affect message meaning?
3. What are some examples of inappropriate workplace attire?
4. How can grooming affect your relationship with customers?
5. What are the four spatial distances observed in Western cultures, and for what people or situations are each typically reserved?
6. What are some of the miscellaneous nonverbal cues that can affect your effectiveness in a customer environment?

7. What are some ways in which men and women differ in their nonverbal communication?

8. What are some examples of unproductive communication?

9. List four strategies for improving nonverbal communication.

10. What are five examples of customer-focused behavior?

Search It Out

Use the Internet to Further Your Knowledge of Nonverbal Communication

Now that you have learned some of the basics of nonverbal communication and the impact it can have on your customer relationships, use the Internet to explore the topic further.

Select two topics from the following list, check out as many reputable sites as you can find, and prepare a report of at least two pages in length to present to your peers.

Body language
Nonverbal cues
Albert Mehrabian
The impact of gender differences on nonverbal communication
Spatial distances
The role of vocal cues in nonverbal communication
Professional appearance and grooming for the workplace
The impact of culture on nonverbal cues

Note: A listing for additional research on specific URLs is provided on the Customer Service website at **<www.mhhe.com/Lucas05>.**

Collaborative Learning Activity

Focus on Your Speech Patterns

Set up an audiocassette player. Then pair up with someone to discuss what you believe are the benefits of understanding and using nonverbal cues for building customer relations (spend at least 5 minutes presenting your ideas). Your partner should then present his or her views to you. Once both of you have presented your ideas, listen to the audiocassette with your partner and focus on your speech patterns.

1. Are you using appropriate verbal cues in your relationships with others? In what ways?

2. Do you use silence effectively? If so, how?

3. How did you sound in regard to the following?
   Rate
   Pitch
   Volume
   Articulation

4. Once you've identified positive and negative areas in your communication, set up an action plan for improvement by targeting the following:

Area(s) for improvement

Target improvement date

Resources needed to improve (assistance of others, training, training materials)

Support person(s)—who will coach or encourage you toward improvement?

Face to Face

Handling Customer Complaints at Central Petroleum National Bank

Background

Central Petroleum National Bank is one of the largest financial institutions in the Dallas–Fort Worth, Texas, area. With revenues of more than $200 million and investment holdings all over the world, the bank does business with many individuals and organizations in the region and other parts of Texas. The bank has 17 branch offices in addition to the home office in downtown Dallas.

Your Role

As one of the 125 employees of Central Petroleum's Western Branch Office, you provide customer service and establish new checking and savings accounts.

On Tuesday, a new customer, Mr. Gomez, came in to open an account. He stated that he was moving his money, over $200,000, from an account at a competing bank because of poor service. As you spoke with Mr. Gomez, one of your established patrons, Mrs. Wyatt, came into the office. As she signed in, you looked over, smiled, nodded, and held up one finger to indicate that you'd be with her momentarily. She smiled in return as she went to sit in the waiting area. As you were finishing the paperwork with Mr. Gomez, his teenage son came in and joined him. The son had been working at a summer job and had saved several hundred dollars. He also wished to establish a checking account. He placed his money on your desk and asked what he needed to do. He stated that he was on his lunch break and had only 20 more minutes to fill out the necessary forms. By then, you noticed that Mrs. Wyatt was looking at her watch and glancing frequently in your direction. Shortly thereafter, she left abruptly.

When you arrived at work the next day, the branch vice president called you into her office to tell you that she had received a complaint letter from Mrs. Wyatt concerning your lack of customer service and uncaring attitude.

Critical Thinking Questions

1. What did you do right in this situation?
2. What could you have done differently?
3. Do you believe that Mrs .Wyatt was justified in her perception of the situation? Explain.
4. Could Mrs. Wyatt have misinterpreted your nonverbal messages? Explain.

PLANNING TO SERVE

CHAPTER 4

Based on the content of this chapter, create a Personal Action Plan focused on improving your nonverbal service to customers. Begin by taking an objective assessment of your current nonverbal skill strengths and areas for improvement. Once you have identified deficit areas, set goals for improvement.

Start your assessment by listing as many strengths and areas for improvement as you are aware of. Share your list with other people who know you well to see if they agree or can add additional items. Keep in mind that you will likely be more critical of yourself than other people will. Additionally, you may be sending nonverbal signals that you are not aware of. For those reasons, keep an open mind when considering their comments.

Once you have a list, choose two or three items that you think need the most work and can add the most value when interacting with others. List these items on a sheet of paper along with specific courses of action you will take for improvement, the name of someone you will enlist to provide feedback on your behavior, and a specific date by which you want to see improvement. Related to the latter, keep in mind that research shows that it takes on average 21 to 30 days to see behavioral change; therefore, set a date that is at least in this range.

Nonverbal Communication Strengths	Areas for Improvement

Top Three Items	Who Will Help	Date for Change
1.		
2.		
3.		

CHAPTER FIVE

Listening to the Customer

From the Frontline Interview

Begum Tolgay recently started a position as an administrative support specialist for the Environmental Protection Department with the State of Florida. In that capacity she provides service to a variety of internal customers and responds to requests from individuals outside the organization.

Prior to moving to the United States, Begum was an account director for 7 years with Worldwide Advertising Agencies in Turkey. During that time, she worked in close partnership with the Planning, Creative, Media, Production departments, and external clients to craft tightly focused advertising strategies, based on an understanding of each client's products, goals, competition, and insights into contemporary consumer behavior.

While with Worldwide, Begum was also responsible for developing marketing strategies for multinational clients and took an active role in directing her team on implementation of these strategies and in follow-up of day-to-day business with clients.

BEGUM TOLGAY,
Administrative Support
Specialist, Environmental
Protection Department,
State of Florida

1 What is the biggest challenge you witness related to listening to customers (internal and external) in your environment?

Getting a clear brief from customers is the most important part of the advertising process. To create a successful advertising strategy, both the client and the agency have to agree on the content of the campaign. Sometimes the client makes the message too complex, either by including too many unnecessary details or too many general issues. As a result, agency representatives become distracted, forget the point, and start to get interested in what they want to say instead of listening to the customer. They rush the speaker, often interrupt him or her, and do not pay close attention.

The client company has to give a clear and effective brief to the agency. They need to be specific rather than general. On the other hand the agency representatives have to focus on the content. They have to ask for clarification, check on possible misunderstandings, and have to use active listening techniques.

2 In your experience, when listening breaks down, what has been the result?

Poor listening causes us many personal and professional problems. When listening breaks down, conversations end without anything being accomplished; therefore, it is hard to fulfill the needs of the customer. When this occurs, account directors cannot take the agency brief correctly and the agency would not be able to create a correct advertising strategy. This would cause both sides a loss of time and money and also would damage the reputation of the agency.

Chapter Learning Objectives

After completing this chapter, you will be able to:

- Describe the four steps in the listening process.
- Actively gather and provide information in customer contact situations.
- Recognize internal and external obstacles to effective listening.
- Develop strategies to improve your listening ability.
- Create relationships with customers through effective listening.

3 **What are some pitfalls that service providers should remember to avoid when listening to customers?**

Service providers should avoid the following pitfalls:

Rushing and interrupting the clients, since the clients want to emphasize certain points on their agency brief.

Failing to listen effectively in order to understand the brief clearly and thus, successfully transfer the message to the creative team.

Controlling of the conversation; instead, let the customer finish speaking before responding.

Failing to ask questions for clarifications related to insights about the product, target audience, product differentiation, market information, media source alternatives, and deadlines of the advertising campaign.

Reacting to the person instead of the message.

Maintaining self-confidence is of utmost importance. When you know your subject well, your customers trust you and this opens the door to success.

4 **What strategies have you developed to ensure that you effectively listen to your customers?**

Being an account director in an advertising company, I communicated mainly with manufacturers. I had to get a clear brief to start the advertising process, so I needed to listen to my customers effectively. To this purpose I developed the following strategies:

I looked at the speaker and maintained eye contact in addition to being positive all through the communication.

To get the insights of the products, I used multiple techniques to fully comprehend what my customers said. For example, I asked questions, repeated what I heard them say, and took notes.

I was keen on showing concern about my client's feelings when it came to the product differentiation process.

Some customers were difficult to deal with, so I learned to handle them by means of listening between the lines and with empathy. Nonverbal language was definitely one of the tools I used when dealing with customers.

5 **What advice related to listening would you give someone entering the customer service profession?**

My advice is to recognize that being a good listener is a challenge; however, listening is the vital part of good communication and of successful customer service. Developing listening strategies is as important as developing marketing and advertising strategies. Improving listening skills by concentrating on conversation content, avoiding interruptions and distractions, paying close attention, and being patient and positive are considered to be significant steps in achieving successful customer service.

Critical Thinking

How can what Begum described be applied to customer environments with which you are familiar? Explain. What are the benefits of implementing some of the strategies outlined by Begum?

Quick Preview

Before reviewing the chapter content, respond to the following questions by placing a "T" for true or an "F" for false on the rules. Use any questions you miss as a checklist of material to which you will pay particular attention as you read through the chapter. For those you get right, congratulate yourself, but review the sections they address in order to learn additional details about the topic.

_____ 1. Listening is a passive process similar to hearing.

_____ 2. Listening is a learned process.

_____ 3. During the comprehending stage of the listening process, messages received are compared and matched to memorized data in order to attach meaning to the messages.

_____ 4. The two categories of obstacles that contribute to listening breakdowns are personal and professional.

_____ 5. Biases sometimes get in the way of effective customer service.

_____ 6. A customer's inability to communicate ideas effectively can be an obstacle to effective listening.

_____ 7. A faulty assumption arises when you react to or make a decision about a customer's message based on your past experiences or encounters.

_____ 8. A customer's refusal to deal with you, coupled with a request to be served by someone else, could indicate that you are viewed as a poor listener.

_____ 9. Many people can listen effectively to several people at one time.

_____ 10. By showing a willingness to listen and eliminate distractions, you can encourage meaningful customer dialogue.

_____ 11. Two types of questions that are effective for gathering information are reflective and direct.

_____ 12. Open-ended questions elicit more information than closed-ended questions do because they allow customers to provide what they feel is necessary to answer your question.

Answers to Quick Preview can be found at the end of the chapter.

1   Why Is Listening So Important?

Concept: To be a better customer service professional, it is necessary to improve your listening skills.

Listening effectively is the primary means customer service professionals use to determine the needs of their customers. Needs are whatever the customer wants or expects you to provide. Many times, these needs are not communicated to you directly but through inferences, indirect comments, or nonverbal signals. A skilled listener will pick up on these cues and conduct follow-up questioning or probe deeper to determine the real need.

Most people take the listening skill for granted. They incorrectly assume that anyone can listen effectively. Unfortunately, this is untrue. Many people are complacent about listening and only go through the motions of listening. According to Andrew Wolvin and Carolyn Coakley in their book *Listening,* one survey found that three-fourths (74.3 percent) of 129 managers surveyed perceived themselves to be passive or detached listeners.

To help reinforce the concept that many customer messages are implied rather than actually spoken to service providers, form a group with two other students and role-play the following scenarios. Choose one in which you play the customer, one in which you play the service provider, and one in which you are the observer.

When you are the customer, simply state your issue or need in a way that does not ask the service provider to do something. Also, do not suggest a solution to the problem or issue. Let the person playing the provider role figure out your need and offer one or more solutions.

At the end of each scenario, you and your teammates should take time to answer the following questions:

1. What unspoken need was the customer sending to the service provider?
2. How well did the service provider do in identifying the customer's issue or need?
3. Specifically, what did the service provider do or say to address the customer's need or issue?
4. What could the service provider have done differently to improve service or satisfy the customer?

Possible answers to these scenarios can be found on page 145.

Scenario #1

A customer has a mortgage payment due on the 1st day of each month. In the past, payday was on the 10th and 25th; however, he/she started a new job and now gets paid on the 15th and 30th of each month.

Scenario #2

You work in a customer care center as a call center representative. A customer contacts you because he/she just placed an order on your company's website but forgot to enter a coupon code for free shipping that he/she received in the mail last week. His/her credit card had already been charged for the shipping when the order was sent.

Scenario #3

A customer moved into her/his newly built house in February and subsequently requested the cable company (your organization) to install cable service to the home. The installers came out with a backhoe, dug a trench, and installed the cable. It is now June and service has been fine until the customer turned on her/his lawn sprinkler system. The water pressure dropped immediately and upon investigation soggy ground was found where the cable company dug to install the cable months ago.

FIGURE 5.1
Missed
Opportunities
(based on a 75
percent efficiency
rate)

Opportunities	Action Taken	Impact
100 customers a day, each with a $10 order	25 orders were filled successfully	Loss of $750 per day ($273,750 per year)
1,000 customers went to a store in one day	250 were serviced properly	750 were dissatisfied
1,000,000 members were eligible for membership renewal in an association	250,000 returned their application	750,000 members were lost

In a classic study on listening conducted by Dr. Ralph G. Nichols, who is sometimes called the *father of listening*, data revealed that the average white-collar worker in the United States typically has only about a 25 percent efficiency rate when listening. This means that 75 percent of the message is lost. Think about what such a loss in message reception could mean in an organization if the poor listening skills of customer service professionals led to a loss of 75 percent of customer opportunities. Figure 5.1 gives you some idea of the impact of this loss.

Think about experiences you have had as a customer in which the provider did not do a good job listening to you. Be prepared to share these in class.

Describe some of these experiences.

How did the behavior of the provider make you feel?

How did you react to the behavior of the provider?

Did you take your business elsewhere?

What did you tell others about your experience?

2 What Is Listening?

Concept: Listening is a learned process, not a physical one.

Listening is your primary means of gathering information from a customer or any other person. True listening is an active learned process, as opposed to hearing, which is the physical action of gathering sound waves through the ear canal. When you listen actively, you go through a process consisting of various phases—hearing or receiving the message, attending, comprehending or assigning meaning, and responding. Figure 5.2 illustrates the process.

Hearing and Receiving the Message

Hearing is a passive physiological process of receiving sound waves and transmitting them to the brain, where they are analyzed. This is usually a simple process. Because of external noises and internal distracters (psychological and physical), however, a customer's message(s) may be lost or distorted. Using some of the strategies for improvement given in this chapter can help change your ability to listen more effectively.

Attending

Once your ears pick up sound waves, your brain goes to work focusing on, or **attending** to, what was heard. In the process, it sorts out everything being heard. The effort involves deciding what's important so that you can focus attention on

FIGURE 5.2
The Listening Process

LEADERSHIP INITIATIVE 5.1

One of the best tools that supervisors have for improving employee listening performance is on-the-job observation (for example, monitoring customer calls and watching face-to-face interactions) followed by immediate coaching. By discovering firsthand how frontline service staff members interact with customers, supervisors can provide more targeted and effective performance feedback. Such feedback should occur regularly (for example, weekly) to prevent patterns of poor listening behavior from becoming set.

FIGURE 5.3
Questions for the Listener

In analyzing your customer's message(s), ask yourself the following questions:

- Am I practicing active listening skills?
- What message is the customer trying to get across?
- What does the customer want or need me to do in response to his or her message?
- Should I take notes or remember key points being made?
- Am I forming premature conclusions, or do I need to listen further?
- Are there biases or distractions I need to avoid?
- Is the customer failing to provide information needed to make a sound decision?
- What other feedback clues are being provided in addition to words? Are they important to message meaning?
- What questions do I need to ask as a follow-up to the customer's message?

the proper sound. This becomes extremely difficult when you are receiving multiple messages or sounds. That is why it's important to eliminate as many distractions as possible. For example, during a meeting you could forward phone calls, or turn off your computer, or shut your door—or you could find a quiet place to meet.

Comprehending or Assigning Meaning

Once you've decided which message or customer you will listen to, your brain begins a process of **comprehending**, or **assigning meaning** to, what you heard. Just like a computer, your brain has files of information—sounds, sights, shapes, images, experiences, knowledge on various topics—it sorts through. As it compares what was heard to what is stored, it tries to match the pieces. For example, when you hear a voice on the phone that sounds familiar, the brain goes to work trying to match the voice to a name or person you've dealt with before. This is called *memory* and *recognition*.

Responding

The last phase of the listening process is **responding**. Selecting an appropriate response is crucial to the success of your customer interactions. The words you select, the way you deliver them, the timing and location, and the nonverbal signals you send all have meaning, and all affect the way others perceive and interpret your message. This is why you should be careful to consciously select the appropriate response and method of delivery when dealing with customers. A wrong choice could mean lost business or worse (the customer could get angry or violent).

Figure 5.3 gives some suggested questions you might ask yourself to check on your listening skills.

3   Characteristics of a Good Listener

Concept: Listening will improve as you "learn" in the customer's shoes.

To help in your efforts in improving your listening skills, use information you entered in Worksheet 5-2 (see <http://www.mhhe.com/lucas05>) as a checklist as you read through this chapter.

Successful listening is essential to service excellence. Like any other skill, listening is a learned behavior that some people learn better than others. Some common characteristics possessed by most effective listeners are discussed in the following sections. The characteristics of effective and ineffective listeners are summarized in Figure 5.4.

Empathetic. By putting yourself in the customer's place and trying to relate to the customer's needs, wants, and concerns, you can often reduce the risk of poor service. Some customer service professionals neglect the customer's need for compassion, especially when the customer is dissatisfied. Such negligence tends to magnify or compound the effect of the initial poor service the customer received.

Understanding. The ability to listen as customers verbalize their needs, and to ensure that you understand them, is essential in properly servicing the customer. Too often, you hear people say, "I understand what you mean," when it is obvious that they have no clue as to the level of emotion being felt. When this happens while a customer is upset or angry, the results could be flared tempers, loss of business, bad publicity, and at the far end of the continuum, acts of violence. Some techniques for demonstrating understanding will be covered later in this chapter.

Patience. Many people spend time thinking about what they will say next rather than listening to what is being said. Taking time to slow down and actively listen to customers makes them feel important and allows you to better meet their needs. Patience is especially important when a language barrier or speech disability is part of the situation. Your job is to take extra care to determine the customer's needs and then respond appropriately. In some cases, you may have to resort to the use of an interpreter or written communication in order to determine the customer's needs.

Attentiveness. By focusing your attention on the customer, you can better interpret his or her message and satisfy his or her needs. Attentiveness is often displayed through nonverbal cues (nodding or cocking of the head to one side or the other, smiling, or using paralanguage), which were discussed in detail in Chapter 4. When you are reading, talking on the phone to someone while servicing your customer, or doing some other task while "listening" to your customer, you are not really focusing. In fact your absorption rate will fall into the 25 percent category discussed earlier.

Objectivity. In dealings with customers, avoid subjective opinions or judgments. If you have a preconceived idea about customers, their concerns or questions, the environment, or anything related to the customers, you could mishandle the situation. Listen openly and avoid making assumptions. Allow customers to describe their needs, wants, or concerns, and then analyze them fairly before taking appropriate action.

FIGURE 5.4
Characteristics of Effective and Ineffective Listeners

Many factors can indicate an effective or ineffective listener. Over the years, researchers have assigned the following characteristics to effective and ineffective listeners:

Effective Listeners	Ineffective Listeners
Focused	Inattentive
Responsive	Uncaring
Alert	Distracted
Understanding	Unconcerned
Caring	Insensitive
Empathetic	Complacent
Unemotional	Emotionally involved
Interested	Self-centered
Patient	Judgmental
Cautious	Haphazard
Open	Defensive

Attention in Listening. Active listening involves complete attention, a readiness and willingness to take action, and an open mind to evaluate customers and determine their needs. *What should customer service professionals do to achieve these goals of active listening?*

4   Causes of Listening Breakdown

Concept: Poor customer service may result from a breakdown of the listening process.

Many factors contribute to ineffective listening. Some are internal, but others are external and you cannot control them. The key is to recognize actual and potential factors that can cause ineffective listening and strive to eliminate them. The factors discussed in the following sections are some of the most common.

Personal Obstacles

As a listener, you may have individual characteristics or qualities that get in the way of listening effectively to the customer. Some of these **personal obstacles** are discussed in the following sections.

Biases

Your opinions or beliefs about a specific person, group, situation, or issue can sometimes cloud your ability to listen objectively to what is being said. These **biases** may result in preconceived and sometimes incorrect assumptions. They can also lead to service breakdown, complaints, and angry or lost customers.

Psychological Distracters

Your psychological state can impede effective listening. **Psychological distractors,** such as being angry or upset, or simply not wanting to deal with a particular person or situation, may negatively affect your listening. Think about a time when you had a negative call or encounter with a customer or someone else and you became frustrated or angry. Did your mood, and possibly your voice tone, change as a result? Did that emotion then carry over and affect another person later?

Often when people become upset, time is needed to cool off before they deal with someone else. If you do not cool off, the chance that you will raise your voice or become frustrated with the next person you encounter is increased greatly. And,

When a customer service professional gets angry, his or her tone and mood may likely carry over to a customer. *How do you feel when a customer service professional is angry and raises his or her voice?*

if this second encounter escalates because of the person's reaction to a negative tone or attitude, you might respond inappropriately. Thus, a vicious cycle is started. You get angry at a person, your tone carries over to a second, who in turn gets upset with your tone, your emotions escalate, and you carry that mood to a third person, and so on. All of this lessens your ability to listen and serve customers effectively.

Physical Condition

Another internal factor that can contribute to or detract from effective listening is your state of wellness and fitness. When you are ill, fatigued, in poor physical condition, or just not feeling well, listening can suffer. According to a study by the National Sleep Foundation, one-third of respondents say they experience daytime sleepiness and over 80 percent of American adults link inadequate sleep with impaired daytime performance and behavior.[1] We often hear that a good diet and exercise are essential to good health. They are also crucial for effective listening. Try not to skip meals when you are working, stay away from foods high in sugar content, and get some form of regular exercise. These all affect physical condition. Try something as simple as using the stairs rather than the elevator or escalator. Another option is a brisk walk at lunchtime. All of these can help you maintain your "edge" so that you will be better prepared for a variety of customer encounters.

---

[1]2002 NSF Sleep in America Poll, the National Sleep Foundation, <http://www.sleepfoundation.org>.

Take a few minutes to think about your personal nutritional and exercise habits; then create a list of the ones that are positive and negative.

Circadian Rhythm

All people have a natural 24-hour biological pattern (**circadian rhythm**) by which they function. This "clock" often establishes the body's peak performance periods. Some people are said to be morning people; their best performance typically occurs early in the day. They often wake early, "hit the ground running," and continue until after lunch, when the natural rhythm or energy level in their body begins to slow down. For such people afternoons are often a struggle. They may not do their best thinking or perform physically at peak during that point in the day.

Evening people often have just the opposite pattern of energy. They struggle to get up or perform in the morning; however, during the afternoon and in the evening they are just hitting their stride. They often stay awake and work or engage in other activities until the early hours of the next day, when the morning people have been sound asleep for hours. From a listening standpoint, you should recognize your own natural body pattern so that you can deal with the most important listening and other activities during your peak period if possible. For example, if you are a morning person, you may want to ask your boss to assign you to customer contact or to handling problem situations early in the day. At that time, you are likely to be most alert and productive, less stressed, and less apt to become frustrated or irritated by abusive or offensive behavior by others.

Preoccupation

When you have personal or other matters on your mind (related to financial matters, school, marriage, family, or personal or work projects), it sometimes becomes difficult to focus on the needs and expectations of the customer. This can frustrate both you and the customer. It is difficult to turn off personal problems, but you should try to resolve them before going to work, even if you must take time off to deal with them. Many companies offer programs to assist employees in dealing with their personal and performance issues. Through employee assistance programs (EAPs), many organizations are offering counseling in such areas as finance, mental hygiene (health), substance abuse, marital and family issues, and workplace performance problems. Check with your supervisor to identify such resources in your organization, or ask about these services during the interview process when you apply for a position.

Hearing Loss

Many people suffer from hearing loss caused by physiological (physical) problems or extended exposure to loud noises. Sometimes they are not aware that their hearing is impaired. Often, out of vanity or embarrassment, people take no action to remedy the loss. If you find yourself regularly straining to hear someone, having to turn one ear or the other toward the speaker, or having to ask people to repeat what they said because you didn't get the entire message, you may have a hearing loss. If you suspect that you have hearing loss, go to your physician or an audiologist (hearing specialist) quickly to avoid complications or further loss of hearing.

Listening Skill Level

People communicate on different levels depending on their knowledge and experiences in the area of communication. Adults are influenced by the experiences they had as children; that is, they are likely to repeat behavior they learned during childhood. For example, if you grew up in an environment where the people around you practiced positive skills related to listening, providing feedback and using nonverbal communication (covered in Chapter 4), and effective interpersonal skills for dealing with others, you will likely use similar techniques as an adult. On the other hand, if your childhood experiences were negative and you did not have good communication role models, the chances are that you struggle in dealing with others effectively.

Listening is the primary skill most people have for gathering information. Unfortunately, in the United States, listening as a skill is not taught in most public school systems. People learn the proper techniques involved in the skill only if they read, listen to audiotapes, watch videos, and attend seminars or college courses on listening. Too often, even though an adult's intentions might be well meant, techniques used to teach listening to children are often ineffective.

Think about your own experiences or times when you have observed an adult "teaching" a child to listen. You might have seen the adult grasp the child, look directly at the child, and say something like, "Look at me when I'm talking to you." Or the adult might have used a harsh tone to say the same kind of thing without touching the child. Now think of this from an adult standpoint. If someone treated you like that today, would you want to focus your attention and say, "Yes, what is it?" Or would a barrier go up and listening stop as your emotions escalated? Remember, if you learned the negative behavior as a child, you will likely repeat it as an adult unless new behavior replaces the old.

Thought Speed

Your brain is capable of comprehending messages delivered at rates of as much as four to six times faster than the speed at which the average adult in the United States speaks (approximately 125 to 150 words per minute, or wpm). The difference between the two rates can be referred to as a **lag time** or **listening gap** during which the mind is actually idle. The result is that your brain does other things to occupy itself (for example, daydreaming). To prevent or reduce such distraction, you must consciously focus on your customer's message, look for key points, ask pertinent questions, and respond appropriately. If the customer has a complaint or suggestion, you may even want to take notes. This not only helps you focus on and recall information but also can demonstrate to the customer that you are truly interested in the ideas or subject of the conversation.

Faulty Assumptions

Because of past experiences or encounters with others, you may be tempted to make **faulty assumptions** about your customer's message(s). Don't. Each customer and each situation is different and should be regarded as such. Because you had a certain experience with one customer does not mean that you will have a similar experience with another. Suppose, for example, that you are a college registrar. You see lots of students and hear lots of stories when they try to change from one class to another or drop a course. One day a student comes into your office and asks to cancel her registration in one class in order to register for another even though the designated time for such a change has passed. Your immediate inclination might be to quote policy

Think about a situation in which you were talking to a customer or someone else and another person arrived, interrupted, and started asking questions or talking to you.

What was the reaction of the first person to whom you were talking?

What was your reaction?

How did you handle the situation?

since you've "heard this one before." Your response might sound like, "I'm sorry, Ms. Molina, the period for adds or drops has passed." Don't respond so quickly; instead, hear the customer out. She may provide information (verbally or nonverbally) that will change your view. For example, Ms. Molina (crying) might say, "I've got to get out of that class. I need one more course to graduate, but I can't stay in this class."

If you are proactive in this situation and practicing active listening, you will pick up on the emotions and ask some questions in order to find out her real need or issue. For example, you might say, "Ms. Molina, you seem very upset, is anything wrong?" She might respond, "Yes. I need to graduate this semester and return to my country to help support my family. But I can't stay in Mr. Broward's class. He's . . . he's always leering at me and making lewd remarks." Obviously, the rules don't apply in this case. If you didn't listen, you'd never know, and there would be a dissatisfied and distraught customer as a result. Also, you might be setting up the institution for a harassment lawsuit by forcing Ms. Molina to stay in the class or to seek other solutions (lawsuit, violence, or going to the media to expose the teacher).

External Obstacles

You cannot remove all barriers to effective listening, but you should still try to reduce them when dealing with customers. Some typical examples of **external obstacles** include the following.

Information Overload

Each day you are bombarded with information from many sources. You get information in meetings, from the radio and television, from customers, and in a variety of public places. In many instances, you spend as much as 5 to 6 hours a day listening to customers, coworkers, family members, friends, and strangers. Such **informational overload** can result in stress, inadequate time to deal with individual situations, and reduced levels of customer service.

Other People Talking

It is not possible for you to give your full attention to two speakers simultaneously. In order to serve customers effectively, deal with only one person at a time. If someone else approaches, smile, acknowledge him or her, and say, "I'll be with you in just a moment" or at least signal that message by holding up your index finger to indicate "1 minute" while you smile.

Ringing Phones

Ringing telephones can be annoying, but you shouldn't stop helping one customer to get into a discussion with or try to serve another customer over the phone. This creates a dilemma, for you cannot ignore customers or others who depend on you to serve their needs over the telephone.

LEADERSHIP INITIATIVE 5.2

Workplaces in service environments can be chaotic and stressful because of the combination of job responsibilities, customer personalities, noise, change, and many other factors. Supervisory and peer pressure in the form of additional requests for assistance and a push to improve service (for example, call times) and meet goals add to employee stress.

Supervisors can help reduce some workplace pressure and aid service staff in delivery of quality service to customers. One way to accomplish this is to continually reevaluate personal leadership and management styles, policies, and procedures. Additionally, ensuring that employees have state-of-the-art equipment and tools that function properly (for example, telephones, answering machines/voice mail, cash registers, heavy equipment, machinery, fork lifts) can alleviate frustration. This allows service providers to be less distracted so that they can carefully listen to customer needs and requests.

Several options are available. You might arrange with your supervisor or coworkers to have someone else take the calls. Those people can either provide service or take messages (as we'll explore in Chapter 9), depending on the business your organization conducts. Another option is the use of a voice mail system, answering service, or pager for message collection. Still another possibility would be to ask the person to whom you are speaking face-to-face to excuse you, professionally answer the phone, and either ask the caller to remain on hold or take a number for a callback.

No one solution is best. You can only try to provide the best service possible, depending on your situation. Before such situations develop, it is a good idea to speak with your supervisor or team leader and peers to determine the policy and procedures for handling customers in these instances.

Speakerphones

These devices allow for hands-free telephone conversations. They are great because you can continue your conversation while searching for something the customer has requested. Unfortunately, many people put callers on the loudspeaker while continuing to do work not related to the caller. This not only is rude but it results in ineffective communication. Because the speakerphone picks up background noise, it is often difficult to hear the caller, especially if you are moving around the room and are not next to the phone. Many people dislike speakerphones. Be aware that improper use of the speakerphone could cause customers to stop calling. An additional issue with the speakerphone is confidentiality. Since others can hear the caller's conversation, the caller may be reluctant to provide certain information (credit card and social security numbers, medical information, or personal data). Whenever you use a speakerphone, inform the caller if someone else is in the room with you and/or close your office door, if possible.

Office and Maintenance Equipment

Noisy printers, computers, photocopying machines, electric staplers, vacuum cleaners, and other devices can also be distractions. When servicing customers, eliminate or minimize the use of these types of items. If others are using noisy equipment, try to position yourself or them as far away from the customer service area as possible.

Physical Barriers

Desks, counters, furniture, or other items separating you from your customer can stifle communication. Depending on your job function, you might be able to eliminate barriers. If possible, do so. These obstacles can distance you physically from

To help you improve your listening skills and offer better service to your customers, complete the following activity. Think of a time when you were trying to verbally communicate ideas to someone but you realized (based on verbal and nonverbal responses) that this person was not listening to you.

1. What led you to believe that this person was not paying attention to your message(s)? How was your ability to get your message across affected? How did you feel?

Next, think of times when you were involved in conversations but were not really focused and listening to the other person.

2. What was going on that prevented you from listening effectively? What reaction did your listener have to your distraction or lack of focus?

Use your responses to these questions to improve your listening skills.

your customer or depersonalize your service. Be conscious of how you arrange your office or work space. Side-by-side (facing the customer at an angle) seating next to a table is preferable to sitting across from a customer in most situations. An exception to this approach would be appropriate if you provide service to customers who might become agitated or violent. Some examples: city or state clerks who deal with people who have been charged with traffic or other violations of the law; public utility employees who deal with people who are complaining about service problems; employees in motor vehicle offices where people may have frustrating problems with drivers' licenses or vehicle registration.

An Additional Obstacle

In addition to the issues already addressed, customers themselves can negatively affect communication—through their inability to convey a message.

Although it is not specifically a listening issue, if customers are unable to deliver their message effectively, you will be unable to receive and properly analyze their meaning. No amount of dedication and effort on your part will make up for a language barrier, a disability (speech, physical) that limits speech and nonverbal body language, or poor communication skills. In these situations, it is often necessary to seek out others to help (translators, signers) or to use alternative means of communication (gestures, written, symbols, or a text telephone, or TTY/TDD) to discover the customers' meaning and satisfy their needs.

By recognizing these limiting factors, you can improve your chances of communicating more effectively. Use Worksheet 5-4 (see <http://www.mhhe.com/lucas05>) to evaluate listening distractions in your environment.

5 Indicators of Poor Listening

Concept: Improve your listening skills through self-analysis.

You cannot afford the luxury of failing to listen to your customer. Periodically, you should do a self-check on your listening style to see whether you need to improve. If any of the following events occur, you may need to refocus.

Customers specifically ask to speak to or be served by someone else.

You find yourself missing key details of conversations.

You regularly have to ask people to repeat information.

You end phone calls or personal encounters not knowing for sure what action is required of you.

Customers often make statements such as, "Did you hear what I said?" "Are you listening to me?" or "You're not listening."

You find yourself daydreaming or distracted as a customer is speaking.

You miss nonverbal cues sent by the customer as the two of you communicate.

You answer a question incorrectly because you didn't actually hear it.

6 Strategies for Improved Listening

Concept: You can improve your listening skills in several different ways. One important way is to listen more than you talk.

Numerous techniques can be used to become a more effective listener. The following tips can be used as a basis for improvement.

Stop Talking!

You cannot talk and actively listen at the same time. When the customer starts talking, stop talking and listen carefully. One common mistake that many people make is to ask a question, hesitate, and if no answer is immediately offered, ask a second question or "clarify" the meaning by providing additional information. A habit like this is not only confusing to the listener, but rude.

Some people like to reflect on what they have heard and then formulate just the right answer before responding. People who speak another language, or who have a disability, may either be translating the information received into their own language or trying to assimilate your message before making an appropriate response. If you interrupt with additional information or questions, you may interfere with their thought patterns and cause them to become frustrated. The end result is that the listener may not speak or respond at all because he or she believes that you aren't really listening or interested in the response anyhow, or because he or she is embarrassed or confused. To avoid such a scenario, plan what you want to say, ask the question, and then stop speaking. You might ask, "Mr. Swanson,

Work It Out 5.6

Correcting Common Listening Problems

Here are some common listening problems. Try to think of one or two means for reducing or eliminating them in your customer service.

Listening to words, not concepts, ideas, or emotions.

Pretending interest in a customer's problem, question, suggestion, or concern.

Planning your next remarks while the customer is talking.

Being distracted by external factors.

Listening only for what you perceive is the real issue or point.

Reacting emotionally to what the customer is saying.

Think about strategies used by people whom you believe are listening to you. List some of the behaviors and techniques they use.

how do you think we might resolve this issue?" Once you have asked the question, stop talking and wait for a response. If a response does not come in a minute or so, try asking the question another way (paraphrase), possibly offering some guidance to a response and concluding with an open-ended question (one that encourages the listener to give opinions or longer responses). You might say, "Mr. Swanson, I'd really like to help resolve this issue. Perhaps we could try _____ or _____. How do you think that would work?"

Prepare Yourself

Before you can listen effectively to someone, you must be ready to receive what this person has to say. Stop reading, writing, talking to others, thinking about other things, working on your computer, answering phones, and dealing with other matters that distract you. For example, if a customer approaches while you're using a calculator to add up a row of figures, smile and say, "I'll be with you in just a moment" or smile and hold up your index finger to indicate "1 minute." As quickly as possible, complete your task, apologize for the delay, and then ask, "How may I assist you?"

Listen Actively

Use the basics of sound communication when a customer is speaking. The following strategies are typically helpful in sending an "I care" message when done naturally and with sincerity:

SMILE!

Do not interrupt to interject your ideas or make comments unless they are designed to clarify a point made by the customer.

Sit or stand up straight and make eye contact with the customer.

Lean forward or turn an ear toward the customer, if appropriate and necessary.

Paraphrase their statements occasionally.

Nod and offer affirmative paralanguage statements ("I see," "Uh-huh," "Really," "Yes") to show that you're following the conversation.

Do not finish a customer's sentence. Let the customer talk.

In addition, focus on complete messages. A complete message consists of the words, nonverbal messages, and emotions of the customer. If a customer says that she's satisfied with a product but is sending nonverbal signals that contradict her statement, you should investigate further. Suppose that the supply of blue bowls being given away as gifts to people who stop by your trade show exhibit is gone. The customer might say, "Oh, that's okay. I guess a green one will do." Her tone and facial expression may, however, indicate disappointment. You could counter with, "I'm sorry we're out of the blue bowls, Mrs. Zagowski. If you'd like one, I can give you a certificate that will allow you to pick one up when you visit our store, or I can take your address and ship one to you when I get back to the store. Would you prefer one of those options?" By being "tuned in" to your customer and taking this extra initiative, you have gone beyond the ordinary and moved into the realm of exceptional customer service. Mrs. Zagowski will probably appreciate your gesture and tell others about the wonderful, customer-focused person she met at the trade show exhibit.

Show a Willingness to Listen

By eliminating distractions, sending positive verbal and nonverbal responses, and actively focusing on what is being said, you can help the customer relax and have a more meaningful dialogue. For example, when dealing with customers, you should make sure that you take some of the positive approaches to listening outlined earlier (turning off noisy equipment, facing the person, making eye contact, and smiling while responding in a positive manner). These small efforts can pay big dividends in the form of higher satisfaction, lower frustration, and a sense of being cared for on the customer's part.

Show Empathy

Put yourself in the customer's place by empathizing, especially when the customer is complaining about what he or she perceives to be poor service or inferior products. This is sometimes referred to as "walking a mile in your customer's shoes." For example, if a customer complains that she was expecting a specific service by a certain date but didn't get it, you might respond as follows: "Mrs. Ellis, I apologize that we were unable to complete _____ on the tenth as promised. We dispatched a truck, but the driver was involved in an accident. Can we make it up to you by _____? (Offer a gift, suggest an alternative such as hand delivery and so on.) This technique, known as **service recovery,** is a crucial step in delivering quality service and remaining competitive into the twenty-first century.

Service recovery is discussed in detail in Chapter 13.

Listen for Concepts

Instead of focusing on one or two details, listen to the entire message before analyzing it and responding. For example, instead of trying to respond to one portion of a message, wait for the customer to provide all the details. Then ask any questions necessary to get the information you need to respond appropriately. For example, "Mr. Chi, if I understand you correctly, you'd like us to build a new prototype part to replace the one currently being used in the assembly. You're looking for a total cost for development and manufacture not to exceed $10,000. Is that correct?"

Be Patient

Not everyone communicates in the same manner. Keep in mind that it is your job to serve the customer. Do your best to listen well so that you can get at the customer's meaning or need. Don't rush a customer who seems to be processing information and forming opinions or making a decision. This is especially important after you have presented product information and have asked for a buying decision. Answer questions, provide additional information requested, but don't push. Doing so could frustrate, anger, and ultimately alienate the customer. You could end up with a complaint or lost customer.

Listen Openly

Avoid the biases discussed earlier. Remember that you don't have to like everyone you encounter, but you do have to respect and treat customers fairly and impartially if you want to maintain a business relationship. For example, whenever you encounter a person who is rude or is the type of person for whom you have a personal dislike, try to maintain your professionalism. Remember that you represent your organization and that you are paid by your employer to serve the customer (whoever he or she is). If a situation arises that you feel you cannot or prefer not to handle, call in a coworker or supervisor. However, be careful in taking this action because you will likely reveal a personal preference or bias that could later be held against you when you apply for other positions in your organization or positions in other companies. Try to work through your differences or biases rather than letting them hinder your ability to deal with others. Your ability to serve each customer fairly and competently is important to your job success.

Send Positive Nonverbal Cues

Be conscious of the nonverbal messages you are sending. Even when you are verbally agreeing or saying yes, you may be unconsciously sending negative nonverbal messages. When sending a message, you should make sure that your verbal cues (words) and nonverbal cues (gestures, facial expressions) are in **congruence**. For example, if you say, "Good morning. How may I help you?" in a gruff tone, with no smile, and while looking away from the customer, that customer is not going to feel welcome or believe that you are sincere in your offer to assist. (Nonverbal cues were covered in detail in Chapter 4.)

Don't Argue

Remember the "Did not," "Did too" quarrels you had when you were a child? Such verbal exchanges got heated, voices rose and tempers escalated, and someone might have started hitting or pushing. Who won? No one. You should avoid similar childish behaviors in dealing with others—especially your customers or potential customers.

Note-taking can help focus listening and later aid recall of what was discussed. What system do you use to take notes while talking on the phone or to follow-up on customer issues?

When you argue, you become part of the problem and cannot be part of the solution. Learn to phrase responses or questions positively (as discussed in Chapter 3). Even when you go out of your way to properly serve customers, some of them will respond negatively. Some people seem to enjoy conflict. In such situations, maintain your composure (count to ten silently before responding), listen, and attempt to satisfy their needs. If necessary, refer such customers to your supervisor or a peer for service.

Take Notes, if Necessary

If information is complicated, or if names, dates, numbers, or numerous details are involved in a customer

LEADERSHIP INITIATIVE 5.3

Role modeling effective listening skills is one of the best ways to help employees improve their listening skills. Supervisors send a message of appreciation and respect for their staff by showing employees that they are listening. They also provide positive models for employees to emulate when talking to their customers.

If supervisors have not been formally trained in effective listening, they should attend communication courses focused on listening skills. They should also arrange for frontline service representatives to attend classes. At the very least, supervisors should attend and share their knowledge with their employees so that everyone can benefit and service to customers can be enhanced.

encounter, you may want to take notes for future reference. Notes can help prevent your forgetting or confusing information. Once you have made your notes, verify your understanding of the facts with your customer before proceeding. For example, in an important client or customer meeting, you may want to jot down key issues, points, follow-up actions, or questions. Doing so shows that you are committed to getting it right or taking action.

Ask Questions

Use questions to determine customer needs and to verify and clarify information received. This will ensure that you thoroughly understand the customer's message prior to taking action or responding. For example, when you first encounter a customer, you must discover his or her needs or what is wanted. Through a series of open-ended questions (typically they start with words such as *when, what, how,* or *why,* and seek substantial amounts of information) and closed-ended questions (they often start with words such as *do, did, are,* and *will,* and elicit one-syllable or single-word responses), you can gain useful information.

7 Information-Gathering Techniques

Concept: Use questions to sort out facts from fiction.

Your purpose in listening to your customers is to gather information about their needs on which you can base decisions on how to best satisfy them. Sometimes, you will need to prompt your customers to provide additional or different types of information. To generate and gather information, you can use a variety of questions. Most questions are either open-ended or closed-ended.

Open-ended Questions

This type of questioning follows the time-tested approach of the 5 Ws and 1 H used by journalists who ask questions that help determine who, what, when, where, why, and how. Basically, **open-ended questions** establish a number of facts. They:

Identify Customer Needs

By asking questions, you can help determine **customer needs,** what he or she wants or expects. This is a crucial task because some customers are either unsure of what they need or want or do not adequately express their needs or wants.

Examples:

"Ms. Deloach, what type of car are you looking for?"

"Mr. Petell, why is an extended warranty important to you?"

Gather a Lot of Information

Open-ended questions are helpful when you're just beginning a customer relationship and aren't sure what the customer has in mind or what's important. By uncovering more details, you can better serve your customer.

Example:

"Mr. and Mrs. Milton, to help me better serve you, could you please describe what your ideal house would look like if you could build it?"

Uncover Background Data

When a customer calls to complain about a problem, often he or she has already taken unsuccessful steps to solve it. In such cases, it is important to find out the background information about the customer or situation. By asking open-ended questions, you allow customers to tell you as much information as they feel is necessary to answer your question. This is why open-ended questions are generally more effective for gathering data than are closed-ended questions. If you feel you need more information after your customer responds to an open-ended question, you can always ask further questions.

Example:

"Mrs. Chan, will you please tell me the history behind this problem, including all of your previous contacts with this office?"

Uncover Objections During a Sale

If you are in sales or cross-selling or upselling products or services (getting a customer to buy a higher quality or different brand of product or extend or enhance existing service agreements) to current customers as a service representative, you will likely encounter **objections**. The reasons for a customer not wanting or needing your product and/or service can be identified through the use of open-ended questions. Such questions can be used to determine whether your customer has questions or objections. Many times, people are not rejecting what you are offering outright; they simply do not see an immediate need for the product or cannot think of appropriate questions to ask. In these cases, you can help them focus their thinking or guide their decision through the use of open-ended questions. Be careful to listen to your customer's words and tone when he or she offers objections. If the customer seems adamant, such as, "I really don't want it," don't go any further with your questions. The customer will probably become angry because he or she will feel that you are not listening. A fine line exists between helping and pushing, and if you cross it, you could end up with a confrontation on your hands. Often active listening and experience will help you determine what course of action to take.

Example:

"Ms. Williams, from what you told me, all the features of the new RD10 model that we talked about will definitely ease some of your workload, so let me get the paperwork started so you can take it home with you. What do you think?"

Give the Customer an Opportunity to Speak

Although it is important to control the conversation in order to save time and thus allow you to serve more customers, sometimes you may want to give the customer an opportunity to talk. This is crucial if the customer is upset or dissatisfied about something. By allowing a customer to "vent" as you listen actively, you can sometimes reduce the level of tension and help solve the problem.

Examples of open-ended questions:

"What suggestions for improving our complaint-handling process should I present to my boss?"

"Why is this feature so important to you?"

"How has the printer been malfunctioning, Jim?"

"What is the main use of this product?

"When would you most likely need to have us come out each month?"

"Where have you seen our product or similar ones being used?"

"Why do you feel that this product is better than others you've tried?"

"How do you normally use the product?"

"Mr. O'Connell, I can see you're unhappy. What can I do to help solve this problem?"

Closed-Ended Questions

Open-ended questions are designed to draw out a lot of information. Traditionally, **closed-ended questions** elicit short, one-syllable responses and gain little new information. Many closed-ended questions can be answered yes or no or with a specific answer, such as a number or a date. Closed-ended questions can be used for:

Verifying Information

Closed-ended questions are a quick way to check what was already said or agreed on. Using them reinforces that you're listening and also helps prevent you from making mistakes because you misinterpreted or misunderstood information.

Example:

"Mr. Christopherson, earlier I believe you said you've used our service before. Is that correct?"

Closing an Order

Once you've discovered needs and presented the benefits and features of your product and service, you need to ask for a buying decision. This brings closure to your discussion. Asking for a decision also signals the customer that it is his or her turn to speak. If the customer offers an objection, you can use the open-ended questioning format discussed earlier.

Example:

"Mr. Jones, this tie will go nicely with your new suit. May I wrap it for you?"

Gaining Agreement

When there has been ongoing dialogue and closure or commitment is needed, closed-ended questions can often bring about that result.

Example:

"Veronica, with everything we've accomplished today, I'd really like to be able to conclude this project before we leave. Can we work for one more hour?"

Clarifying Information

Closed-ended questions can also help ensure that you have the details correct and thus help prevent future misunderstandings or mistakes. Closed-ended questions also help save time and reduce the number of complaints and/or product returns you or someone else will have to deal with.

Example:

"Ms. Jovanovick, if I heard you correctly, you said that the problem occurs when you increase power to the engine. Is that as soon as you turn the ignition key or after you've been driving the car for a while?"

Examples of closed-ended questions:

"Do you agree that we should begin right away?" (obtaining agreement)

"Mrs. Leonard, did you say this was your first visit to our restaurant?" (verifying understanding)

"Mr. Morris, did you say you normally travel three or four times a month and have been doing so for the past ten years?" (verifying facts)

"How many employees do you have, Mr. Carroll?" (obtaining information)

8   Additional Question Guidelines

Concept: Use questions to further your feedback.

In order to generate meaningful responses from customers, keep the following points in mind.

Avoid Criticism

Be careful not to seem to be critical in the way you ask questions. For example, a question like, "You really aren't going to need two of the same item, are you?" sounds as if you are challenging the customer's decision making. And the bottom line is that what customers choose should not be your concern. Your job is to help them by providing excellent service. Also, as you read in Chapter 4, nonverbal messages delivered via tone or body language can suggest criticism, even if your spoken words do not.

Ask Only Positively Phrased Questions

You can ask for the same information in different ways, some more positive than others. As you interact with your customers, it is crucial to send messages in an open, pleasant manner. This is done by tone of voice and proper word selection. In the examples, you can see how a negative or positive word choice affects meaning.

Examples:

"You really don't want that color do you, Mrs. Handly?" (potentially negative or directive)

"We offer a wide selection of colors. Would you consider another color as an alternative, Mrs. Handly?" (positive or suggestive)

Ask Direct Questions

You generally get what you ask for. Therefore, being very specific with your questions can often result in your receiving useful information. Being specific can also save time and effort. This should not be construed to mean that you should be abrupt or curt in your communication with customers or anyone else.

Example:

If you want to know what style of furniture the customer prefers, but you know that only three styles are available, don't ask a general open-ended question, such as, "Mrs. Harris, what style of furniture were you looking for?" Instead, try a more structured closed-ended question such as, "Mrs. Harris, we stock Colonial, French provincial, and Victorian styles. Do any of those meet your needs?"

This approach prevents you from having to respond, "I'm sorry, we don't stock that style," when Mrs. Harris answers your open-ended question by telling you that she's looking for Art Deco style furniture.

Ask Customers How You Can Better Serve

You will find no better or easier way to determine what customers want and expect than to ask them. They'll appreciate it, and you'll do a better job serving them. *Note:* If appropriate, a good follow-up question to gain additional information after a customer has responded to a question is, "That's interesting, will you please explain to me why you feel that way or believe that's true?"

Chapter Summary

No matter what your current level of listening skill is, there is usually room for improvement. Customers expect and should receive your undivided attention in any encounter they have with you. You should continually reevaluate your own listening style, decide which areas need development, and strive for improvement. In addition, you should keep in mind that active listening involves more than just focusing on spoken words. Remember that there are many obstacles that can impede listening. To overcome them, you need to develop the characteristics of an effective listener and strive to minimize negative habits. Through the use of the active listening process and positive questioning, you can better determine and satisfy customer needs.

SERVICE IN ACTION   General Electric   CHAPTER 5

http://www.ge.com

Formed in 1876 by Thomas Alva Edison, General Electric (GE) has become a household word, manufacturing everything from appliances, light bulbs, and medical equipment to airplane engines. Today GE operates facilities in over 100 countries and employs more than 315,000 people worldwide. Its 2002 revenues were over 131 billion dollars (40 percent from its international initiatives), which would rank it as a powerhouse in any industry.

Because of the company's focus on quality, employees, consumer service, and development of products that make people's lives better, GE has won dozens of awards over the years. *Forbes* magazine recognized the company as number one in their Super 500 corporation listing in 2003 and in previous years as Global Most Admired Company (four years). *Fortune* magazine rated GE as America's Most Admired Company (four years). In 2003, *Working Mother* ranked GE as one of the 100 Best Companies for Working Mothers.

The guiding premise behind GE's success is its stated corporate values: *Respecting Always the Three Traditions of GE… Unyielding Integrity, Commitment to Performance and Thirst for Change.* On its website GE states that it has a passion for its customers and that it measures its own success by that of its customers. Obviously their strategy is working as a global product and service provider.

Key Terms and Concepts

attending	external obstacles	open-ended questions
biases	faulty assumptions	personal obstacles
circadian rhythm	hearing	psychological
closed-ended questions	informational overload	distracters
comprehending or	lag time or listening gap	responding
assigning meaning	listening	service recovery
congruence	objections	thought speed
customer needs		

Quick Preview Answers

1. F	5. T	9. F
2. T	6. T	10. T
3. T	7. T	11. F
4. F	8. T	12. T

Work It Out 5.1 Implied Messages (Possible Solutions)

Scenario #1

Issues/Needs   The customer is now unable to meet the due date for his/her mortgage since there is only one day between payday and the payment due date. He/she needs more time.

Possible Solution   Empathize with the customer (for example, I can understand how the dates present a problem) then offer to change the mortgage due date (for example, to the 10th of each month) to allow more time to make the payment. Ask if there is anything else with which you can assist and thank the customer for his/her business.

Scenario #2

Issues/Needs   To agree to accept the coupon for free shipping and then issue a refund of the shipping cost.

Solution   Take ownership for the problem (for example, I can help with that) and then modify the order to provide free shipping. Next, you need to issue a credit card refund for the amount of shipping. Ask if there is anything else you can assist with and thank the customer for his/her order.

Scenario #3

Issues/Needs   To have you (your organization) assume responsibility for the damage and pay to have it repaired.

Solution   Apologize for the inconvenience and empathize (for example, I know how frustrating that must be). Explain that while you do not doubt what the customer has said, you will have to do some research on the initial service call and get back to him/her. When you do call back after ascertaining that your employees caused the damage, apologize again. Next, either offer to have a sprinkler repair company come out to fix the system or to reimburse the customer if he/she has a sprinkler company that normally handles their system. Finally, offer further assistance and thank the customer for his/her business. You can also offer a free month of cable service for the inconvenience.

Chapter Review Questions

1. What phases make up the active listening process?
2. How does hearing differ from listening?
3. According to studies, what is the average rate of listening efficiency for most adults in the United States? Why is this significant in a customer service environment?

4. List 14 characteristics of effective listeners.

5. What is an important reason for practicing good listening skills in a customer service environment?

6. Of the characteristics common to good listeners, which do you consider the most important in a customer service organization? Explain.

7. What obstacles to effective listening have you experienced, either as a customer service professional or as a customer?

8. How can you determine when someone is not listening to what you say?

9. What techniques or strategies can be used to improve your listening skills?

10. How is the outcome of customer service encounters improved by using a variety of questions?

Search It Out

Search the Internet for Items on Listening Skills

To find out more about the listening process and how you can improve your listening skills, log on to the Internet and type in Listening or any of the other topic headings or subheadings in this chapter. Search for the following items:

Listening activities

Quotations about listening

Books and articles on listening (create a bibliographic list) or interpersonal communication

Research data on listening

Any other topic covered in this chapter (open-ended or closed-ended questions, handling sales objections)

Note: A listing for additional research on specific URLs is provided on the Customer Service website at **<www.mhhe.com/lucas05>.**

Collaborative Learning Activity

Bring your findings to class and be prepared to discuss them with your group.

Developing Team Listening Skills

To give you some practical experience in using the techniques described in this chapter, you will now have an opportunity to interact with others in your group. The activity will be done in groups of three or four members. One person will be the listener, one the speaker, and one or two observers. Each person will have an opportunity to play the different roles. For example, if there are four people in the group, there will be four rounds of activity. In the first round one member of the group will be the listener, one will be the speaker, and the other two will be observers. The roles will change in each of the next three rounds so that everyone will have had a turn at each role.

The speaker will spend about five to seven minutes sharing a customer service experience he or she has had in the past few weeks (it can be positive or negative).

The experience should have been one that lasted for several minutes so that there will be enough detail to share with the other members of the group. The speaker should describe the type of organization, why he or she was there, how he or she was greeted, the behavior of the customer service provider, how the provider dealt with concerns and questions, and any other important point the speaker can recall.

As the speaker talks, the listener should pay attention and use as many of the positive listening skills discussed in this chapter as possible. The observers should watch and take notes on what they see. Specifically, they should look for use of the positive listening skills and any other behaviors exhibited (positive or negative). After each speaker has finished his or her story, the listener, then the speaker, and finally the observers (in that order) should answer the following questions about the listener's behavior:

> What was done well from a listening standpoint?
> What needed improvement?
> What comments or suggestions came to mind?

 Face to Face

Handling an Irate Customer at Regal Florists

Background

Regal Florists is a small, third-generation family-owned flower shop in Willow Grove, Pennsylvania. Most customers are local residents, but Regal has a website and an FTD delivery arrangement so that it serves customers throughout the United States. Mr. and Mrs. Raymond Boyle have been doing business with Regal for more than 20 years and know the owners well. Quite often they order centerpiece arrangements for holidays and dinner parties, which they host frequently because of Mr. Boyle's position with a public relations firm. They also occasionally send flowers to their six children and four grandchildren living in various parts of the United States and overseas. Regal's owners and employees are usually especially cheerful, helpful, and efficient. That's one of the reasons the Boyles are loyal customers even though Regal's prices have risen about the industry average in recent years.

Your Role

During the past four years you have worked part-time at Regal's, at first delivering arrangements and for the past year creating arrangements and managing the shop.

Mr. Boyle stopped by first thing this morning, just as you were opening the store. He was irate, demanding to know what happened with the arrangement delivered yesterday to his assistant for Secretary's Day, and swearing he'd never patronize Regal's again. Apparently, he had phoned in the order last week. The order was taken by a 16-year-old part-time employee who has since resigned. According to Mr. Boyle, he'd ordered a small arrangement with carnations and various other bright spring flowers for his assistant. Instead, his assistant received a dozen red roses along with a card, on the outside of which was a border of little hearts and the statement "Thinking of you." Inside the card was a message intended for his wife: "I don't know what I'd do without you." Unfortunately, Mrs. Boyle had dropped by Mr. Boyle's office and was near the assistant's desk when the flowers arrived, saw the card and flowers, and was quite upset. Rumor has it that Mr. and Mrs. Boyle are having marital problems. You were the only person in the shop when Mr. Boyle came in. Answer these questions.

Critical Thinking Questions

1. Do you think that Mr. Boyle should take Regal's past performance record into consideration? Why or why not?
2. What listening skills addressed in this chapter should you use in this situation? Why?
3. What can you possibly do or say that might resolve this situation positively?
4. Based on information provided, how would you have reacted in this situation if you were Mr. Boyle? Why?
5. If you were Mr. Boyle, what could be done or said to convince you to continue to do business with Regal?

PLANNING TO SERVE   CHAPTER 5

Based on the content of this chapter, create a Personal Action Plan focused on improving your listening skills when providing service to your customers. Begin by taking an objective assessment of your current listening strengths and areas for improvement. Once you have identified deficit areas, set goals for improvement.

Start your assessment by listing as many strengths and areas for improvement as you are aware of. Share your list with other people who know you well to see if they agree or can add additional items. Keep in mind that you will likely be more critical of yourself than other people will. Additionally, you may be sending nonverbal signals related to listening

that you are not aware of. For those reasons, keep an open mind when considering their comments.

Once you have a list, choose two or three items that you think need the most work and can add the most value when interacting with others. List these items on a sheet of paper along with specific courses of action you will take for improvement, the name of someone you will enlist to provide feedback on your behavior, and a specific date by which you want to see improvement. Related to the latter, keep in mind that research shows that it takes on average 21 to 30 days to see behavioral change; therefore, set a date that is at least in this range.

Listening	Areas for Improvement

Top Three Items	Who Will Help	Date for Change
1.		
2.		
3.		

Customer Service and Behavior

From the Frontline Interview

Jason Grimard is a nutritional fitness specialist who states that his customer service career is rooted in his need to interact with the public. He has worked in customer service at restaurants, retail in the health, fitness and nutritional sales and service areas, and at an athletic franchise facility.

JASON GRIMARD,
Nutrition Specialist/
Personal Fitness Trainer

1 **What has been some of your most pleasurable experiences related to dealing with customers? Why?**

I learned several years ago that I cannot have a profession where I am "behind closed doors." I have tried jobs which did not require direct customer contact and did not like them. Early on, it became clear to me that I did not like my profession at all. The realization set in that I was much happier when I was dealing with the public. Thus, I sought jobs interacting with the public in positions that required tasks such as funds transaction and quality control (dealing with complaints and problems). All of my jobs have demanded a high customer-service-oriented attitude.

Some of my most pleasurable experiences have come when I was helping someone with their needs, no matter how significant or insignificant their need. The reason this is so enjoyable to me is that I have to put myself on both sides of the fence where I know how it feels to be the customer and the relief of being assisted by someone who cares. When you realize that you are truly helping someone's

personal needs it becomes more than your job and turns into a pleasure.

2 **What are some of the biggest challenges that you have faced in dealing with customer behavior? Why?**

My biggest challenges have involved nonresponsive, close-minded customers. This occurs when I have already used all the training tips related to helping the customer, but I am now in a corner where I cannot consult someone for further advice and am forced to go beyond training to study the customer to find a resolution. This is done in steps. First, I read the customer's emotional state. If it seems unstable, I try to comfort him or her. Then, I try to relate to the customer so that he or she will feel that I understand his or her needs. Then I can tell if the customer is becoming responsive. Finally, I agree with the person in order to show understanding. The goal of all this is for the customer to be more responsive and explain his or her needs. I must get the person to listen to suggestions from me as a trusted friend.

3 **What are some of the typical mistakes you see others make when they are dealing with customer behavior in negative situations?**

I see others make a number of mistakes. First, they lose their compassion for their customers, adopting an "I don't care attitude." Second, they lose their temper when dealing with

Chapter Learning Objectives

After completing this chapter, you will be able to:

- Recognize four key behavioral styles and the roles they play in customer service.

- Use techniques outlined to interact with various customer behavioral styles.

- Develop strategies for communicating effectively with customers.

- Interpret customer nonverbal cues effectively on the basis of behavioral styles.

- Respond to customer problems effectively.

---

a customer. They become frustrated, and it shows through facial and body expressions and their words. The third mistake is when customer service reps are close-minded about a situation and unwilling to seek further help from someone higher up with more experience.

4 What techniques or strategies do you use to get customers to cooperate and not cause problems when you interact with them?

I try to gain cooperation by first addressing their needs in an attempt to understand exactly what they require. I do this to try to identify their emotional state to see whether they are angry, depressed, or happy. This can give me the upper hand by not provoking an argument and gaining cooperation. A good technique in studying someone is to look into his or her eyes. Another strategy is to watch body language for signs of anxiety, nervousness, or any kind of tension. All of those mental states are unpredictable, but easily addressed if done properly. Dealing with an angry customer is somewhat of an art that can help ensure that I get to provide service to the person in the future.

To deal with an angry customer you *must* keep smiling, and not fake a "my job depends on it" smile. It must be a compassionate, sincere smile. If you lose your temper you are doomed. You have to find out exactly why a customer is angry. It may not even be with you or your company. After you have found what the customer is angry about, you must comfort his or her displeasure and continue to be kind and compassionate. This will show that you actually do care and that he or she is not just another person to you. Kindness, comfort, and

compassion will defuse anger when used properly. Next, you should try to relate to the customer in order to gain friendship. You do this to promote further business with the customer in the future. The result of all this is that you can successfully overcome a customer's anger, gain a professional friendship, and secure continued business.

5 What advice would you give other service providers regarding ways to be more effective in dealing with customer behavior?

To be more effective in dealing with customer behavior you must always, I mean *always,* stay positive. Being positive can uplift a customer's day. Never bring your personal life to the job. Be compassionate. This is essential. The minute a customer feels you are not compassionate, that automatically translates into "you don't care one bit about me." People have a tendency to jump to negativity; do not give them an option. Try to understand how they display their emotions. This will be essential for dealing with a difficult customer service situation.

Critical Thinking

According to what Jason has said, what role does the use of a "second sense" to determine someone's emotional state play in delivering quality customer service? What are some of the key tools for doing this based on his comments?

Quick Preview

Before reviewing the chapter content, respond to the following questions by placing a "T" for true or an "F" for false on the rules. Use any questions you miss as a checklist of material to which you will pay particular attention as you read through the chapter. For those you get right, congratulate yourself, but review the sections they address in order to learn additional details about the topic.

_____ 1. Understanding behavioral styles can aid in establishing and maintaining positive customer relationships.

_____ 2. You should treat others as individuals, not as members of a category.

_____ 3. People whose primary behavioral style category is "E" focus their energy on working with people.

_____ 4. People whose primary behavioral style category is "D" focus their energy on tasks or getting the job done.

_____ 5. Some behavioral styles are better than others.

_____ 6. People who exhibit the "D" style often tend to move slowly and speak in a low-key manner.

_____ 7. People who exhibit the "E" style often tend to be highly animated in using gestures and speaking.

_____ 8. People who exhibit the "R" style often tend to be very impatient.

_____ 9. People who exhibit the "I" style often tend to express their emotions easily.

_____ 10. You should attempt to determine a customer's behavioral style and then tailor your communication accordingly.

_____ 11. To deliver total customer satisfaction, you need to make your customers feel special.

_____ 12. When you say no to a customer, it is important to let him or her know what you cannot do and why.

_____ 13. Service to your customers should be seamless; customers should not have to see or deal with problems or process breakdowns.

_____ 14. Perceptions are based on education, experiences, events, and interpersonal contacts, as well as a person's intelligence level.

_____ 15. Once you've made a perception, you should evaluate its accuracy.

Answers to Quick Preview can be found at the end of the chapter.

1 Why Be Concerned With Behavioral Styles?

Concept: Behavioral styles are observable tendencies. An awareness of your own style can lead you to understand customers and improve your relationships with customers.

As a customer service professional, you need to understand human behavioral style characteristics. The more proficient you become at identifying your own behavioral characteristics and those of others, the better you will be at establishing and maintaining positive relationships with customers. Self-knowledge is the starting point. To help in this effort, we will examine some common behavior that you exhibit and that you may observe in various other people.

A key to successfully dealing with others is recognizing your own style. Too often we try to impose our *beliefs, values, attitudes,* and *needs* on others. This can lead to frustration for them and us. When dealing with your customers, you should recognize that someone else doing something or acting differently from the way you do doesn't mean that that person is wrong. Relationships are built on accepting the characteristics of others. In customer service, adaptability is crucial, for many people do not always act the way you want them to. As you will read later in this chapter, there are many strategies that can be used to help modify and adapt your behavior so that it does not clash with that of your customers. This does not mean that you must make all the concessions when behaviors do not mesh. It simply means that, although you do not have control over the behavior of others, you do have control over your own behavior. Use this control to deal more effectively with your customers.

2   What Are Behavioral Styles?

Concept: Behavioral styles are actions exhibited when you and others deal with tasks or people. As a customer service professional, you need to be aware that everyone is not the same.

Behavioral styles are observable tendencies (actions that you can see or experience) that you and other people exhibit when dealing with tasks or people. As you grow from infancy, your personality forms, based on your experiences and your environment. For example, if you had a lot of interaction with others as a child and were exposed to "people-based" activities, you likely will relate well to others in the workplace as an adult. On the other hand, if your childhood was a lonely one, as an adult you may have difficulties interacting with people.

For thousands of years, people have devised systems in an attempt to better understand why people do what they do and how they accomplish what they do—and to categorize behavioral styles. Many of these systems are still in use today. For example, early astrologers grouped the 12 signs into the four categories Earth, Air, Fire, and Water. Hippocrates, and other ancient physicians and philosophers, observed and categorized people (for example, sanguine, phlegmatic, melancholy, and choleric). Modern researchers have examined behavior from a variety of perspectives.

Have you ever come into contact with someone with whom you simply did not feel comfortable or someone with whom you felt an immediate bond? If so, you were possibly experiencing and reacting to the impact of behavioral style. As a customer service professional, you need to be aware that everyone is not the same, or behaviorally just like you. For this reason, you should strive to provide service in a manner that addresses others' needs and desires, not the ones you prefer.

Because you have certain behavioral preferences, you may want to impose them on others. This type of action from a service provider may cause a customer to become angry, withdrawn, or even disruptive. You will be better informed about yourself if you learn your own behavior preferences. The next section addresses how to do that.

3   Identifying Behavioral Styles

Concept: Each contact in a customer service environment has the potential for contributing to your success. Each person should be valued for his or her strengths and not belittled for what you perceive as shortcomings.

Through an assessment questionnaire you can discover your own behavioral tendencies in a variety of situations. An awareness of your own style preferences can

LEADERSHIP INITIATIVE   6.1

Supervisors have to take a lead in preparing service employees to deal with a multitude of personalities and human behavior. An easy way to accomplish this is by personally becoming aware of various aspects of human behavior. This can be accomplished through self-assessment surveys, reading on the topic, and attending training classes or seminars.

Once knowledge has been gained, it should be freely shared with employees so that they too can benefit. Additionally, by sending employees to training on behavioral styles and other aspects of diversity, they can gain new insights about themselves and others. This can lead to a reduction in misunderstandings with others and to enhanced customer service.

then lead you to a better understanding of customers, since they also possess style preferences. By understanding these characteristics, you can improve communication, build stronger relationships, and offer better service to the customer.

Many self-assessment questionnaires and research related to behavioral styles are based on the work begun by psychiatrist Carl Jung and others in the earlier part of the twentieth century. Jung explored human personality and behavior. He divided behavior into two "attitudes" (introvert and extrovert) and four "functions" (thinking, feeling, sensing, and intuitive). These attitudes and functions can intermingle to form eight psychological types, a knowledge of which is useful in defining and describing human behavioral characteristics.

From Jung's complex research have come many variations, additional studies, and a variety of behavioral style self-assessment questionnaires and models for explaining personal behavior. Examples of these questionnaires are the Myers-Briggs Type Indicator (MBTI), the Personal Profile System (DiSC), and the Social Styles Profile (SSP).

Although everyone typically has a **primary behavior pattern** (the way a person acts or reacts under certain circumstances) to which he/she reverts in stressful situations, people also have other characteristics in common and regularly demonstrate some of the other behavioral patterns. Identifying your own style preferences helps *you* identify similar ones in others.

To informally identify some of your own behavioral styles preferences, complete Work It Out 6.1.

Note: Keep in mind that this is only a quick indicator. A more thorough assessment, using a formal instrument (questionnaire), will be better at predicting your style preferences. For more information or to obtain written or computer-based surveys and reports, write the author at the address shown in the author information section of this book.

You should be aware that you should not try to use behavioral characteristics and cues as absolute indicators of the type of person you are dealing with. (This is similar to the situation with nonverbal cues.) Human behavior is complex and often unpredictable. You have some of the characteristics listed for all four style categories; you simply have learned through years of experience which behavior you are most comfortable with and when adaptation is helpful or necessary. Generally, most people are adaptable and can shift style categories or exhibit different characteristics based on the situation. For example, a person who is normally very personable and amiable can revert to more directive behavior, if necessary, to manage an activity or process for which he or she will be held accountable. Similarly, a person who normally exhibits controlling or task-oriented behavior can socialize and react positively in "people" situations. People are adaptable.

To determine your behavioral style preference, make a copy of this page and then complete the following survey.

Step 1 Read the following list of words and phrases and rate yourself by placing a number (from 1 to 5) next to each item. A 5 means that the word is an accurate description of yourself in most situations, a 3 indicates a balanced agreement about the word's application, and a 1 means that you do not feel that the word describes your behavior well. Before you begin, refer to the sample assessment in Figure 6.1.

Relaxed

Logical

Decisive

Talkative

Consistent

Nonaggressive (avoids conflict)

Calculating

Fun-loving

Loyal

Quality-focused

Competitive

Enthusiastic

Sincere

Accurate

Pragmatic (practical)

Popular

Patient

Detail-oriented

Objective

Optimistic

TOTAL   R =   I =   D =   E =

Step 2 Once you have rated each word or phrase, start with the first word, *Relaxed,* and put the letter "R" to the right of it. Place an "I" to the right of the second words, an "D" to the right of the third word, and an "E" to the right of the fourth word. Then start over with the fifth word and repeat the RIDE pattern until all words have a letter at their right.

Step 3 Next, go through the list and count point values for all words that have an "R" beside them. Put the total at the bottom of the grid next to "R=." Do the same for the other letters.

Once you have finished, one letter will probably have the highest total score. This is your natural style tendency. For example, if "R" has the highest score, your primary style is Rational. If "I" has the highest score, you exhibit more Inquisitive behavior. "D" indicates Decisive, and "E" is an Expressive style preference.

If two or more of your scores have the same high totals, you probably generally put forth similar amounts of effort in both these style areas.

An important point to remember is that there is no "right" or "wrong" style. Each person should be valued for his or her strengths and not belittled because of what you perceive as shortcomings. In a customer environment, each contact has the potential for contributing to your success and that of your organization. By appreciating the behavioral characteristics of people with whom you interact, you can avoid bias or prejudice and better serve your customer.

FIGURE 6.1
Sample Completed
Self-Assessment

5	Relaxed	R
3	Logical	I
1	Decisive	D
4	Talkative	E
5	Consistent	R
3	Nonaggressive (avoids conflict)	I
5	Calculating	D
3	Fun-loving	E
5	Loyal	R
1	Quality-focused	I
3	Competitive	D
2	Enthusiastic	E
5	Sincere	R
1	Accurate	I
3	Pragmatic (practical)	D
1	Popular	E
5	Patient	R
2	Detail-oriented	I
1	Objective	D
1	Optimistic	E
TOTAL	R = 25　　I = 10　　D = 13　　E = 11	

4　Style Tendencies

Concept: A person may demonstrate strong tendencies toward one style preference or another. By being familiar with these styles and their general characteristics, you can adapt to various behaviors your customers may exhibit.

How can a person who demonstrates one of the four styles be described? How might this person act, react, or interact? Some generalizations about behavior are listed in this section. Keep in mind that even though people have a primary style, they demonstrate other style behaviors too. By becoming familiar with these style characteristics, and observing how others display them, you can begin to learn how to better adapt to various behaviors.

R: Rational 理性

People who have a preference for the **rational style** may tend to:

- Be very patient.
- Wait or stand in one place for periods of time without complaining, although they may be irritated about a breakdown in the system or lack of organization.
- Exhibit congenial eye contact and facial expressions.
- Prefer one-on-one or small-group interactions over solitary or large-group ones.
- Seek specific or complete explanations to questions (e.g., "That's our policy" does not work well with an "R" customer).
- Dislike calling attention to themselves or a situation.
- Avoid conflict and anger.
- Often wear subdued colors and informal, conservative, or conventional clothing styles.
- Ask questions rather than state their opinion.

- Listen and observe more than they talk (especially in groups).
- Communicate more in writing and like the use of notes, birthday, or thank-you cards just to stay in touch.
- Like to be on a first-name basis with others.
- Have intermittent eye contact with brief, businesslike handshake.
- Have informal, comfortable office spaces, possibly with pictures of family in view.
- Like leisure activities that involve people (often family).

I: Inquisitive 好奇为.

People who have a preference for the **inquisitive style** may tend to:

- Rarely volunteer feelings freely.
- Ask specific, pertinent questions rather than making statements of their feelings.
- Rely heavily on facts, times, dates, and practical information to make their point.
- Prefer to interact in writing rather than in person or on the phone.
- Prefer formality and distance in interactions. They often lean back when talking, even when emphasizing key points.
- Use formal titles and last names as opposed to first names. They may also stress the use of full names, not nicknames (e.g., Cynthia instead of Cindy or Charles instead of Chuck).
- Use cool, brief handshakes, often without a smile. If they do smile, it may appear forced.
- Wear conservative clothing although their accessories are matched well.
- Be impeccable in their grooming but may differ in their choice of styles from those around them (e.g., hair and makeup).
- Be very punctual and time-conscious.
- Carry on lengthy conversations, especially when trying to get answers to questions.
- Be diplomatic with others.
- Prefer solitary leisure activities (e.g., reading or listening to relaxing music).
- Keep their personal life separate from business.

D: Decisive 坚定

People who have a preference for the **decisive style** may tend to:

- Move quickly.
- Seek immediate gratification of needs or results.
- Work proactively toward a solution to a problem.
- Be forceful and assertive in their approach (sometimes overly so).
- Project a competitive nature.
- Display a confident, possibly arrogant demeanor.
- Ask specific, direct questions and give short, straight answers.
- Discuss rather than write about something (e.g., call or come in rather than write about a complaint).
- Talk and interrupt more than listen.

- Display symbols of power to demonstrate their own importance (e.g., expensive jewelry, clothes, cars, power colors in business attire such as navy blue or charcoal gray).
- Be solemn and use closed, nonverbal body cues.
- Have firm handshakes and strong, direct eye contact.
- Have functionally decorated offices (all items have a purpose and are not there to make the environment more attractive).
- Prefer active, competitive leisure activities.

E: Expressive 长此河

People who have a preference for the **expressive style** may tend to:

- Look for opportunities to socialize or talk with others (e.g., checkout lines at stores, bus stops, waiting areas).
- Project a friendly, positive attitude.
- Be enthusiastic, even animated when talking, using wide, free-flowing gestures.
- Use direct eye contact and enthusiastic, warm (often two-handed) handshake.
- Smile and use open body language.
- Get close or touch when speaking to someone.
- Talk rather than write about something (e.g., call or come in with a complaint rather than writing to complain).
- Initiate projects.
- Wear bright, modern, or unusual clothes and jewelry because it gets them noticed or fits their mood.
- Dislike routine.
- Share feelings and express opinions or ideas easily and readily.
- Get distracted in conversations and start discussing other issues.
- Prefer informal use of names and like first-name communication.
- Not be time conscious and may often be late for appointments.
- Speak loudly and expressively with a wide range of inflection.
- Like action-oriented, people-centered leisure activities.

5   Communicating With Each Style

Concept: Each behavior style features various indicators of this style in practice. Remember, these cues are indicators, not absolutes, as you begin to use them to interact appropriately with others.

Once you recognize people's style tendencies, you can improve your relationships and chances of success by tailoring your communication strategies. As you examine Figure 6.2, think about how you can use these strategies with people you know in each style category. Keep in mind that these and other characteristics outlined in this chapter are only general in nature. Everyone is a mixture of all four styles and can change to a different style to address a variety of situations. Use these examples as indicators of style and not as absolutes. Also, be careful *not* to label a person as being one style (for example, Toni is a high "R"), since people use all four styles.

FIGURE 6.2
Communicating
With Different
Personality Styles

Style	Behaviors	Strategy
RATIONAL	*Nonverbal Cues* Gentle handshake, flowing, nondramatic gestures. Fleeting eye contact.	Return firm, brief handshake; avoid aggressive gestures. Make intermittent (3 to 5 seconds) eye contact.
	Verbal Cues Steady, even delivery. Subdued volume. Slower rate of speech. Keeps communication brief. Communication follows a logical pattern (e.g., Step 1, Step 2).	Mirror their style somewhat. Relax your message delivery. Slow your rate if necessary; be patient. Ask open-ended questions to draw out information. Use structured approach in communications.
	Additional Cues Avoids confrontation.	Attempt to solve problems without creating a situation in which they feel challenged or obliged to defend themselves.
INQUISITIVE	*Nonverbal Cues* Deliberate body movements. Uses little physical contact. Correspondence is formal and includes many details.	Use careful, restrained body cues. Avoid touching. Respond similarly.
	Verbal Cues Quiet, slow-paced speech (especially in groups). Minimal vocal variety.	Mirror rate and pattern. Use subdued tone and volume.
	Additional Cues Values concise communication. Uses details to make points. Prefers confirmation and backup in writing. Uses formal names instead of nicknames.	Use brief, accurate statements. Provide background information and data. Respond in writing and provide adequate background information. Address them by title and last name unless told otherwise.
	Additional Cues Sharing of personal information is minimal. Focuses on task at hand.	Communicate on business level unless they initiate personal conversation. Organize thoughts before responding.
DECISIVE	*Nonverbal Cues* Steady, direct eye contact. Writing tends to be short and specific. Gestures tend to be autocratic (e.g., pointing fingers or hands on hips).	Return eye contact (3 to 5 seconds) and smile. Respond in similar fashion; minimize small talk and details. Stand your ground without antagonizing. Maintain a professional demeanor.

FIGURE 6.2
continued

	Verbal Cues	
	Forceful tone.	Don't react defensively or in a retaliatory manner.
	Speaks in statements.	Use facts and logic and avoid unnecessary details.
	Direct and challenging (short, abrupt).	Listen rather than defend.
	Fast rate of speech.	Match rate somewhat.
	Additional Cues	
	Short attention span when listening.	Keep sentences and communication brief.
	Very direct and decisive.	Support opinions, ideas, and vision.
EXPRESSIVE	*Nonverbal Cues*	
	Enthusiasm and inflection in voice.	Listen and respond enthusiastically.
	Active body language.	Use open, positive body language and smile easily.
	Enthusiastic, possibly two-handed handshake.	Return firm, professional one-handed shake.
	Uses touch to emphasize points.	Acknowledge but use caution in returning touch (this action could be misinterpreted by them or others).
	Very intense, dramatic.	Show interest and ask pertinent questions.
	Writing tends to be flowery and includes many details.	When writing, use a friendly reader-focused style.
	Verbal Cues	
	Excessive details when describing something.	Ask specific open-ended questions to help them refocus.
	Fast rate of speech.	Mirror or match their rate and excitement where appropriate.
	Emphasizes storytelling and fun.	Relax, listen, and respond appropriately.
	Additional Cues	
	Inattentive to details in tasks.	Ask questions to involve them.
	Shares personal information and virtually anything else freely.	Reciprocate if you are comfortable doing so; however, stay focused on task at hand.

People send verbal and nonverbal clues to their behavioral style preference. Observe your customers' eye contact, level of directness or evasiveness, how quickly or slowly they speak, and their level of warmth versus formality. Once you can read these and other clues, you'll be better able to individualize the customer service you provide. *Can you think of a person in your life who exhibits clues to his or her behavioral style?*

To practice matching behavior with styles, try this activity. Make four or five copies of Worksheet 6-1 (see website http://www.mhhe.com/lucas05). Select four or five friends or coworkers whom you see and interact with regularly. Write one of their names at the top of each worksheet copy. Covertly (without their knowledge) observe these people for a week or so and make notes about their behavior under each category listed on the worksheet. Focus specifically on the following areas:

- Writing pattern or style
- Interpersonal communication style (e.g., direct, indirect, specific or nonspecific questions, good or poor listener)
- Body movements and other nonverbal gestures
- Dress style (e.g., flashy, conservative, formal, informal)
- Surroundings (e.g, office decorations or organization, car, home)
- Personality (e.g., activities and interactions preferred—solitary, group, active, passive)

At the end of the week, decide which primary and/or secondary style of behavior each person exhibits most often. Then ask these people to assist you in an experiment that will involve them completing the quick style assessment that you did earlier (Work It Out 6.1).

After they have rated themselves, explain that you have been observing them for the past week.

Compare their ratings to the characteristics described in this chapter, and to your own assessment. Were you able to predict their primary or, at least, their secondary style?

6 Building Stronger Relationships by Problem Solving

Concept: Sometimes building stronger customer relationships means that you discover customer needs, seek opportunities for service, and respond appropriately to customers' behavioral styles. Occasionally you will need to de-emphasize a no and say it as positively as you can.

Recognizing and relating to customers' behavioral styles is just the first step in providing better service (see Figures 6.2 and 6.3). To deliver total customer satisfaction, you will need to make the customer feel special, which often entails **problem solving.** Whether a situation involves simply answering a question, guiding someone to a desired product or location, or performing a service, customers should leave the interaction feeling good about what they experienced. Providing this feeling is not only good business sense on your part but also helps guarantee the customers return or favorable word-of-mouth advertising. There are many ways of partnering with either internal or external customers to solve problems and produce a **win-win situation** (one in which the customer and you and your organization succeed). Whatever you do to achieve this result, your customers should realize that you are their advocate and are acting in their best interests to solve their problems (see problem-solving model on pages 194–198). Some suggestions for building stronger customer relationships follow.

Discover Customer Needs

Using the communication skills addressed in earlier chapters, engage customers in a dialogue that allows them to identify what they really want or need. If you can determine a customer's behavioral style, you can tailor your communication strategy to that style. Keep in mind that some customer needs may not be expressed aloud. In these instances, you should attempt to validate your impressions or suspicions

FIGURE 6.3

Strategies for Responding to Customer Problems

Figure 6.3 provides some strategies to use when responding to customer complaints and solving problems involving people who demonstrate the four behavioral styles you have learned about. By tailoring customer service strategies to individual style preferences, you address the customer's specific needs. As you read in Chapter 5, active listening is a key skill in any service situation. As you review these strategies, think of other things you might do to better serve each behavioral type.

Style	Behaviors	Strategies
RATIONAL	Seeks systematic resolution to the situation. Avoids conflict or disagreement. Strives for acceptance of ideas. Intermittent eye contact. Uses hand and subdued body movements and speech to emphasize key points.	Stress resolution and security of the issue. Smile, when appropriate. Provide references or resources. Listen actively; make eye contact. Focus on personal movements to convey your feelings about the incident (e.g., "How do you feel we can best resolve this problem?").
INQUISITIVE	Listens to explanations. Demands specifics. Mild demeanor. Intermittent eye contact. Gives list of issues, in chronological order. Exhibits patience. Seeks reassurance. Focuses on facts.	Focus on the problem, not the person. Have details and facts available. Approach in nonthreatening manner. Listen actively, make eye contact, and focus on the situation. Be specific in outlining actions to be taken by everyone. Follow through on commitments. Offer guarantees of resolution if possible. Give facts and pros and cons of suggestions.
DECISIVE	Seeks to avoid conflict; just wants resolution. Loud voice. Finger pointing or aggressive body gestures. Firm, active handshake. Directly places blame on service provider. Direct eye contact. Sarcasm. Impatient. Demanding verbiage (e.g., "You'd better fix this"; "I want to see the manager *now*!"). Irrational assertions (e.g., "You people *never* or *always*...") Threats (e.g., "If you can't help, I'll go to a company that can.").	Use low-pitched, unemotional speech; be patient; listen. Be patient; listen empathetically. Don't internalize; they are angry with the product or service, not necessarily you. Return a firm businesslike handshake. Be brief; tell them what you can do; offer solutions. Be formal, businesslike. Don't take a happy-go-lucky or flippant approach. Be time-conscious; time is money to a "D." Project competence; find the best person to solve problem. Ask questions that focus on what they need or want (e.g., "What do you think is a reasonable solution?"). Reassure; say what you can do.

FIGURE 6.3
continued

EXPRESSIVE	Intermittent smiling along with verbalizing dissatisfaction. Uses nonaggressive language (e.g., "I'd like to talk with someone about . . .").	Be supportive; tell them what you *can* do for them. Allow them to vent frustrations or verbalize thoughts.
	Steady eye contact.	Smile, if appropriate; return eye contact while conversing.
	Elicits your assistance and follow-up (e.g., "I really don't want to run all over town searching. Will you please call . . ."). Shows sincere interest.	Take the time to offer assistance and comply with their requests, if possible. Focus on feelings through empathy (e.g., "I feel that . . .")
	Enthusiastic active handshake. Enthusiastically explains a situation.	Return a firm businesslike handshake. Patiently provide active listening; offer ideas and suggestions for resolution.

by asking questions or requesting feedback. Gather information about a customer from observing vocal qualities, phrasing, nonverbal expressions and movements, and emotional state. For example, while providing service to Mr. Delgado, you told him that the product he was ordering would not arrive for three weeks. You noticed that he grimaced and made a concerned sound of "Um." At this point, a perception check would have been appropriate. You could have said, "Mr. Delgado, you looked concerned or disappointed when I mentioned the delivery date. Is that a problem for you?" You might have discovered that he needed the item sooner but resigned himself to the delay and didn't ask about other options. In effect, he was exhibiting "I" or possibly "R" behavior (silence and low-key reaction). Rather than have a confrontation, he accepted the situation without voicing disappointment or concern. He might then have gone to a competitor. By reacting positively to his non-verbal signals, you could identify and address a concern and thus prevent a dissatisfied and/or lost customer.

Say "Yes"

If you must decline a request or cannot provide a product or service, do so in a positive manner. De-emphasizing what you cannot do and providing an alternative puts the customer in a power position. That is, even though she may not get her first request, she is once again in control because she can say yes or no to the alternative you have offered, or she can decide on the next step. For example, when a customer requests a brand or product not stocked by your organization, you could offer alternatives. You might counter with, "Mrs. Hanslik, although we don't stock that brand, we do have a comparable product which has been rated higher by *Consumer's Report* than the one you requested. Let me show you." This approach not only serves the customer but also (sometimes) results in a sale.

Seek Opportunities for Service

View complaints as a chance to create a favorable impression by solving a problem. Watch the behavioral characteristics being exhibited by your customer. Based on what you see and hear, take appropriate action to adapt to the customer's personality needs and solve the problem professionally. For example, Mrs. Minga complained loudly to you that the service woman who installed her new washing machine tracked oil onto the dining room carpet. As she is speaking, Mrs. Minga is pointing her finger and threatening to go to the manager if you do not handle this situation immediately. You can take the opportunity to solve the problem and strengthen the relationship at the same time. You might try the following. Make direct eye contact (no staring), smile, and empathize by saying, "Mrs. Minga, I'm terribly sorry about your carpet. I know that it must be very upsetting. If you'll allow me to, I'll arrange to have your dining room carpet cleaned, and for your inconvenience, while they're at it we'll have them clean all the carpets in your house at no cost to you. How does that sound?" In reacting this way, you have professionally and assertively taken control of the situation. This is important because Mrs. Minga is exhibiting high "D" behavior. Responding in a less decisive manner might result in an escalation of her emotions and a demand to see someone in authority.

The process just described, which involves an attempt at righting a wrong and compensating for inconvenience, is called *service recovery*. The concept will be addressed in detail in Chapter 13.

Focus on Process Improvement

Customers generally do not like being kept waiting when your system is not functioning properly. They rightfully view their time as valuable. To expect them to patiently wait while a new cashier tries to figure out the register codes, someone gets a price check because the product was coded incorrectly, you have to call the office for information or approvals, and so on, is unfair and unreasonable. Defects or delays should be handled when the customer is not present. Service should be seamless to customers. This means that they should get great service and never have to worry about your problems or breakdowns. When breakdowns do occur, they should be fixed quickly, and the customer relationship smoothed over. In addition, it is important to recognize that customers with different behavioral styles will react differently to such breakdowns. "R" style customers are likely to complain in an inoffensive manner and may even smile but may also seek out a supervisor. Those with "I" styles may seem to be patient and not say anything or cause a confrontation but will possibly request directions to the supervisor's office and/or later send a detailed letter of complaint. Someone who exhibits "D" behavior may get loud, aggressive, and vocal and demand a supervisor after only a brief delay. The "E" types may get upset but will often make the best of their time complaining to other customers and comparing notes on similar past experiences. No matter what style the customer exhibits, you should strive to reduce or eliminate customer inconvenience and distress.

In all cases, after a delay you may want to compensate the customer for the inconvenience. At the least, such a situation warrants a sincere apology. Such an occurrence might be handled in the following manner. "Mr. Westgate, I am sorry for the delay. We've been experiencing computer problems all day. I'd like to make up for your inconvenience by giving you a 10 percent discount off your meal check. Would that be acceptable?" Although this is not a significant offering, your intention is to show remorse and to placate the customer so that he or she will continue to use your products and/or services. You will read more about this technique in Chapter 13.

After you have dealt with the situation, your next concern should be to personally fix the process that caused the breakdown or make a recommendation to your supervisor or other appropriate person. Quality and **process improvement** are the responsibility of all employees.

Make Customers Feel Special

No matter which style tendencies a customer has, everyone likes to feel appreciated. By taking the time to recognize customers' value and by communicating effectively, you can bolster their self-esteem. When customers feel good about themselves as a result of something you did or said, they are likely to better appreciate what you and your organization can offer them. For example, as appreciation for long-term patronage, you may want to recognize a customer as follows: "Mr. and Mrs. Hoffmeister, we really appreciate your loyalty. Our records indicate that you've been a customer for over 20 years. In recognition, on behalf of _____ I'd like to present you with a complimentary weekend stay at _____ and two tickets to see the opening night of _____, along with a coupon for $50 toward dinner for two at _____. Please accept these with our compliments." This type of strategy goes a long way in guaranteeing customer loyalty.

Be Culturally Aware

The reality of a multicultural customer service environment further challenges your ability to deal with behaviors. This is because in today's multicultural business environment, it is likely that you will come into contact with someone of a different background, belief system, or culture. Many problems that develop in these encounters are a result of diversity ignorance. Even after you master the concepts of behavioral styles, you must remember that because values and beliefs vary from one culture to another, behavior is also likely to vary. For example, in many countries or cultures, the nonverbal gestures that Americans use have completely different meanings. Also, the reactions to such gestures will differ based on the recipient's personality style. Variations of symbols such as joining the thumb and index finger to form an O, signaling "Okay," have sexual connotations in several countries (e.g., Germany, Sardinia, Malta, Greece, Turkey, Russia, the Middle East, and parts of South America). Likewise, variations of the V symbolizing "victory" or "peace" to many people in Western cultures have negative connotations in some parts of the world (e.g., British Isles and parts of Malta).[1] Symbols and gestures, therefore, might anger or offend some customers. Also, seemingly innocent behaviors such as crossing your legs so that the sole of your shoe points toward someone or patting a small child on the top of his or her head may cause offense. The sole of the foot is the lowest part of the body and touches the ground. In some parts of the world, pointing the sole of the foot toward a person implies that the person is lowly. Males from a Western culture, and specifically males who have "D," "I," and "R" styles and tend to adopt a formal posture when seated, should be aware of the effect of crossing their legs might have on certain customers. ("E" style people tend to be more relaxed and sprawling in their posture.) As for the head, many countries (e.g., in the Far East, especially Thailand)[2] view it as a sacred part of the body. Patting a child on the head is sometimes considered to invite evil spirits or bad omens. This action might easily be taken by people who have high "E" behavioral tendencies, for they tend to be touchy-feely.

Some books listed in the Bibliography address these kinds of issues. Also, we will explore other culturally related subjects in Chapter 8.

[1] Desmond Morris, *Bodytalk: The Meaning of Human Gestures* Crown Trade Paperbacks, New York, 1994, pp. 118–119; 130–131.
[2] Ibid., p. 142.

To help send a positive message to customers from other cultures, you can do simple things that might have major impacts. For example, if you work in a restaurant and want to show appreciation for the large numbers of customers from another country who patronize the restaurant, you might recommend to your boss that a special dish from that area of the world be added to the menu. This offering could be promoted through flyers or advertisements. Such a strategy shows appreciation of the customers and their culture while encouraging them to eat at your establishment. However, be sure that the special dish is correctly prepared and uses the correct ingredients. Otherwise, you might offend rather than please the customer.

All these strategies, combined with a heightened knowledge of behavioral styles, can better prepare you to serve a wide variety of customers.

Know Your Products and Services

Customers expect that you will be able to identify and describe the products and services offered by your company. Depending on the behavioral style of the customer, the type of questions will vary. For example, an "R" personality may want to know who uses your services and products and ask to see the instructions, an "I" may ask many questions related to options, testing, rebates, and similar detailed technical information, a person with a strong "D" behavioral tendency may want to know the "bottom line" of using your service or product, and an "E" may want to talk about uses, colors, and sizes. If you cannot answer their questions, frustration, complaints, and/or loss of a customer may result.

Service providers need to know the products they are offering so that they can provide the best customer service possible. For example, when a new product line is introduced, orientation classes for employees can be arranged. In the classes, the features, benefits, and operation of the new items can be explained and demonstrated. Taking this approach increases knowledge of products and helps ensure better customer service.

Continue to Learn About People

To better prepare yourself for serving others, read whatever you can get your hands on related to customer service and take classes on how to interact and communicate with a variety of different types of people. Courses in psychology, sociology, and interpersonal communication are invaluable for providing a basis of understanding why people act as they do. Focus on issues of differences and similarities between men and women, cultural diversity, behavioral styles, and any other topic that will expand and round out your knowledge of people.

Of course, each person is unique, but the more you know about human behavior in general, the more successful you will be in dealing with the individuals you serve.

Prepare Yourself

Before you come into contact with customers, take a minute to review your appearance. Ask yourself, "What image do I project?" Think about how well your appearance is in tune with that of your typical customer. Evaluate your knowledge of your job and of the products and services offered by your organization. Are you ready and able to describe them to people regardless of their style preference? If not, start getting ready by learning as much as you can and practicing your message delivery by reviewing and implementing some of the strategies related to each style preference discussed earlier in this chapter.

Read the following descriptions and then determine which behavioral style you are dealing with. Keep in mind that each person can switch behavioral styles depending on the situation. To help you determine styles, refer to the style tendencies described in previous sections of this chapter. Suggested answers are given below the situation.

Situation 1

You are a salesperson at a jewelry counter and observe a professionally dressed female customer waiting in line for several minutes. She is checking her watch frequently, anxiously looking around, and sighing often. When she arrives at the counter, she makes direct eye contact with you and without smiling states, "I want to buy a 16-inch 14-karat gold twisted-link necklace like the one advertised in today's paper. I also want a small gold heart pendant and would like these to cost no more than $125. Can you help me? Oh yes, I almost forgot. Wrap that in birthday paper. This gift is for my daughter's birthday."

Situation 1 = D
Impatience, directive "D" language, direct eye contact, and no indication of smiling.

Answers
The behavioral styles and telltale indicators are described for each situation.

Situation 2

You stop by the office of a director of a department that provides data you use to prepare your end-of-month reports. As you look around, you see a photograph of his family. Your coworker smiles weakly and asks you to have a seat. As you begin to state your purpose by saying, "Thanks for taking the time to see me Mr. Cohen," he interrupts and says, "Call me Lenny, please."

Situation 2 = R
Low-key, friendly approach to communicating, smiling, offering a seat, suggesting that the less formal name *Lenny* be used, family photos present.

Situation 3

As a customer service representative for an automobile dealer, you return a phone message from Cynthia McGregor. When the phone is answered, you say, "Good morning, may I speak with Cindy McGregor?" The curt response is, "This is *Cynthia* McGregor. How may I help you?" During the conversation, Ms. McGregor asks a variety of very specific questions about an automotive recall. Even though it seems obvious that the recall does not apply to her car, she asks very detailed follow-up questions such as why the recall was necessary, who was affected, and what was being done. Throughout the conversation, she is very focused on facts, times, dates, and technical aspects of the recall.

Situation 3 = I
Insistence on formal name *Cynthia* as opposed to more informal *Cindy*, direct, to the point, specific questions, detail-focused approach to gathering information.

Situation 4

You are a teller in a bank. Mrs. Vittelli, one of the customers, comes into your branch several times a week. You know that she has just become a grandmother because she has brought along photos of her grandson. She has shared them, and all the details of her daughter's pregnancy, in a loud, exuberant manner with several of your coworkers. As she speaks, you have noticed that she has a beautiful smile, and that throughout conversations she is very animated, using gestures and often reaching over to lightly touch others as they speak.

Situation 4 = E
Freely sharing personal information about her family with strangers, outgoing demeanor, smiling, gesturing, and communicating in a loud, animated voice.

LEADERSHIP INITIATIVE

6.2

Supervisors can use information provided in the previous section to raise employee consciousness of the need to prepare for and deal with varied customer behaviors. This can be accomplished by using each subsection of information as a basis for group discussions and planning to serve.

7   Dealing With Perceptions

Concept: Often there are many different perceptions of an event. Our perceptions are often influenced by many factors such as physical qualities, social roles and behaviors, psychological qualities, and group affiliations.

Everyone has **perceptions** about the people and events he or she encounters. A person's background, based on education, experiences, events, and interpersonal contacts, influences how he or she view the world. In effect, there are sometimes as many different perceptions of an event as there are people involved.

Factors Affecting Perceptions

How are our perceptions shaped within a customer service framework? In essence, there are five categories that form the basis of many perceptions. We tend to base our perceptions of others and categorize people by thinking about the following:

- *Physical qualities.* What does a person look like? What gender? What body shape? Color of skin? Physical characteristics (hair color or type, facial features, height or weight)?
- *Social roles.* What is a person's position in society? Job title? Honors received? Involvement in social or volunteer organizations?
- *Social behaviors.* How does this person act, based on the behavioral style characteristics? What social skills does he or she exhibit in social and business settings? How well does he or she interact with people (peers, customers, seniors, subordinates, and people of other races, gender, or backgrounds)?
- *Psychological qualities.* How does he or she process information mentally? Is this person confident? Stressed out? Insecure? Curious? Paranoid?
- *Group affiliations.* Does this person belong to a recognizable religious, ethnic, or political group? What kinds of qualities are associated with each group? Does he or she assume leadership roles and demonstrate competence in such roles?

Perceptions and Stereotypes

People's perceptions of events vary greatly, as do their perceptions of each other. As a customer service provider, you should be aware of how you perceive your customers and, in turn, how they perceive you.

In some cases, you may **stereotype** people and, in doing so, adversely affect delivery of services. For example, your perception of older customers may be that they are all slow, hard of hearing, cranky, and politically conservative. This perception may be based on past experiences or from what you've heard or seen on television. This view might cause you to treat most older people in the same way, rather than treating each person as unique. However, you are basing your behavior on a

Many preconceived ideas about an individual or group can lead to disparate treatment and poor service. *What preconceived ideas do you have that might impact service to a diverse customer base?*

stereotype, not on reality. Think about it—aren't there many older people who don't have these characteristics? Thus, you need to be very careful that your perceptions are not influenced by stereotypes, because this clearly works against treating each customer as an individual.

Stereotyping people affects our relationships with customers. For this reason, you should consciously guard against stereotyping when you interact with others. If you pigeonhole people right away because of preconceptions, you may negatively affect future interactions. For example, suppose you use your new knowledge about behavioral styles to walk up to a coworker and say something like, "I figured out what your problem is when dealing with people. You're a 'D.' " Could this create a confrontational situation? Might this person react negatively? What impact might your behavior have on your relationship with your coworker (and possibly others)? Based on what you have read regarding communication in earlier chapters, several things are wrong with such an approach. First of all, no one is always a "D." Although a person might exhibit this behavior a lot, he or she draws from all four styles, just as you do. Second, exhibiting any particular style is not a "problem." As you have seen in this chapter, "D" behavior can provide some valuable input to any situation. And finally, although a behavioral style may contribute to a person's actions, many other factors come into play (communication ability, timing, location, situation, etc.).

To avoid categorizing people, spend time observing them, listen to them objectively, and respond based on each situation and person. Doing this can lead to better relationships and improved customer service.

8   Strategies for Success

Concept: Being aware of the possible behavioral styles of others can help you determine which strategies for success will be most useful to you.

Now that you have a better understanding about behavioral style(s), you can improve your chances of building successful relationships with others. In order to successfully deal with customers, try focusing on the following strategies:

Rational

People who demonstrate the "R" behavioral style often want to maintain peace and group stability. To help them accomplish this:

- Focus on their need for security and amiable relationships.
- Show a sincere interest in them and their views.
- Organize your information in a logical sequence and provide background data, if necessary.
- Take a slow, low-key approach in recommending products or services.
- Use open-ended questions to obtain information.
- Explain how your product or service can help simplify and support their relationships and systems.
- Stress low risk and benefits to them.
- Encourage them to verify facts, and so on, with others whose opinions they value.
- When change occurs, explain the need for the change and allow time for them to adjust.
- Provide information on available warranties, guarantees, and support systems.

Inquisitive

People whose style is "I" often desire quality, efficiency, and precision. To help them attain these things:

- Focus on their need for accuracy and efficiency by methodically outlining steps, processes, or details related to a product or service.
- Tie communication into facts, not feelings.
- Prepare information in advance and be thoroughly familiar with it.
- Approach encounters in a direct, businesslike, low-key manner.
- Avoid small talk and speaking about yourself.
- Ask specific open-ended questions about their background or experiences related to the product or service.
- Present solutions in a sequential fashion, stressing advantages, value, quality, reliability, and price. Also, be prepared to point out and discuss disadvantages.
- Have documentation available to substantiate your claims.
- Don't pressure their decisions.
- Follow through on promises.

Decisive

People whose style is "D" often want to save time and money. To help them accomplish this:

- Focus on their need for control by finding out what they wish to do, what they want or need, or what motivates them.
- Provide direct, concise, and factual answers to their questions.
- Keep explanations brief and provide solutions, not excuses.
- Avoid trying to "get to know them." They often perceive this as a waste of time, and they may distrust your motives.
- Be conscious of time, by making your point and then concluding the interaction appropriately.

Refer to Work It Out 6.1 (Describing Your Behavior). Select four to eight friends or coworkers and ask them to rate themselves using Work It Out 6.1. Next, ask each person to answer the following questions:

What do I look for when I shop?

What is my main reason for shopping?

What do I do when I need to buy or replace something?

What is the most important thing to me when I'm looking to replace something?

Once everyone has finished, gather in a group to compare and discuss answers. Focus on the fact that each person and each style is unique but that we all have common characteristics and needs. Discuss how this knowledge of common needs or drives can be used to provide customer service more effectively.

- Provide opportunities for the customer to talk by alternately providing small bits of information and asking specific questions aimed at solving the problem and serving the customer.
- Be prepared with information, necessary forms, details, warranties, and so on, before they arrive.
- When appropriate, provide options supported by evidence and focus on how the solution will affect their time, effort, and money.
- Focus on new, innovative products or services, emphasizing especially those that are environmentally sensitive or responsive.

Expressive

People exhibiting the "E" style are typically people-oriented and want to be around people. To help them succeed in this goal:

- Focus on their need to be liked and accepted by appealing to their emotions.
- Give positive feedback, acknowledging their ideas.
- Listen to their stories and share humorous ones about yourself.
- Use an open-ended, friendly approach.
- Ask questions such as "What attracted you to this product or service?"
- Keep product details to a minimum unless they ask for them.
- Describe how your product or service can help them get closer to their goals or to fulfilling their needs.
- Explain solutions or suggestions in terms of the impact on them and their relationships with others.
- If appropriate, provide incentives to encourage a decision.

Chapter Summary

Everything a customer experiences from the time he or she makes contact with an organization, in person, on the phone, or through other means, affects that customer's perception of the organization and its employees. To positively influence the customer's opinion, customer service professionals must be constantly alert for opportunities to provide excellent service. Making a little extra effort can often mean the difference between total customer satisfaction and service breakdown.

As you have seen in this chapter, people are varied and have different behavioral styles. Recognizing the differences and dealing with customers on a case-by-case basis is the foundation of solid customer service. By examining individual behavioral tendencies, actions, communication styles, and needs, you can better determine a course of action for each customer. The test of your effectiveness is whether your customers return and what they tell their friends about you and your organization.

SERVICE IN ACTION   Ritz-Carlton Hotel Company   CHAPTER 6

http://www.ritzcarlton.com

When asked what they think is the finest luxury hotel, many people would name the Ritz-Carlton, even though most have likely never stayed there or known anyone who has. Yet, the reputation of this top-of-the-line travel venue often sets the limit for competitors to reach. As an indication of its success, the Ritz-Carlton Hotel Company earned the highest ranking in the luxury segment of the J. D. Power and Associates 2003 North America Hotel Guest Satisfaction Index Study. This marks the first time Ritz-Carlton has received highest category honors in this study.

To determine the award winner, J. D. Power surveyed over 13,000 business and leisure guests who stayed at major hotel chains in the United States during a 12-month period. The Ritz-Carlton was awarded the highest scores in not only overall "Guest Satisfaction" but in every factor in the luxury segment, including prearrival, guestroom, food and beverage, hotel services, and departure. In addition to the Power's ranking, the Ritz-Carlton has twice won the prestigious Malcolm Baldrige National Quality Award given by the U.S. Chamber of Commerce.

The fact that the Ritz-Carlton has received these highly coveted awards is a telling accomplishment since the hotel has only 54 properties worldwide. It employs over 23,000 employees worldwide to deliver exemplary service.

So, what does this 20-year-old hotel chain do that sets it apart from the competition? In a word—SERVICE. Not just ordinary service but the type that legends are made of. Nothing is left to chance in a Ritz hotel. Minute details and an atmosphere that includes such amenities as lighter fabrics in the guest rooms to allow for more thorough washing, white tie and apron uniforms for the wait staff, black tie for the maitre d' and morning suits for all other staff, conducive to a formal, professional appearance, extensive fresh flowers throughout the public areas, and a lá carte dining, providing choices for diners.

The Ritz-Carlton motto of "we are ladies and gentlemen serving ladies and gentlemen" coupled with its credo, help set the standards by which every employee functions.

THE RITZ-CARLTON CREDO

"The Ritz-Carlton is a place where the genuine care and comfort of our guests is our highest mission. We pledge to provide the finest personal service and facilities for our guests who will always enjoy a warm, relaxed yet refined ambience. The Ritz-Carlton experience enlivens the senses, instills well-being, and fulfills even the unexpressed wishes and needs of our guests."

Key Terms and Concepts	behavioral styles	perceptions	process improvement
	decisive style	primary behavior	rational style
	expressive style	pattern	stereotype
	inquisitive style	problem solving	win-win situation

Quick Preview Answers			
1. T	6. F	11. T
2. T	7. T	12. F
3. T	8. F	13. T
4. T	9. F	14. F
5. F	10. T	15. T

Chapter Review Questions

1. What are behavioral styles?
2. What are the four behavioral style categories discussed in this chapter?
3. What are some of the characteristics that can help you identify a person who has the following style preferences: R, I, D, E?
4. When communicating with someone who has an "R" preference, what can you do to improve your effectiveness?
5. When communicating with someone who has an "I" preference, what can you do to improve your effectiveness?
6. When communicating with someone who has a "D" preference, what can you do to improve your effectiveness?
7. When communicating with someone who has an "E" preference, what can you do to improve your effectiveness?
8. What are some strategies for eliminating service barriers by using your knowledge of behavioral styles?
9. What are perceptions?
10. How can perceptions affect customer relations?

Search It Out

Search for Behavioral Styles on the Internet

Log onto the Internet and look for information and research data on behavioral styles. Specifically look for the various theories and surveys that describe and categorize behavior. Also try to find information about some of the people who have done research on behavior:

Sigmund Freud
Carl Jung
Alfred Adler
Abraham Maslow
William Moulton Marston
Ivan Pavlov
B. F. Skinner

Be prepared to present some of your findings at the next scheduled class.

Note: A listing for additional research on specific URLs is provided on the Customer Service website at **<http://www.mhhe.com/Lucas05>.**

Collaborative Learning Activity

Observing and Analyzing Behavioral Styles

With a partner or team, go to a public place (park, mall, airport, train or bus station, or restaurant) to observe three different people. Using the Worksheet 6-5 on the McGraw-Hill website shown above, note the specific behaviors each person exhibits. After you have finished this part of the activity, take a guess at each person's behavioral style preference based on behaviors you saw. Compare notes with your teammates and discuss similarities and differences among findings. Also, discuss how this information can be helpful in your workplace to deliver better customer service.

Face to Face

Working Through Technology and People Problems at Child's Play Toy Company

Background

Since opening its newest store in Princeton, New Jersey, Child's Play Toy Company of Minneapolis, Minnesota, has been getting mixed customer reviews. Designed to be state-of-the-art, open, and customer-friendly, the store includes an attended activity area where small children can play while parents shop. In addition, an innovative system makes it possible for local customers to order products from catalogs or from the company's website and then go to a drive-up window to pick up their purchases without leaving their cars. Another creative feature involves interactive television monitors in the store—where customers can see a customer service representative at the same time the representative sees them. To reduce staffing costs, the customer service representatives are at a Philadelphia, Pennsylvania, location and are remotely connected via satellite and computer to all new stores. This system is used for special ordering, billing questions, and complaint resolution. Customers can use a computer keyboard to enter data.

In recent months, the number of customer complaints has been rising. Many people complain about not getting the product that they ordered over the system, they are uncomfortable using the computer keyboard, they dislike the lack of personal touch and the fact that they have to answer a series of standard questions asked by a "talking head" on the screen, they have encountered system or computer breakdowns, and they cannot get timely service or resolution of problems.

Your Role

As a customer service representative and cashier at the store, you are responsible for operating a cash register when all lines are operational and more than two customers are in each line. You are also responsible for supervising other cashiers on your shift and dealing with customer questions, complaints, or problems. You report directly to the assistant store manager, Meg Finochio. Prior to coming to this store, you worked in two other New Jersey branches during the five preceding years.

This afternoon, Mrs. Sakuro, a regular customer, came to you. She was obviously frustrated and pointed her finger at you as she shouted, "You people are stupid!" She also demanded to speak with the manager and threatened that, "If you people do not want my business, I will go to another store!" Apparently, a doll that Mrs. Sakuro had ordered two weeks ago over the in-store system had not arrived. The doll was to be for her daughter's birthday, which is in two days. Although Mrs. Sakuro has a heavy accent, you understood that she had been directed by a cashier to check with a customer service representative via the monitor to determine the status of the orders. When she did this, she was informed that there was a problem with the order. The representative who took the order wrote the credit card number incorrectly, and the order was not processed. When Mrs. Sakuro asked the customer service representative why someone hadn't called her, the representative said that the customer service department was in another state and that long-distance calls were not allowed. She was told that the local store is responsible for verifying order status and handling problems.

Mrs. Sakuro's behavior and attitude are upsetting to you.

Critical Thinking Questions

1. Based on the behavioral style information in this chapter and other subjects discussed in this book, what do you think is causing the complaints being made?
2. What system changes would you suggest for Child's Play? Why?
3. What can you do at this point to solve the problem?
4. What primary behavioral style is Mrs. Sakuro exhibiting? What specific strategies should you use to address her behavior?

PLANNING TO SERVE

CHAPTER 6

In order to ensure that you are prepared to provide premium service to your customers, take some time to think about typical customer situations in which you were personally involved or witnessed. Answer the following questions based on situations recalled.

1. What types of behaviors do the average customer exhibit?
2. Based on what you learned about behavioral styles in general, and your preferred style, what service strategies could you use if you were involved with the behaviors identified in question 1?
3. In difficult or emotional service situations, what behaviors often manifest themselves?
4. What strategies might help you in dealing with such customer behaviors?

Handling Difficult Customer Encounters

From the Frontline Interview

Christy Street is the manager of Davinco, Inc. (Shady Brook Cinemas), in Columbia, Tennessee. She is the person external customers contact with problems or compliments. She also interacts, and resolves issues, with internal customers (employees).

1 What is your perspective on the importance of customers in your industry?

In my view, without external customers, our company would not be in business, so it is always very important to explain to employees the importance of taking care of these customers and making sure their experience at our business is as enjoyable as possible. Additionally, I believe that internal customers are very important as well. Without them, I could not complete some of the tasks the organization strives to reach. It is very important to recognize and reward our internal customers for jobs well done. After all, they are the ones that make a difference in our business.

CHRISTY STREET,
Manager,
Davinco, Inc.

2 How do you define "difficult" customers? Why?

A difficult customer in my mind is a person who tries to provoke you to react in an uncontrollable manner. The important thing to remember—always have control of the situation!

3 What is the most common types of difficult customer situations that you and your staff encounter? How do you typically handle them?

The most common types of difficult customer situations at our business would be problems with customers disturbing others in an auditorium. Our business is a 12-plex movie theater and for some reason, customers want to talk on cell phones or talk loud enough to disturb others while watching a movie. We try to improve these disturbances by making announcements before each movie starts asking our guests to turn of all cell

"Working with people is difficult, but not impossible." Peter Drucker, author and management consultant

Chapter Learning Objectives

After completing this chapter, you will be able to:

- Recognize a variety of difficult personality types.
- Use the Emotion-Reducing Model to help keep difficult situations from escalating.
- Determine appropriate strategies for dealing with various types of customers.

- Exhibit confidence when involved in difficult customer interactions.
- Develop better relationships with internal customers.
- Use the six-step Problem-Solving Model in handling difficult customer situations.

phones and pagers. We also go in each auditorium numerous times throughout the night to check for other disturbances. Sometimes parents bring young children to see a movie. The child can be a disturbance by crying or running around the auditorium. When this happens we ask the parent to take the child to the lobby area so other customers can enjoy the movie. Very seldom, we will get a complaint that the popcorn is too salty. Of course in this situation we pop a batch of popcorn with no salt. This usually solves the problem.

4 What type of training do you feel is needed by service personnel to help them better deal with difficult customer situations in today's service-oriented world?

Give your employees examples of situations that arise from time to time and ask how they would handle them. Have discussions on ways to please the customer in these difficult situations. Make sure you have videos or DVDs available that employees can watch during slow periods. This will enhance their knowledge of customer service and enhance their confidence when dealing with difficult customer situations.

5 What advice can you give to someone who wants to get into a customer service occupation?

Read lots of literature on customer service, always be in control of your emotions and the situation, have lots of patience, and stay calm. In short, be prepared to handle any type of situation.

Critical Thinking

What issues, described by Christy, can you relate to? Explain. How can effectively dealing with difficult customer situations effectively enhance customer service for your organization or those with which you are familiar?

Quick Preview

Before reviewing the chapter content, respond to the following questions by placing a "T" for true or an "F" for false on the rules. Use any questions you miss as a checklist of material to which you will pay particular attention as you read through the chapter. For those you get right, congratulate yourself, but review the sections they address in order to learn additional details about the topic.

_____ 1. An important realization that will assist you in better serving customers is to acknowledge that they all have needs and expectations.

_____ 2. Customer needs are driven by internal motivators and can be broken down into five categories.

_____ 3. Behavioral style preferences do not affect customer needs or satisfaction levels.

_____ 4. An upset customer is usually annoyed with a specific person rather than the organization or system.

_____ 5. An effective strategy for dealing with angry customers is to let them know exactly what your company policy is.

_____ 6. When you cannot comply with the demands of an angry customer, you should try to negotiate an alternative solution.

_____ 7. In some cases, indecisive customers truly do not know what they need or want.

_____ 8. Demanding customers often act in a domineering manner because they are very self-confident. This is a function of behavioral style.

_____ 9. Rude customers need to be controlled or "put in their place" to prevent a repetition of the behavior.

_____ 10. Some service providers have difficulty handling talkative customers.

_____ 11. Adopting a "good neighbor policy" can help in dealings with internal customers.

_____ 12. As part of trying to help solve a customer problem, you should assess its seriousness.

Answers to Quick Preview can be found at the end of the chapter.

1 Difficult Customers

Concept: Successful service will ultimately be delivered through effective communication skills, positive attitude, patience, and a willingness to help the customer.

You may think of **difficult customer** contacts as those in which you have to deal with negative, rude, angry, complaining, or aggressive people. These are just a few of the types of potentially difficult interactions. From time to time, you will also be called upon to help customers who can be described in one or more of the following ways:

Lack knowledge about your product, service, or policies.

Dissatisfied with your service or products.

Demanding.

Talkative.

Handling difficult customers will be one of your biggest challenges, so be prepared. *How would you deal with an unhappy customer?*

Internal customers with special requests.

Speak English as a second language (discussed on website <http://www.mhhe.com/Lucas05>).

Elderly and need extra assistance (discussed on website <http://www.mhhe.com/Lucas05>).

Have a disability (discussed on website <http://www.mhhe.com/Lucas05>).

Each of the above categories can be difficult to handle, depending on your knowledge, experience, and abilities. A key to successfully serving all type of customers is to treat each person as an individual. Avoid stereotyping people according to their behavior. Do not mentally categorize people (put them into groups) according to the way they speak or act or look—and then treat everyone in a "group" the same way. If you stereotype people, you will likely damage the customer-provider relationship.

Ultimately, you will deliver successful service through your effective communication skills, positive attitude, patience, and willingness to help the customer. Your ability to focus on the situation or problem and not on the person will be a very important factor in your success. Making the distinction between the person and the problem is especially important when you are faced with difficult situations in the service environment. Although you may not understand or approve of a person's behavior, he or she is still your customer. Try to make the interaction a positive one, and if necessary ask for assistance from a coworker or refer the problem to an appropriate level in your operational chain of command.

Many difficult situations you will deal with as a service provider will be caused by your customer's needs, wants, and expectations. You will read about service challenges in this chapter, along with their causes and some strategies for effectively dealing with them.

2   Why People Buy

Concept: Understanding the drive behind customers' needs, wants, and emotional reactions will help you know why people buy. You will be able to give better customer service once you understand the customer better.

Factors such as needs, wants, and emotional reaction cause customers to buy things. Each of these factors provides a stimulus for the customer to shop, compare, and possibly purchase a product or service.

Needs are things that a customer feels compelled to address or believes are necessary. Needs are an individual matter and arise from internal sources or motivations that vary from one customer to the next according to their situation and background. **Wants** are desired objects or experiences that a customer would like to have. They are not necessary, yet often bring personal appreciation, value, or satisfaction.

You will be helped in serving your customers if you understand that all people have needs. Since each person's needs are different, no two customers are going to like the same thing or buy the same product or service for the same reason. Therefore, although some of the basic customer service techniques discussed in earlier chapters will help you in determining and addressing customer needs, there will be times when these techniques will not help you at all. Customer diversity, which you will read about in Chapter 8, along with customer expectations and the various circumstances in which you and your customers find yourselves, also affects your success. Depending on the customer, situation, emotions, and other factors, you will find that some customer contacts are challenging or difficult. These situations are not hopeless if you plan ahead and mentally prepare yourself for them.

You should understand, too, that needs alone do not cause customers to make purchases. Research has shown that emotion often influences buying decisions. A classic example of this was demonstrated when the Coca-Cola Company decided to introduce the "New Coke." Company executives had become concerned about sales. They were losing ground to their major competitors, Pepsi and 7UP, and also to their own Diet Coke. Also, they had seen the price of sugar rise and were looking for ways to reduce costs and increase revenue. They decided that they would introduce a new product and gradually take the original Coca-Cola off the market. The decision was affected also by the fact that Pepsi and Diet Coke had a smoother, sweeter taste than Coca-Cola.

Before making such an important decision, Coca-Cola managers did all the right things. They experimented to find just the right combination of ingredients, and they market-tested their product through blind taste tests (in which consumers were blindfolded and asked to sample various products including the original Coke, Pepsi, and Diet Coke). During the tests, consumers overwhelmingly selected the "New Coke" as their product of choice. Coca-Cola then put together fancy advertisements and an advertising campaign to introduce the product with great fanfare.

Coca-Cola executives were sure that they had a huge success on their hands and believed that they would leave Pepsi far behind in the market ratings. Instead, they failed partly because Coca-Cola had kept secret its plan to remove the original Coke from the shelves the same week that the new product was released. The public was outraged. Coca-Cola had one of the greatest marketing fiascoes of the twentieth century on its hands. What Coca-Cola had failed to reckon with was the emotional reaction of the public. Even before people tasted the new product, they felt betrayed by a company they trusted. As a result, they rebelled. They wanted the original Coke back. After all, they had grown up with this product. The New Coke was introduced on April 23, 1985. Within days, Coca-Cola received thousands of calls and letters of complaint. On July 11, 1985, at a press conference, the chairman of Coca-Cola, Roberto Goizeuta, and president and CEO, Donald Keough, announced, "We have heard you." New Coke faded into oblivion and "Classic Coke," made with the original formula, was born. The public celebrated (with a Coke of course!).

FIGURE 7.1
Maslow's Hierarchy
of Needs Theory

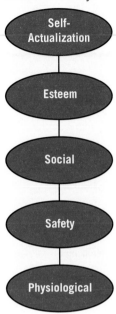

The Basis of Customer Needs

To address customer needs, you must first understand the origin of needs and why people buy different products. As psychologist Dr. **Abraham Maslow** once stated, "The human being is a wanting animal and rarely reaches a state of complete satisfaction except for a short time. As one desire is satisfied, another pops up to take its place. When this is satisfied, still another comes to the foreground and so on. It is characteristic of human beings throughout their whole lives that they are practically always desiring something."[1]

Figure 7.1 illustrates Maslow's **Hierarchy of Needs Theory** that also applies to customers' needs. Needs are often derived from internal motivators or things that make us happy and satisfy us. A classic study on human motivation conducted by Maslow after World War II might help you understand human needs. Although his work focused on the needs of employees in the workplace, it has application in many other environments.

In his research, Maslow found that people have specific needs starting at the basic or *physiological* level, at which they need items that will sustain life (e.g., food, shelter, clothing, water, and air). Once people have satisfied their basic needs, they can move up the hierarchy to other needs, such as the second level, *safety* or *security.* At that level, people focus on products and services that will help them feel protected (e.g., insurance, firearms, security devices, and fault-free electrical or mechanical products). The third level identified by Maslow was *social,* which concerns the need to feel accepted or loved. Products or services that can help people fulfill their social needs can go a long way toward making them feel successful (e.g., flowers, gifts, or other items that demonstrate love, affection, and caring). Anything that makes people feel as if they belong to a group or **subculture** will help fulfill this need. The fourth level of need is that of *esteem* or *ego.* Items that can help customers feel better about themselves (self-esteem), project status or prestige, or gain the respect of others are important (e.g., clothing, cars, furniture, jewelry, body adornments, or grooming products).

The highest level on Maslow's hierarchy is *self-actualization* or, in the words of a U.S. Army recruiting slogan, "Be all you can be." Anything that can help customers attain their highest potential addresses this final need category (e.g., educational software, professional development seminars, or tools that enhance effectiveness and efficiency).

To relate this theory to reasons why customers become dissatisfied and difficult to deal with, think about a situation like the following: A customer goes into a convenience store on the way home from work. He has a very stressful job. He earns minimum wage, and his wife is unemployed. Recently, he had to quit taking classes at a local college, where he was trying to get an associate degree in order to qualify for a higher-paying job, because he had to take a second job to help support the family. He has two sick toddlers at home and has stopped in at the store to get cough medicine. He specifically chose this store because he had seen a flyer in the morning paper indicating that cough syrup was on sale. When he checked the shelf, the product was out of stock. The customer is not happy!

A knowledge of Maslow's work can help you determine your customer's level of need. Try completing Worksheet 7.1 (see website <http://www.mhhe.com/lucas05>) to see how well you can guess which level of need is being demonstrated.

---

[1]Abraham H. Maslow, *Motivation and Personality,* Harper & Row, New York, NY, 1970, p. 7.

FIGURE 7.2
Typical Customer
Expectations

Customers come to you expecting that certain things will occur related to the products and services they obtain. Customers typically expect the following:

Expectations related to people

Friendly, knowledgeable service providers

Respect (they want to be treated as if they are intelligent)

Empathy (they want their feelings and emotions to be recognized)

Courtesy (they want to be recognized as "the customer" and as someone who is important to you and your organization)

Equitable treatment (they do not want to feel that one individual or group gets preferential benefits or treatment over another)

Expectations related to products and services

Easily accessible and available products and services (no lengthy delays)

Reasonable and competitive pricing

Products and services that adequately address needs

Quality (appropriate value for money and time invested)

Ease of use

Safe (warranty available and product free of defects that might cause physical injury)

State-of-the-art products and service delivery

Easy-to-understand instructions (and follow-up assistance availability)

Ease of return or exchange (flexible policies that provide alternatives depending on the situation)

Appropriate and expedient problem resolution

Customer Expectations

As you have read in earlier chapters, today's customers are more discerning, better educated, have access to more up-to-date and accurate information, and are often more demanding than in the past. They have certain **expectations** about your products and services, and the way that you will provide them. Figure 7.2 shows some common expectations customers might have of a service organization. Failure to fulfill some or all of these expectations can lead to dissatisfaction and in some cases confrontation and/or loss of business.

3 The Role of Behavioral Style

Concept: Behavioral preferences have a major impact on the interactions of people. The more you know about style tendencies, the better you will understand your customers.

As you read in Chapter 6, behavioral style preferences play a major part in how people interact. Styles also affect the types of things people want and value. For example, people with high expressive tendencies will probably buy more colorful and people-oriented items than will people who have high decisive tendencies.

The more you know about style tendencies, the easier it becomes to deal with people in a variety of situations and to help match their needs with the products and services you and your organization can provide. Take a few minutes to go back and review Figure 6.3 before going further in this chapter. The suggested strategies found there can assist you in dealing with customers who exhibit a specific

LEADERSHIP INITIATIVE   7.1

behavioral style preference and are upset, irrational, or confrontational. Keep in mind that everyone possesses all four behavioral styles discussed in Chapter 6 and can display various types of behavior from time to time. Therefore, carefully observe your customer's behavior and use the information you learned about each style as an indicator of the type of person with whom you are dealing. Do not use such information as the definitive answer for resolving the situation. Human beings are complex and react to stimuli in various ways—so adapt your approach as necessary. In addition, learn to deal with your emotions so that you can prevent or resolve heated emotional situations.

Handling Emotions With the Emotion-Reducing Model

It is important to remember when dealing with people who are behaving emotionally (e.g., irritated, angry, upset, crying, or raising their voice) that they are typically upset with the structure, process, organization, or other factors over which you and/or they have no control. They are usually not upset with you (unless you have provoked them by exhibiting poor customer service skills or attitude).

Before you can get your customer to calm down, listen, and address the situation, you must first deal with her or his emotional state. Once you do this, you can proceed to use problem-solving strategies (discussed later in this chapter) to assist in solving the problem. Until you reduce the customer's emotional level, he or she will probably not listen to you or be receptive to what you are saying or your attempts to assist. In some cases, she or he may even become irritated because you seem nonempathetic or uncaring.

To help calm the customer down, you must send customer-focused verbal and nonverbal messages. You need to demonstrate patience and use all the positive communication skills you read about in Chapters 3 to 5. Most important among those skills are the ability and the willingness to listen calmly to what the customer has to say without interrupting or interjecting your views. This lesson is taught to many law enforcement officers to help them deal with crisis situations such as domestic disturbances. If your customer perceives that you are not attuned to his or her emotional needs or thinks that you are not working in his or her best interest, you become part of the problem, rather than part of the solution.

Keep in mind that a customer generally wants to be respected and *acknowledged* as an individual and as being important. As you interact with the customer, you can soften the situation and reduce emotion by providing customer-focused responses. Simple customer-focused messages can put you on a friendly (human) level while at the same time helping to calm the emotion.

Here's how the **Emotion-Reducing Model** works: Assume a customer has a problem. As the customer approaches (or when you answer the telephone), greet him or her with "Good morning (or afternoon)," a smile, and open body language

FIGURE 7.3
Emotion-Reducing
Model

and gesturing (customer-focused message). Then, as the customer explains the problems (emotion), you can offer statements such as, "I see," "I can appreciate your concern, frustration, or anger," or "I understand how that can feel (customer-focused)." Such statements can help you connect psychologically with the customer. Continue to use positive reinforcement and communication throughout your interaction. Once the problem has been defined and resolved (problem resolution), take one more opportunity at the end of your interaction to send a customer-focused message by smiling and thanking the customer for allowing you to assist. Also, one last apology may be appropriate for inconvenience, frustration, mistreatment, and so on (customer-focused). Figure 7.3 provides a visual model of this process.

4 Working With Difficult Customers

Concept: You will need to be calm and professional when dealing with difficult customers.

Most customers have a specific type of product or service in mind when they make contact with your organization. They are also willing to let you help them if you do so in a positive, pleasant, and professional manner. There are others who, because of their outlook on life, attitude, personal habits, or background, may cause you frustration and require additional effort. You should expect to encounter difficult people and try to serve them to the best of your ability. With **difficult customers,** you should remain calm and professional.

Angry Customers

Dealing with angry people requires a certain amount of caution. For you to effectively serve an **angry customer,** you must move beyond the emotions to discover the reason for his or her anger. Here are some possible tactics:

- *Be positive.* Tell the customer what you can do, rather than what you cannot do. If you say, "Our policy won't permit us to give you a refund," you can expect an angry response. On the other hand, you might offer, "What I can do is issue a store credit that may be used at any of our 12 branch stores in the city."

Note: Before dealing with customers, check with your supervisor to find out what your policies are and what level of authority you have in making decisions. This relates to empowerment discussed earlier in the book.

By having this information before a customer encounter, you will have the tools and knowledge necessary to handle your customers effectively and professionally.

- *Acknowledge the customer's feelings or anger.* You cannot and should not try to deny the customer's anger. Doing so could result in a serious confrontation. Instead of saying, "You really don't have to be upset," try, "I can see you're upset. I want to help solve this problem, so could you please help me understand what's happened?"

By taking this approach, you've acknowledged the customer's feelings, demonstrated a willingness to assist, and asked the customer to participate in solving the problem.

- *Reassure.* Reassure the customer. Indicate that you understand why he or she is angry and that you will work to solve the problems. Statements such as these can help ease the frustration of your customers: "I'm going to do my best to help resolve this quickly," "I can assure you that this will be resolved by Monday," "You can rest assured that I am going to make this a priority."
- *Remain objective.* As mentioned earlier, becoming part of the problem is not the answer. Even if the customer raises his or her voice or uses profanity, remain calm. This may be difficult, but it will help keep the situation from escalating. If necessary, count to ten in your head and take a deep breath before responding. Remember, angry customers are usually angry at the organization, product, or service that you represent, not at *you.* If they do not settle down, calmly but assertively explain that although you want to assist, you cannot do so until they help by providing information. If possible, suggest moving to a private area away from other customers and ask for help from a supervisor or team leader, if appropriate.
- *Determine the cause.* Through a combination of asking questions, listening, feedback, and analyzing the information you receive, try to determine the cause of the problem. The customer may simply have misunderstood what was said. In such an instance, a clarification may be all that is required. Try something like, "There seems to be some confusion. May I explain?" or possibly, "It appears that I was unclear. May I explain?"
- *Listen actively.* When people are angry, they need a chance to vent their frustration and be heard. Avoid interrupting or offering "Yes, but . . ." types of remarks. This only fuels their anger. Suppose that a customer calls to make an appointment for an oil change and is told that the special sale ended yesterday. The customer then says that there was no indication in the newspaper advertisement that there was an expiration date. You respond with, "Yes, that's true, but we always run our sale ads for only one week. Everybody knows that." Naturally, the customer is now upset. A better response would be something like, "Although that sale ended yesterday, we will honor the coupon because the expiration date was inadvertently omitted from the advertisement." Whether the customer is

"right" or "wrong" makes no difference in situations like these. You will build stronger customer relationships when you make this kind of concession, because you are bringing in money you might not have received if the customer got upset. Moreover, the customer is now satisfied, may tell others, and will likely return.

In cases such as this, inform your supervisor of the problems caused by the omission of expiration dates in ads.

- *Reduce frustrations.* Don't say or do anything that will create further tension. For instance, don't transfer a caller to another extension if the customer told you he or she has already been transferred several times, interrupt to serve another customer (especially for a telephone caller—unless your organization's policy requires that you do so), or put the person on hold repeatedly to handle other customers or tasks not related to serving the original customer.

- *Negotiate a solution.* Elicit ideas from the customer on how to solve the problem. If the customer's suggestions are realistic and feasible, implement them. Or negotiate an alternative. By using customers' suggestions, you are likely to gain their agreement. Also, if something goes wrong later, they may be less likely to complain again since it was their idea in the first place.

- *Conduct a follow-up.* Don't assume that the organization's system will work as designed. If there is a breakdown, the customer has your name and may complain to your supervisor. Or, the customer may not complain but instead go to a competitor. Either way, you lose.

Once an agreed-upon solution has been implemented, take the time to follow up to ensure that all went well. This may involve personally calling the accounting department to ensure that proper credits were made, delivering an order or materials or shipping them yourself, or calling or writing the customer after a period of time to make sure the customer is satisfied and to offer future assistance. Whatever it takes, do it to ensure customer satisfaction. As a rule of thumb, *under*promise and *over*deliver.

Dissatisfied Customers

Occasionally, you will encounter customers who are **dissatisfied** or unhappy when you meet them. Possibly they have been improperly served by you or one of your peers, or by a competitor in the past. Even if you were not personally involved in their previous experience, you represent the organization or you may be considered "just like that last service employee." Unfair as this may be, you have to try to make these customers happy. To do so, try the following strategies:

- *Listen.* Take the time to listen actively, as discussed in Chapter 5. Often, when people are upset, all they want to know is that you're willing to attend to their concerns.

FIGURE 7.4
Positive Wording

When faced with a customer encounter that isn't going well, remain positive in language. This will help you avoid escalating the situation.

Negative Words or Phrases	Positive Alternatives
Problem	Situation, issue, concern, challenge
No	What I (or) we can do is . . .
Cannot	What I (or) we can do is . . .
It's not my job (or my fault)	Although I do not normally handle that, I'm happy to assist you.
You'll have to (or you must . . .)	Would you mind . . . ? Can I get you to . . . ?
Our policy says . . .	While I'm unable to . . . What I can do is . . .

- *Remain positive.* Even though angry customers drain your energy, don't get drawn into mirroring their anger or agreeing with their putdowns of your company, competitors, peers, products, or services. This only fuels the fire. If appropriate, smile and interject positive comments into the conversation as you listen, and try to determine an effective course of action.

Keep in mind what you read about the power of **positive wording** in Chapter 3. Figure 7.4 shows some examples of negative wording and some possible alternatives.

- *Smile, give your name, and offer assistance.* Sometimes a typically cheerful greeting is not possible because a customer verbally attacks first (e.g., you pick up a ringing phone or a customer walks up as you are serving another customer or looking down or away). In such instances, listen to what the customer is saying, use positive nonverbal cues (e.g., nodding, open or nonthreatening body posture, and possibly smiling) and inject paralanguage (e.g., Uh-huh, Hmmmm, Ahhhh, or other vocalizations). By demonstrating positive nonverbal behaviors, you may be able to psychologically "bond" with the customer. People usually do not attack a "friend," someone they know, or someone who is trying to assist them. This is why many law enforcement officers are trained to introduce themselves and to use a person's name.
- *Don't make excuses.* Typically, customers are not interested in why they did not get the product or service they wanted or thought they paid for; they just want the problem solved (in their favor). Look for ways to correct a mistake rather than cover it up.

Remember: if you get defensive, you become part of the problem and not part of the solution.

- *Be compassionate.* Try to remain warm, compassionate, empathetic while you are trying to uncover the cause of the problem. You can then attempt to service the customer properly and promptly. An approach often used by service and sales professionals to help defuse a customer's emotion when he or she is upset or frustrated (not really angry) is known as the **"feel, felt, found" strategy.** When using it, the service provider might state something like: "I know how you *feel* Ms. Winston. Others have said they *felt* the same way when they experienced this problem. However, we have *found* that by making a small adjustment to the _____ that the problem is quickly resolved." In effect, what this strategy does is empathize with the customer, shows he or she is not alone in the way he or she feels and shows there is a solution. Many times this strategy can begin by using statements such as:

Take a few minutes to think about your organization or one with which you are familiar. Look for factors that might contribute to customer dissatisfaction. Make a list of them, and then list some strategies for eliminating or reducing them. As an alternative, you might want to work with someone else and compare lists.

I see.

I can relate to that.

I understand what you're saying.

I can appreciate your point.

I know how you feel. (Use caution with this statement if someone is very emotional. This type of comment could increase the customer's anger and escalate the situation).

- *Ask open-ended questions.* By using specific open-ended questions, you can obtain the information you need to serve the customer. For example, "Mr. Washington, can you explain exactly what you expected from our service contract?"

- *Verify information.* To prevent misunderstandings or the possibility of escalating an uncomfortable situation, be sure that you received the correct message. Too often, we believe we understand the meaning of a message, only to find out later that we misinterpreted it. Test your interpretation of a customer's message by stating it in your own words. For example, "Mr. Rasheed, if I heard you correctly, you were told by the clerk who sold you this table that it would be assembled upon delivery, but the driver refused to do so. Is that correct?"

- *Take appropriate action.* After you have gathered all pertinent information you need to make a decision, work with the customer to satisfy his or her needs.

Indecisive Customers

You will encounter people who cannot or will not make a decision. They sometimes spend hours vacillating. In some cases, **indecisive customers** truly do not know what they want or need, as when they are looking for a gift for a special occasion. Sometimes such customers are afraid that they will choose incorrectly. In these situations, use all your communication skills. Otherwise, indecisive customers will occupy large amounts of your time and detract from your ability to do your job effectively or to assist other customers.

Be aware, however, that some people really *are* just looking as they check out sales, kill time between appointments, relax, or they may be lonely and want to be around others. Strategies for dealing with an indecisive person are given in the following sections.

- *Be patient.* Keep in mind that, although indecisive people can be frustrating (especially if you have a high D behavioral style preference), they are still customers. Greet such customers just as you would any other customer and offer assistance. If the customer refuses your help or wants to browse, that's fine, but indicate where you will be and watch for the customer to signal for assistance.

Think about a recent time when you were indecisive about purchasing a product or service, and then respond to the following questions:

1. What caused your indecisiveness?
2. What ultimately helped you to make a decision?
3. How can you use your own strategies to help satisfy an indecisive customer?

Indecisive people can be frustrating as you try to serve their needs. What steps would you take to help a customer make a decision?

- *Ask open-ended questions.* Just as you would do with a dissatisfied customer, try to get as much background information as possible. The more data you can gather, the better you can evaluate the situation, determine needs, and assist in the solution of any problems.
- *Listen actively.* Focus on verbal and nonverbal messages for clues to determine emotions, concerns, and interests.
- *Suggest other options.* Offer alternatives that will help in decision making and reduce the customer's anxiety. For example, "Ms. Sylvester, if you find that the color of the fabric doesn't match your wallpaper, you have 30 days to return it." This approach shows that you are informed and trying to assist, and it may help the person make up his or her mind. Suggesting a warranty or exchange possibility may make the customer more secure in the decision-making process.
- *Guide decision making.* By assertively, not aggressively, offering suggestions or ideas, you can help customers make a decision. Note that you are helping them, not making the decision for them. If you push your preferences on them, they may be dissatisfied and return the item. Then you, or someone else, will have to deal with an unhappy customer.

Demanding or Domineering Customers

Customers can be **demanding** or **domineering** for a number of reasons. Many times, domineering behavior is part of a personality style, as discussed in Chapter 6. In other instances, it could be a reaction to past customer service encounters. A demanding customer may feel a need to be or stay in control, especially if he or she has felt out of control in the past. Often, such people are insecure. Some strategies for effectively handling demanding customers are discussed in the following sections:

- *Be professional.* Don't raise your voice or retaliate verbally. Children engage in name-calling, which often escalates into shoving matches. Unfortunately, some adults "regress" to childish behavior. Your customer may revert to negative behavior learned in the past. Both you and the customer lose when this happens.

- *Respect the customer.* Showing respect does not mean that you must accommodate your customer's every wish. It means that you should make positive eye contact (but not glare), remain calm, use the customer's name, apologize when appropriate and/or necessary, and let the customer know that he or she is important to you and your organization. Work positively toward a resolution of the problem.

- *Be firm and fair and focus on the customer's needs.* As you read in Chapter 3, assertive behavior is an appropriate response to a domineering or demanding person; aggression is not. Also, remember the importance of treating each customer as an individual.

- *Tell the customer what you can do.* Don't focus on negatives or what can't be done when dealing with your customers. Stick with what is possible and what you are willing to do. Be flexible and willing to listen to requests. If something suggested is possible and will help solve the problem, compliment the person on his or her idea (e.g., "Mr. Hollister, that's a good suggestion, and one that I think will work"), and then try to make it happen. Doing this will show that you are receptive to new ideas, are truly working to meet the customer's needs and expectations, and value the customer's opinion. Also, remember that if you can psychologically partner with a customer, he or she is less likely to attack. You do need to make sure that your willingness to assist and comply is not seen as giving in or backing down. If it is, the customer may make additional demands or return in the future with similar demands. To avoid this, you could add to the earlier statement by saying something like, "Mr. Hollister, that's a good suggestion, and although we cannot do this in every instance, I think that your suggestion is one that will work at this time." This puts the customer on alert that although he or she may get his or her way this time, it will not necessarily happen in the future. Another strategy is to make a counteroffer.

If you are thoroughly familiar with your organization's policies and procedures and your limits of authority, you will be prepared to negotiate with demanding customers. If they want something you cannot provide, you might offer an alternative that will satisfy them. Remember that your goal is customer satisfaction.

Work It Out 7.4

Handling the Demanding Customer

Survey customer service professionals in various professions to see how they handle demanding or domineering customers. Make a list for future reference and role-play a variety of scenarios involving demanding customers with a peer.

Before you can deal with a customer's business needs, you must first address the customer's emotional issues and try to calm him or her. *What would you do to calm such customers?*

Rude or Inconsiderate Customers

Some people seem to go out of their way to be offensive or to get attention. Although they seem confident and self-assured outwardly, they are often insecure and defensive. Some behaviors they might exhibit are raising the voice, demanding to speak to a supervisor, using profanity, cutting in front of someone else in a line, being verbally abrupt (snapping back at you) even though you're trying to assist, calling you by your last name, which they see on your name tag (e.g., "Listen, Smith"), ignoring what you say, or otherwise going out of the way to be offensive or in control. Try the following strategies for dealing with **rude** or **inconsiderate customers:**

- *Remain professional.* Just because the customer is exhibiting inappropriate behavior does not justify your reacting in kind. Remain calm, assertive, and in control of the situation. For example, if you are waiting on a customer and a rude person barges in or cuts off your conversation, pause, make direct eye contact, smile, and firmly say, "I'll be with you as soon as I finish with this customer, sir or madam." If he or she insists, repeat your comment and let the person know that the faster you serve the current customer, the faster you can get to the person waiting. Also, maintaining decorum may help win over the person or at least keep him or her in check.
- *Don't resort to retaliation.* Retaliation will only infuriate this type of customer, especially if you have embarrassed him or her in the presence of others. Remember that such people are still customers, and if they or someone else perceives your actions as inappropriate, you could lose more than just the battle at hand.

Talkative Customers

Some people phone or approach you and then spend excessive amounts of time discussing irrelevant matters such as personal experiences, family, friends, schooling, accomplishments, other customer service situations, and the weather. The following tips might help when dealing with **talkative customers:**

Work It Out 7.5

Responding to Rudeness

Working with a partner, develop a list of rude comments that a customer might make to you (e.g., "If you're not *too* busy, I'd like some assistance") along with responses you might give (e.g., "If you could please wait, I'll be happy to assist you as soon as I finish, sir (or madam). I want to be able to give you my full attention and don't want to be distracted.").

Go on a field trip to a variety of businesses or stores (possibly a mall). As you visit these establishments, play the role of a customer and engage customer service professionals in lengthy conversation. Take note of the techniques they use to regain control of the conversation. Chances are, most, especially the more experienced, will allow you to talk and will respond to you rather than risk being rude. Remember the effective techniques described and jot them down.

- *Remain warm and cordial, but focused.* Recognize that this person's personality style is probably mainly expressive and that his or her natural inclination is to connect with others. You can smile, acknowledge comments, and carry on a brief conversation as you are serving this customer. For example, if the person comments that your last name is spelled exactly like his or her great aunt's and then asks where your family is from, you could respond with "That's interesting. My family is from . . . but I don't believe we have any relatives outside that area." You have responded but possibly cut off the next question. Anything less would probably be viewed as rude by the customer. Anything more could invite additional discussion. Your next statement should then be business-related (e.g., "Is there anything else I can assist you with today?").
- *Ask specific open-ended questions.* These types of questions can assist in determining needs and addressing customer concerns.
- *Use closed-ended questions to control.* Once you have determined the customer's needs, switch to closed-ended questions to better control the situation and limit the opportunity for the customer to continue talking.
- *Manage the conversation.* Keep in mind that if you spend a lot of time with one customer, other customers may be neglected. You can manage a customer encounter through questioning and through statements that let the customer know your objective is to serve customers. You might say, "I know you said you have a lot of shopping to do, so I won't keep you any longer. Thanks for coming in. Please let me know if I can assist in the future." Imply that you are ending the interaction to benefit the customer.

5 Working With Internal Customers (Coworkers)

Concept: Relationships with your internal customers are important. You should meet your commitments and build a professional reputation.

As we discussed in earlier chapters, you have to deal with internal as well as **external customers**. Although your interactions with **internal customers** may not be difficult, they can often be more sensitive than your dealings with outsiders.

After all, you see peers and coworkers regularly, and because of your job, office politics, and protocol, your interactions with them are ongoing. Therefore, extend all the same courtesies to internal customers that you do to external ones—in some cases, more so. Some suggestions that might help you enhance your interactions with internal customers are given in the following sections.

Stay Connected

Since relationships within the organization are so important, go out of your way to make contact with internal customers periodically. You can do this by

LEADERSHIP INITIATIVE   7.2

Creating an environment where employees learn to recognize and treat peers and coworkers as customers can go a long way toward enhancing the service environment. When employees learn the importance of building rapport and personal relationships with their internal customers, the quality of work life improves and everyone benefits. Service can also become exceptional.

dropping by their work area to say hello, sending an e-mail, or leaving a voice mail message. This helps keep the door to communication open so that if service does break down someday, you will have a better chance of hearing about it and solving the problem amiably. You might describe your coworkers as your "normal" internal customers, but do not forget the importance of your relationships with the cleaning crew (they service your office and work area), security force (they protect you, your organization, and your vehicle), and the information technology people (they maintain computer equipment). All these groups and many others within the organization add value and can be a big help to you.

Meet All Commitments

Too often, service providers forget the importance of internal customers. Because of familiarity, they sometimes become lax and tend to not give the attention to internal customers that they would give to external customers. This can be a big mistake. For example, if you depend on someone else to obtain or send products or services to external customers, that relationship is as crucial as the ones you have with external customers. Don't forget that if you depend on internal suppliers for materials, products, or information, these people can negatively affect your ability to serve external customers by delaying or withholding the items you need. Such actions might be unintentional or intentional, depending on your relationship.

To prevent, or at least reduce, the possibility of such breakdowns, honor all commitments you make to internal customers. If you promise to do something, do your best to deliver, and in the agreed-upon time. If you can't do something, say so when your customer asks. If something comes up that prevents you from fulfilling your commitment, let the internal customer know of the change in a timely manner.

Remember, it is better to *under*promise and *over*deliver than vice versa. If you beat a deadline, they will probably be pleasantly surprised and appreciative.

Don't Sit on Your Emotions

Some people hold on to anger, frustration, and other negative emotions rather than getting their feelings out into the open and dealing with them. Not only is this potentially damaging to your health, for it might cause stress-related illnesses, but it can also destroy working relationships. Whenever something goes wrong or you are troubled by something, go to the person and, using the feedback skills you learned in Chapter 3, talk about the situation. Failure to do so can result in disgruntled internal customers, damage to the customer-supplier relationship, and damage to your reputation. Don't forget that you will continue to rely on your customer in the future, so you cannot afford a relationship problem.

Build a Professional Reputation

Through your words and actions, go out of your way to let your customer and your boss know that you have a positive, can-do, customer-focused attitude. Let them know that you will do whatever it takes to create an environment in which internal and external customers are important. Also, regularly demonstrate your commitment to *proactive* service. This means gathering information, products, and other tools before coming into contact with a customer so that you are prepared to deal with a variety of situations and people. It also means doing the unexpected for customers and providing service that makes them excited about doing business with you and your organization.

Adopt a Good-Neighbor Policy

Take a proactive approach to building internal relationships so that you can head off negative situations. If your internal customers are in your department, act in a manner that preserves sound working relationships. You can accomplish this in part by avoiding the following negative work habits:

- *Avoid gathering of friends and loud conversation in your work space.* This can be especially annoying if the office setup consists of cubicles as sound travels easily. Respect your coworkers' right to work in a professional environment. If you must hold meetings or gatherings, go to the cafeteria or some other place away from the work area.

- *Maintain sound grooming and hygiene habits.* Demonstrate professionalism in your dress and grooming. Avoid excessive amounts of colognes and perfumes.

- *Don't overdo call forwarding.* Sometimes you must be away from your work space. Company policy may require that you forward your calls. Do not overdo forwarding your calls. Your coworkers may be inconvenienced and resentful if you do.

- *Avoid unloading personal problems.* Everyone has personal problems now and then. Do not bring personal problems to the workplace and burden coworkers with them. If you have personal problems and need assistance, go to your supervisor or team leader or human resources department and ask for some suggestions. If you get a reputation for often having personal problems—and bringing them to the workplace—your career could suffer.

- *Avoid office politics and gossip.* Your purpose in the workplace is to serve the customer and do your job. If you have time to spread gossip and network often with others, you should approach your supervisor or team leader about the job opportunities in which you can learn new skills. This can increase your effectiveness and marketability in the workplace.

- *Pitch in to help.* If you have spare time and your coworkers need assistance with a project, volunteer to help out. They may do the same at some point in the future when you are feeling overwhelmed with a project or assignment.

- *Be truthful.* One of the fastest ways for you to suffer a damaged relationship, or lose the trust and confidence of your coworkers and customers, is to be caught in a lie. Regard your word as your bond.

6   The Problem-Solving Process

Concept: To solve a problem, you need to first identify the problem and determine if the problem is one that should be solved. Once you decide to solve the problem, follow the six proven steps to problem solving.

FIGURE 7.5   The Problem-Solving Model

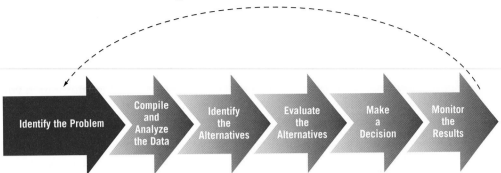

When customers have a complaint or a problem to be solved, they want solutions, not excuses. To ensure that you address customer needs effectively in these situations, you need to be effective at problem solving. Figure 7.5 shows a concise six-step **Problem-Solving Model**.

Before you being to solve a customer's problem, consider the fact that he or she may not really want you to "solve the problem." In some cases, a person simply wants to vent frustration or be heard. This is where the empathetic listening you have read about will come in handy. In many cases, your customer will often have a solution in mind when he or she calls or comes in. Your role may be to simply listen and offer to facilitate the implementation of the suggested solution. In some situations, you may have to "plant a seed" by asking an open-ended question that suggests a solution. If the customer picks up on your "seed" and nourishes it, you end up with an outcome for which he or she feels ownership. For example, assume that a customer wants a product that you do not have in stock. Instead of saying, "I'm sorry, that item is out of stock," you could ask a question such as, "How do you think _____ would work as an alternative?" You have now subtly made a suggestion without saying, "You could use _____ instead. It does the same thing."

If you jointly solve a problem, the customer feels ownership—that he or she has made the decision. This customer is likely to be a satisfied customer. The following sections describe some key actions involved in this process.

Step 1: Identify the Problem

Before you can decide on a course of action, you must first know the nature and scope of the problem you are facing. Often, a customer may not know how to explain his or her problem well, especially if he or she speaks English as a second language or has a communication-related disability. In such cases, it is up to you to do a little detective work and ask questions or review available information.

Begin your journey into problem solving by apologizing for any inconvenience you or your organization has caused. The customer probably wants someone to be responsible. A simple "I'm sorry you were inconvenienced. How may I assist you?" coupled with some of the other techniques covered in this book can go a long way toward mending the relationship. Take responsibility for the problem, even if you didn't actually cause it. Remember that, in the customer's eyes, you represent the organization. Therefore, you are "chosen" to be responsible. Don't point fingers at other employees, policies, or procedures. It is also important to let the customer know that you are sincerely regretful that the problem has occurred and will do whatever possible to quickly and effectively solve it.

To learn as much about the problem as you can, start by speaking directly to the customer, when possible. Collect any documentation or other background information available.

Ask Questions

Ask specific questions so that you can gather the information you need to help identify and solve a customer's problem. The only way to get the information you want is to ask the right questions. You might use a variety of question types. Here are some examples.

- *Open-ended.* As discussed in Chapter 5, open-ended questions are good for defining issues, clarifying, gathering information, and getting involvement. When asking open-ended questions, phrase them in a manner that allows the customer to respond as he or she feels necessary. You are not making a decision or forcing a response, as you can do with other types of questions; you are providing a vehicle for sharing information. Help focus the customer's response by asking specific open-ended questions. Note the difference between the sample questions that follow.

  Nonspecific: "How do you like this new product?"

  Specific: "What uses can you see for this new product?"

Although the first question may yield a useful response, you have not asked for a specific, focused piece of information. On the other hand, the second question will get the same bit of information but will also lead the customer to think of specific applications. You have thereby created a need (in the customer's mind) and she or he may now buy your product or service.

- *Closed-ended questions.* As you also saw in Chapter 5, closed-ended questions are sometimes valuable for getting a quick response, gaining minimal involvement, controlling the conversation, verifying information, and clarifying or confirming points. For example:

  Mr. Ho, didn't you say that your son would be the primary user of this product? (yes or no)

  Mrs. Lacata, how many times have you used our services? (a specific number)

  Ms. Hyland, do you prefer the blue or yellow one? (a choice between two items)

An important aspect of asking questions is to find out the customer's true concerns and solve his or her problems. For example, a customer may call and say that he or she wants to return a television set because it doesn't work. By asking questions, you may be able to help the person solve the problem without the added expense of shipping or having a service technician call on the customer. You may ask for background information about the television set and then ask some specific questions about the problem. Questions such as the following might be appropriate:

What model is it?

What, exactly, is wrong?

Does it have an antenna attached?

Is there a remote control?

Have you checked to see that the power cord is firmly attached?

Have you tried using a different electrical outlet?

Have you checked to make sure that the power strip is turned on?

Step 2: Compile and Analyze the Data

收集

To be able to effectively determine a course of action, you need as much information as possible and a thorough understanding of what you are dealing with. To get that data requires active listening and a little investigative work. You may need to collect information from a variety of sources, such as sales receipts, correspondence, the customer, public records, the manufacturer, and files.

In gathering data, you should also do a quick assessment of how serious the problem is. You may hear about one instance of a defective product, or you may hear about a pattern of inefficient service.

Once you have collected information through questioning and from other sources, spend some time reviewing what you have found. If time permits and you think it necessary or helpful (e.g., the customer is not present or on the telephone), ask for the opinions of others (e.g., coworkers, team leader or supervisor, technical experts). Ultimately, what you are trying to do is determine the choices available to you that will help satisfy the customer and solve the problems.

Step 3: Identify Alternatives

Let customers know that you are willing to work with them to find an acceptable solution to the problem. Tell them what you can do, gain their agreement, and then set about taking action.

Since you are new to the situation when a customer notifies you of a problem or their dissatisfaction, you have an objective perspective. Use this perspective as a basis on which to offer suggestions or viewpoints that the customer may not see or has overlooked. Also, make sure that you consider various possibilities and alternatives when thinking about potential solutions. Look out for the best interests of your customer and your organization. To do this, be willing to listen to the customer's suggestions and to think creatively. Perhaps you will come up with ideas other than the ones that you and your organization typically use. Don't sacrifice customer satisfaction for convenience. If necessary, seek approval from higher authority to use creative solutions (e.g., to make a special purchase of an alternative item for the customer, or to give a refund even though the time frame for refunds has expired).

Step 4: Evaluate Alternatives

Once you have collected all the facts, examine your alternatives or options. Be careful not to let cost be the deciding factor. A little extra time and money spent to solve a problem could save a customer and prevent recurring problems. Consider the following factors in this evaluation process:

What is the most efficient way to solve this problem?

Which are the most effective options for solving this problem?

Which options are the most cost-effective?

Will the options being considered solve the problem and satisfy the customer?

Step 5: Make a Decision

Based on the factors in step 4, and any others you wish to use in your evaluation process, make a decision on what your course of action will be. To do this ask the customer "Which option would you prefer?" This simple question puts the customer into the decision-making position and makes the customer feel empowered. The customer chooses. If the request is reasonable and practical, proceed and solve the problem. If not, negotiate a different alternative.

Step 6: Monitor the Results

Once you make a decision, monitor the impact or results. Do not assume your customer is satisfied, especially if any negotiation occurred between the two of you.

You can monitor the situation with a follow-up call, asking if he or she needs anything else when you see him or her, or sending a written follow-up (e.g., thank-you letter with query concerning satisfaction, service survey, or e-mail).

If you determine that your customer is not satisfied or additional needs are present, go back to step 1 and start over.

Chapter Summary

Dealing with various types of people can be frustrating, but it can also be very satisfying. Many times, you will have to deal with a variety of external and internal customers, including those who are angry, indecisive, dissatisfied, demanding, domineering, rude, or talkative. Your goal in all your efforts should be to work harmoniously with all customers. Whenever you can address customer needs in a variety of situations and find acceptable solutions, you, the customer, and the organization win. To assist customers effectively doesn't take magic; all it takes is a positive attitude, preparation, and a sincere desire to help others. If you use the techniques outlined in this chapter, and others in this book, you're on your way to providing stellar customer service and satisfying customer needs.

SERVICE IN ACTION   Southwest Airlines   CHAPTER 7

http://www.southwest.com

"The mission of Southwest Airlines is dedication to the highest quality of Customer Service delivered with a sense of warmth, friendliness, individual price, and Company Spirit." The company mission statement says a lot about the Southwest culture. As a result, after 30 years of passenger service, the airline is the fourth largest in the United States, flying more than 64 million passengers a year out of 59 airports.

The approach to business and customers is what makes Southwest a popular airlines with passengers. In 1988, 1992, 1993, 1994, 1995, and 1996, the airline won the coveted industry Triple Crown—Best On-Time Record, Best Baggage Handling, and Fewest Customer Complaints. It was the first airline to accomplish this feat. They have since spearheaded other customer-focused initiatives by being the first airline to award frequent flyer points for number of trips flown with them instead of based on miles. Southwest also pioneered senior discounts, Fun Fares, Fun Packs, a same-day air freight delivery service, ticketless travel, and many other unique programs. The airline's emphasis is not just on travel, but on making the journey fun.

The result of doing business that is attuned to customer needs and preferences has been a growth to over 33,000 employees, 375 aircraft, and net income of over $240 million in 2002. That year was the 30th consecutive year that the company posted a profit in an industry where competitors have struggled and disappeared.

Key Terms and Concepts

- angry customers
- customer expectations
- demanding or domineering customers
- difficult customers
- dissatisfied customers
- Emotion-Reducing Model
- external customers
- feel, felt, found strategy
- Hierarchy of Needs Theory
- indecisive customers
- internal customers
- Maslow, Abraham
- needs
- positive wording
- Problem-Solving Model
- rude or inconsiderate customers
- subculture
- talkative customers
- wants

Quick Preview Answers

1. T	5. F	9. F
2. T	6. T	10. T
3. F	7. T	11. T
4. F	8. T	12. T

Chapter Review Questions

1. What are the five levels of needs identified in Maslow's hierarchy of needs, and how do they affect customer service?
2. What causes customers to become dissatisfied?
3. What tactics can you use to deal with angry customers?
4. What can you do to assist indecisive people in coming to a decision?
5. Why might some customers feel they have to demand things from others?
6. How can you effectively deal with rude or inconsiderate customers?
7. What are some steps to help regain control of a conversation with a talkative customer without causing offense?
8. What strategies can you use to build strong relationships with coworkers?
9. List the strategies for effective problem solving.

Search It Out

Search the Internet for Information on Problem Solving

Log onto the Internet and locate information on providing customer service to irate customers. Also look for information on the following topics:

> Conflict resolution
> Problem solving
> Handling stressful situations

Be prepared to share what you find with your classmates at the next scheduled class.

Note: A listing of additional research on specific URLs is provided on the Customer Service website at **<http://www.mhhe.com/lucas05>.**

Collaborative Learning Activity

Role-Playing Difficult Customer Situations

Work with a partner and role-play one or more of the following scenarios. Each of you should choose at least one scenario in which you will play the service provider role. The other person will play the customer. In each instance, discuss what type of difficult customer you are dealing with and how such an encounter might go. At the end of each role-play, both persons should answer the following questions and discuss ideas for improvement:

Questions

1. How well was service provided?
2. Were any negative or unclear messages, verbal or nonverbal, communicated? If so, discuss.
3. How can you incorporate the improvements you have identified into a real customer service encounter?
4. What open-ended questions were used to discover customer needs? What others could have been used?

Scenario 1: Terry Welch entered your shoe store over 30 minutes ago and seems to be having trouble deciding the style and color of shoes he wants.

Scenario 2: Chris Dulaney is back in your lawn mower repair shop. This is the third time in less than two weeks that she has been in for repairs on a riding mower. Chris is getting upset because the problem stems from a defective carburetor that has been repaired on each previous visit. She is beginning to raise her voice, and her frustration is becoming evident.

Scenario 3: You are a telephone service representative for a large retail catalog distribution center. You've been at work for about an hour when you receive a call from Pat Mason, who immediately starts making demands (e.g., "I've only got a few minutes for you to tell me how to order." "Look, I've read all the articles about the scams telemarketers pull. I'll tell you what I want, and you tell me how much it will cost." "Listen, what I want you to do is take my order and get me the products within the next two days. I need them for a conference."

Scenario 4: You are a cashier in the express lane at a supermarket. As you are ringing up a customer's order, a second customer approaches, squeezes past several people in line and says, "I'm in a hurry. All I have is a quart of milk. Can you just tell me how much it costs, and I'll leave the money right here on the register."

Scenario 5: You are a very busy switchboard operator for ComTech, a large corporation. A vendor whom you recognize from previous encounters has just called to speak with your purchasing manager. As in previous calls, the vendor starts a friendly conversation about the weather, how things are going, and other topics not related to business.

Face to Face

Handling a Dissatisfied Customer at Newsome Furniture and Appliances

Background

Newsome Furniture and Appliances is a small family-owned store that has been in operation for 47 years in Billings, Montana. The store employs 16 employees in two locations. Most customers are local residents, but there is a steady flow of customers from nearby smaller towns and cities. Most customers shop at Newsome's store that is located in a large shopping mall outside of Billings.

On an average weekday, Newsome's two stores, combined, get 80 to 150 walk-through customers. On Saturdays several hundred customers patronize the two stores.

Of the frontline employees (sales, customer service, and credit staff), most have been with the company at least five years. No formal classroom training on effective customer service techniques is offered to the staff. However, each employee is encouraged to attend one professional development workshop or community college course each year. Mr. Newsome pays 75 percent of the cost of such courses. You were hired as a customer service assistant eight months ago after you graduated from high school. You report to the customer service supervisor, Ginny Hall. In school, you took a couple of business courses and have read numerous books on sales and customer service. You hope for career advancement in this field.

On Saturday morning Mr. and Mrs. Wyland Sommers came into your store. Both are senior citizens and longtime Billings residents. They have made numerous purchases at Newsome's over the past 18 years.

The Sommers bought a sofa bed last week, and it was delivered on Friday. The sofa had been a floor model, and the price had been reduced by 50 percent. The tag on the sofa said "as is" because there was a large tear in the mattress cover.

Your Role

When Mr. and Mrs. Sommers came into the store, they proceeded directly to the customer service department. As they approached, you smiled, said good morning, and offered to assist them. The following conversation occurred:

Mr. Sommers **[without acknowledging your greeting]:**	Where's Ginny?
You [smiling]:	Ginny's off today, sir. May I help you?
Mr. Sommers:	Where's Tom Newsome?
You [still smiling]:	He had to go to our other store. Can I help you?
Mrs. Sommers:	We bought a sofa bed here, and when they delivered it, I found a big hole in the mattress. My son and his wife will be here on Wednesday. I can't have them sleep on that old thing. I'd be too embarrassed.
Mr. Sommers:	I can't believe you'd sell something like that to a loyal customer. Do you have any idea how much money we've spent in this store over the past 18 years?
You:	Eighteen years is a long time to shop at a store. We appreciate your business. I'm terribly sorry that the sofa was damaged, I can't believe our warehouse would ship a damaged piece of furniture.
Mr. Sommers **[raising his voice]:**	Well they sure did! I just told you they did! Don't you believe me?
You:	I'm sorry sir. I didn't mean that you weren't telling the truth. I meant that I was surprised that we'd do that. Do you have your sales receipt? I'll see if I can't help work this out.
Mrs. Sommers:	We've got to have a sofa by Wednesday. My daughter-in-law comes from a very nice family in Virginia. I'd die if she saw that old thing you sent.

You:	Yes, ma'am. I'm sure we can fix the problem.
Mr. Sommers:	I don't want anything fixed. I want a new sofa before Wednesday. The last time I bought something here, you people messed up the order too. I guess I should have learned my lesson then.
You:	I apologize for any inconvenience we've caused. I can assure you we'll get this worked out. If you'll just give me your receipt, I'll get started.
Mr. Sommers:	I'll have to go see if it's in the pickup. Hold on. Ma, you wait here.
You [Mr. Sommers has returned with the receipt]:	I think I understand why your sofa has a damaged mattress. The sofa was a floor model discounted 50 percent and sold as is.
Mrs. Sommers [voice raised]:	What do you mean, "as is"? We paid a lot of money for that sofa!
You:	Yes, ma'am, I see you did. What I mean is that because the sofa had some damage, we reduced the price significantly to sell it.
Mr. Sommers:	Well nobody told us the thing was damaged. I want to talk to Tom right now. You call him at the other store!
You:	I think I have an idea. We have another sofa exactly like yours that is on sale. Since you saved 50 percent off your sofa, if we could exchange mattresses for say, 50 extra dollars, you'd still be saving hundreds off the original price. You could have the mattress by Monday, and your daughter-in-law would never know. What do you think?
Mr. Sommers:	Well, I don't know. I didn't want to spend any more money.
Mrs. Sommers:	Lou, that young salesman did say that we were getting a really special price because of some minor damage.
Mr. Sommers:	Yeah, I guess maybe he might have mentioned the damage. We just didn't know the hole would be as big as it is.
You:	I am truly sorry for any misunderstanding, and I wouldn't want Mrs. Sommers to be embarrassed. That's why I suggested the exchange. What do you think, folks?
Mr. Sommers:	Okay. But you better have it there by Monday at the latest.
You [smiling]:	Yes, sir. You'll have it by 3 P.M., or I'll deliver it myself.
Mr. Sommers [smiling]:	Thanks, kid.

Critical Thinking Questions

1. What were the needs of these customers?
2. What considerations about the customers did you have to take into account during this exchange?
3. What worked well here?

PLANNING TO SERVE

CHAPTER 7

To help better prepare yourself to deal with difficult customer service situations, respond to the following statements. On the basis of any "no" responses, seek out resources (e.g., materials, training programs, and people) that can help broaden your knowledge on these topics. If you answered "yes" to all the questions, congratulate yourself, then work to share your knowledge with others in your workplace. This can ultimately help improve employee morale and service to customers.

1. I approach what I believe to be a difficult customer with a positive attitude and believe that I can turn the situation around.	Yes	No
2. In dealing with customers, I seek to determine their true needs before offering a service solution.	Yes	No
3. I have done additional research on behavioral styles and recognize their importance in delivering quality service.	Yes	No
4. When emotions are high during a service transaction, I use strategies, such as those shown in the Emotion-Reducing Model.	Yes	No
5. I consciously monitor my language, and elicit feedback from peers on it to ensure that I typically use positive words and phrases when communicating.	Yes	No
6. When dealing with the types of difficult customers described in this chapter, I maintain my professionalism and actively listen in order to better serve their needs.	Yes	No
7. When working with coworkers, I afford the same courtesies and professionalism that is required for external customers.	Yes	No
8. To assure that I fully understand and react appropriately to problems in the workplace, I use the six-step Problem-Solving Model (or one like it).	Yes	No

Customer Service in a Diverse World

不同的.

From the Frontline Interview

Karen Buchan, is the Community Relations Coordinator at Webster University–Orlando. Webster University is an internationally known university based in St. Louis, Missouri. In her position, she interacts with internal customers—staff and faculty at the Orlando campus and at the more than 100 campuses worldwide in 19 states and seven other countries.

Karen's external customers are primarily adult students. In working in both student recruitment and marketing she deals with a diverse customer base: prospective students, alumni, numerous community organizations and chambers of commerce, corporate representatives, and vendors.

KAREN BUCHAN,
Community Relations
Coordinator,
Webster
University–Orlando

larger percentage of international students than in past years. The diversity of this group has changed also with students who represent a growing number of countries and a real melting pot of previous educational experiences. The students as a whole have a greater range of ages and a much more global perspective. Additionally, we have a large percentage of minority students at our two Orlando campus locations.

2 **What has been the impact of changing customer and workplace demographics on your profession?**

Changing demographics have impacted my profession in several ways. My community involvement includes a large number of organizations with an ever-increasing diverse membership. Whether dealing with internal or external customers it has become more important to stay current or at least have some knowledge of current events—globally and locally, and in every arena from television and the Internet to

1 **In what ways have you seen the workplace and your customer base change in recent years?**

The most noteworthy change to our customer base in recent years has been in the increasing diversity of our student body. Webster University's Orlando campus has a much

Chapter Learning Objectives

After completing this chapter, you will be able to:

- Recognize that differences are not bad.
- Develop a sensitivity to the fact that we are all unique.
- Understand the need to treat customers as individuals.
- Determine actions for dealing with various types of people.

- Identify a variety of factors that make people diverse and that help better serve them.
- Comply with legal requirements in assisting customers with disabilities.
- Serve all customer groups effectively.

business and sports. To retain a competitive edge in higher education I feel there is a greater need to educate myself and others on the values, beliefs, and motivations of the individuals and groups we service.

3 What skills and knowledge do you and your peers need to deliver quality service to a diverse customer base? Why?

Good communications and patience are the most important skills needed to deliver quality service to a diverse customer base. In communications, choosing words carefully, being unbiased, and avoiding slang or jargon lead to greater understanding. Being polite, showing empathy and always listening attentively will facilitate good service. Additionally, promoting multicultural understanding by learning as much as possible about the culture and customs of the groups dealt with most often and sharing what you learn with your coworkers is critical. Keeping an open mind and learning not to make assumptions about groups as a whole is crucial since every individual is unique and deserves your respect.

4 What advice can you give customer service personnel related to dealing with a broad customer base?

The best advice I can give customer service personnel dealing with a broad customer base is first, to understand others, second, accept all aspects of the diversity around you, and third, value and embrace diversity. Celebrate the differences as well as the similarities while being a positive role model and encouraging others to do likewise. Find ways to take advantage of the opportunities that a diverse customer base may provide, such as the ability to use the resources and talents of a wide cross section of society.

Critical Thinking

In what ways can you relate what Karen described to service environments with which you are familiar? Explain. How has the issue of diversity impacted you personally from a customer and service provider perspective?

Quick Preview

Before reviewing the chapter content, respond to the following questions by placing a "T" for true or an "F" for false on the rules. Use any questions you miss as a checklist of material to which you will pay particular attention as you read through the chapter. For those you get right, congratulate yourself, but review the sections they address in order to learn additional details about the topic.

_____ 1. Diversity is an important aspect of everyone's life that presents many negative challenges.

_____ 2. Many people associate the term *diversity* with the word *cultural,* which describes the differences between groups of people from various countries and with differing beliefs.

_____ 3. The diverse nature of your customer population requires you to be aware of the various ways people from different cultures interact in the business setting.

_____ 4. Values are the "rules" that people use to evaluate situations, make decisions, interact with others, and deal with conflict.

_____ 5. In some cultures, direct eye contact is often discouraged, for it suggests disrespect.

_____ 6. Today, many cultures use less formality in the business environment and do not stress the importance of using titles and family names as often as they did in the past.

_____ 7. When encountering someone who speaks English as a second language, you should avoid jokes, words, or acronyms that are uniquely American or tied to sports, historical events, or specific aspects of American culture.

_____ 8. In serving customers from other cultures, it is important to avoid the use of the word *no* because this word may cause the customer to become embarrassed or experience a "loss of face."

_____ 9. According to the U.S. Census Bureau, approximately 54 million Americans have some level of disability.

_____ 10. When a customer has a disability, the disability should be deemphasized by thinking of the person first and the disability second.

_____ 11. When dealing with an elderly customer, you should always be respectful.

_____ 12. Young customers are as valuable as those in any other group and should be professionally served.

Answers to Quick Preview can be found at the end of the chapter.

1   The Impact of Diversity

Concept: Diversity is an important aspect of everyone's life. Encounters with others give us an opportunity to expand our knowledge of others.

As the world grows smaller economically or otherwise (e.g., world trade, international travel, and technologically transmitted information exchange), the likelihood that you will have contact on the job with people from other cultures, or who

Take a few minutes to think about diversity and what it means to you. Write your own definition of diversity.

During the past week, in what situations have you encountered someone from a different culture (someone whose values or beliefs differed from yours or who looked or dressed differently from you or your group)? Make a list of the diversity and the situations encountered.

Once you have created your responses, form a group with two to three other students, share your responses, and discuss the implications of providing quality service to customers.

are different from you in other ways, increases. This likelihood also carries over into your personal life. **Diversity** is encountered everywhere (supermarkets, religious organizations, public transportation) and so is an important aspect of everyone's life. Although it presents challenges in making us think of differences and similarities, it also enriches our lives—each encounter we have with another person gives us an opportunity to expand our knowledge of others while growing personally.

2 Defining Diversity

Concept: Diversity is not a simple matter; it is not difficult to deal with if you are fair to people and keep an open mind.

The word *diversity* encompasses a broad range of differences. Many people associate the term **diversity** with the word **cultural**, which has to do with the differences between groups of people depending on their country of origin and their beliefs. They fail to recognize that diversity is not just cultural. Certainly, diversity occurs within each cultural group; however, many other characteristics are involved. For example, within a group of Japanese people are subgroups such as males, females, children, the elderly, athletes, thin people, gay or lesbian people, Buddhists, Christians, married people, and unmarried people, to mention just a few of the possible characteristics, beliefs, and values.

Diversity is not a simple matter, yet it is not difficult to deal with, if you are fair to people and keep an open mind. In fact, when you look more closely at, and think about, diversity, it provides wonderful opportunities because people from varying groups bring with them special knowledge, experience, and value. This is because even though people have differences, they have many traits in common. Their similarities form a solid basis for successful interpersonal relationships if you are knowledgeable and think of people as unique individuals. If you cannot think of the person instead of the group, you may stereotype people—lump them together and treat them all the same. This is a recipe for interpersonal disaster and service breakdown.

The basic customer service techniques related to communication found in this book can be applied to many situations in which you encounter customers from various groups. Coupled with specific strategies for adapting to special customer needs, these techniques provide the tools you need to provide excellent customer service.

A key point to remember is that the concept of treating others as you would like to be treated (a Christian value) can lead to service breakdowns. This is because your customers are unique and may not value what you do. To better ensure service success, find out what customers want and treat them as *they* want to be treated. This concept has been termed the **Platinum Rule.**[1]

Some factors that make people different are innate, such as height, weight, hair color, gender, skin color, physical and mental condition, and sibling birth order. All these factors contribute to our uniqueness and help or inhibit us throughout our lives depending on the perceptions we and others have. Other factors that make us unique are learned or gained, for example, religion, **values, beliefs,** economic level, lifestyle choices, profession, marital status, education, and political affiliation. These factors are also used to assign people to categories. Caution must be used when considering any of these characteristics since grouping people can lead to stereotyping and possibly discrimination.

The bottom line is that all of these factors affect each customer encounter. Your awareness of differences and of your own preferences are crucial in determining the success you will have in each instance.

3   Customer Awareness

Concept: Applying Western practices to a situation involving someone from another culture can result in frustration, anger, poor service, and lost business.

Aren't all customers alike? Emphatically, no! No two people are alike, no two generations are alike, and no two cultures are alike. In addition, as we discussed in Chapter 7, each customer has needs based on his or her own perceptions and situation.

In our highly mobile, technologically connected world, it is not unusual to encounter a wide variety of people with differing backgrounds, experiences, religions, modes of dress, values, and beliefs within the course of a single day. All these factors affect customer needs and create situations in which you must be alert to the verbal and nonverbal messages that indicate those needs. Moreover, the diverse nature of your customer population requires you to be aware of the various ways people from different cultures interact in the business setting. Applying Western practices to a situation involving someone from another culture can result in frustration, anger, poor service, and lost business.

4   The Impact of Cultural Values

Concept: Values often dictate which behaviors and practices are acceptable or unacceptable. These values may or may not have a direct bearing on serving the customer.

Although many cultures have similar values and beliefs, specific cultural values are often taught to members of particular groups starting at a very young age. This does not mean that a particular group's values and beliefs are better or worse than those of any other culture; they are simply important to that particular group. These values often dictate which behaviors and practices are acceptable or unacceptable. These values may or may not have a direct bearing on serving the customer, but they can have a very powerful influence on what the customer wants, needs, thinks is important, and is willing to seek or accept. Values can also influence your perceptions and actions. Being conscious of differences can lead to a better understanding of customers and potentially reduce conflict or misunderstandings in dealing with them.

[1]Tony Alessandra and Michael J. O'Connor, *The Platinum Rule,* Warner Books, 1996.

The mobility of modern-day society may put you in regular contact with customers from a variety of cultures. The more informed you are about similarities and differences, the greater the likelihood that you will provide quality service. *How should you provide customer service to someone from another culture?*

Many service providers take values for granted. This is a mistake. Values are the "rules" that people use to evaluate issues or situations, make decisions, interact with others, and deal with conflict. As a whole, a person's value system often guides thinking and helps him or her determine right from wrong or good from bad. From a customer service perspective, values often strongly drive customer needs and influence the buying decision. Values also differ from one culture to another based on its views on ethics, morals, religion, and many other factors. For example, if customers perceive clothing as too sexy or too conservative, they may not purchase the items, depending on what need they are trying to meet. Or, they may not buy a house because it's in the "wrong" neighborhood.

Values are based on the deeply held beliefs of a culture or subculture. These beliefs might be founded in religion, politics, or group mores. They drive thinking and actions and are so powerful that they have served as the basis for arguments, conflicts, and even wars.

To be effective in dealing with others, service providers should not ignore the power of values and beliefs, nor should they think that their value system is better than that of someone else's. The key to success is to be open-minded and accept that someone else has a different belief system that determines his or her needs. With this in mind, you as a service provider should strive to use all the positive communication and needs identification you have read about thus far in order to satisfy the customer.

Cultural values can be openly expressed or subtly demonstrated through behavior. They can affect your interactions with your customers in a variety of ways. Figure 8.1 shows the results of one study that compared the top five personal values of Asian respondents to those of their American counterparts. In the next few pages, consider the connection of values with behavior, and how you can adjust your customer service to ensure a satisfactory experience for diverse customers. Keep in mind that the degree to which customers have been acculturated to Western standards will determine how they act.

The goal is to provide service to the customer. In order to achieve success in accomplishing this goal, service providers must be sensitive to, tolerant of, and empathetic toward customers. You do not need to adopt the beliefs of others, but you should adapt to them to the extent that you provide the best service possible to all of your customers. As mentioned earlier, apply the Platinum Rule of service when dealing with customers.

FIGURE 8.1
Top Five Asian and American Personal Values

A survey of 101 Asians from eight countries and 28 Americans from U.S. foreign affairs offices in Washington and East Asia revealed the differences in values shown here, ranked from top to bottom.

Asian	American
Hard work	Self-reliance
Respect for learning	Hard work
Honesty	Achieving success in life
Self-discipline	Personal achievement
Self-reliance	Helping others

Source: David J. Hitchcock, *Asian Values and the United States: How Much Conflict?* Center for Strategic and International Studies, Washington, D.C., 1994, pp. 21–22.

Modesty

Modesty is exhibited in many ways. In some cultures (e.g., Muslim) conservative dress by women is one manifestation of modesty. For example, in many Arab cultures women demonstrate modesty and a dedication to traditional beliefs by wearing a veil. Such practices are tied to religious and cultural beliefs that originated hundreds of years ago. In other cultures, nonverbal communication cues send messages. For example, direct eye contact is viewed as an effective communication approach in the many Western cultures, and lack of eye contact could suggest dishonesty or lack of confidence to a Westerner. In some cultures (India and Japan), direct eye contact is often discouraged, in particular between men and women and between people who are of different social or business status, for it is considered disrespectful. Often a sense of modesty is instilled into people at an early age (more so in females). Modesty may be demonstrated by covering the mouth or part of the face with an open hand, or through avoiding direct eye contact in certain situations.

Impact on Service

When encountering such behavior, evaluate the situation for the true message being delivered. The person may really be exhibiting suspicious behavior. However, instead of assuming that the customer is being evasive or dishonest, consider the possible impact of culture. Don't force the issue or draw undue attention to a customer's nonverbal behavior, cultural dress, or beliefs being demonstrated. Instead, continue to verbally probe for customer needs and address them. In addition, provide the same quality of friendly service as you would to others who display behavior or cultural characteristics that do not differ from your own.

Expectations of Privacy

Based on your personality and prior life experiences, you may be more or less likely to disclose personal information, especially to people you do not know well. You should be aware that disclosing personal information about oneself is often a cultural factor and that **expectations of privacy** vary. According to research, people who are British, German, Australian, Korean, or Japanese display a tendency to disclose less about themselves than Americans do.[2]

---

[2]Carley H. Dodd, *Dynamics of Intercultural Communication*, 4th ed., Brown & Benchmark, Madison, Wis., 1995, pp. 243–244.

Impact on Service

If you tend to be gregarious and speak freely about virtually any topic, you should curtail this tendency in the customer service environment. Failure to do so could make your customer feel uneasy and uncomfortable. This is true in part because, in Western cultures, when someone asks a question or shares information, there is an expectation that the other party will reciprocate. Reluctance to do so is sometimes perceived as being unfriendly or even rude. A good rule of thumb is to stay focused on the business of serving your customer in an expeditious and professional manner. Keeping your conversations centered on satisfying the customers' needs can accomplish this. This should not be construed to mean that you should totally avoid "small talk," just keep it under control and watch customer reactions closely.

Forms of Address

Although Americans often pride themselves on their informality, people from other countries see informality as rudeness, arrogance, or overfamiliarity. Many cultures stress formality in the business environment and place importance on the use of titles and family names when addressing others (e.g., Argentina, European countries, China).

To further confuse the issue of how to address a customer, some cultures have differing rules on how family names are listed and used. For example, in China, each person is given a family name, a generational name (for the period during which they are born), and a personal name at birth. The generational and personal names might be separated by a hyphen or space (a female might be named Li Teng Jiang or Li Teng-Jiang). Women typically do not take their husband's surnames. When addressing someone from the Chinese culture, use an appropriate title such as *Mr.* or *Mrs.* followed by their family name (Mrs. Li) unless you are asked to use a different **form of address**. Many people adopt a Western first name when they immigrate to the United States (Amanda or Richard). In Argentina (and most **Hispanic** or **Latino cultures**), people have two surnames: one from their father (listed first) and one from their mother (Jose Ricardo Gutierrez Martinez). Usually, when addressing the person, use a title only with the father's surname (Mr. or Mrs. Gutierrez).[3]

Impact on Service

A customer's preference for a particular name or form of address has an impact upon your ability to effectively deal with him or her. If you start a conversation with someone and immediately alienate the person by incorrectly using his or her name, you may not be able to recover. Moreover, informality or improper use of family names could send a message of lack of knowledge or concern for the customer as an individual or as being important to you.

Respect for Elders

In most cultures, some level of respect is paid to older people. Often this **respect for elders** is focused more on males (when older men are viewed as superior, as among Chinese).[4] This arises from a belief that, with age, come knowledge, authority, and

---

[3]Terri Morrison, Wayne A. Conaway, and George A. Borden, *Kiss, Bow, or Shake Hands: How to Do Business in 60 Countries*, Adams Media Corporation, Holbrook, Mass., pp. 5, 61.

[4]Guo-Ming Chen and William J. Starosta, *Foundations of Intercultural Communication*, Allyn & Bacon, Needham Heights, Mass., 1998, p. 47.

higher status. Thus, respect for or deference to elders is normal. Also, in many cultures age brings with it unique privileges and rights (such as the right to rule or to be the leader). This is true in many Native American cultures.[5]

Impact on Service

You must be careful to pay appropriate respect when speaking to older customers. Further, you should be sensitive to the fact that if the customer demands to speak to a senior person or to the manager or owner, he or she may be simply exhibiting a customary expectation for his or her culture or generation.

If you can assist without creating conflict, do so; if not, honor the request when possible.

Importance of Relationships

In many Asian, Latin American, and Middle Eastern cultures, the building of a strong interpersonal **relationship** is extremely important before business is conducted. For example, in Malaysia, Indonesia, Myanmar, Korea, and Japan it is not unusual to have a number of meetings with people in an organization before coming to an agreement. Lunch, dinner, and office meetings often occur for weeks before an agreement is reached. Also, unless you reach the right level of management in the organization for these meetings, all your efforts may be wasted. Figure 8.2 shows a partial listing of some of the world's more relationship-focused countries.

Impact on Service

Failure to establish support or an environment of trust could lead to a breakdown in service and/or lost customers. This does not mean that you should not assume a quicker familiarity with customers from such cultures. This could also alienate them. Instead, when you will be having ongoing contact or be doing repeat business, follow the customers' lead. Get to know them and share information about your organization and yourself that can lead to mutual respect and trust. You may find that you have to take time at the beginning of each encounter with your established customer to reestablish the relationship. This may involve spending time in conversations related to nonbusiness topics (sports, hobbies, pets, or other topics in which the customer is interested).

Relationship building may also involve presenting gifts to persuade various people in the organization that you are a friend and have their interests at heart. Only then can you proceed to determine need(s) and provide service.

Gender Roles

Culturally, and individually, people view the role of men and women differently. And, although **gender roles** are continually evolving throughout the world, decision making and authority are often clearly established as male prerogatives within a culture, subculture, or family.[6] For example, in many Middle Eastern, Asian, South American, and European countries, women have not gained the respect or credibility in the business environment that they have achieved in many parts of North America. In some countries it is not unusual for women to be expected to take a "be seen and not heard" role or to remain out of business transactions. In Korea and other Pacific Rim countries, it is rare for women to participate in business. Men still have

---

[5]Dan C. Locke, *Increasing Multicultural Understanding: A Comprehensive Model,* Sage Publications, Thousand Oaks, Calif., 1998, p.67.

[6]Dodd, p. 43.

FIGURE 8.2
Relationship-
Focused Countries
(partial listing)

Bangladesh	Iran	Pakistan	Singapore
Brazil	Iraq	Philippines	South Korea
China	Japan	Poland	Thailand
Egypt	Kuwait	Qatar	Turkey
Greece	Malaysia	Romania	Vietnam
India	Mexico	Russia	
Indonesia	Myanmar	Saudi Arabia	

higher social status than females. Among many Israelis, men are prohibited from touching a woman in the business environment. Thus Israeli women cannot shake hands and exchange business cards in the Western fashion. To exchange a business card, they often must place the card on a table so that a man can pick it up.[7]

You don't have to agree with this behavior, but you will need to take it into consideration when facing it in customer encounters. People leave a country, but they take their culture with them. Failure to consider alternative ways of dealing with people in certain instances might cause you to react negatively to a situation and nonverbally communicate your bias.

Impact on Service

If you are a female dealing with a male whose cultural background is like one of the ones just described, he may reject your assistance and ask for a male service provider. If you are a male dealing with a male and female from such a culture, don't be surprised if your conversation involves only the male. Attempts to draw a woman into such a transaction may embarrass, offend, or even anger customers and their family members.

Attitude Toward Conflict

Conflict is possible when two people come together in a customer environment, but it does not have to happen. By recognizing your biases and preferences, and being familiar with those of people from other cultures, you can reduce the potential for disagreement. Certainly, there will be times when a customer initiates conflict. In this case all you can do is to use the positive communication techniques described throughout this book.

Many times, **attitudes** toward conflict are rooted in the individual's culture or subculture and based on behavioral style preference (discussed in Chapter 6). Some cultures are **individualistic** (emphasis is placed on individuals' goals, as in Western countries), and some are **collective cultures** (individuals are viewed as part of a group, as in Japan or in Native American cultures). Members of individualistic cultures are likely to take a direct approach to conflict, whereas people whose culture is collective may address conflict indirectly, using an informal mediator in an effort to prevent loss of face or embarrassment for those involved. Even within subcultures of a society, there are differing styles of communication and dealing with conflict.[8] For example, cross-cultural studies have shown that many African Americans prefer a controlling (argumentative) **conflict resolution style,** but Americans of European ancestry prefer a solution-oriented (discussion) approach. Of course, regardless of culture or group, people choose different forms of conflict resolution on the basis of personality style preferences (see Chapter 6).

[7]Larry A. Samovar, Richard E. Porter, and Lisi A. Stefani, *Communication Between Cultures,* Wadsworth, Belmont, Calif., 1998, p. 191.

[8]William B. Gudykunst, *Bridging Differences: Effective Intergroup Communication,* 3rd ed., Sage, Thousand Oaks, Calif., 1998, pp. 246–268.

Impact on Service

Depending on the individuals you encounter and their cultural background, you and your customers may deal differently with conflict. If you use the wrong strategy, emotions could escalate and customer dissatisfaction could follow. The key is to listen and remain calm, especially if the customer becomes agitated.

The Concept of Time

In relation to time, people and societies are often referred to as being either **monochronic** or **polychronic**. People from monochronic societies tend to do one thing at a time, take time commitments seriously, are often focused on short-term projects or relationships, and adhere closely to plans. On the other hand, polychronic people are used to distractions, juggle multiple things (e.g., conversations) without feeling stressed, consider time as a guide and flexible commodity, work toward long-term deadlines, and base promptness on relationships.

Americans are typically very time-conscious (monochronic). You often hear such phrases as "Time is money," "Faster than a New York minute," and "Time is of the essence." In Germany, punctuality is almost a religion, and being late is viewed as very unprofessional and rude. In most business settings in the United States, anyone over 5 minutes late for a meeting is often chastised. In many colleges and universities, etiquette dictates that students wait no longer than 15 to 20 minutes when an instructor (depending on whether he or she is a full or associate professor) is late. Americans tend to expect people from other cultures to be as time-conscious as they are. This is not the case, however. For example, it is not unusual for people from Arab countries (polychronic) to be a half hour or more late for an appointment or for a person from Hispanic and some Asian cultures to be an hour late. A phrase used by some Asian Indians sums up the concept and justifies the lateness: "Indian standard time." Such tardiness is not viewed as disrespect for the time of others or rudeness; it is simply indicative of a cultural value or way of life. In fact, in some Latin American countries, one is expected to arrive late for an appointment as a show of respect.[9] Figure 8.3 shows countries based on their **concept of time.**

Impact on Service

In Western and other monochronic cultures you are expected to be punctual. This is a crucial factor in delivering effective service. Although others may not have the same beliefs and may be late for meetings, you must observe time rules in order to project an appropriate image and to satisfy the needs of your customers and organization.

Ownership of Property

In many cultures (e.g., Buddhist, certain African tribes, and the Chickasaw Indian nation) **ownership of property,** or accumulation of worldly goods or wealth, is frowned upon. In the case of the Chickasaw Indians, such things as the earth, nature, natural resources, possessions, and individual skills are shared among the tribal group. They are not to be owned or kept from others, for the Creator gave them.[10] Many devout Buddhists believe that giving away personal belongings to others can help them reach a higher spiritual state. Thus the amassing of material things is not at all important to them.

---

[9]Samovar, Porter, and Stefani, p. 167.
[10]Chickasaw Nation home page.

FIGURE 8.3
Monochronic and
Polychronic
Countries

Most cultures can be described as either monochronic or polychronic. Some are both in that people exhibit one focus in the workplace and another with relationships. In some countries, a monochronic approach is prevalent in major urban areas, whereas a polychronic view is taken elsewhere. The following is a sampling of countries and their perspective on time.

Monochronic	Polychronic		Both
Australia	Africa	Latvia	Brazil
England	Bahrain	Lebanon	France
Canada	Bangladesh	Mexico	Japan
Czech Republic	Cambodia	Myanmar	Spain
Germany	China	Native American tribes	
Hungary	Croatia	Pakistan	
New Zealand	Ethiopia	Philippines	
Norway	Estonia	Portugal	
The Netherlands	Greece	Romania	
Poland	India	Russia	
Slovakia	Indonesia	Saudi Arabia	
Sweden	Ireland	Serbia	
Switzerland	Italy	South Korea	
United States	Java	Thailand	
	Jordan	Turkey	
	Kuwait	Ukraine	
	Laos	Vietnam	

Impact on Service

People have differing levels of needs. Ask customers what their needs are and listen to their responses. Don't persist in upgrading a customer's request to a higher level or more expensive product if he or she declines your suggestion. You may offend and lose a customer. Of course, if you are in sales, you must make a judgment on whether an objection is one that you should attempt to overcome or whether it is culturally based and means no.

5   Providing Quality Service to Diverse Customer Groups

Concept: As a service provider, you should become proficient in working with customers with language differences and disabilities; you also need to work with young and elderly customers.

Given the potential diversity of your customer base, it may be impossible to establish a service strategy for each group. However, you should think of what you might do to address the needs of some of the larger categories of customer with whom you will probably come into contact. The next few sections provide some strategies for dealing effectively with people from four diverse groups: customers with language differences, customers with disabilities, elderly customers, and young customers.

Customers With Language Differences

One major obstacle for service providers in the United States is that many adult Americans believe that just over half (52%) of the world's population speaks English. Based on findings from the National Foreign Language Center in Washington D.C., the number is closer to 20 percent.

LEADERSHIP INITIATIVE   8.1

Providing Spanish language training for supervisors and employees, along with cultural awareness materials can increase knowledge of and service levels to an increasing number of foreign-born customers and coworkers. It can also reduce frustration and confusion between employees and customers. At a minimum, words and phrases related to serving customers in the industry in which your organization markets can be helpful, for example, terms related to auto, home, and life insurance for those in the insurance industry. These terms could be posted on small job aids at each workstation for quick reference following training.

FIGURE 8.4
Foreign-Born Population Living in the United States by Sex and World Region of Birth (numbers in thousands)
Source: U.S. Census Bureau, *Current Population Survey,* Ethnic and Hispanic Statistics Branch, Population Division, March 2002. Extracted from Table 3.14.

Sex	Foreign-Born	World Region of Birth			
		Europe	**Asia**	**Latin America***	**Other Areas***
Total	32,453	4,547	8,281	16,943	2,680
Male	16,352	2,097	3,975	8,919	1,360
Female	16,101	2,450	4,306	8,024	1,320

*The majority of those born in Latin America are from Mexico. Those born in other areas are from Africa, Oceania, Bermuda, and Canada.

According to U.S. Census Bureau figures, about 32+ million **foreign-born people** live in the United States. These numbers equate to consumer spending of about $223 billion dollars on goods and services in 1990, with a projected increase to over $926 billion by 2007.[11] Figure 8.4 gives an idea of how these numbers break down by country or origin. The key to effectively serving people from different cultures is flexibility. Since you are likely to encounter customers from virtually any country in the world, you need to be prepared. You need to have a way to use alternative methods or strategies for providing service. For example, you might identify people in your organization who speak languages other than English so that you can call upon them, if necessary. Or, you can do research on the Internet and at the library to learn about different cultures or countries. You might subscribe to publications that focus on cultural issues and a variety of countries, such as *National Geographic.*[12] If a customer speaks a little English or has a heavy accent, try the strategies described in the following sections.

Let Your Customer Guide the Conversation

When possible, let your customer take the lead in guiding the service interaction. Some customers may want to spend time getting to know you, others may take a rigid or formal approach and get right down to business by taking the lead, and still others may choose to have someone else act as a mediator or an intermediary. Learn to recognize the cues and follow along when you can.

[11]Holmes, Tamara E., *The Changing Language of Customer Service,* National Federation of Independent Businesses, <http://www.nfib.com>, July 22, 2003.

[12]National Geographic Society, Washington, D.C.

Be Flexible

Communicating with people from other cultures who do not speak English fluently can be frustrating and complicated. Even if you do not understand their culture or language, using the positive listening, nonverbal, and verbal techniques you read about in Chapters 3 to 6 can help. If you are having difficulties, try some of the specific ideas included in this section of the book. Part of being flexible is recognizing that your views are not the way of the world. Making the mistake of believing that everyone has the same experiences and sees things the way you do can lead to communication and relationship breakdown. It is probably wise to assume that people from other cultures with whom you come into contact do not have the same knowledge and experience that you have. You can then proceed to share information with each other openly and freely. Listen for points of agreement or commonality.

Listen Patiently

You may be frustrated, but so is the other person. Focus on what he or she is saying and try to understand the meaning of the message and the needs being communicated by your customer.

Speak Clearly and Slowly

Most adults in the United States speak at a rate of about 125 to 150 words a minute. Speak at a rate slow enough that allows understanding without being insulting.

Speak at a Normal Volume and Tone

Yelling or changing tone does nothing to enhance understanding. A customer who is unable to speak English is not deaf. You may naturally raise your voice if a customer cannot speak English, but if you do, the customer may become offended or think that you are hard of hearing and raise his or her voice also. This is not an effective way to communicate or provide effective customer service.

Use Open-Ended Questions

Open-ended questions encourage customers to share information. On the other hand, closed-ended questions do not allow you to accurately gauge a customer's viewpoint or understanding. Either because of embarrassment or to avoid saying no, some customers from other cultures may not admit that they do not agree, have an answer, or want to do something if you used a closed-ended question. This reluctance can lead to misunderstandings and possibly resentment if you do not recognize a customer's nonverbal signals.

Pause Frequently

Pausing allows your customer to translate what you have said into her or his language, comprehend, and then respond in English or ask questions.

Use Standard English

Avoid technical terms, contractions (e.g., *don't, can't*), slang (e.g., *like, you know, whoopee, rubberneck*), or broken English (e.g., sentences that fail to follow standard rules of grammar or syntax). Some people, when encountering non-English-speaking customers, revert to an insulting singsong, almost childish, form of English. This does nothing to aid communication, for it is offensive and any English the customer understands gets lost in translation. Remember, some people understand English though they may not be able to speak it well. Also, some people do not speak English because they are self-conscious about their ability or choose not to. Many cultures value and use silence as an important aspect to communication, something that people of Western cultures find difficult to understand. Many Westerners often believe that silence means that a person does not understand.

A scene in the movie *Rush Hour*, with Chris Tucker and Jackie Chan, was a perfect example of how some people make assumptions about people from other cultures and end up communicating ineffectively. Tucker (playing a Los Angeles police officer) is sent to the airport to pick up a Chinese police officer. Tucker immediately makes assumptions about Chan's ability to communicate in English:

> Tucker [upon meeting Chan]: "Please tell me you speak English."
>
> Chan [gives no response; just looks at a Chinese airline pilot standing next to him].
>
> Tucker [raises his voice]: "I'm Detective Carter. You speaka any English?"
>
> Chan [again looks at others and says nothing]
>
> Tucker [in a loud, exaggerated voice and gesturing toward his mouth]: "Do you understand the words coming out of my mouth?"
>
> Chan [smiles and says nothing]
>
> Later in the movie, as the two are riding in Tucker's car, Chan finally speaks in English.
>
> Tucker: "All of a sudden, you're speaking English now."
>
> Chan: "A little."
>
> Tucker: "You lied to me."
>
> Chan: "I didn't say I didn't speak English. You assumed I didn't. Not being able to speak is not the same as not speaking."

Use Globally Understood References

To reduce the risk of misunderstandings by people who speak English as a second language, stick with basic verbiage. Avoid jokes, words, or acronyms that are uniquely American or tied to sports, historical events, or American culture. For example, avoid these types of statements: "I'll need your John Hancock (referring to Hancock signing the Declaration of Independence) on this form," "If plan A fails, we'll drop back and punt (referring to American football)" or "We scored a base hit with that proposal yesterday (referring to baseball)." These phrases might be understood by someone acculturated to American society but will likely make no sense to others.

Be Conscious of Nonverbal Cues

Continually monitor nonverbal reactions as you converse with a customer. If you sense confusion or lack of comprehension, stop and try to reestablish a bond. Also, be aware of the cues you send and make sure that they are in line with your verbal message.

Paraphrase the Customer's Message

After focusing on what you think is the customer's message, you may convey your understanding to the customer in your own words. When you think that you don't understand, either paraphrase the part of the customer's message up to the point at which you did understand or ask clarifying questions. For example, "Mr. Rasheed, I understand your complaint, but I'm not sure I understand what you expect us to do. How can I help make this better for you?"

Try Writing Your Message

Some people understand written English better than they speak it. If a customer seems to be having trouble understanding what you are saying, try printing your message (legibly) to see if they can understand your meaning. You might even try using recognizable symbols, if appropriate (e.g., a stop sign when you are giving directions or a picture of an object if you are describing something).

Try Another Language

If you speak a second language, try using it. Your non-English-speaking customers may understand, since many countries require students to learn multiple languages in school. At the very least, they will appreciate your efforts to communicate with them.

Avoid Humor and Sarcasm

Humor and sarcasm do not work well with customers whose first language is not English. They could lead to customer confusion and embarrassment. Differing cultural values and beliefs result in different points of view about what is socially acceptable. Also, jokes and other types of humor are typically based on incidents or people connected to a specific culture. They do not "travel well" and may not be understood by someone not of that culture.

Look for Positive Options

Americans are often very direct. Many tend to use an abrupt *no* in response to a request they cannot fulfill. This behavior is viewed as rude, arrogant, and closed-minded in many cultures. Some countries do not even have a word in their language for *no* (e.g., Burmese). In many cases (e.g., parts of Asia) the response *no* in a conversation may cause a person embarrassment or loss of **face** (the esteem of others). Many people try to avoid such embarrassment at all costs. In some instances, people from certain parts of Asia may say yes to your proposal and then not follow through on your suggestion rather than tell you no. Such behavior is acceptable in some cultures.

If you are dealing with customers who might react to your saying no in these ways—and you must decline—smile, apologize, and then try something like, "I am not sure we can do this" or "That will be difficult to do." Then, offer an alternative.

Be Less Critical

If a customer makes a mistake (e.g., improperly fills out a form or uses the wrong word), do not point out the mistake. Instead, take responsibility for correcting the error or clearing up the misunderstanding (e.g., "I am sorry that these forms are so confusing. I have trouble with them too."). This strategy helps them avoid embarrassment (save face) and sends a nonjudgmental message that you are there to assist them.

Use Questions Carefully

As mentioned earlier, phrase questions simply and avoid the use of closed-ended questions that require a yes or no. Watch your customer's nonverbal responses so that you will be able to gauge his or her reactions to your questions.

In some cultures, people believe that questioning someone is intrusive, and they therefore avoid it. This is especially true if the questions are personal (e.g., "How is your family?").

Use a Step-by-Step Approach

When explaining something, outline exactly what you will do or what will be expected of the customer. Write this information down for the customer's future reference in order to prevent misunderstandings. If the customer cannot read it, and does not want to admit this out of embarrassment, he or she now has something to take to someone else for translation.

Keep Your Message Brief

Avoid lengthy explanations or details that might frustrate or confuse your customer. Use simple one-syllable words and short sentences. But also avoid being too brisk. Make sure you allow time for interpretation of, translation of, and response to your message.

Check Frequently for Understanding

In addition to using short words and sentences, pause often to verify the customer's understanding of your message before continuing. Avoid questions such as "Do you understand?" Not only can this be answered with a "yes" or "no" as you read earlier, but it can also offend someone who speaks and understands English reasonably well. The nonverbal message is that the person may not be smart enough to get your meaning. Instead, try tie-in questions such as "How do you think you will use this?" or others that will give you an indication of whether the customer understands the information you have provided. These types of questions help you and the customer visualize how the information will be put to use. They also give you a chance to find out if the person has misunderstood what you explained.

Keep Smiling

Smiling is a universal language. Speak it fluently!

Customers With Disabilities

According to the U.S. Census Bureau, approximately 50 million (one in five) Americans over the age of five and noninstitutionalized have some level of disability. It is also estimated that about one in ten Americans have what are defined as severe disabilities. These numbers are projected to continue to grow as the population ages.

From a customer service perspective, it is a certainty that you will at some point encounter someone who has a disability that requires your assistance in serving him or her. Some customer service professionals are uncomfortable working with **customers with disabilities** because they have had little prior exposure to people who have disabilities, they are uninformed about various disabilities, or they have unfounded fear or anxiety. Even though you may be unfamiliar with how people with disabilities adapt to life experiences, you should provide excellent service to them. In most cases, customers who have disabilities do not want to be treated differently; they want to be treated equally.

In addition to all the factors you have read about previously, to be effective in dealing with customers, you must be aware of the **1990 Americans With Disabilities Act** (ADA) and other legislation passed by Congress to protect individuals and groups. You should also understand the court interpretations of these laws that require businesses to provide certain services to customers with disabilities and to make

FIGURE 8.5
General Strategies for Servicing Customers With Disabilities

In addition to the suggestions offered in this chapter for serving customers with specific disabilities, here are some general guidelines for success:

Be prepared and informed. You can find a lot of literature and information about disabilities. Do some reading to learn about the capabilities and needs of customers with disabilities.

Note: If you deal with customers who use computers (e.g., computer training or sales) a free video entitled *Enable* is available through the Internet at www.microsoft.com/enable/productions. The video helps increase awareness about the capabilities of people with various disabilities and how computers can help them compensate for lost abilities.

Be careful not to patronize. Customers with disabilities aren't your children; don't talk down to them. Just because they have a physical or mental disability does not mean that they should be valued less as a customer or person.

Treat them equally, not differently. Just as you would other customers, work to discover their needs and then set about satisfying them.

Refer to the person, not the disability. For example, instead of referring to the *blind man,* refer to the *man with a sight loss* or *man who is blind,* or better yet, *the man.*

Offer assistance; do not rush to help without asking. Just as you would ask someone without a disability whether you might hold a door or carry a package, do the same for a person with a disability. Unsolicited assistance can be offensive and might even be dangerous, if it is unexpected and causes the person to lose his or her balance, for example.

Be respectful. The amount of respect you show to all customers should be at a consistently high level. This includes tone of voice (showing patience), gestures, eye contact, and all the other communication techniques you have learned about.

certain premises accessible to them. The laws also prohibit any form of discrimination or harassment.

Since the passage of the ADA, much has been published about the rights of and accommodations for people with disabilities. Figure 8.5 provides general strategies for working with customers and others with disabilities and complying with the ADA. In addition, the following sections discuss specific approaches you can take to work well with people with certain disabilities.

Customers With Hearing Disabilities

Customers who have **hearing disabilities** have special needs, but they also have certain abilities. Do not assume that people who are hearing impaired are helpless. In interactions with such customers, you can do a variety of things to provide effective service:

- Provide written information and instructions where appropriate and possible.
- Use pictures, objects, diagrams, or other such items to communicate more clearly.
- To get the person's attention, use nonverbal cues such as gesturing.
- Use facial expressions and gestures to emphasize key words or express thoughts.
- Face the person directly.
- Enunciate your words and speak slowly so that the customer can see your mouth form words.
- Use short sentences and words.
- Check for understanding frequently by using open-ended questions to which the customer must provide descriptive answers.

- Communicate in a well-lighted room when possible.
- Watch backlighting (light coming from behind you which can cast a shadow on your face), which may reduce the ability to see your mouth.
- Reduce background noise, is possible.

Customers With Vision Disabilities

According to the National Eye Institute in Bethesda, Maryland, approximately 3 million Americans have low vision, almost 1 million are "legally blind," and another 220,000 are totally blind. This means that you are likely to encounter someone with a vision impairment. Like people who have hearing impairments, customers with **vision disabilities** may need special assistance but are not helpless. Depending on your organization's product and service focus, you can do things to assist visually impaired customers. Be aware that, depending on the type of impairment, a person may have limited vision that can be used to advantage. Here are some strategies to use:

- Talk to a visually impaired person the same way you would talk to anyone else.
- You do not have to raise your voice; the person is *visually* impaired.
- Do not feel embarrassed or change your vocabulary. It is okay to say things like "Do you see my point?" or "Do you get the picture?"
- Speak directly to the customer.
- If the customer uses a guide dog, do not pet, feed, or otherwise distract the animal without the owner's permission. A guide dog is especially trained to perform specific functions. If you interfere, the dog might become confused. The owner could possibly be injured as a result.
- Speak to the person as he or she enters the room or approach the person so that he or she knows where you are. Also, introduce others who are present, or at least inform the customer of their presence.
- If appropriate, ask how much sight he or she has and how you can best assist.
- Give very specific information and directions (e..g, "A chair is approximately ten feet ahead on your left").
- If you are seating the person, face him or her away from bright lights that might interfere with any limited vision he or she may have.
- When walking with someone who is blind, offer your arm. Do not take the person's arm without permission; this could startle him or her. Let the person take your elbow and walk slightly behind you.
- When helping a blind person to a chair, guide his or her hand to the back of the chair. Also, inform the person if a chair has arms to prevent him or her from overturning the chair by leaning or sitting on an arm.
- Leave doors either completely closed or open. Partially open doors pose a danger to visually impaired people.

Customers With Mobility or Motion Impairments

Customers who have **mobility or motion impairments** often use specially designed equipment and have had extensive training in how to best use assistive devices to compensate for the loss of the use of some part of their body. You can best assist them by offering to help and then following their lead or instructions. Do not make the assumption that they need your assistance and then set about giving it. You can

Check with local advocacy groups or on the Internet for information on the types of accommodations you might make for people with various disabilities and how best to interact with people who have specific disabilities (e.g., sight, mobility, hearing impairment). Collect and read literature on the subject. Share the information with other students and/or coworkers (if you currently work in a customer service environment).

What to look for:

Definitions of various disabilities.

Strategies for better communication.

Accommodations necessary to allow customer access to products and services.

Resources available (e.g., tools, equipment, training, or organizations).

Bibliographic information on disabilities (e.g., books or articles).

Customers with mobility impairment have typically learned to overcome or compensate for their disability. Offer assistance without interfering. *In what ways would you offer assistance to someone with a mobility impairment?*

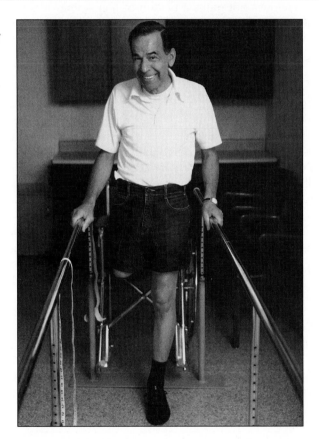

cause injury if you upset their balance or routine. Here are some strategies for better serving these customers:

Prior to a situation in which you may have to accommodate someone who uses a walker, wheelchair, crutches, or other device(s), do an environmental survey of your workplace. Note areas where space is inadequate to permit mobility (a minimum of 36 inches is needed for a standard wheelchair) or where hazards exist. If you can correct the situation, do so. For example, move or bring in a different table or chair or rearrange furniture for better access. Otherwise, make suggestions for improvements to the proper people in your organization. Remind them that the ADA and state regulations require an organization to accommodate customers with such disabilities.

Do not assume that someone who has such an impairment cannot perform certain tasks. As mentioned earlier, people who have disabilities are often given extensive training. They have learned how to overcome obstacles and perform various tasks in different ways.

Make sure that you place information or materials at a level that makes it possible for the person to see without undue strain (e.g., eye level for someone in a wheelchair so that he or she does not have to look up).

Stand or sit so that you can make direct eye contact with a person in a wheelchair without forcing the person to look up at an uncomfortable angle for extended periods.

Do not push or lean on someone's wheelchair without his or her permission.

Elderly Customers

Being elderly does not make a person or a customer less valuable. In fact, many older customers are in excellent physical and mental shape, are still employed, and have more time to be active now than when they were younger. Studies show that senior citizens have more disposable income now than at any other time in history. And, as the **baby boomer** population (people born between 1946 and 1964) ages, there are more senior citizens than ever. Moreover, as the population ages, there will be a greater need for services—and service providers—to care for people and allow them to enjoy a good quality of life. Figure 8.6 shows the U.S. population aged 65 and older by sex between 1990 and 2000. Consider the following strategies when you are interacting with an **elderly customer.**

Be Respectful

As you would with any customer, be respectful. Even if the customer seems a bit arrogant, disoriented, or disrespectful, don't lose your professionalism. Recognize that sometimes these behaviors are a response to perceptions based on your cues. When this happens, quickly evaluate your behavior and make adjustments, if necessary. If an older customer seems abrupt in his or her response, think about whether you might have nonverbally signaled impatience because of your perception that he or she was slow in acting or responding.

Be Patient

Allow older customers the time to look around, respond, react, or ask questions. Value their decisions. Also, keep in mind that as some people age, their ability to process information lessens and their attention span becomes shorter. Do not assume that this is true of all older customers, but be patient when it does occur.

FIGURE 8.6
Population 65 Years and Over by Age and Sex: 1990 and 2000 (numbers in thousands)

Source: U.S. Census Bureau, Census 2000 Summary File 1; 1990 Census of Population, General Population Characteristics, United States (1990 CP-1-1).

	65 to 74 years		75–84 Years		85 Years and Over	
	1990	2000	1990	2000	1990	2000
Men	7,942	8,303	3,766	4,879	858	1,227
Women	10,165	10,088	6,289	7,482	2,222	3,013
Total	18,107	18,391	10,055	12,361	3,080	4,240

Answer Questions

Providing information to customers is crucial in order to help them make reasoned decisions. Even though you may have just explained something, listen to the customer's questions, respond, and restate. If it appears that the customer has misunderstood, try repeating the information, possibly using slightly different words.

Try Not to Sound Patronizing

If you appear to talk down to older customers, problems could arise or you could lose a customer. Customers who are elderly should not be treated as if they are senile! A condescending attitude will cause any customer, elderly or otherwise, to take his or her business elsewhere.

Remain Professional

Addressing senior citizens accompanied by their children or grandchildren with "Good morning, Grandma" because one of their family members used that language is inappropriate, disrespectful, and rude.

Guard Against Biases

Be careful not to let biases about older people interfere with good service. Don't ignore or offend older customers by making statements such as "Hang on, old timer. I'll be with you in a minute."

Communicate Effectively

Even if an elderly customer does not exhibit the common symptoms of hearing loss (e.g., incorrect responses or facial expressions indicating that she or he is straining to hear or may have missed the message), use the following to help enhance communication:

- Face the person.
- Talk slowly and enunciate words clearly.
- Keep your hands away from your mouth.
- Talk without food or chewing gum in your mouth.
- Observe the customer's nonverbal cues.
- Reword statements or ask questions again, if necessary.
- Be positive, patient, and practice the good listening skills covered in Chapter 5.
- Stand near good lighting, and keep background noise to a minimum, when possible.
- If an interpreter is with the customer, talk to the customer and not the interpreter. The interpreter will know what to do.

Younger Customers

You have heard the various terms describing the "younger generation"—Generation Y, Nexters, MTV generation, millennial generation, cyberkids. Whatever the term, this group follows Generation X (born 1964–1977) and is now entering the workplace as employees and as consumers in great numbers. Financially, the group accounts for billions of dollars in business revenue for products such as clothes, music, videos, and electronic entertainment equipment. Generation Y is a spending force to be reckoned with, and marketers are going after them with a vengeance. If you don't believe this, pick up a magazine and look at the faces of the

Pair up with a peer and use the following scenarios as the basis of role-plays to give you practice and feedback in dealing with various categories of customers. Before beginning, discuss how you might deal with each customer in a real-life situation. After the role-plays, both persons should answer the following questions and discuss any ideas for improvement.

Questions:

1. How well do you feel that service was provided?
2. Were any negative or unclear messages, verbal or nonverbal, communicated? If yes, discuss.
3. What open-ended questions were used to discover customer needs? What others could have been used?
4. How can identified areas for improvement be incorporated into a real customer service encounter?

Scenario 1   Farooq Khan was recently hired as a telecommunications specialist for a local telephone company. Your company is providing and installing equipment at a new relay station, and you will be working closely with Farooq, who is the project manager, over the next three months. On several occasions during the past week, you have spoken with Farooq over the phone and are now going to meet him in person for the first time. You are not impressed by him since, as you told a coworker, "He's an ignorant foreigner who doesn't even understand English." Your purpose for meeting with Farooq is to get to know him and discuss an implementation schedule for the project. You also want to find out his expectations for you and your company on the project.

Scenario 2   You are a shuttle driver for the airport and just received a call from your dispatcher to proceed to 8172 Dealy Lane to pick up Casandra Fenton. You were told that Ms. Fenton is blind and will need assistance getting her bags from the house to the bus. Upon arrival, you find Ms. Fenton waiting on her front porch with her bags.

Scenario 3   Mrs. Zagowski is 62 years old and is in the library where you are working at the circulation desk. As you observe her, you notice that she seems a bit frustrated and confused. You saw her browse through several aisles of books, then talk briefly with the reference librarian, and finally go to the computer containing the publication listings and their locations. You are going to try to assist her. Upon meeting her, you realize that she has a hearing deficit and has difficulty hearing what you are saying.

Scenario 4   You are the owner of a small hobby shop that specializes in coins, stamps, comics, and sports memorabilia. Tommy Chin, whom you recognize as a regular "browser," has come in while you are particularly busy. After looking through numerous racks of comic books and trading cards, he is now focused on autographed baseballs in a display case. You believe that he cannot afford them, although he is asking about prices and for other information.

models, look at the products being sold, and watch the shows being added to television lineups each year. All of this affects the way you will provide service to this generation of customers. Depending on your own age, your attitude toward them will vary. If you are of Gen Y, you may make the mistake of being overly familiar with your age group in delivering service. If you are a baby boomer or older, you may feel paternalistic or maternalistic or might believe some of the stereotypical rhetoric about this group (e.g., low moral values, fragmented in focus, overprotected by legislation and programs). Although some of these descriptions may be accurate, it is dangerous to pigeonhole any group or individual. This is especially true when providing service, for, as you have read, service is based on satisfying personal needs and wants.

LEADERSHIP INITIATIVE   8.2

To help raise awareness of potential stereotypes of and offensive language toward customers, some supervisors spend time brainstorming lists of negative terms or phrases typically applied to individuals and groups. They create lists of these and give them to each employee for posting in workstations. This helps the employees remember to watch their language when dealing with others.

Remember when you were young and felt that adults didn't understand or care about your wants or needs? Well, your **younger customers** probably feel the same way and will remember how you treat them. Their memories could prompt them to take their business elsewhere if their experience with you is negative. If you are older, you may be tempted to talk down to them or be flippant. Don't give in to the temptation. Keep in mind that they are customers. If they feel unwelcome, they will take their business and money elsewhere, and they will tell their friends of the poor treatment they received. Just as with older customers, avoid demeaning language and condescending forms of address (*kid*, *sonny*, *sweetie*, or *sugar*).

An additional point to remember when dealing with younger customers is that they may not have the product knowledge and sophistication in communicating that older customers do. You can decrease confusion and increase communication effectiveness by using words that are appropriate for their age group and by taking the time to explain and/or demonstrate technical points. Keep it simple without being patronizing.

6 Communicating With Diverse Customers

Concept: Many considerations need to be taken into account when you are delivering service to a diverse customer base. Appropriate language usage is a meaningful tool that you should master for good customer service.

Given all this diversity, you must be wondering how to provide service that is acceptable to all of these customer groups. As you've seen, there are many considerations in delivering service to a diverse customer base. Therefore, consider the following basic guidelines for communicating; these tips are appropriate for dealing with all types of customers.

Be Careful With Your Remarks and Jokes

Comments that focus on any aspect of diversity (religion, sexual preference, weight, hair color, age) can be offensive and should not be made. Also, humor does not cross cultural boundaries well. Each culture has a different interpretation of what is humorous and socially acceptable.

Make Sure That Your Language Is "Inclusive"

When speaking, address or refer to the people from various groups that are present. If you are addressing a group of eight men and one woman, using the term *guys* or *fellows* excludes the woman and thus is not **inclusive**.

Respect Personal Preferences When Addressing People

As you read earlier, don't assume familiarity when addressing others. (Don't call someone by her or his first name unless he or she gives permission.) Don't use *Ms.* if a female customer prefers another form of address. Also, avoid terms such as *honey, sugar,* and *sweetheart* or other overly familiar language.

Use General Terms

Instead of singling a customer out or focusing on exceptions in a group, describe people in general terms. That is, instead of referring to someone as a *female supervisor, black salesperson,* or *disabled administrative assistant,* say *supervisor, salesperson,* or *administrative assistant.*

Recognize the Impact of Words

Keep in mind that certain words have a negative connotation and could insult or offend. Even if you do not intend to offend, the customer's perception is the deciding factor of your actions. For example, using the terms *handicapped* or *crippled, boy, girl, queer,* or *idiot* may conjure up a negative image to some groups or individuals. Using such terminology can also reflect negatively upon you and your organization.

Use Care With Nonverbal Cues

The nonverbal cues that you are familiar with may carry different meanings in other cultures. Be careful when you use symbols or gestures if you are not certain how your customer will receive them. Figure 8.7 lists some cues that are common in Western cultures but have negative meanings in other cultures.

Cultural Awareness Tips for Service Providers

The challenge is that, in a multicultural world, there has been a constant blending of people and heritage. The result is that it is virtually impossible to find terms or names to accurately describe all people. This is the struggle that the U.S. Census Bureau has each time it tries to accurately categorize the people residing in the United States. In 2000, for the first time since taking the census, respondents were allowed to choose more than one descriptor for their ethnic background.

   While it is dangerous to generalize and lump people and cultures together when interacting with someone, there are some general characteristics and common values shared by many people from various countries and cultural backgrounds. By keeping these similarities in mind when interacting with your customers you can enhance the opportunities of successful service. Remember that the characteristics provided in this section are only general guidelines and *do not* apply to all members of the groups identified. It is *always* better to ask customers their preference and observe their reactions when you need to know something about them. If you note annoyance or discomfort during a conversation, do a perception check to see if you have said or done something to cause the reaction or if there is another reason. Also, keep in mind that exposure to other cultures (**acculturation**) will impact what a person believes and how he or she acts. For example, a second- or third-generation Asian American in the United States may relate more closely to Western values than those of his or her native heritage.

   For purposes of this book, the following are definitions of the cultural groups described in this section.

FIGURE 8.7
Nonverbal Cue Meanings

The following are symbols and gestures that are commonly used in the United States but have different—and negative or offensive—meanings in other parts of the world:

American Gesture or Symbol	Meaning in Other Cultures	Country
Beckoning by curling and uncurling index finger[1,2]	Used for calling animals or ladies of the evening	Hong Kong, Australia, Indonesia, Yugoslavia, Malaysia
V for victory sign (with palm facing you)[1,2]	Rude gesture	England
Sole of foot pointed toward a person [1,3]	You are lowly (the sole is lowest part of the body and contacts the ground)	Thailand, Saudi Arabia, Singapore, Egypt
"Halt" gesture with palm and extended fingers thrust toward someone[1,2,3]	Rude epithet	Greece
Thumb up (fingers curled) indicating *okay, good going,* or *everything is fine*[1,3]	The number 5 Rude gesture	Japan Nigeria, Australia
Thumb and forefinger forming an O, meaning *okay*[1,3]	Zero or worthless Money Rude gesture	France Japan Brazil, Malta, Greece, Tunisia, Turkey, Italy, Paraguay, Russia
Waving good-bye with fingers extended, palm down, and moving the fingers up and down toward yourself[1,3]	Come here	Parts of Europe, Myanmar, Colombia, Peru
Patting the head of a child	Insult, inviting evil spirits	Parts of the Far East
Using red ink for documents	Death; offensive	Parts of Korea, Mexico, and China
Passing things with left hand (especially food)	Socially unacceptable	India, Pakistan

[1]R. Axtell, *Gestures: The Do's and Taboos of Body Language Around the World,* John Wiley and Sons, N.Y., 1991.
[2]A. Wolfgang, *Everybody's Guide to People Watching,* International Press, Yarmouth, Mass., 1995.
[3]D. Morris, *Bodytalk, The Meaning of Human Gestures,* Crown Trade Paperback, N.Y., 1994.

Hispanic, Latino, or Chicano includes groups that trace their origins or background to Spain, Latin America, or Mexico. *Note:* The U.S. Census Bureau uses the term *Hispanic* for all these groups.

African American or black includes groups that trace their origins or background to Africa (sub-Saharan area). The descriptive term *African American* is often used in the United States while *black* is often used by people in Latin America or the Caribbean.

Asians or Asian Americans includes groups that trace their origins or background to the Asian continent or to the Pacific Islands (e.g., China, Korea, Japan, or Samoa).

Native American includes groups that trace their origins or background to the continents of America.

European American, Anglo American, or white includes groups that trace their origins or background to Europe, other than Spanish.

Hispanic/Latino/Chicano Cultures

Different terms are assigned to people of Hispanic background based on the region of the world from which they originate. Each country has its own unique culture; however, because of a common heritage, they share a number of general characteristics and values. The following are some things to keep in mind when serving people from this group:

- Family and group loyalty is an important concept in many Hispanic cultures. Long-term relationships are valued.
- Women are often admired and respected, especially mothers.
- Respect for elders and authority (e.g., teachers) is important. Direct eye contact is often avoided when talking with people who are older or of higher status as a show of respect. Additionally, many people often look away rather than make direct eye contact while listening.
- Time is viewed as flexible and the concept of hurrying to meet a deadline at the expense of disregarding others and what someone values can cause problems.
- Generally, people live in the moment and want to see what happens next. Also, many take a more casual, spontaneous and impulsive approach to life. This can influence buying decisions.
- Religious affiliations often strong.
- Courtesy (use of diplomacy and tact), dignity, honor, and loyalty are valued in business as well as in family affairs.
- Men tend to be more assertive than women in business although women are often more assertive and men are more aggressive in their communication approach.
- Direct argument or contradiction are typically viewed as rude and disrespectful.
- Emotions readily displayed (e.g., crying, laughing, touching, and smiling).
- Material objects are often viewed as a necessity versus an end in themselves.
- Many Hispanics are in tune with their environment. They tend to touch, smell, feel, taste, and come in close proximity with objects or people that have their attention.

African-American/Black Cultures

Depending on the country of origin and personal background, there will be differences among individuals; however, there are some general characteristics shared by many African Americans or black people.

- Communication is more emotional or expressive. Voice volume and inflection is often elevated.
- Focus on unity or group is strong.
- Close relationships with group and family are valued.
- Assertiveness and directness are common and valued.

- Religious affiliations are often strong.
- Direct eye contact when speaking, rather than when listening is common. This is often as a show of respect and learned at a young age. Contrarily, a prolonged glance may be viewed as sexual interest or disrespect, depending on the parties involved.
- More spatial distance when talking to others, especially strangers, is preferred.
- Touching or patting of a child's head, especially by a white person, is often viewed as condescending.
- Use of nonverbal cues are often limited (e.g., head nodding while listening).
- Use of direct questions is sometimes considered harassment. For example, asking an African-American customer who is trying to decide between two items or choices, "Can I assist in your decision making" might appear as if you are rushing them.
- Conversations between two people who know one another are typically viewed as private. Therefore, anyone who interrupts without permission is viewed as an eavesdropper and is often rebuked. For example, if two African-American customers were discussing the benefits that they recognize for an item you had shown them and you interrupted to emphasize additional benefits or features, you would likely offend them.
- When speaking to each other, conversations can get loud and animated.
- Time is viewed as flexible, not linear. Life issues may take priority over keeping appointments and many people are "present-oriented." Older African Americans tend to be more punctual and more willing to wait than their younger counterparts.
- Adoption and use of a "black" dialect or terminology by people outside the cultural group without authorization is often viewed as mocking and an insult.
- Interrupting during conversation is usually tolerated. Competition to speak is often granted to the person who is most assertive.
- Asking personal questions of a person met for the first time may be seen as improper and intrusive.
- Emotions not readily displayed by men (e.g., crying), especially among strangers.
- The term *you people* is typically seen as pejorative and racist.
- Men may wear sunglasses and hats indoors as adornments, much like jewelry might be worn by other groups.

Asian/Asian-American Cultures

Some shared values and characteristics by people with Asian heritage include:

- "Family" is important since many Asians typically value collectivism.
- Maintaining a low personal profile and working for the betterment of family or the group is important. This can sometimes be tied to face.
- In regards to group orientation, many Asians prefer terms like *we, us,* and *ours* to *I, me,* and *mine.*
- Ranks and titles are important and used.
- Face, harmony, and obligation are important elements in dealing with others. Doing things that caused someone else to be embarrassed, ridiculed, or put in a lower position can damaged a relationship with an Asian person.
- Time and the idea of hurrying to meet a deadline at the expense of disregarding others and what they value is a foreign concept.

- Religious affiliations are often strong.
- Physical contact and facial expressions are often minimal. Patting someone on the back or putting an arm around someone's shoulder in the workplace is not typically done.
- Touch between strangers (especially those of the opposite sex) is frowned upon.
- The head is often considered the residence of the soul; therefore, touching a person's head potentially places them in jeopardy or invites evil.
- Personal cleanliness is valued and expected.
- Sitting with legs crossed and the sole of feet facing someone is considered rude and insulting in a number of countries since the foot is the lowest part of the body.
- Space between individuals is often at least six inches farther than what many Westerners consider comfortable.
- Some see animated expressions or gestures as a sign of a lack of control.
- Respect and humility are key cultural values. This is often demonstrated by avoiding direct eye contact or lowering eyes when talking, especially to someone older or who is an actual or perceived superior (socially or in the workplace).
- Privacy is valued, especially among strangers. Discussions or inquiries regarding a person's occupation, income, politics, current events, controversial topics, family life, or spouse should be avoided. Any of these could potentially lead to disharmony or a loss of face.
- Trust is a crucial element in business. Before getting down to business, you will need to spend time (possibly months and numerous meetings) to establish trust before broaching negotiations or business topics.
- An indirect style of communication is often used, along with silence. For example, instead of saying "no" (which could cause someone to lose face) to a pushy salesperson, an Asian customer might agree to purchase an item. They may later regret or resent the purchase and stop doing business with an organization.
- Facial expressions are often suppressed.
- Belching after a meal is often considered a show of satisfaction.
- Some people of this group use laughter or giggling to hide embarrassment, anger, sorrow, discomfort with a situation, or displeasure. A hand is often used to cover the mouth when laughing or giggling.

European/White/Westernized Cultures

- Direct nonverbal communication prominent (e.g., eye contact, nodding while listening, sitting facing a speaker).
- Use of direct questions for personal information is permissible and often appreciated.
- Emotions are not publicly expressed (e.g., crying), especially among strangers.
- Hand gestures are prominent during communication (e.g., "A-okay" symbol).
- Touching in public between opposite sexes is viewed as rude in many countries (e.g., England, Germany, and Scandinavia).
- Spatial distance preferences tend to be wider (in northern Europe), especially among strangers.
- Sunglasses and hats are considered functional items to be worn only outside and removed when coming indoors.

- "Taking turns" in conversation dictates that one person has the floor until all of his or her points are made.
- Showing emotions during disagreements is perceived as the beginning of conflict which can escalate if left unchecked.
- Inquiring about jobs, family, and so forth, of a new customer from this group is often viewed as being friendly.
- Many cultures are past-oriented and resist change in their lives.
- Many are more individualistic in their approach to relationships or handling problems rather than relying on others.
- Long-term business relationships are often preferred over "quick sales."

Middle Eastern Cultures

- Emotion is expressed easily (e.g., smiling, laughing, crying).
- Grief or sadness are often exaggerated.
- Direct eye contact is often used to show interest and help someone understand truthfulness of another person. Failure to reciprocate is often seen as a lack of trustworthiness.
- Speaking loudly often indicates strength while a soft voice sends a message of weakness.
- Touching or passing items, especially food, with the left hand is a social insult since that is the "bathroom" hand used for toilet functions.
- In Islamic cultures, touching between genders (even handshakes) is inappropriate; however, touching (e.g., hand-holding and hugs) between the same sex is appropriate.
- Body odors are often considered normal and appropriate (e.g., breath that smells heavily of garlic or perspiration/body odor).
- Standing in close proximity is common when talking.
- Time is viewed as fluid; therefore, taking time to get to know someone and building trust are important elements in business. People and relationships are more important than a company or job.
- Honor and dignity are important personal characteristics; therefore, you should avoid expressing doubts or criticism about a person or their possessions when others are present.
- A circuitous speech pattern is common and it may take a while to "get to the point." Be patient and professional while listening.
- Changes in plans, schedules, and meetings are common.
- Giving special treatment to friends and family members is considered an obligation.
- Religious festivals and events normally supersede other events and business.
- Eating pork is forbidden by law in countries where Islam and Judaism is the primary religion.
- Islamic law frowns on profiteering, therefore product pricing should not be viewed as excessive.
- Women have a lesser role in Islamic cultures and normally do not participate in business dealings. Also, when traveling in Islamic countries they are required to dress in such a way that their arms, legs, torso, and faces are concealed. This includes foreign visitors.
- Asking a host about the health of his spouse is insulting.

Chapter Summary

Opportunities to deal with a diverse customer base will increase as the global economy expands. With continuing immigrations, an aging U.S. population, changes in values, and increased ease of mobility, the only thing certain is that the next customer you speak with *will* be different from you. Remember, however, that he or she will also be similar to you in many ways and that both of you will have a basis for discussion.

The success you have in the area of dealing with others is totally dependent on your preparation and attitude toward providing quality service. Learn as much as you can about various groups of people in order to effectively evaluate situations, determine needs, and serve all customers on an equal basis.

SERVICE IN ACTION   LensCrafters   CHAPTER 8

http://www.lenscrafters.com

In 1983, LensCrafters started a new approach to the eyewear industry. It consolidated the eye doctor, a wide selection of frames and lenses, and the lens-making laboratory together in one convenient location. With over 850 stores located through the United States, Canada, and Puerto Rico, convenient hours of operation, and the ability to craft eyewear on-site, LensCrafters became a one-stop shop for eyeglasses. Stores carry a wide variety of frames with prices clearly marked to allow customers to comparison-shop. This is something that typical eyeglass providers do not provide. Customers have responded favorably and the company has become the largest optical retailer (based on revenues) in the world.

LensCrafters stresses the service mentality in its mission, vision, and core values that emphasize extraordinary customer service and associated satisfaction. These elements are shared with all new employees to the company.

On January 1, 2000, the company unveiled a new marketing campaign, entitled "My Personal Vision Place," that focuses on the Vision, Mission, and Core Values of LensCrafters in addition to its high-quality service and products. Rather than focusing on discounts and price points as most competitors do, LensCrafters now focuses on a message that speaks to the importance and value of vision care. The strategy seems to be paying off since corporate revenues continue to grow.

Key Terms and Concepts

acculturation	elderly customers	individualistic cultures
Americans With Disabilities Act of 1990	expectations of privacy	mobility or motion impairments
attitudes	face	modesty
baby boomer	foreign-born people	monochronic
beliefs	forms of address	ownership of property
collective cultures	gender roles	Platinum Rule
concept of time	hearing disabilities	polychronic
conflict resolution style	Hispanic or Latino cultures	respect for elders
cultural diversity	inclusive	values
customers with disabilities	importance of relationships	vision disabilities
diversity		younger customers

Quick Preview Answers

1. F	5. T	9. T
2. T	6. F	10. T
3. T	7. T	11. T
4. T	8. T	12. T

Chapter Review Questions

1. What are some innate qualities or characteristics that make people unique?
2. What external or societal factors affect the way members of a group are seen or perceived?
3. What are values?
4. Do beliefs differ from values? Explain.
5. Why would some people be reluctant to make eye contact with you?
6. When dealing with customers with a disability, how can you best help them?
7. How can recognition of the cultural value of "importance of family" be helpful in customer service?
8. What are some considerations for improving communication in a diverse environment?
9. How can you effectively communicate with someone who has difficulty with the English language?
10. What are some techniques for effectively providing service to older customers?

Search It Out

Search the Internet for Diversity Information

Log on to the Internet to locate information and articles related to topics covered in this chapter. Be prepared to share what you found at your next scheduled class or session. The following are some key words you might use in your search:

> Diversity
> Cultural diversity
> Cultural values
> Beliefs
> Disabilities
> Disability advocacy
> Intercultural communication
> Intercultural dynamics
> Any country name (e.g., Australia, Canada, Sri Lanka)
> Elderly
> Generation X
> Generation Y
> Population projections

Note: A listing for additional research on specific URLs is provided on the Customer Service website at **<http://www.mhhe.com/lucas05>**.

Collaborative Learning Activity

Awareness of Diversity

To help raise your awareness related to diversity in the customer service environment, try the following activities:

1. Pair up with someone to role-play scenarios in which you are a service provider and have customers from the following groups:

An elderly person who has a hearing loss and wants directions on how to use some equipment (you choose the equipment and provide instruction).

Someone who speaks English as a second language (with a heavy accent) and needs to fill out a credit card application or some other form.

Someone with a sight impairment who wants to "see" several blouses or shirts or needs directions to another part of your store.

A 10-year-old who wants a new computer and has questions about various types, components, and how they work.

2. Interview a variety of people: from different cultures, from various age groups, with disabilities, male or female (opposite of your sex), or gay or lesbian. Find out whether they have preferences in the type of customer service they receive or in the kind of language used to refer to their group. Also, ask about ways you can better communicate with and understand them and people from their group.

3. Suggest to your supervisor, team leader, or work group peers that employees meet as a group to discuss situations in which all of you have encountered people from different cultures or groups. Exchange ideas on how to better serve such people in the future. Report the results of your efforts to your class members at the next scheduled meeting.

4. Working in teams assigned by your instructor, set up an appointment to visit a local advocacy group for the disabled or aging, or contact a national group (e.g., the National Society to Prevent Blindness, assisted-living facilities, World Federation of the Deaf, National Information Center on Deafness, National Eye Institute, National Institute on Aging). Focus on gathering information that will help you understand various disabilities and develop strategies for effectively communicating with and serving people who have disabilities. Write a brief summary of your experience and report back to your peers.

Face to Face

Dealing With Difficult People on the Phone at MedMobile

Background

MedMobile is a medical supply business located in Los Angeles, California, employing 62 full-time and 11 part-time workers. The company specializes in equipment designed to improve patient mobility (walkers, motorized carts, wheelchairs, mechanized beds and chairs). Average yearly sales are in the area of $1.5 million.

The primary client base for the company is insurance companies that pay for rehabilitation following worker accidents or injuries. Medical professionals who conduct the patient medical case file reviews and recommend treatment programs are in regular contact with the account representatives for MedMobile.

Your Role

As an account representative with MedMobile, you have been with the company for about 18 months. Your main job is to help clients determine and obtain the correct equipment needed to assist their patients. To do this, you spend hours on the phone daily and often know clients by voice. In recent months you have become extremely frustrated, almost to the point of anger. A new claims adjuster works for one of your primary account companies, TrueCare Insurance Company. His name is Abeyola Pepukayi, and he has been with TrueCare eight weeks. He has been an adjuster for a little over a year.

You just got off the phone after a lengthy conversation with Abeyola and you are agitated. For over half an hour you tried unsuccessfully to explain why you felt the equipment being ordered by Abeyola was not the best for the patient's injury, as he described it to you.

Because this isn't the first time such an encounter has taken place, you are now in your supervisor's office venting. While discussing the situation with your boss, you note the following about Abeyola:

> He doesn't listen. No matter what you say, he asks totally irrelevant questions about other equipment.
>
> He usually has no idea what you're talking about.
>
> He is rude and interrupts, often making statements such as "One moment, please. That makes no sense."
>
> You have spent hours discussing equipment design and function because he doesn't know anything about it.
>
> He spends endless amounts of time getting off track and trying to discuss other issues or topics.

After your conversation, your boss called a friend at TrueCare to see what he knew of the situation. The friend, David Helmstedter, supervises Abeyola. Apparently, Abeyola has been venting to David about you. From what David has been told:

> You are rude and abrupt and aren't very friendly. Abeyola has tried to establish a relationship, but you have ignored his efforts.
>
> Abeyola is trying hard to learn the terminology and equipment but you are unwilling to help.
>
> You speak rapidly, using a lot of technical language that you don't explain.

Critical Thinking Questions

1. What seems to be happening here? Does Abeyola have any legitimate complaints? If so, what are they?
2. What steps or process can you use to clarify understanding?
3. What cultural differences might be involved in this scenario?

PLANNING TO SERVE

CHAPTER 8

IDENTIFYING YOUR BIASES

We sometimes have biases that interfere with our interactions with others. Typically, these biases on learned behavior (something we have personally experienced or have been taught by others). By thinking of your biases and bringing them to a conscious level, you can better control or eliminate them in dealing with your customers and others.

Think about the qualities of other people or groups that you do not like or prefer to avoid. List them, along with the basis (why you believe them to be true) for each.

Customer Service via Technology

From the Frontline Interview

Ana Bertoli has worked at the McGraw-Hill Companies for the past three years. She started as a senior administrative assistant with daily internal and external customer contact by phone and e-mail and, today, is a software support coordinator. Her main contact is still e-mail and phone. Prior to coming to McGraw-Hill, Ana worked in a medical research center as a secretary for ten years. During that time, she had daily contact with patients.

**ANA BERTOLI,
Software Support
Coordinator,
*The McGraw-Hill
Companies***

1 **How have you seen technology aid service providers in delivering quality customer service? Please explain/give example(s).**

The Internet has been playing a very important role in delivering quality customer service. Technology aids providers by making them available by phone and e-mail, thus, ensuring that customers have a possible quick solution to questions and problems.

In 2004 we will be installing and using a new customer relationship management solution that will enable us to autoroute customers to the analyst most skilled for the problem. This new system will also autoretrieve voice mail and e-mail messages and route to open analysts, saving us hours of time and enabling faster responses. Additionally, we will be creating a customer self-help community on our website. This site will be searchable by common language questions and will pull from a knowledge database we create. This will give customers a quick way to get resolution to simple problems.

2 **In what ways have you seen service negatively impacted by technology? Please explain/give example(s).**

It is very challenging for the companies to comply with the advances in technology, which is changing on average every year. The changes are impacting the quality of service

Chapter Learning Objectives

After completing this chapter, you will be able to:

- Understand the extent to which customer service is facilitated by the effective use of technology.
- Use technology to enhance service delivery capabilities.
- Communicate effectively via e-mail, the Internet, and facsimile.
- Deliver quality service through effective telephone techniques.
- Recognize the impact of verbal cues during telephone conversations.
- Send and receive message via voice mail.

and it is requiring most companies to make a reasonable investment to get skilled, motivated, and enthusiastic employees to perform specific customer-related functions.

Technology is only as good as what you put into it. Most negative issues arise based upon poor data in the system. There is always the issue of systems going down unexpectedly. When this happens, there needs to be a manual backup system which service representatives are trained to use. This training requires more time and can be another challenge.

3 What trends have you seen related to changing service technology? Please explain/give example(s).

Technology brings many benefits allowing companies to serve more customers in a shorter period of time. With the technology improving constantly, speed will be the main drive. More and more companies are moving to customer self-help options. By letting customers help themselves, analysts can be reserved for more complex issues. It also helps companies service more people at one time. We do have multiple contact points for customers, like mail, phone, fax, e-mail, and websites as we are in a mobile world.

One concern that I have is related to the personal contact that today is provided via customer service to many customers. Maybe in the future the contact will not be necessary, but time will tell us.

4 What advice can you offer for new service representatives?

If you like computers, technology, and to help others, you will have a great time in the customer service field. You need to be okay with yourself and others to be successful. You also need to care about people, smile, listen, speak slowly, want to ask questions, and have a high desire to work with others. Otherwise, the job can be very frustrating.

Critical Thinking

In what ways have you experienced some of the issues described by Ana as a customer? As a service provider? Do you believe that service is improved or hurt by the use of technology? Explain.

Quick Preview

Before reviewing the chapter content, respond to the following questions by placing a "T" for true or an "F" for false on the rules. Use any questions you miss as a checklist of material to which you will pay particular attention as you read through the chapter. For those you get right, congratulate yourself, but review the sections they address in order to learn additional details about the topic.

_____ 1. According to the U.S. Department of Commerce, over 94 percent of U.S. homes have telephones.

_____ 2. *E-commerce* is a term that means that the commerce of the United States is in excellent condition.

_____ 3. A customer service representative might also have one of the following job titles: associate, sales representative, consumer affairs counselor, consultant, technical service representative, operator, account executive, attendant, or engineer.

_____ 4. The acronym TTY is used by call center staff members to indicate that something is *to* be *done* *today.*

_____ 5. Many organizations think of technology as a way to reduce staff and save money.

_____ 6. One way to improve your image over the telephone is to continually evaluate your speech.

_____ 7. Jargon, slang, and colloquialisms can distort message meaning.

_____ 8. Adjusting your rate of speech to mirror a customer's rate can aid comprehension.

_____ 9. Quoting policy is one way to ensure that customers understand why you can't give them what they want.

_____ 10. To ensure that accurate communication has taken place, you should summarize key points at the end of a telephone conversation.

_____ 11. Blind transfers are effective if you don't take too much time explaining who is calling.

_____ 12. Chewing food and gum, drinking, or talking to others while on the telephone can be distracting and should be avoided.

_____ 13. Using voice mail to answer calls is an effective way to avoid interruptions while you are speaking to a customer.

_____ 14. Planning calls and the information you will leave is an effective way to avoid telephone tag.

Answers to Quick Preview can be found at the end of the chapter.

1 The Increasing Role of Technology in Customer Service

Concept: Customer service is a 24/7 responsibility, and technology can assist in making it effective.

To say that technology has permeated almost every aspect of life in most developed countries would be an understatement. Computers are continually becoming smaller, more complex, and powerful; we have only started to see the impact

FIGURE 9.1   Estimated Wireless Subscribers: June 1985 to June 2003

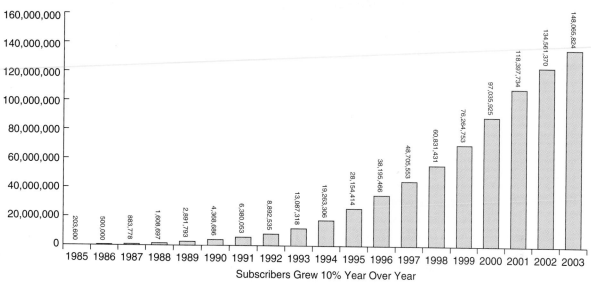

Subscribers Grew 10% Year Over Year

Source: Cellular Telecommunications Industry Association Semi-Annual Wireless Industry Survey. Used with permission of CTIA.

that technology will have on shaping the future. Most businesses in the United States are technologically dependent in some form. Calculators, cash registers, maintenance equipment, telephones, radios, cellular phones, pagers, computer systems, and handheld personal planners are typical examples of technology that we rely upon. We have become a 24/7 society (we access technology 24 hours a day, 7 days a week) and can communicate at any time and any place. Roughly two-thirds (69 percent) of American adults owned a cellular phone in 2002 according to Scarborough Research. That is up 29 percent from 1999. According to the Cellular Telecommunications Industry Association, nearly 150 million people subscribe to wireless telephone service[1] (Figure 9.1). By the year 2010, it is projected that 70 percent of the population will be using wireless devices. This is in addition to the more than 94 percent of U.S. households that have telephones.[2] A result is that more people are accessing telephone-related customer service. There are about 100,000 **call centers** in the United States, with over 3 million agents to answer those calls and serve the people who have access to technology.

This means that companies that are not prepared to meet the future will lose business as customers migrate to providers that are better prepared. With access to products and services at almost any time through telephones, e-mail, facsimile machines, and the Internet, customers are in a power position as never before. They will likely use alternative resources considering the fact that the United States has enjoyed the lowest unemployment rate in almost two decades. Thus, fewer service providers are available to fill jobs. That translates to longer wait times and increased frustration that many customers will simply not accept.

[1]Cellular Telecommunications Industry Association.

[2]U.S. Department of Commerce, National Telecommunications and Information Administration.

2 The Call Center or Help Desk

Concept: Electronic commerce is a new and powerful way to employ technology to conduct business.

The growing trend to reduce staff and costs, while maintaining or increasing service effectiveness, necessitates employing technology in addition to people. In the past, operations that used technology were seen as labor-intensive (because of the need to maintain and operate equipment) and behind-the-scenes or "back-office" functions. They typically supplemented the frontline service providers and were not viewed as a strategic initiative related to the overall operation of the organization. With the availability of technically literate and trained employees, and a shift in expectations of customers who are capable of accessing products and services through technology, customer support through call centers is now an integral part of business. Corporate and organizational officers now recognize the potential of such operations and are pumping billions of dollars into the development, maintenance, and improvement of call center operations. Call centers or **help desks**, are more powerful and complicated than ever before. They also provide more functions than their rather ineffectual predecessors.

The influence is so significant in terms of dollars that the way that organizations do business using technology has been labeled **electronic commerce (e-commerce)**.

Even with all the technological advances, one thing remains clear: customers still appreciate old-fashioned personalized customer service. Successful service organizations realize that each customer is unique. Some people are *high touch* while others are *low touch*, therefore, offering a variety of service delivery systems is smart business. Whether service is delivered face-to-face or via technology, there is often no substitute for a dedicated, knowledgeable, and well-trained employee. You and your peers are the lifeline of your organization.

Types of Technology

Technology is advancing at such a rapid rate that the typical organization and its employees are unable to cope with the changes. Previously when a customer had a question or needed assistance, he or she would call an 800 number. When the call arrived at the call center, a customer service representative would answer, and after obtaining various information, might be able to handle the customer's situation.

Today, the representatives have a vast amount of technology at their disposal. Some of the typical systems found in call centers nowadays are described in the following sections.

Automatic Call Distribution (ACD) System

An **automatic call distribution (ACD) system** routes incoming calls to the next available agent when lines are busy. This is the typical system. A recording may cue you to select a series of numbers on the phone to get to certain people or information.

Automatic Number Identification (ANI)

Automatic number identification, or **ANI** (pronounced "Annie"), is a form of caller ID similar to home telephones. The system allows customers to be identified and their call directed appropriately before an agent talks to them. For example, a customer could be routed to a special agent who is multilingual or who has specialized product or service knowledge. This saves time for the agent, for the customer's telephone number does not have to be keyed in and the agent can identify the

customer's geographic location before speaking with him or her. The agent might also be able to access information on a computer screen about the customer's history with the organization. Also, calls can be routed to the same agent who most recently handled a specific caller. Finally, with ANI, calls can be routed to the service center closest to the customer's home.

Electronic Mail (E-Mail)

This form of technology provides an inexpensive, rapid way of communicating with customers in writing worldwide. **Electronic mail (e-mail)** allows customers to access information via telephone and then, through prompting (using the telephone keypad), have the information delivered to them via e-mail. A big advantage of e-mail is that you can write a single message and have it delivered to hundreds of people worldwide in a matter of minutes at little or no cost.

Facsimile (Fax) Machine

A **facsimile (fax) machine** allows graphics and text messages to be transported as electronic signals via telephone lines or from a personal computer equipped with a modem. Information can be sent anywhere in the world in minutes, or a customer can make a call, key in a code number, and have information delivered to his or her fax machine or computer without ever speaking to a person (**fax-on-demand** system).

Internet Call Back

An **Internet call-back** system allows someone browsing the Internet to click on words or phrases (e.g., *Call me*), enter his or her phone number, and continue browsing. This triggers the predictive dialing system (discussed later in this chapter) and assigns an agent to handle the call when it rings at the customer's end.

Internet Telephony

Internet telephony allows users to have voice communications over the Internet. Although widely discussed in the industry, call center Internet telephony is in its infancy, lacks standards, and is not currently embraced by consumers.

Interactive Voice Response (IVR) or Voice Response Unit (VRU)

An **interactive voice response (IVR) system** or a **voice response unit (VRU)** allows customers to call in 24 hours a day, 7 days a week, even when customer service representatives are not available. By keying in a series of numbers on the phone, customers can get information or answers to questions. Such systems also ensure consistency of information. Banks and credit card companies use such systems to allow customers to access account information.

Media Blending

Media blending allows agents to communicate with a customer over a telephone line at the same time information is displayed over the Internet to the customer. As with Internet telephony, this technology has not yet been taken to its fullest potential.

Online Information Fulfillment System

An **online information fulfillment system** allows customers to go to the World Wide Web, access an organization's website, and click on desired information. This is one of the fastest-growing customer service technologies. Every competitive business will eventually use this system so that customers can get information and place orders.

Predictive Dialing System

A **predictive dialing system** automatically places outgoing calls and delivers incoming calls to the next available agent. This system is often used in outbound (telemarketing) operations. Because of numerous abuses, the government is continually restricting its use.

Screen Pop-Ups

Screen pop-ups are used in conjunction with ANI and IVR systems to identify callers. As a call is received and dispatched to an agent, the system provides information about the caller that "pops" onto the agent's screen before he or she answers the telephone (e.g., order information, membership data, service history, contact history).

Teletype Systems (TTY)

Partly because of the passage of the 1990 Americans With Disabilities Act, which required that telecommunication services be available to people with disabilities, organizations now have the technology to assist customers who have hearing and speech impairments. By using a **teletype system (TTY)**—a typewriter-type device for sending messages back and forth over telephone lines—a person who has a hearing or speech impairment can contact someone who is using a standard telephone. The sender and the receiver type their messages using the TTY. To do this, the sender or receiver can go through an operator-assisted relay service provided by local and long-distance telephone companies for example, 1-800-855-1155 (AT&T) and 1-800-855-4000 (Sprint), to reach companies and individuals who do not have TTY receiving technology, or the user can get in touch directly with companies that have TTYs. The service is free of charge. Operators can help first-time hearing users understand the rules in using TTY. Also, local speech and hearing centers can often provide training on the use of TTY in a call center environment.

The federal government has a similar service (Federal Information Relay Service, or FIRS) for individuals who wish to conduct business with any branch of the federal government nationwide.

Video

For customers and call centers equipped with video camera-computer hookups, this evolving technology allows customers and agents to interact via the computer. Like the interactive video kiosks discussed earlier in this book, this technology allows customers and agents to see one another during their interactions. Because of privacy concerns or preference, some software allows customers to block their image, yet they still see the agent to whom they are speaking.

Voice Recognition

This relative newcomer to the market is advancing rapidly. The technology is incorporated into a call center's voice response system. It is typically used by individuals to dictate data directly into a computer, which then converts the spoken words into text. There are potential applications of voice-recognition systems for all call centers. Some companies are recording customers' voices (passwords and phrases) as a means of identification so that customers can gain access to their accounts. With other applications agents speak into a computer, rather than typing data, and people who have disabilities can obtain data from their accounts by speaking into the computer.

Advantages and Disadvantages of Technology

Like anything else related to customer service, technology offers advantages and disadvantages. The following sections briefly review some of the issues resulting from the use of technology.

Organizational Issues

Distinct advantages accrue to organizations that use technology. Through the use of computers, software, and various telecommunication devices, a company can extend its presence without physically establishing a business site and without adding staff. Simply by setting up a website, organizations can become known and develop a worldwide customer base. Information and services can be provided on demand to customers. Often, many customers can be served simultaneously through the telephone, fax, and so on.

The challenge for organizations is to have well-maintained, state-of-the-art equipment and qualified, competent people to operate it. In a low unemployment era, this can be a challenge and can result in disgruntled customers who have to wait on hold for service until an agent is available to help them.

Staying on top of competition with technology is an expensive venture. New and upgraded software and hardware appear almost every day. If a company is using systems that are six months old, these systems are on their way to becoming obsolete. Also, new technology typically brings with it a need to train or retrain staff. The end result is that employees have to be taken away from their jobs for training.

Employee Issues

Technology brings many benefits to employees. The greatest benefit is that it frees them from mundane tasks such as taking information and mailing out forms, information, or other materials. These tasks can be done by using fax-on-demand,

IVR, or online fulfillment systems. Technology also allows employees to serve more people in a shorter period of time—and to do it better.

The downside for employees is that many organizations see technology as a way to reduce staff costs and overhead related to employees, and they therefore eliminate positions. Moreover, as mentioned before, new technology requires new training and skills. Some people have difficulty using technology and are not able to master it. This in turn can lead to reassignment or dismissal. To avoid such negative outcomes, you and your peers should continually work to stay abreast of technology trends by checking the Internet or taking refresher courses through your organization's training department or local community resources.

Another problem created is an increase in stress levels of both employee and customer. This arises from the increased pace of business and daily life, from the need for employees to keep up to date with technology, and so on. Stress accounts for some of the high turnover rate in call center staff and for customer defection. But, it doesn't necessarily have to be that way. Read Chapter 10 carefully for tips on controlling and reducing stress.

Customer Issues

From a customer standpoint, technology can be a blessing. From the comfort and convenience of a home, office, car, or anywhere a customer may have a telephone or laptop computer, he or she can access products and services. More people than ever have access to the Internet and computers (Figure 9.2). Technologies allow a customer to get information, order products, have questions about billing or other matters answered, and access virtually anything she or he wants on the World Wide Web.

However, this convenience comes with a cost to customers, just as it does for organizations. To have the latest gadgets is costly in terms of time and money. For example, when a customer calls an 800 or 888 support number, or must pay for a call to a support center, it is not unusual for the customer to wait on hold for the next available agent. Also, technology does not always work as it is designed to. For example, a website might not provide clear instructions about how to enter an account number or how to get a password. Even if a customer follows the instructions exactly, he or she might repeatedly get a frustrating error message instruc-

FIGURE 9.2
Percent of U.S. Households With a Computer and Internet Access: 1994, 1997, 1998, 2000

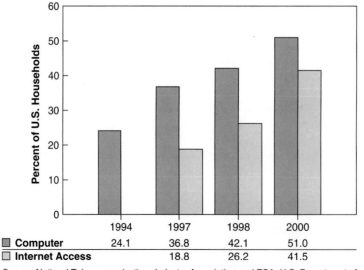

	1994	1997	1998	2000
■ Computer	24.1	36.8	42.1	51.0
□ Internet Access		18.8	26.2	41.5

Source: National Telecommunications Industry Association and ESA, U.S. Department of Commerce, using U.S. Bureau of Census current population survey supplements.

ting him or her to reenter the data. At some point, the customer will simply give up and go to another website. Another example would be to get caught in "voice mail jail." In this situation the customer follows the instructions, pressing the appropriate phone keys to get to a representative, only to find that the representative has forwarded his or her calls to another voice mail box. Eventually the instructions lead the customer back to the first message.

Additional Issues

Just as with any system, there are people who will take advantage of it. Technology, especially the Internet, has spawned a new era of fraud and manipulation. This is a major concern for consumers and can create many challenges for you and your peers when you work in a call center. One of the biggest problems you must deal with is customers' fear of fraud and violation of privacy. According to the National Fraud Information Center, a division of the National Consumers League in Washington, D.C., the number of Internet fraud complaints has risen over 600 percent since 1997.

Informed customers go to great lengths to protect credit card, merchant account, and social security numbers, addresses, and personal data (e.g., arrest records, medical history, and family data). Many news stories have warned of criminal activity associated with technology. The result is that customers, especially those who are technically naive, have a level of distrust and paranoia related to giving information via the Internet. This is why many websites involved in e-commerce offer the option of calling an 800 number instead of entering credit card and other personal information into an Internet order form. If you, as a customer service provider, encounter a lot of this type of reluctance, notify your supervisor. Some systemic issues may be adding to your customers' fears. Helping identify these issues and dealing with them can make life easier for you and your customers while helping the organization improve the quality of service delivered.

One thing to remember is that a customer's reluctance to provide you with information is not necessarily a reflection on you or your service-providing peers; it is based more on a distrust in the system. Figure 9.3 lists some strategies you can use to help reduce customer fears related to communicating via technology.

3   Technology Etiquette and Strategies

Concept: Using technology ethically and with correct etiquette is important.

As with any other interaction with people, you should be aware of some basic dos and don'ts related to using technology to interact with and serve your customers. Failure to observe some commonsense rules can cause loss of a customer.

E-Mail

The e-mail system was designed as an inexpensive, quick way of communicating via the World Wide Web. E-mail was not designed to replace formal written correspondence. E-mail has its own set of guidelines for effective usage to ensure that you do not offend or otherwise create problems when dealing with customers via e-mail. Here are some e-mail tips to remember, as well as some etiquette for effective usage.

- *Use abbreviations and initials.* Since e-mail is an informal means of communicating, using acronyms and other short forms or abbreviations (e.g., USA versus United States of America) works fine in some cases. Just be sure that your

FIGURE 9.3
Reducing Customer Fears About Technology

Avoiding customer concerns is often as simple as communicating effectively. Try some of the following approaches to help reassure your customers about the security of technology:

- Emphasize the organization's policy on security and service (e.g., if customers voice concerns about providing a credit card number over the phone, you might respond with "This is not a problem. You can either fax or mail the information to us.").
- Stress participation in consumer watchdog or community organizations (e.g., Better Business Bureau or Chamber of Commerce).
- Ask for only pertinent information.
- Answer questions quickly and openly (e.g., if a customer asks why you need certain information, respond in terms of customer service, e.g., "We need that information to ensure that we credit the right account.").
- Explain why you need information (e.g., "To verify your account information, could I please have the last four digits of your social security number or your account password?").
- Inform customers of security devices that are in place to protect information.
- Avoid asking for personal and account information when possible.
- Offer other options for data submission, if they are available.
- When using the telephone, smile and sound approachable in order to establish rapport (customers can "hear" a smile over the telephone).
- Listen carefully for voice tones that indicate hesitancy or uncertainty and respond appropriately (e.g., "You sound a bit hesitant about giving that information, Mr. Hopkins. Let me assure you that nothing will be processed until we have actually shipped your order.").
- Communicate in short, clear, and concise terms and sentences. Also, avoid technical or "legal" language that might confuse or frustrate the customer.

FIGURE 9.4
Common Abbreviations

LOL	Lots of luck	ROTFL	Rolling on the floor laughing
BCNU	Be seeing you	TTFN	Ta ta for now
FYI	For your information	TTYL	Talk to you later
IMHO	In my humble opinion	BTW	By the way
FWIW	For what it's worth	ASAP	As soon as possible

receiver knows what the letters stand for; otherwise miscommunication could occur. Figure 9.4 lists some common abbreviations employed by e-mail users who typically know one another and e-mail one another frequently (e.g., internal customers). When communicating with external customers, you may want to use abbreviations sparingly or avoid them altogether in order to prevent confusion, communication breakdown, and the perception that you are unprofessional.

- *Proofread and spell-check before sending a message.* Checking your message before sending an e-mail may help prevent damage to your professional image. This is especially true when writing customers, for you represent your organization. Poor grammar, syntax, spelling, and usage can paint a poor picture of your professionalism.
- *Think before writing.* This is especially important if you are answering an e-mail when you are upset or emotional. Take time to cool off before responding to a negative message (An insulting or provocative e-mail message is called a *flame*.)

or when you are angry. Remember that once you send an e-mail, you cannot take back your words. Your relationship with your receiver is at stake.

- *Use short, concise sentences.* The average person will not read lengthy messages sent by e-mail. Scrolling up and down pages of text is time-consuming and frustrating. Therefore, put your question or key idea in the first sentence or paragraph. Keep your sentences short and use new paragraphs often, for easier reading. A good rule of thumb is that if the entire message does not fit on a single viewing screen, consider whether another means of communication is more appropriate. An option would be to use the attachment feature so that lengthy documents can be printed out.

- *Use both upper- and lowercase letters.* With e-mail, writing a sentence or message in all-capital letters is like shouting at a person and could offend or cause relationship problems.

- *Be careful with punctuation.* As with all-capital letters, you should use caution with punctuation marks, especially exclamation points, which can cause offense because, like all-capital letters, they indicate strong emotion.

- *Use e-mail only for informal correspondence.* Do not use e-mail when a more formal format is appropriate. For example, it would be inappropriate to send a cancellation notice via e-mail. The receiver might think that the matter is not significant enough to warrant your organization's buying a stamp to mail a letter. However, this caution does not mean that you should not attach letters or other documents to an e-mail. Just consider the impact on the recipient.

  Another important thing to remember about e-mail is that it is sometimes unreliable. Many people do not check their e-mail regularly, computer systems fail, and individuals often change service providers without notifying you. If your message is critical and delivery is time-sensitive, choose another method (e.g., a telephone call or express mail). In some cases, e-mail that is not delivered is not returned to the sender, so you may not know why the recipient did not respond.

- *Use organization e-mail for business only.* Many companies have policies prohibiting sending personal e-mail via their system. Some companies have started to monitor outgoing messages. Avoid violating your company's policy on this. Remember, too, that while you are sending personal messages, you are wasting productive time and your customers may be waiting.

- *Use care in the type of information you send.* Avoid sending personal information (e.g., account numbers, personal data) or proprietary information via e-mail. Unless you have security software that will decode and mask the information, hackers or others who do not have a right or need to know such information can gain access to it. A good rule of thumb is to never send anything by e-mail that you would not want to see in tomorrow's newspaper.

- *Use blind courtesy copies (BCCs) sparingly.* Most e-mail systems allow you to send a copy to someone without the original addressee knowing it (a blind courtesy copy, or bcc). If the recipient becomes aware of the bcc, your actions might be viewed as suspicious, and your motives brought into question. They might view your actions as an attempt to hide something from them. Thus, a relationship breakdown could occur if the original recipient discovers the existence of the bcc or if the recipient of the bcc misuses the information.

- *Copy only necessary people.* Nowadays, most people are overloaded with work and do not have the time to read every e-mail. If someone does not need to see a message, do not send them a copy with the "reply to all" function available in e-mail programs.

FIGURE 9.5
Some Emoticons

:-)	Happy	:-}	Embarrassment or sarcasm
:-(	Sad	:-D	Big grin or laugh
;-)	Flirting or wink	<:-)	Stupid question (dunce cap)
0 <> /\	Defiant or determined	0:-)	Angel or saint
:-0	Yelling or surprise	>:-)	Devil
:-x	Lips are sealed	:~/	Really confused

- *Get permission to send advertisements or promotional materials.* As mentioned earlier, people have little time or patience to read lengthy e-mail messages, especially from someone trying to promote or sell them something. This is viewed the same way you probably think of unsolicited junk mail or telemarketing calls at home.

- *Be cautious in using emoticons.* **Emoticons** (for *emot*ional *icons*) are the faces created through the use of computer keyboard characters. Many people believe that their use in business correspondence is inappropriate and too informal. Also, since humor is a matter of personal point of view, these symbols might be misinterpreted and confusing. This is especially true when you are corresponding with someone from a different culture. Figure 9.5 shows examples of emoticons.

- *Fill in your address line last.* This is a safety mechanism to ensure that you take the time to read and think about your message before you send the e-mail. The message cannot be transmitted until you address it. You will have one last chance to think about the impact of the message on the recipient.

Facsimile

As with any other form of communication, there are certain dos and don'ts to abide by when using a fax machine to transmit messages. Failing to adhere to these simple guidelines can cause frustration, anger, and a breakdown in the relationships between you and your customers or others to whom you send messages.

- *Be considerate of your receiver.* If you plan to send a multipage document to your customer, telephone in advance to make sure that it is okay to send it. This is especially true if you will be using a business number during the workday or if there is only one line for the telephone and fax machine. It is frustrating and irritating to customers when a fax is tied up because large documents are being transmitted. If you must send a large document, try to do so before or after working hours (i.e., before or after 9 A.M. to 5 P.M.). Also, keep in mind geographic time differences. Following these tips can also help maintain good relationships with coworkers who may depend on the fax machine to conduct business with their customers.

- *Limit graphics.* Graphic images that are not needed to clarify written text waste the receiver's printer cartridge ink, tie up the machine unduly, and can irritate your receiver. Therefore, delete any unnecessary graphics, including your corporate logo on a cover sheet if it is heavily colored and requires a lot of ink to print. (If appropriate, create a special outline image of your logo for your fax cover sheets. See sample in Figure 9.6.)

LEADERSHIP INITIATIVE 9.1

Supervisors should create, communicate, and administer prudent policies that provide logical and customer-focused guidelines for technology usage by employees. Such proce- dures can reduce the chances of misuse and misunderstandings while helping ensure that employees are available, and can effectively serve customers.

FIGURE 9.6
Sample Fax Cover Sheet

Creative

　　Presentation

　　　　Resources, Inc.

P.O. Box 180487 Casselberry, FL 32718-0487

(407)695-5535/(800)308-0399 FAX (407)695-7447 email: blucas@presentationresources.net

Date:　　　　　　　　　　　　　　　　　　　　**#Pages (Including cover)**
To:
From: Bob Lucas, President
Re:

- *Limit correspondence recipients.* As with e-mail and memorandums, limit the recipients of your messages. If they do not have a need to know, do not send them messages. Check your broadcast mailing list (a list of people who will receive all messages, often programmed into a computer) to ensure that it is limited to people who "have a need to know." This is also important from the standpoint of confidentiality. If the information you are sending is proprietary or sensitive in any way, think about who will receive it. Do not forget that unless the document is going directly to someone's computer fax modem, it may be lying in a stack of other incoming messages and accessible by people other than your intended recipient.

4 The Telephone in Customer Service

Concept: The telephone is the second most important link in customer service.

Not all service via technology, and specifically the telephone, is delivered from a call center. Although many small- and medium-sized organizations have dedicated customer service professionals to staff their telephones, others do not. In the latter cases, the responsibility for answering the telephone and providing service falls on anyone who is available and hears the telephone ring (e.g., administrative assistant, salesperson, driver, partner, owner, CEO). Remember that in order to provide quality customer service, everyone in the organization has to take ownership for customer satisfaction.

Modern businesses rely heavily on the use of telephones to conduct day-to-day operations and communicate with internal as well as external customers. Effective use of the telephone saves employee time and effort. Employees no longer have to

Telephones have changed the way that organizations do business. *How have telephones impacted your job?*

take time to physically travel to another location to interact with customers and vendors. By simply lifting the telephone receiver and dialing a number, you are almost instantaneously transported anywhere in the world. And with the use of the fax and computer modem, documents and information can also be sent in minutes to someone thousands of miles away—even during nonbusiness hours.

With these tools, more businesses are setting up inbound (e.g., order taking, customer service, information sources) and outbound (e.g., telemarketing sales, customer service, customer surveys) telephone staffs. Through these groups of trained specialists, companies can expand their customer contact and be more likely to accomplish total customer satisfaction.

Advantages of Telephone Customer Service

Even though there are some disadvantages to telephone communication (for example, lack of face-to-face contact with the customer), there are many advantages. Some of the advantages are discussed in the following sections.

- *Convenience.* Sales, information exchange, money collection, customer satisfaction surveys, and complaint handling are only a few of the many tasks that can be effectively handled using the telephone and related equipment. If a quick answer is needed, the telephone can provide it without the need to travel and meet with someone face-to-face or to endure the delays caused by the mail.
- *Ease of communication.* Although some countries have more advanced telephone systems and capabilities than others, you can call someone in nearly any country in the world. And, with advances in cellular phone technology, even mobile phones have international communication capability.
- *Economy.* Face-to-face visits or sales calls are expensive and can be reduced or eliminated by making contacts over the telephone as opposed to traveling to a customer's location. With competitive rates offered by many telephone companies since the deregulation of the telecommunication industry years ago, companies and customers have many options for calling plans. For example, customers can purchase a calling card and use it from any telephone. All of this makes accessing customer services a simple and relatively inexpensive task, especially when combined with the other technology discussed in this chapter.
- *Efficiency.* You and your customer can interact without being delayed by writing and responding. Telephone usage is so simple that it is taught to kindergarten and grade school children.

Communication Skills for Success

In Chapters 3 to 5, you read about the skills you need in face-to-face customer service. The same skills apply to providing effective customer service over the telephone, especially the use of vocal quality and listening skills. Your customer cannot communicate with or understand you if she or he doesn't accurately receive your message. To reduce the chances of message failure, think about the communication techniques discussed below.

- *Speak clearly.* By pronouncing words clearly and correctly, you increase the chances that your customer will accurately receive your intended message. Failure to use good diction could decrease a customer's comprehension of your message and be interpreted as a sign that you are lazy, unprofessional, or lack intelligence and/or education. If you are unsure how to improve your diction, review Chapter 3.

- *Limit jargon, slang, and colloquialisms.* Technical jargon (terms related to technology, an industry, a specific organization, or a job), slang (informal words used to make a message more colorful; e.g., *whoopee, blooper, groovy*), and colloquialisms (regional phrases or words such as, "fair to middling," "if the good Lord's willing and the creek don't rise," or "faster than a New York minute") can distort your message and detract from your ability to communicate effectively. This is especially true when your recipient speaks English as a second language (see Chapter 8 for more information on this topic). By using words or phrases unfamiliar to the customer, you draw the customer's attention away from listening to your message. This is because, when people encounter a word or phrase that is unfamiliar, they tend to stop and reflect on that word or phrase. When this occurs, the next part of the message is missed while the mind tries to focus on and decipher the unfamiliar element it encountered. You must then repeat the missed portion or end up with a miscommunication.

- *Adjust your volume.* As your conversation progresses, it may become apparent that you need to speak more loudly or more softly to your customer. Obvious cues are statements from the customer, such as, "You don't have to yell" or "Could you speak up?" Or if your customer is speaking really loudly, he or she may have a hearing impairment. To find out if this is the case, you could say, "I'm sorry, Mrs. _____ , are you able to hear me clearly? I'm having trouble with loud volume on my end."

- *Speak at a rate that allows comprehension.* Depending on the person to whom you are speaking, you may find yourself having to adjust your rate of speech (covered in Chapter 3) by either speeding up or slowing down. A good rule of thumb is to mirror or match the other person's rate of speech to some extent, since he or she is probably comfortable with it. Otherwise you risk boring the customer by speaking too slowly, or losing the customer by speaking too rapidly. Be careful not to be too obvious or unnatural when doing this; otherwise, some customers may think that you're making fun of them.

- *Use voice inflection.* By using inflection and avoiding a tendency to speak in a monotone, you can help communicate your message in an interesting manner that will hold your customer's attention. The result might be saved time since your message may be received correctly the first time and you will not have to repeat it.

- *Use correct grammar.* Just as important as enunciation, good grammar helps project a positive, competent image. When you fail to use good grammar in your communication, you may be perceived as lazy or uneducated. Keep in mind that your customer forms an image of you and the company you represent simply by listening to you and the way you speak. (Grammar is covered in more detail on website **<http:/www.mhhe.com/lucas05>**).

- *Pause occasionally.* This simple yet dramatic technique can sometimes affect the course of a conversation. By pausing after you make a statement or ask a question, you give yourself time to breathe and think. You also give your customer an opportunity to reflect on what you have said or to ask questions. This practice can greatly aid in reducing tension when you are speaking with an upset customer or one who does not speak your language fluently.

- *Smile as you speak.* By smiling, you project an upbeat, warm, and sincere attitude through the phone. This can often cheer the customer, diffuse irritation, and help build rapport. A technique some telephone professionals use to remind themselves to smile when placing or answering a call is to put a small mirror or a picture of a "smiling face" in front of them or next to their telephone. This reminds them to smile as they talk.

- *Project a positive image and attitude.* All the tips related to using your voice that were presented in earlier chapters contribute to how people envision you. Customers generally do not want to hear what you cannot do for them or about the bad day you're having. They want a timely, affirmative answer to their questions or solution of their problems. Giving anything less is likely to discourage or annoy them and result in a service breakdown.

- *Wait to speak.* Many people tend to interrupt a customer to add information or ask a question. As you read in Chapter 5, this is not only rude but can cause a breakdown in communication and possibly anger the customer. If you ask a question or if the customer is speaking, allow him or her to respond or to finish speaking before interjecting your thoughts or comments.

- *Listen actively.* Just as with face-to-face communication, effective listening is a crucial telephone skill for the customer service provider. The need to focus is even more important when you are speaking on the phone since you do not have nonverbal cues or visual contact to help in message delivery or interpretation. Information on active listening was covered in Chapter 5.

   To help prevent breakdowns in communication, avoid distractions while you are on the phone. It is difficult to listen effectively when you are reading something, writing notes to yourself, using a cash register, typing, polishing your fingernails, and so on.

Tips for Creating a Positive Telephone Image

People form an opinion of you and your organization quickly. The message they receive often determines how they interact with you during the conversation and in your future relationship. Keep in mind that when you answer your organization's telephone, or call someone else as part of your job, you represent yourself *and* the organization. And, since many telephone calls are short, you have limited opportunity to make a positive impression.

When you feel good about yourself, you normally project a naturally confident and pleasant image. On days when things aren't going so well for you, your self-image may tend to suffer. Here are some suggestions to help serve your customers effectively and leave them thinking well of you and your organization.

- *Continually evaluate yourself.* You are your own best critic. From time to time, think about your conversation—what went well, what could have been improved. If possible, occasionally tape-record your conversations and evaluate your voice qualities and message delivery. Have someone else listen to the tape and provide objective feedback. To help in your self-assessment, you may want to make copies of Worksheet 9.1 (see website **<http://www.mhhe.com/lucas05>**) and evaluate all your calls for a specific period of time (for example, a couple of hours or a day).

- *Use proper body posture.* The following can negatively affect the sound and quality of your voice:

  Slouching in your chair.

  Sitting with your feet on a desk with your arms behind your head as you rock back and forth in your chair.

  Looking down, with your chin on your chest, to read or search through drawers.

  Resting the telephone handset between your cheek and shoulder as you do other work (e.g., type data into a computer, look for something, writing, or doodling).

  Strive to sit or stand upright and speak clearly into the mouthpiece whether you are using a headset or handheld receiver. If you are using a handheld receiver, make sure that the earpiece is placed firmly against your ear and the mouthpiece is directly in front of your mouth.

- *Be prepared.* Answer a ringing phone promptly and use a standard greeting as outlined later in this chapter.

- *Speak naturally.* Whether you are calling someone or providing information to a caller, speak in a conversational voice. Don't use a "canned" or mechanical presentation, and don't read from a prepared script, unless you are required to do so by your company. If you must read from a script, *practice, practice, practice.* Before you connect with a customer, become very comfortable with your presentation so that you can deliver it in a fluid, warm, and sincere manner. Nothing sends a more negative message than a service provider who mispronounces a customer's name, stumbles through opening comments, and seems disorganized.

- *Be time-conscious.* Customers appreciate prompt, courteous service. Be aware that time is money—yours, your organization's, and the customer's. Have your thoughts organized when you call a customer. It is a good idea to use a list of questions or key points (see Worksheet 9.2 [see website **<http:/www.mhhe. com/lucas05>** as an example). If a customer calls you and you don't have an answer or information readily available, offer to do some research and call back instead of putting the customer on hold. Respect your customer's time. Chances are that customers will prefer to hold if they will be waiting only a short time, but give them the option. In addition to helping better organize your calls, a written call-planning sheet will provide a good record of the call.

- *Be proactive with service.* If you must say no to a customer, do so in a positive manner without quoting policy. Tell the customer what you can do. For example, if your policy prohibits refunds on one-of-a-kind or closeout items, you might make an offer such as this (depending on your level of authority or empowerment):

  "Mr. _____ , I see that the computer you ordered from our website was a closeout item. I understand that you have decided that you need more RAM. Although I cannot give refunds on a closeout item, I can give you a voucher good at any of our retail locations for a $50 discount on a memory chip upgrade or free installation, whichever you prefer."

Doing more than the customer expects following a breakdown (this is called *service recovery* and is discussed in Chapter 13) is important, especially if you or your company made an error. When you or your company is not responsible for the error, but you want to maintain a positive customer-provider relationship, going out of your way to help make it better is just good business practice.

• *Conclude calls professionally.* Ending a call on an upbeat note, using the caller's name, and summarizing key actions to be taken by both parties are all recommended practices. For example, you might say, "All right, Ms. _____ , let me confirm what we've discussed. I'll get _____ by the 23d, and call you to confirm _____ . You'll take care of _____ . Is that correct?" Once agreement has been reached, thank the customer for calling, ask what other questions he or she has or what else you can assist with, and then let the customer hang up first. By following this type of format, you can reduce misunderstandings and elicit any last-minute questions or comments the customer might have. If you fail to bring the conversation to a formal close and hang up abruptly, the customer may feel you are in a hurry to service him or her (regardless of the fact that you have just spent 15 minutes talking with him or her!). Think of this final step as wrapping a gift: it looks fine, but adding a nice ribbon and bow makes it look even better. The thank-you and polite sign-off are your ribbon and bow.

Effective Telephone Usage

One basic strategy for successfully providing effective customer service over the telephone is to thoroughly understand all phone features and use them effectively. This may seem to be a logical and simple concept, but think about times when you

Dealing with customers effectively requires focus and skills. Eliminating outside distractors is crucial for service success. *What do you do to eliminate distractors when dealing with customers?*

called a company and someone attempted to transfer you, or put you on hold, or did not communicate clearly. If the transfer was successful, you were lucky. If not, you probably couldn't understand what happened, got disconnected, were connected to the wrong party, or heard the original person come back on the telephone to apologize and say something like, "The call didn't go through. Let me try again." Sound familiar? If so, use the following strategies to ensure that you do not deliver similar poor service.

- *Eliminate distractions.* Don't eat food, chew gum, drink, talk to others, read (unless for the purpose of providing the customer with information), or handle other office tasks (filing, stapling, stamping, sealing envelopes, etc.) while on the phone. Your voice quality will alert the customer to the fact that you are otherwise occupied.

- *Answer promptly.* A lot is communicated by the way a phone call is handled. One tip for success is to always answer by the third or fourth ring. This sends a non-verbal message to your customers of your availability to serve them. It also reduces the irritating ringing that you, coworkers, or customers have to hear.

- *Use titles with names.* It has been said that there is nothing sweeter than hearing one's own name. However, until you are told otherwise, use a person's title (e.g., Mr., Mrs., Ms., or Dr.) and last name. Do not assume that it is all right to use first names. Some people regard the use of their first name as insolent or rude. This may especially be true of older customers and people from other cultures where respect and use of titles are valued. When you are speaking with customers, it is also a good idea to use their name frequently (don't overdo it, though, or you'll sound mechanical). Repeat the name directly after the greeting (e.g., "Yes, _____ , how may I help you?"), during the conversation (e.g., "One idea I have, _____ , is to . . ."), and at the end of the call (e.g., "Thanks for calling, _____ . I'll get that information right out to you.").

- *Ask questions.* You read about the use of questions earlier in the book. Use them on the telephone to get information or clarify points made by the customer. Ask open-ended questions; then listen to the response carefully. To clarify or verify information, use closed-ended questions.

- *Use equipment properly.* Your success or failure in receiving and delivering messages often hinges on simply holding the receiver or wearing a headset properly. Ensure that the earpiece and mouthpiece rest squarely against your ear and in front of your mouth, respectively. This allows you to accurately hear what is said and accurately transmit your words to the customer clearly.

- *Use speakerphones with caution.* Speakerphones make sense for people who have certain disabilities and in some environments (where you need free hands or are doing something else while you are on hold or are waiting for a phone to be answered). From a customer service standpoint, they can send a cold or impersonal message, and their use should be minimal. Many callers do not like them and even think that speakerphone users are rude. Also, depending on the equipment used and how far you are from the telephone, the message received by your customer could be distorted, or it might seem as though you are in an echo chamber. Before using a speakerphone, ask yourself whether there is a valid reason for not using a headset or handheld phone. When you are using a speakerphone, make sure that your conversation will not be overhead if you are discussing personal, proprietary, or confidential information. Also, if someone is listening in on the customer's conversation, make sure that you inform the customer of that fact and explain who the listener is and why he or she is listening. As you read earlier, some people are very protective of their privacy and their feelings should be respected.

- *Transfer calls properly.* Be sure you understand how the telephone transfer (sometimes called the *link*) and hold functions work. Nothing is more frustrating or irritating for callers than to be shuffled from one person to the next or to be placed on what seems to be an endless hold. Here are some suggestions that can help to increase your effectiveness in these areas:

  Always request permission before transferring a caller. This shows respect for the caller and psychologically gives the caller a feeling of control over the conversation. You can also offer options (you can ask the caller to allow a transfer or let you take a message). This is especially helpful when the customer is already irritated or has a problem. Before transferring the call, explain why you need to do so. You might say, "The person who handles billing questions is Shashandra Philips at extension 4739. May I transfer you, or would you rather I take a message and pass it along to her?" This saves you and the caller time and effort, and you have provided professional, courteous service. If the caller says, "Yes, please transfer me," follow by saying something like, "I'd be happy to connect you. Again, if you are accidentally disconnected, I'll be calling Shashandra Philips at extension 4739."

  Once you have successfully reached the intended person, announce the call by saying, "Shashandra, this is (your name), from (your department). I have (customer's name) on the phone. She has a (question, problem). Are you the right person to handle that?" If Shashandra answers yes, connect the caller and announce, "(Customer's name), I have Shashandra Philips on the line. She will be happy to assist you. Thanks for calling (or some similar positive disconnect phrase)." You can then hang up, knowing that you did your part in delivering quality customer service.

  If the call taker is not available or is not the appropriate person, reconnect with the customer and explain the situation. Then offer to take a message rather than trying to transfer to different people while keeping the customer on hold. You would make an exception if the call taker informed you of the appropriate person to whom you should transfer, or if the customer insisted on staying on the line while you tried to transfer to the right person.

  You should avoid making a **blind transfer.** This practice is ineffective, rude, and not customer-focused. A blind transfer happens when a service provider asks a caller, "May I transfer you to _____?" or may even say, without permission, "Let me transfer you to _____ ." Once the intended transfer party answers, the person transferring the call hangs up. Always announce your caller by waiting for the phone to be picked up and saying, "This is (your name) in (your department). I have (customer's name) on the line. Can you take the call?" Failure to do this could result in a confrontation between the two people. If the calling customer is already upset, you have just set up a situation that could lead to a lost customer and/or angry coworker.

  If you place someone on hold, it is a good idea to go back on the line every 20 to 30 seconds to let the person know that you have not forgotten the call. This action becomes more important if the phone system you are using does not offer information that the customer hears during the holding time.

  One final word about holds. Once you return to the phone to take the call, thank the caller for waiting.

- *Use call waiting.* A useful feature offered by many phone systems is call waiting. While you are on the phone, a signal (usually a beep) indicates that there is an

LEADERSHIP INITIATIVE **9.2**

Effective supervisors set up systems to periodically evaluate the effectiveness of the way in which frontline employees are using service technology systems. They either personally scrutinize or use internal or external resources to ensure that telephone call routing, voice messaging, and other tools in the service environment are being used correctly and according to organizational guidelines.

incoming call. When you hear the signal, you have a couple of options: Excuse yourself from your current call, by getting permission to place the person on hold, or ignore the second caller. If you have a voice mail system, the system makes the choice for you by transferring incoming calls to your message system. Both options have advantages and disadvantages.

By taking the second call, you may irritate your current caller, who might hang up. This results in lost business. (On the other hand, by not taking the second call, you might miss an important message and/or irritate that caller.)

By ignoring the signal, you might offend the second caller. Research indicates that many customers forget to or decide against placing later calls to busy numbers, especially if they have already made several attempts. Customers may feel that you're too busy to properly serve them.

So, how do you handle the dilemma? Make a judgment about how the customer to whom you are speaking might react and then act accordingly. In some instances, company policies tell you what to do, so you don't have to decide.

Voice Mail and Answering Machines or Services

Although voice mail is hailed by many people as a time-saver and vehicle for delivering messages when an intended recipient is unavailable, many other people have difficulty dealing with voice mail (including answering machines). Let's take a look at some ways to use voice mail.

- *Managing incoming calls.* To effectively use voice mail, you must first understand how your system works. Check the manuals delivered with your system or speak with your supervisor and/or the technical expert responsible for its maintenance.

  A key to using voice mail effectively is to keep your outgoing message current, indicating your availability, the type of information the caller should leave, and when the caller can expect a return call. If your system allows the caller the option of accessing an operator or another person, you should indicate this early in your outgoing message to save the caller from having to listen to unnecessary information. Figure 9.7 provides a sample outgoing message. Also, Work It Out 9.1 can be used to evaluate the voice mail messages of others when you call them. Another key to effective voice mail usage is to retrieve your calls and return them as soon as possible. Usually 24 hours, or by the next working day, is a good guideline for returning calls. Doing so sends a positive customer service message.

To help increase your awareness of the impact of voice mail messages, make note of the following questions during the coming week. As you call people or organizations, consider the outgoing messages that they leave on their voice mail or answering machines and evaluate them using the following questions.

1. Was the call answered by the fourth ring?
2. Did the announcement contain the following:

Greeting (Hello, Good morning, or Good afternoon)?

Organization's name?

Departmental name?

A statement of when the person would return?

An early announcement of an option to press a number for assistance?

Instructions for leaving a message?

When calls would be returned?

FIGURE 9.7
Sample Outgoing Message

"Hello. This is the voice mail of (your name) of (company and department). I'm unavailable to take your call at the moment, but if you will leave your name, number, and a brief message, I'll call you as soon as possible. Thanks for calling." If you know when you will be returning calls (e.g., at the end of the workday), tell the caller so. If your voice mail system offers callers the option to press a number to speak with someone else, let them know this right after you tell them whose voice mail they have reached. This avoids requiring them to listen to a lengthy message before they can select an option.

- *Placing calls to voice mail.* Many normally articulate people cannot speak coherently when they encounter an answering machine or voice mail. One technique for success is to plan your call before picking up the phone. Have a 30-second or less "sales" presentation in mind that you can deliver whether you get a person or machine. For example, if you get a person, try, "This is (your first and last name) from (company) calling (or returning a call) for _____. Is he available?" Also, have available a written list of the key points you want to discuss so you don't forget them as you talk.

  If you get a machine, try, "This is (first and last name) from (company) calling (returning a call) for _____. My number is _____. I will be available from _____ to _____." If you are calling to get or give information, you may want to add, "The reason I am calling is to _____." This allows the return caller to leave information on your voice mail or with someone else and thus avoid the game of telephone tag.

- *Avoiding telephone tag.* You have probably played telephone tag. The game starts when the intended call receiver is not available and a message is left. The game continues when the call is returned, the original caller is not available, a return message is left, and so on.

Telephone tag is frustrating and a waste of valuable time. It results in a loss of efficiency, money, and in some cases, customers. To avoid telephone tag, plan your calls and make your messages effective by giving your name, company name, phone number, time and date of your call, and a succinct message, and by indicating when you can be reached. If appropriate, emphasize that it is all right to leave the information you have requested on your voice mail or with someone else. Also, you may suggest that your message recipient tell you a time when you can call or meet with him or her face-to-face. By doing this, you end the game and get what you need. Use Worksheet 9-3 (see website **<http://www.mhhe.com/lucas05>**) to help plan your calls effectively.

Taking Messages Professionally

If you have ever received an incomplete or unreadable telephone message, you can appreciate the need for practice in this area. At a minimum, when you take a message you should get the following information from the caller:

Name (correctly spelled)

Company name

Phone number (with area code and country code, if appropriate)

Brief message

When call should be returned

Time and date of the call and your name (in case a question about the message arises)

If you are answering someone's phone while he or she is away, let the caller know right away. This can be done by using a statement such as, "Hello, (person's name) line. This is (your name). How may I assist you?" In addition, be cautious of statements you make regarding the intended recipient's availability. Sometimes, well-meant comments can send a negative message to customers. See Figure 9.8 for typical problem messages and better alternatives.

General Advice

Don't communicate personal information (someone is at the doctor's, on sick leave, etc.), belittle yourself (i.e., "I' don't know", "I'm only . . .") or the company (i.e., "Nobody knows"), or use weak or negative language (i.e., "I think," "I can't"). Instead, simply state "_____ is unavailable. May I take a message?" or if appropriate, "I'd be happy to assist you." After you have taken the message, thank the caller before hanging up and then deliver the message to the intended receiver in a timely manner. If you discover that the receiver will not be available within a 24-hour period, you may want to call the customer and convey this information. If you do so, again offer to assist or suggest some other alternative, if one is available.

FIGURE 9.8
Communicating Messages

Message	Possible Interpretation	Alternative
"I'm not sure where he is" or "He's out roaming around the building somewhere."	"Don't they have any control or structure at this company?"	"He's not available. May I take a message?"
"I'm sorry. She is *still* at lunch."	(Depending on the time of the call.) "Must be nice to have two-hour lunch breaks!"	Same as above or "I'm sorry, She is at lunch. May I assist you or take a message?"
"We *should* have that problem taken care of soon."	"Don't you know for sure?"	"I apologize for the inconvenience. We'll attempt to resolve this by ____."
"He isn't available right now. He's taking care of a crisis."	"Is there a problem there?"	"He isn't available right now. May I assist you or take a message?"
"She's not in today. I'm not sure when she'll be back."	Same as above.	"She's not in today. May I assist you or take a message?"
"He left early today."	"Obviously, you people are not very customer-focused or she would be there during normal business hours to assist me."	"He is out of the office. May I assist you or take a message?"
"I don't know where she is. I was just walking by and heard the phone ringing."	"Nice that you're so conscientious. Too bad others are not."	"She isn't available right now, but I'd be happy to take a message."
"I'll give him the message and try to get him to call you back."	"So there's a 50–50 chance I'll be served."	"I'll give him the message when he returns and ask him to call you back."
"Hang on a second while I find something to take a message with."	"Doesn't sound as if people at this company are very prepared to serve customers."	"Would you please hold while I get a pen and paper?"

Chapter Summary

Delivering customer service via technology can be an effective and efficient approach to use to achieve total customer satisfaction. However, you must continually upgrade your personal technology knowledge and skills, practice their application, and consciously evaluate the approach and techniques you use to provide service.

In the quality-oriented cultures now developing in the United States and in many other countries, service will make the difference between survival or failure for individuals and organizations. You are the front line, and you are often the first and only contact a customer will have with your company. Strive to use technology to its fullest potential, but do not forget that you and your peers ultimately determine whether expectations are met in the eyes of your customer.

SERVICE IN ACTION | Dell Computers

CHAPTER 9

http://www.dell.com
In 2003, customers purchased over 140 million Dell servers, personal computers, and workstations in an economy that was stalled and headed for a recession. Revenue for 2003 was over $35 billion compared to just over $18 billion in 1999. In 2002 and 2003 Dell supplied more computers to customers than any competitor.

To ensure that they stay in a leadership position, Dell constantly monitors its customer-focused measures (e.g., delivery timeliness, product reliability, and speed and quality of service and support). Its efforts in these and other customer support areas have regularly earned the company a number one rating in overall satisfaction among computer hardware vendors according to Technology Business Research. Additionally, according to its 2003 annual report to shareholders, Dell stresses its commitment to colleagues, customers, direct relationships, global citizenship, and winning with integrity as key elements of its culture. These beliefs have earned praise from noted sources. *Forbes* magazine rated Dell as the fourth-most-admired global and U.S. company, while it rated number nine (and the only technology company) in the top ten companies in a Harris Interactive survey of corporate reputation.

Key Terms and Concepts

automatic call distribution (ACD) system
automatic number identification (ANI) system
blind transfer
call center
electronic commerce (e-commerce)

electronic mail (e-mail)
emotional icons or emoticons
facsimile (fax) machine
fax on demand
help desk
interactive voice response (IVR) system
Internet call back

Internet telephony
media blending
online information fulfillment system
predictive dialing system
screen pop-ups
teletype systems (TTY)
voice response unit (VRU)

Quick Preview Answers

1. T	6. T	11. F
2. F	7. T	12. T
3. T	8. T	13. T
4. F	9. F	14. T
5. T	10. T	

Chapter Review Questions

1. In what ways can technology play a role in the delivery of effective customer service? Explain.
2. What are some advantages of using technology for service delivery?
3. What are some disadvantages of using technology for service delivery?
4. What are some of the communication skills for success?
5. How can you project a more positive image over the telephone?
6. What information should you always get when taking telephone messages?
7. When transferring calls, what should you avoid and why?
8. When you leave a message on voice mail, what information should you give?
9. What is telephone tag, and how can it be avoided or reduced?

Search It Out

Search the Internet for Customer Service Technology

1. Log onto the Internet and search for sites that deal with customer service and the technology used to deliver quality customer service. Also, look for the websites and organizations that focus on the technology and people involved in the delivery of customer service.

2. Log onto the Internet to search for books and other publications that focus on customer service and technology. Develop a bibliographic listing of at least seven to ten publications, make copies of the list, and share it with your classmates.

Note: A listing for additional research on specific URLs is provided on the Customer Service website at **<http://www.mhhe.com/lucas05>**.

Collaborative Learning Activity

Practice Customer Service With Your Team Members

Get together in teams of three members each. One person will take the role of a customer service provider, one will be a customer, and one will be the observer. Use the following scenarios to practice the skills you have learned in this chapter. Incorporate other communication skills covered in previous chapters as you deal with your "customer." Use three of the four scenarios so that each person in a group has a chance to play each of the three roles. Depending on the scenario, you might use copies of Worksheet 9-2 (see website **<http://www.mhhe.com/lucas05>**) to plan your call.

Scenario 1: You are a customer service representative in a call center that provides service to customers who have purchased small appliances from your company. A customer is going to call complaining that she purchased a waffle iron from one of your outlet stores two weeks ago and it no longer works. She is upset because her in-laws and family are arriving in two days for an extended visit and they love her "special" waffles.

Scenario 2: You are a customer care specialist for a company that provides answers to travel-related questions for a national membership warehouse retail store. A customer will call to find out about the types of travel-related discounts for which he qualifies through his membership.

Scenario 3: You are a telemarketing sales representative for a company that sells water filtration systems. You are calling current customers who purchased a filtration system seven to ten years ago to inform them of your new Oasis line of filters, which is better than any other system on the market. You can offer them:

A 30-day money-back guarantee.

Billing by all major credit cards or invoice.

A one-year limited warranty on the system that replaces all defective parts but does not cover labor.

If they find a less expensive offer for the same product, a refund for the difference and an additional 50 percent of the difference.

Scenario 4: This scenario has two parts. In Part 1, you are a mechanic in an automotive repair shop. You answer a phone call from a customer calling to complain about what he perceives is an inflated billing charge for a recent air-conditioning repair. He is calling for your manager, who is at lunch and won't be back for 45 minutes. You take the incoming call, using the message-taking format covered in this chapter. In Part 2, you are the manager. You have just returned from lunch and find a message from the irate customer described in Part 1 and must call the customer. Use Worksheet 9.3 (see website <http://www.mhhe.com/lucas05>) to plan your return call based on the message you received.

Face to Face

Telephone Techniques at Staff-Temps

Background

Staff-Temps International is a temporary employment agency based in Chicago, Illinois. It has six full-time and three part-time employment counselors. The office is part of a national chain owned by Yamaguchi Enterprises, Ltd., headquartered in Tokyo. The chain annually places over 100,000 temporary employees in a variety of businesses and offices.

Most of Staff-Temps' contacts are made by telephone; therefore, greater emphasis is placed on selecting and training employees who have a good phone presence. Each employee is required to meet certain standards of quality in dealing with customers on the telephone. To ensure that these standards are applied uniformly, an outside quality control company (Morrison and Lewis) is used to make "phantom calls" to staff members. In these calls, Morrison and Lewis staff pretend to be potential clients seeking information. Employee-customer calls are also randomly taped. Through the calls and tapes, levels of customer service are measured.

Your Role

Your name is Chris Walker. As an employment counselor with Staff-Temps, you are aware of the customer service standards, which include the following:

Answer a ringing telephone within three rings.

Smile as you speak.

Use a standard salutation (Good morning, afternoon, or evening).

Give your name and the name of your department and company.

Offer to assist the customer ("How may I assist you?").

On the way back to the office after lunch, you were involved in a minor automobile accident. Even though it was not your fault, you are concerned that your insurance may be canceled since you had another accident and got a speeding ticket earlier this year. Because of the accident, you were an hour late in returning from lunch. Upon your arrival, the receptionist handed you six messages from vendors and customers. Two of the messages were from Aretha Washington, human resources director for an electronics manufacturing firm that has been a good client for over two years. The two of you had spoken earlier in the day.

As you walked into your office, the telephone started to ring. By the time you took your coat off and got to your desk, the phone had rung five or six times.

When you answered, you heard Aretha's voice on the line. Her tone told you that she was upset. This was the conversation:

You: "Staff-Temps. Chris speaking."

Aretha: "Chris, what's going on? You told me when I called first thing this morning that you would find out why my temp didn't show up today and would call me back. I've left messages all day and haven't heard a thing! We've got a major deadline to meet for a very important client, and I can't get the work done. My boss has been in here every half hour checking on this. What is going on?"

You: Aretha, I'm sorry. I just got in from lunch and haven't been able to get back to you."

Aretha: "Just got back from lunch! It's after 2:30! It must be nice to have the luxury of a long lunch break. I didn't even get to eat lunch today!"

You: "Listen, Aretha, I couldn't help . . ." Obviously anxious and raising your voice.

Aretha: "Don't you 'listen' me. I'm the customer, and if you can't handle my needs, I know someone else who can. If I don't hear from you within the next half hour, I don't ever want to hear from you again! Goodbye!" [Slamming receiver down.]

Critical Review Questions

1. How well was this customer call handled? Explain.
2. What should you have done differently?
3. Do you believe that Aretha was justified in how she treated you? Explain.
4. How do personal problems or priorities sometimes affect customer service?

PLANNING TO SERVE

CHAPTER 9

Use the following checklist to ensure that you are delivering the best possible service to customers, using technology effectively, and sending a positive image to others.

Call your own telephone number to determine:

- How many times the telephone rings before being routed to another person or voice mail. Four rings should be the maximum unless your organization has another standard.
- If the "0" (operator) option is chosen, does the call go to a live person at another number? In other words, do you have service coverage when you are away from your telephone?

If you choose the voice mail option, is your outgoing message:

- Upbeat and friendly?
- Concise?

- In compliance with organizational guidelines for voice messages? If no standards exist, does your message comply with the suggested message format in this chapter?

E-mail yourself to determine:

- If the message is delivered properly to your mailbox.
- If your "out of office" message is sent automatically (assuming you have this option on your system and have activated it). For example, a response might be generated that tells correspondents that "I'll be out of the office from (date) until (date) but I will be checking my e-mail during that period and will respond as soon as possible."

Examine your fax cover sheets (if used) to ensure that excessive information and graphics (e.g., bulky logos or icons) have been removed and that your name and phone number are provided (see Figure 9.6 for an example).

Self-Help Skills

Managing Your Stress

From the Frontline Interview

Sharelle Rogers is a customer service supervisor for Westgate Resorts, which sells vacation packages. Prior, she worked in the Verification Department for three years validating vacation packages at the point of sale and, ultimately, supervising. In that role, it was her responsibility to make sure that vacation packages that were deemed invalid, for whatever reason, were corrected. Those that could not be corrected were canceled.

**SHARELLE ROGERS,
Customer Service
Supervisor,
*Westgate Resorts***

1 **Do you believe it is easier to deal with internal or external customers? Why?**

Handling the external customer is often simpler than managing internal customers, although I believe that the sense of ease with external customers may be my own perception. I say that because knowing that a customer just purchased a vacation package and could easily cancel, according to the grace period provided for new packages, was not just an option for the customer; it was also security for me. I found no difficulty explaining the standards and policies of our company to a customer despite the fact that just moments prior a sales agent offered a promise that I could not validate by the standard of the company. If a customer's irritation escalated to fury while trying to "save a deal" I knew that I could offer to void the transaction.

It wasn't until I was promoted to the Customer Service Department that I got a real sense of "dealing" with a situation. In most cases, the vacation packages that customers wanted to cancel were not within the cancel-lation period, so whatever sense of security I once had was gone. At first, I felt a little like I had been thrown to the wolves. I asked myself, "How do I do this?" I did learn how to deal with a variety of personalities and situations through training, but I attribute most of the learning to experience and exposure. I learned to adapt to the customer's situation and exercise my abilities while adhering to the company policies.

2 **What role does stress and the management of it play in your daily job accomplishment? Please explain.**

It is impossible for me to accomplish my daily tasks while ignoring the indicators of stress. Management of stress is vital to getting the job done. Every day, my employees and I work under stress, and occasionally I feel the strain. In the past, I would "bottle" my stress and keep a straight face. Now, I handle my stress by recognizing the symptoms, focusing on the source, and managing my reactions. I also prepare myself for adverse situations before they occur. Prior to getting involved in my daily activities I remind myself who I am and whom I have to be in order to get the task done. In other words, I coach myself. I think I spend more time coping than trying to escape stress.

3 **What are some of the biggest contributors to stress in dealing with customers in your position?**

Providing service to a vast number of culturally diverse customers is very stressful. Trying to adapt to the situation

Chapter Learning Objectives

After completing this chapter, you will be able to:

- Identify leading causes of stress in the customer service environment.

- Describe personal stressors.

- Recognize potentially stressful situations.

- Avoid stressful situations.

- Develop techniques for reducing stress.

---

and the specific needs of the customer (internal or external) is challenging because you cannot be uniform in dealing with all people and situations and achieve successful outcomes. I find that stress gets overwhelming during the times that I rely on my own self-references instead of thinking outside the box. I have learned to overcome stress caused by multitasking by acknowledging what needs to be done and then prioritizing.

4 How have you seen technology add to the stress level faced by employees in today's customer service environment?

Many people believe that technology increases stress levels because people are resistant to change, but in my experience it is the feeling of inadequacy resulting from the change that is the real stress. When major system changes are essential to the duties and mandatory to the job requirement, many employees who have all the current knowledge down pat are back to square one. Without proper preparation and training, capabilities and self-esteem are lowered, prompting mental and emotional stress.

5 In your experience, what do service providers do to increase their stress levels when dealing with customers?

I have noticed that I increase my own stress levels when dealing with upset customers by taking their negative remarks and attitudes personally. I remind myself that I am a representative of the company and thus, I must not react. Instead, I must respond professionally.

6 What are some strategies that you use to reduce or eliminate stress each day?

I have not found a strategy that completely eliminates stress and I am not sure if such a strategy exists. I have been able to work comfortably by implementing two methods. First, I know myself. I have learned to identify those situations that are most probably going to cause me excess stress and I learned how to prepare for instead of avoid them. Second, I've learned to eliminate the stress that comes from other people's negativity by not taking things personally. To do this, I try to maintain a rational thinking mode and keep myself from reverting to emotions.

7 What advice related to stress and its reduction can you give to someone entering a customer service job today?

My advice is to examine yourself, know your job, and understand obstacles that you will frequently have to overcome. Treat every customer and situation individually. Situations that are common in your industry may be an unpleasant surprise to the customer. Understand that tough customers will say things that you promised you would never take from anybody. Recognize that their comments are directed toward the situation, not you. Your attention should focus only on resolving conflict.

Critical Thinking

What is your reaction to what Sharelle has said? Why? In what ways can you relate to her comments as a customer and as a service provider?

Quick Preview

Before reviewing the chapter content, respond to the following questions by placing a "T" for true or an "F" for false on the rules. Use any questions you miss as a checklist of material to which you will pay particular attention as you read through the chapter. For those you get right, congratulate yourself, but review the sections they address in order to learn additional details about the topic.

_____ 1. Both positive and negative stress exist.

_____ 2. Studies do not substantiate employee claims that customer service is a stressful profession.

_____ 3. Stressors do not affect all people in the same manner.

_____ 4. Physical reactions caused by stress are observable.

_____ 5. Environmental factors such as lighting, temperature, and noise can be stress-inducing.

_____ 6. Unresolved personal issues can cause workplace stress.

_____ 7. The way a job is structured has little impact on stress levels.

_____ 8. A lack of time for oneself does not typically create stress.

_____ 9. The use of "I" language can help in reducing stressful situations.

_____ 10. Taking regularly scheduled breaks can add to your stress because you'll probably have work waiting for you when you return.

_____ 11. According to the Better Sleep Council, most people get enough sleep each night.

_____ 12. Each week, an average of 20 people are killed on the job as a result of workplace violence.

Answers to Quick Preview can be found at the end of the chapter.

1   Stress Research

Concept: Stress has been linked to all the leading causes of death, including heart disease, cancer, lung ailments, accidents, and suicide. Dealing with stress is a major health-related issue today.

Stress is a major contributor to loss of workplace efficiency. Each year, millions of dollars and countless worker-hours of productivity are lost because of stress-related illnesses (see Figure 10.1). In all stress-related statistics, customer service is rated among the top most stressful occupations. In fact, many studies have consistently listed customer service in the top ten most stressful occupations in the country. This is because the variety of people and situations you face on any given day require you to call on a multitude of skills and to think quickly. According to the American Institute of Stress, customer service representatives ranked fourth behind air traffic controllers, inner-city high school teachers, and police officers as having the most stressful job in the country. Additional studies conducted by Yale University ranked customer service as the eighth most stressful occupation.

The results of pressures that people are facing in the workplace have been staggering, financially and from a health standpoint (see Figure 10.1).[1] Thus, stress can be a problem, especially if you aren't prepared to handle it.

[1]American Institute of Stress.

FIGURE 10.1
The Impact
of Stress

Percent distribution of all nonfatal injuries and illnesses and of cases of neurotic reaction to stress involving days away from work, by industry, 1997

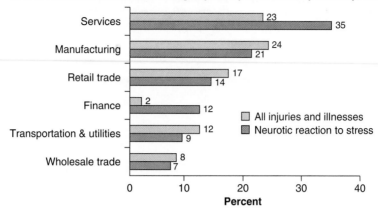

- Stress is America's No. 1 health problem.
- Among adults, 43 percent suffer adverse health effects due to stress.
- Of all visits to primary care physicians, 75 to 90 percent are stress-related.
- Stress has been linked to all the leading causes of death, including heart disease, cancer, lung ailments, accidents, and suicide.
- An estimated 1 million workers are absent on an average workday because of stress-related complaints. Stress is said to be responsible for more than half of the 550 million workdays lost annually because of absenteeism.
- A 32-year study conducted by a large corporation showed that 60 percent of employee absences were due to psychological problems such as stress.
- Nearly half of all American workers suffer from symptoms of **burnout,** a disabling reaction to stress on the job.
- Job stress is estimated to cost U.S. industry $300 billion annually, as measured by absenteeism, diminished productivity, employee turnover, and medical, legal, and insurance fees. Sixty to eighty percent of industrial accidents are due to stress.
- Workers' compensation awards for job stress, rare in the early 1980s, have sky-rocketed and threaten to bankrupt insurance systems in some states. Employers in California shelled out almost $1 billion for medical and legal fees alone. Nine of ten job stress lawsuits are successful, with an average payout more than four times that for regular injury claims.
- It is estimated that 40 percent of worker turnover is due to job stress. The Xerox Corporation estimates that it costs approximately $1 million to $1.5 million to replace a top executive, and average employee turnover costs between $2,000 and $13,000 per individual.
- Workplace violence is rampant. Almost 2 million cases of homicide, aggravated assault, rape, or sexual assaults are reported each year. Homicide is the second leading cause of fatal occupational injury and the leading cause of death for working women.

2   What Is Job Stress?

Concept: Nowadays many workers feel that their job is full of stress. Stress can create problems in the workplace. However, not all stress is bad stress.

Job stress can be defined as the harmful physical and emotional responses that occur when the requirements of a job do not match the capabilities, resources, or needs of the worker.[2] Bad stress, or **distress,** causes problems in dealing with customers

[2]Center for Disease Control, National Institute for Occupational Safety and Health (NIOSH).

Today's workplace contributes to employee stress in many ways. Job and life expectations and responsibilities pressure workers on and off the job. *What things add to your stress in the workplace and what are you doing to eliminate or reduce them?*

FIGURE 10.2
What Workers Say About Stress on the Job

Source: *Stress at Work,* DHHS (NIOSH) Publication No. 99-101, Institute for Occupational Safety and Health, January 1999.

Survey by the Northwestern National Life

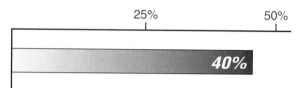

Percentage of workers who report that their job is "very or extremely stressful"

Survey by the Families and Work Institute

Percentage of workers who report that they are "often or very often burned out or stressed by their work."

Survey by Yale University

Percentage of workers who report that they feel "quite a bit or extremely stressed at work."

and other people, reduces your effectiveness, dampens your motivation, makes your life miserable, and can lead to long-term mental and physical problems or death. Although some of the stress that you encounter in the workplace can be eliminated, some cannot; you simply have to work to minimize it as much as possible. Strategies and techniques for doing this are given in this chapter.

You are not alone in feeling stressed on the job. Nowadays, many workers believe that their jobs are stressful (see Figure 10.2).

Not all stress is bad, however. Dr. Hans Selye, a prominent psychologist, coined the term **eustress** a number of years ago to describe "good" stress. You would experience eustress if you set a goal for yourself and achieved that goal (e.g., running three miles in under 20 minutes, graduating from high school or college, delivering a successful presentation to clients). You would feel good about your accomplishment. You might also feel negative stress along the way toward your goal because of the tasks required to achieve your ultimate objective (e.g., the physical conditioning necessary to strengthen your body to run faster, staying up all night to study for an examination, or spending hours researching and rehearsing a presentation). With eustress, you may go through the same physiological stages that you would for negative situations, but at the end, when you reach your goal, you have a sense of accomplishment and a feeling of exhilaration.

3 What Creates Stress?

Concept: What you feel in the environment, on the job, and your personal factors are some of the things that create stress.

In a word, *life* creates stress. Harris Interactive, a worldwide market research and consulting firm, conducted a nationwide telephone survey of 1,010 adults in 2002 to determine what factors tend to stress most people out. The following factors were selected by respondents, from among 13 offered, as the ones that most affect them in daily life:

Rising prices (69 percent)

Too many things to do (62 percent)

Concerns about money emergencies (51 percent)

Health concerns (47 percent)

Figures 10.3 and 10.4 show the percentage of people affected by various "hassles" in the month preceding the poll—by age, sex, and race/ethnicity. These figures show *how respondents replied when asked to respond to:* "Now I'd like to read you a list of things that may have failed you in the last month. For each, please tell me if it has affected you in the last month or not."

As you read in Chapter 9, the world moves at a much faster pace than it did decades ago. People's values, beliefs, and expectations have caused much of this acceleration. Customers have become conditioned to expect quality products and services at competitive prices and in time frames unheard of one or two decades ago. The speed of services is spoiling customers. You can see the impact of customer expectations when you recall a FedEx television advertisement of a few years back. Remember: "When your package absolutely, positively, has to get there overnight?" Customers are also becoming complacent. They assume that if they want something, service providers will provide it instantaneously . . . and in many cases they are right. Organizations realize the value of providing service on demand. Tasks that used to take hours, days, and even weeks are now done almost instantaneously, or certainly in a greatly reduced time frame. The idea of getting it now has so permeated the culture that failure to provide the quickest, most efficient delivery of products and services can be the kiss of death for an organization. As a result of this "get it now" mentality, each new generation has less memory of the long waiting times experienced by their forebears. Today, if customers cannot get what they want from you and your organization, when they want it, they go elsewhere. Increasing schedule pressures can add to stress for you and your coworkers.

FIGURE 10.3
"Hassles" by Age*

Source: Humphrey Taylor, *Poor People and African Americans Suffer the Most from the Hassles of Daily Living*, Harris Interactive® www.harrisinteractive.com (2002). Reprinted with permission.

	All Adults	Age					
		18–24	25–29	30–39	40–49	50–64	65+
Those affected by:							
Rising prices	69%	70%	68%	72%	65%	71%	67%
Too many things to do	62	75	69	71	72	56	30
Concerns about money for emergencies	51	62	64	61	49	44	35
Concerns about health in general	47	44	49	40	47	50	56
Illness of a family member	37	28	48	35	40	39	37
Trouble relaxing	37	44	49	42	41	29	23
Not enough money for basic necessities	35	50	48	37	32	28	28
Problems with aging parents	23	18	19	23	32	30	12
Problems with your work, boss, or fellow workers	20	24	28	25	28	16	2
Frequent or excessive noise	18	20	19	21	16	19	16
Abuse of your personal privacy	18	22	17	15	20	21	12
Problems with your children	18	7	13	22	27	24	8
Being lonely	15	18	24	12	14	15	16

*Base: All adults.

FIGURE 10.4
Hassles by Sex and Race/Ethnicity

Source: Humphrey Taylor, *Poor People and African Americans Suffer the Most from the Hassles of Daily Living*, Harris Interactive® www.harrisinteractive.com (2002). Reprinted with permission.

	All Adults	Sex		Race/Ethnicity		
		Male	Female	White	Black	Hispanic
Those affected by:						
Rising prices	69%	64%	73%	66%	82%	71%
Too many things to do	62	56	67	61	56	69
Concerns about money for emergencies	51	45	57	46	69	66
Concerns about health in general	47	43	50	46	55	40
Illness of a family member	37	33	41	37	33	39
Trouble relaxing	37	32	41	35	35	37
Not enough money for basic necessities	35	33	37	30	62	44
Problems with aging parents	23	24	22	23	22	29
Problems with your work, boss, or fellow workers	20	19	21	18	26	25
Frequent or excessive noise	18	19	18	16	32	22
Abuse of your personal privacy	18	18	19	17	22	16
Problems with your children	18	16	20	16	27	27
Being lonely	15	16	15	15	23	14

It is important to remember that stress affects different people in different ways. You will likely handle an angry customer's response or a tight deadline in a different way than a coworker might. Psychological and physical reactions to stress vary from one person to another. The environmental, job, and personal factors you encounter throughout your day can have a major impact on your mental and physical state and can affect how you react to the stress you experience.

You are a product of evolution when it comes to your brain's reaction to stress. When your brain recognizes or perceives danger (or stress), it triggers a chain reaction of events, starting with the release of chemicals (adrenaline) into the nervous system. Your heart starts beating faster, sending more blood throughout the body. Your breathing accelerates so that you take in more oxygen so that you are ready to deal with the situation (fight), or perhaps to leave the area (flight). This reaction has been called the **fight or flight syndrome**. Typically, after spurts of excessive adrenaline and activity, the body needs to take a break to recoup. Think about times when you have worked very hard (studying all night for an exam or preparing for an interview or presentation). You were able to accomplish the task but subsequently required time to recuperate. You may have heard about how a small person was able to do extraordinary things (lift a car off someone who became trapped when a jack collapsed). Because of body chemistry changes brought on by stressful situations, you, and they, had the necessary tools to accomplish unusual tasks. These are examples of how the fight or flight syndrome works.

In the customer service environment increased levels of adrenaline can be helpful in solving customer problems, or it can cause problems if you lose control. On the positive side, getting excited about a project can work in your favor. This is especially true when deadlines are tight for extended periods. For example, assume that your organization just bought out a rival company and taken over a call center site. A new computer-based communication system will be installed to better handle customer calls and contacts. You have an eight-week window during which you can move into the new facility, hire and train additional staff, and install the communication system before going online to take calls. You and other employees will have to work overtime for the entire period. If eight weeks was a realistic estimate of the time needed, you will probably meet your deadline, but then, you and the others will need time to rest.

On the negative side of the fight or flight syndrome in the customer environment, increased levels of adrenaline can create problems in maintaining the customer-provider relationship. For example, assume that you encounter a very disagreeable customer who has experienced a problem. No matter what positive communication and customer service skills you try, the customer will accept nothing less than what he is demanding. In addition, he is yelling and using profanity directed at you and the organization. In such a situation, the added adrenaline may lead you to react inappropriately (fight). In such instances you must remain professional and maintain control. You may need to excuse yourself and seek a supervisor or someone else to handle the situation (flight).

The speed at which customers expect product and service delivery in the twenty-first century will likely increase. Current systems efficiency is causing customers to keep demanding faster service. Some of the things that fuel such expectations are:

Think of a time when you have experienced the fight or flight syndrome in a customer environment as either a provider or a customer. Answer, then discuss, the following questions with others:

1. What happened?
2. Was the situation handled professionally? Explain.
3. If not, what was done wrong?
4. What could have been done differently?

- Almost instantaneous access to telephone numbers via directory information over the telephone or the Internet.
- ATM banking.
- E-mail.
- Microwave ovens.
- Fax machines.
- One-hour photo processing.
- Automobile oil changes in under a half hour.
- Convenience stores open 24 hours a day.
- Supermarkets with bank services, florists, pharmacies, and delis.
- Express delivery by the U.S. Post Office and other carriers in less than 24 hours.
- Cellular phones.
- Beepers.
- Electronic book publishing for out-of-print or out-of-stock books.
- Drive-up laundry and dry cleaning services.
- Twenty-four-hour automobile club towing services.
- Credit approvals over the telephone, or in person, in less than an hour.
- Electronic IRS filings.
- Laser eye surgery in less than a half hour.

4 Recognizing Stress

Concept: Stress has observable symptoms such as fatigue, aggressiveness, nail biting, and tardiness to name a few.

Stress has many observable symptoms, but some symptoms are difficult to pinpoint. The following are some typical indicators that stress is present:

- Inability to focus or concentrate on a customer problem or workplace situation.
- Irritability in dealing with others in the workplace.
- Excessive fatigue, which causes you to daydream or "nod off" during the day. Fatigue also prevents you from operating at your full potential or exercising initiative.
- Intestinal irritation that can affect your appetite or cause you to be absent from work.

- Tardiness or absenteeism because of physical symptoms or the need to catch up on sleep.
- Being argumentative or aggressive with customers and others.
- Nail biting or other nervous habits (e.g., fidgeting, sighing, playing with hair, wringing hands, constantly tapping the feet or an object).
- Poor attitude, which manifests itself in phrases like "Who cares?," "Is it Friday yet?" "It's not my problem," "Whatever," or "Tell someone who cares."
- Insomnia.
- Rapid or irregular heartbeat.
- Feelings of depression, crying spells, or feelings of uselessness and being underappreciated.
- Bingeing on food, alcohol, or tobacco.
- Pains in the stomach or head, neck or muscle pains, rapid pulse, high blood pressure, or irregular menstrual cycles.

Such symptoms, left unchecked for long periods of time, can cause serious health problems and even death. They can also affect your relationships with others for they can prevent you from performing at peak efficiency. If any one of these symptoms occurs, you may not need to be concerned (unless it lasts for an extended period of time); however, the occurrence of multiple symptoms should raise a red flag that causes you to seek assistance. Such help might be in the form of going to your supervisor or team leader to request reassignment, additional training, or more tools to help you do your job. A trip to a medical professional may be required. The important thing is to take action—quickly. Taking the "ostrich approach" (hiding your head in the sand) will not solve a problem. Such behavior will only expose you to risk.

Environmental Factors

Many **environmental factors affecting stress** are found in the workplace. Some are discussed in the following sections.

People

People can be a major source of stress. This is because you cannot control other people and how they behave. Another person's behavioral style, emotional and mental state, and unwillingness to communicate appropriately and effectively may make it stressful for you to do your job.

Physical factors. Physical factors such as noise, odors, bright or dim lighting, and heat or cold might affect you more than they affect others. Your ability to perform at peak efficiency may be inhibited by these factors. Such situations should be brought to the attention of a supervisor or team leader. In addition, depending on your job and what is permitted, you could take such actions as wearing earplugs or possibly having a radio on your desk that is tuned to an easy-listening or instrumental station. Such music is often subconsciously soothing. Depending on the tasks you are performing, you might be able to relocate to a quieter office, cubicle, or work area for short periods as you complete an assignment (e.g., assembling information packets, counting items, or filing).

Occupational hazards. Hazards that cause you to be concerned for your safety and that of others can be stressful. Such **stressors** (things that cause stress) are dangerous people or situations, heavy equipment or machinery, flammable, caustic, or explosive materials, or heavy lifting. It is important that you and other workers use caution in such environments.

If you are injured, you, the organization, and ultimately the customer suffer. Wear safety equipment, take your time when performing dangerous tasks, read instructions before using equipment, and point out any potentially dangerous situations to supervisors, team leaders, or other appropriate people.

Nonergonomic situations. Physical stress is created in environments in which chairs, tables, computer equipment, and other tools do not conform with industry standards related to employee protection, comfort, and safety. Back, eye, wrist, hand, arm, and leg strain, among other medical problems, can occur when such industry standards are not followed. When assigned a work area, make (or have others make) the necessary adjustments to the level of your desk surface, computer keyboard, computer monitor, telephone, and do anything else that would increase efficiency and reduce repetitive-motion injuries. If you must stand in one place for extended periods (e.g., manufacturing, cashier, or security staff), request a cushioned floor pad or chair as appropriate.

Organizational elements. The organization you work for can play a big role in increasing or decreasing your stress levels. This is especially true if the organization is undergoing various changes—in structure, product and/or service focus, technology, and so on. Employees often help reduce their stress levels in such situations by asking for information and by looking for opportunities to get involved in problem-solving and decision-making meetings. Having some degree of control over your environment can make a lot of difference in reducing stress.

Job Factors

In addition to the environmental aspects of a job that can lead to increased stress levels, other job-related factors can frustrate you and add tension to your day. For example, suppose that your organization provides only one microwave oven in the lunchroom. During the 45-minute lunch period, 30 to 40 people need to use the oven at the same time. Such situations are often not something you can control. You might choose to look for another job. In most instances, however, if you take the time to think of the situation and the interpersonal skills you have read about in this book, you can likely reduce your stress levels by negotiating or brainstorming solutions to the problem.

The key to improving your job and environment is often related to simple, effective interpersonal communication. Working with your team leader or supervisor, move toward changing the way you and your organization view your job and the way you perform it. Do this by openly discussing the following:

- Your level of authority and decision making in dealing with customer situations.
- Realistic and mutually agreed-upon performance goals.
- Specific opportunities for personal and professional growth.
- Recognition and reward for job performance.
- Elimination of unnecessary and repetitive tasks, where possible.
- Increased open communication between all levels within the organization.

Some of the many **job factors affecting stress** include:

Job structures. Organizational structures that require you to work various shifts and/or overtime in order to complete assigned work can be stressful and can lead to physical and mental side effects. Also, whether you work in a hierarchical or team-based environment can have an impact. Both organizational structures have advantages and disadvantages, based on how they are designed, managed, and allowed to function.

To improve your chances for success, become aware of your job responsibilities quickly (especially when they change), try to focus on the positive side of change (e.g., new opportunities to learn, increased opportunity for promotion, and the possibility of streamlining job functions and becoming more effective and efficient), and take advantage of the changing situation. Victims rarely win in changing environments. As organizations try to cut overhead costs, make systems more efficient, and better serve customers, they want employees who can support their goals. Make yourself more marketable by continually gaining new knowledge and skills so that you will be better prepared for the inevitable change that will occur in your organization.

Job insecurity. Employees often go through a period of insecurity when major changes occur within an organization. Some of their insecurity can be attributed to the behavioral style preferences that you read about in Chapter 6, but much of it is simply human nature. Such insecurity is often the result of a lack of adequate and effective communication from upper management. It can also be caused by a volatile industry or job market, as in the case of technology-based organizations that depend on military or government contracts; when government spending is curtailed, employees may be laid off.

If you find yourself in such a situation, use a proactive approach of gathering information, asking questions of your employers, reading materials given to you by the organization, taking the opportunity to get involved on committees or projects, and generally becoming a "player" rather than an "observer" as change occurs.

Unreasonable goals. Goals are part of evaluating job performance in most organizations. There are personal and organizational goals. You will typically be held accountable for personal goals that can ultimately influence the attainment of the goals of the organization.

Unfortunately, many supervisors and team leaders set goals with little or no personal input from the employees who have to meet them. Employees are held accountable for unrealistic production (dollar volume) goals, and in some organizations their results are publicly displayed. This practice can cause disillusionment among employees, as well as low morale, resentment, and frustration.

Help yourself and your organization by jotting down personal and performance goals throughout the year, so that when the time to set your performance goals for the next evaluation period comes around, you can have some input. Your goal might be personal (you want to learn a new software program or skill to better prepare you for job openings that occur from time to time), or it might be job-related (you need additional knowledge or skills to better perform your job and serve customers). By being proactive and demonstrating to your supervisor that you care about the goals set for you, you might rise in the opinion of your supervisor, since most employees do not take such actions.

Think about all the elements of your workplace or one in which you would like to work. What are some of the factors that can lead to personal stress?

Conflicting demands. In today's competitive environment, most employees have multiple responsibilities. Naturally, these demands may sometimes conflict. Although most employees prevail and accomplish their job tasks, there may be times when you may not achieve the degree of success that you prefer and desire. This is often because your need and efforts to provide quality service might be hampered by policies and procedures or by other factors not within your control. In addition, personal demands can cause internal conflict while you are on the job. A good time management system is sometimes the answer. For other situations, you may have to use your interpersonal communication skills to negotiate a settlement or compromise. Remember that you cannot always eliminate sources of stress. Therefore, you must seek ways of dealing with them.

Repetitive tasks. Many positions require employees to do repetitive tasks (e.g., data entry, manufacturing, cashiering, and some call center positions) that provide little or no opportunity for initiative or change in routine. Such responsibilities can sometimes lead to boredom or to a lackadaisical attitude toward job performance and lowered morale. If you find yourself in such a position, you might volunteer for additional assignments, committees, or cross-training in order to break the monotony and better qualify you for other positions.

Limited authority. One of the most frustrating situations for service providers and customers occurs when the provider does not have the authority to make decisions or assist customers. Suppose, for example, that a customer calls or comes to your organization and wants a refund, but you do not have the authority because the cost of the item cost is over your authorization limit (say $100). This type of situation sets up potential customer confrontation and resentment and can ultimately cause lost business.

If you find yourself in this type of situation, try suggesting to your supervisor some alternative systems for dealing with customer returns. There may be reasons why a system cannot be changed, but you will never know unless you ask.

Limited opportunities for advancement. Another job factor that often creates challenges for employees and their organizations occurs when opportunities for professional development are limited. Such roadblocks to professional and personal goal achievement can dampen an employee's desire to excel, use creativity and initiative, or remain in the job. To deal with this problem, many organizations offer on-site as well as computer-based training opportunities. Taking advantage of such opportunities builds your current job efficiency and also prepares you for future situations.

Personal Factors

Many things people do in their lives outside the workplace carry over into the workplace. Habits, activities, and other aspects of their personal life can create stress. Some **personal factors affecting stress** are discussed in the next section.

Personal issues often plague service providers on the job, leading to added stress levels. *What services or tools are available to help you deal with your own personal issues so that they do not impact your job performance?*

Relationships. If organizations could place a box at the entrance to their building with a sign saying "Leave your personal baggage here. Pick it up on your way out," it would be wonderful. In reality, this cannot be done. People are complex creatures. You cannot disassociate yourself from others very easily. As a result, you bring emotional "baggage" with you to work each day. For example, if you have an argument with a spouse or friend, that emotional encounter will stay with you when you report to work. Other aspects of relationships can create stress (for example, a spouse or roommate who does not do his or her part in helping with household chores, grocery shopping, or paying the bills). In such situations, communication skills that you learned earlier in this book can be a great help. Work to negotiate an equitable arrangement. If necessary, bring in an outside intermediary (counselor or financial planner). Such resources are often available through employee assistance programs.

From a positive perspective, your relationships with others outside the workplace can provide you with valuable tools for dealing with customers. In interacting with people outside of the workplace, you learn about behavioral styles, diversity, and human nature. The knowledge you gain outside the workplace can strengthen relationships in the workplace.

Physical condition and nutrition. How well you maintain your body can have a major impact on the way you feel, your energy level, your ability to think clearly and creatively, and ultimately how long you live. Recent reports of the "fattening" of Americans are alarming. After years of healthy eating and exercising, Americans are reverting to a less active lifestyle. If you are not monitoring your food intake and exercising, you could be setting yourself up for problems and lessening the chances that you will be ready to face the various customer service or workplace situations that surface.

Chemical use. Drinking, smoking, taking drugs, or using any other chemical substance can reduce your effectiveness on the job, and actually be deadly. Most health plans nowadays offer assistance in reducing substance depency. If you use any of these substances, you may want to check with your supervisor to find out whether programs to help you change your behavior are available.

Financial problems. If you are like most people, you have financial problems from time to time. Perhaps you don't have enough money in your checking account to cover expenses or you don't have the cash to make a needed purchase. These problems can weigh heavily on your mind and lessen your effectiveness in dealing with customers. If you have financial problems, look for resources (books, classes, employee assistance programs) that can help you get on sound financial footing.

Lack of "alone" time. Taking time for yourself is crucial for good mental hygiene. Sometimes the pressures of work and family responsibilities cause extreme stress levels to build up. When this happens, you can become like a

Develop a list of stressors in your personal life that might carry over to and affect your workplace performance and/or your personal relationships. Share your list with others and brainstorm possible stress-reduction strategies.

bomb with a short fuse waiting to be lit. And, if the match comes in the form of a difficult customer situation, problems for you, your organization, and your customer may be the result.

Build time into your schedule for you. Read a book, watch a movie, or do whatever you want to do. This sometimes takes negotiation with others in your personal and work life, but the dividends are worth the effort.

Overworking. Does the term *workaholic* apply to you? Because of competition in the workplace, concerns about job security, overextension of credit by banks, downsizing or "rightsizing" (or "capsizing") in many organizations, and numerous other factors, a lot of people spend more time at work than elsewhere. If you are such a person, the positive side is that you are doing more work and gaining new skills and knowledge while possibly moving up the career ladder. The downside is that other parts of your life may be suffering. The key to real long-term success is balance. You can obtain some balance through effective time usage (see Chapter 11). Here are some quick questions to help determine whether you fall into the workaholic category. If you answer yes to all or most of these questions, there is a good chance that you are a workaholic.

- Do you arrive early for work, no matter how late you stayed the night before?
- Do you volunteer to take on new tasks, even if you already feel overwhelmed?
- Do you skip lunch and breaks (and sometimes dinner) in order to work on job-related tasks?
- Do you regularly volunteer for overtime or work on weekends and holidays?
- Do you find it difficult to be inactive or relax?
- Do you approach every activity as a competition or challenge (even leisure activities or hobbies)?
- Do you find it hard to take a vacation (and when you do, you take work along)?
- Can you not envision yourself ever retiring?

Inability to solve problems. Customer service can be a stressful occupation. To be successful, you need a wide range of knowledge and skills. As you read in Chapter 7 and will read again later in this book, problem-solving skills are key to your success. Failure to develop and fine-tune skills necessary to assess a wide variety of service situations and to understand different types of customers can dramatically increase stress levels for you and your customers.

5 Avoiding Stress Through Effective Communication

Concept: Effective communication techniques such as politeness, being assertive rather than aggressive, and expressing your feelings are a few ways that you can avoid stress.

As you have discovered in other chapters, your key tool for success when dealing with customers is your ability to communicate in a positive, effective manner. By practicing active listening, selecting words and nonverbal cues carefully, and then

LEADERSHIP INITIATIVE

10.1

By assisting employees identify their own stressors and brainstorming ways to reduce stress, supervisors can help ease workplace tension. In providing meeting or training time for employees to address the issue of stress, organizations can ultimately reduce stress-related health care and turnover, and potentially prevent workplace violence.

A customer may vent frustration by yelling at you. *What can you do to avoid this type of situation?*

selecting the right time and place to deliver your message, you can significantly improve your relationships with customers and reduce stress levels (for you and your customers) at the same time. The following sections discuss specific strategies for communicating with customers.

Be Polite

Think of all the things you have been taught throughout your life related to courtesy. You may have heard statements such as "You can catch more flies with sugar," or you were reminded to always say please and thank-you. Whatever you learned, the concepts are the same—treat people well and with respect, and things will go much better. This is especially helpful in emotional or stressful encounters. The **acknowledgment** of customers as important people can sometimes get them to calm their own emotions and thus reduce stress levels for both of you. If nothing else, they will sometimes start to become embarrassed or feel bad about the way they are treating you and will calm down.

Respond Appropriately to Messages Received

When a customer asks a question or makes a statement, it is crucial that you listen and respond in a suitable manner. Summarizing what was said is one technique to accomplish this. Failure to respond appropriately can frustrate and irritate a customer or lead to escalated emotion.

Recognize that your customers are just like you—they experience pressure and stress. They come to you and your organization to fulfill a need or obtain something they want, not to receive poor service or defective products or to add more stress to their lives. They also do not expect to find you in a nonreceptive mood. If you and the organization disappoint the customer, he or she will likely become irritated or upset. A key point to remember is that although the customer may or may not have a legitimate complaint, it is your job to listen and take action to solve the problem to the best of your ability, and in a manner that will satisfy the customer.

Speak Assuredly

As you learned in Chapter 3, there is a difference between assertive and aggressive language and voice tones. When a customer or someone else is upset, it is best to allow him or her to vent without responding immediately. This can take the edge off an otherwise stressful situation. When you do speak, do so clearly and with authority and confidence. Also, stay calm as you communicate.

Do not let the other person irritate you or draw you into an emotional exchange. This will only heat up the situation, and will not help you to lead the conversation toward resolution.

Use "I" Language

Remember what you have learned about word choice. The word *you* can sound accusatory and challenging, but "I" language sounds as if you are taking on responsibility and are trying to join the other person in solving a problem. For example, suppose that a customer comes into your store complaining that a power tool does not work properly, all the while repeating that he or she had a similar one before and has read the owner's manual. If you say something like, "You're incorrect . . . ," a confrontation is likely to occur. On the other hand, if you say something like, "I'm not sure, but I believe that if you do . . . it will work fine. May I please show you?" In the second example, you are working with the customer in a nonthreatening manner to solve the problem without posing a challenge. You are also asking permission when you use the word *please.*

Communicate Your Feelings

A big factor contributing to stress is caused by failing to give feedback or to express yourself effectively. If you are troubled by something or someone, think about how to address the matter and then tactfully and professionally approach the person. Keeping feelings or emotions bottled up inside can cause stress and ultimately lead to relationship breakdown and illness. Management consultant and author Ken Blanchard calls this storing of feelings *gunnysacking.* He equates carrying around built-up emotions to putting them in an imaginary sack that you carry with you. Whenever someone does something you object to, you (figuratively) put it into your sack. You collect your complaints. You may grumble (to yourself), "I hate it when he does that," or "There he goes again. One of these days, I'm going to talk to him about that." What often happens is that at some point a small thing sets you off and you begin to unpack your gunnysack. You say things to the other person like, "I hate it when you do such and such," or "And another thing you do that makes me crazy . . ." The recipient of your anger is dumbfounded because he had no idea you had stored all the feelings you are now releasing. The result: You may feel better, but your relationship may be irreparably damaged.

As you read in Chapter 3, it is far better to share your feelings in a low-key rational manner than to save them up and explode. The other person may also explode, and you could end up in a highly charged, emotional argument. Instead, when something occurs that bothers you, take the time to provide immediate (or as soon as possible) feedback to the person. Discuss the behavior, the impact it had, your feelings on the subject, and then listen to his or her side of the situation, offer suggestions where appropriate, and reaffirm the value of the relationship to you. These simple things can mean a lot in maintaining a strong relationship with a customer or someone else in your life.

6   Maintaining Your Sanity

Concept: Maintaining your sanity means that you take active and positive steps to reduce your stressful situations. Managing your time effectively, setting realistic goals, and taking frequent breaks are just a few steps that will help.

You can probably identify many things that add stress to your personal life. With the added stress of dealing with difficult customers, how can you keep your sanity? To help cope with the day-to-day pressures brought on by dealing with difficult customers and workplace situations, try the tips given in Figure 10.5.

Stay Calm

Even though a customer or someone else does or says something that angers or upsets you, stay in control. When an incident occurs that makes you frustrated or emotional, keep smiling inside, politely excuse yourself, and take a quick break from the situation. Breathe deeply and think of something pleasant. Either return once you cool down or ask someone else to handle the person.

Manage Your Time Effectively

Chapter 11 will provide you with some ideas and specific tips for effectively managing your time. The key to successful customer service is to establish a system for managing your time. There are many good books, audiotapes, videos, and seminars that teach the skill of organization and task management. Learning and practicing these skills can help relieve stress. For example, taking care of difficult or unpleasant tasks first thing in the day means that you will not dread them all day long.

Avoid Procrastination

As you record tasks that need attention, take care of them. Putting them off only adds the stress of "one more thing to do." If your tasks seem overwhelming, break them into manageable chunks and work on one small piece at a time. For example, assume that you have been given the task of going through all correspondence files

FIGURE 10.5
**Stress-Reduction
Strategies**

There are things you can do to reduce your stress level. Here are a few:

• Stay calm	• Use positive self-talk
• Manage your time effectively	• Vary your activities
• Avoid procrastination	• Get more sleep
• Prioritize tasks	• Find a hobby
• Set realistic goals	• Take a humor break
• Take frequent breaks	• Be a realist
• Exercise regularly	• Take a mental trip
• Eliminate vagueness	• Smile
• Reduce personal tensions	

for the past year to identify recurring complaints. Try asking whether you can do a portion of the job at a time. If you are given permission to divide the work into chunks, you might work on three months of files each day until you have completed the review.

Prioritize Tasks

You will learn strategies for effective time management in Chapter 11. Specific techniques such as making a list of tasks to be accomplished at the end of each day or first thing in the morning and then following through on them can help reduce your stress level. With this technique, tasks not handled by the end of the day can become a high priority on your list for the following day.

Set Realistic Goals

Many people subject themselves to unnecessary stress by reacting as events occur. By setting attainable goals, you stay on track and feel a sense of accomplishment when you reach them. Also, get in the habit of rewarding yourself when you achieve goals. Do this by taking a short break or having a snack.

Take Frequent Breaks

Too many service providers develop the habit of skipping breaks and lunch or speaking to customers for hours at a time. This is a mistake. You need an occasional escape from the routine of dealing with customers and workplace activities. Taking time away from customers and job tasks can revitalize you mentally. If you also build in some exercise, as suggested in the next section of this chapter, you will double the benefit. Moreover, if you spend some time with coworkers occasionally during the day (e.g., breaks, lunch, or brief chats between customers), you will have an opportunity to strengthen workplace relationships while networking and sharing new ideas and information. All of this can be very valuable to your long-term health and success. Take opportunities during lunch or breaks to go outside the building to read, for fresh air, to walk, for a change of scenery, or to meet with friends. You'll return refreshed and ready to deal with customers again.

Exercise Regularly

Even though there are not enough hours in the day to accomplish everything that you have to do in your personal and work life, exercise is one thing that you should try to keep in your schedule. Exercise can provide many benefits, including prevention of emotional trauma brought on by stressful situations. Practices such as using the stairs instead of the elevator or escalator, walking at lunchtime, taking a brisk walk before or after work, and riding a bicycle to the convenience store rather than driving can add significantly to a feeling of good health. You may choose to park in a distant parking lot so that you have farther to walk. Walk in the mall at lunch or at night.

You can even exercise right on the job. Try using some simple isometric exercises (pushing against your chair seat or desk, grasping the edges of your chair seat and pulling firmly as you are seated, or keeping the feet flat on the floor while seated and pushing down against the floor). You can also do simple stretching activities (raising your arms above your head and reaching toward the ceiling, rolling your head slowly, and bending slowly to touch your toes).

Eliminate Vagueness

Much stress is due to uncertainty. To reduce uncertainty, research solutions, ask questions, or set up a system to deal with various situations that occur in your job or personal life. For example, suppose that a certain customer situation comes up periodically, and yet no policy or procedure exists to deal with it. You might check to see what other customer service professionals do in similar situations and then suggest to your team leader or supervisor that your organization implement a standard policy or procedure.

Reduce Personal Tensions

You cannot switch off your personal life while you're at work. Take the time to deal with problems in your personal life as they surface. Ignoring them will only frustrate you. Also, strive for balance in your personal and professional life (instead of spending all your waking hours working, develop a hobby, take a trip, spend time with friends and loved ones, or just relax). If you spend too much time and energy on either work or relaxation, you will neglect the other.

Use Positive Self-Talk

Give yourself a pep talk by saying positive things such as "I can handle this," "I won't let this get to me," or "This is only a temporary event, and a year from now, it will have no meaning." Too often, people get caught up in negative self-talk, which is unhealthy. They tell themselves things such as "I can't do this," "I can't do anything right," "Why can't I be more like . . . ?"

If you tell yourself these types of things often enough, they might become a reality, because initiative fades as defeat is accepted. This can lead to stress and depression.

Vary Your Activities

You may have heard the phrase "Variety is the spice of life." Variety is also crucial for preventing mental **burnout**. Your brain needs stimulation and challenge. If you follow the same routine day in and out, you have little opportunity to develop new ideas, explore other alternatives, and allow the brain to grow.

Be creative in your job and personal life. If you usually get up at 6:30 A.M., try getting up at 6 to read the paper, watch the news, or go for a walk or bicycle ride. If you always eat in the company cafeteria, try getting together with others to go off-site. If you usually follow one route to and from work, try an alternative. By varying routine and what you see or experience, you will gain a new perspective. This can lead to reduced stress, improved job performance, and increased satisfaction.

Making some of the minor routine changes shown in Figure 10.6 can often lead to enhanced creativity, different perspectives, and a feeling of being refreshed or renewed. The reason for this is that the brain is exercised by being exposed to new and different stimuli that cause it to adapt and learn. This can lead to more effective job performance and better interactions with customers and others in the workplace.

Get More Sleep

According to the Better Sleep Council in Alexandria, Virginia, most people do not get enough sleep. Each person is different in the amount of sleep needed to be efficient. Typically, eight hours of sleep has been recommended for years by various experts. If you find yourself trying to "catch up" on your sleep during weekends, your body is telling you that it is sleep-deprived during the week. Instead of staying up to watch the late news, turn off the set and go to bed earlier. If you really

FIGURE 10.6
Mental Stimulators

- Take a shower instead of a bath, or vice versa.
- Get up earlier or later each day.
- Change your morning routine.
- Have something different for breakfast occasionally.
- Take a different route to work.
- Listen to a different radio station in the car.
- Watch a different television channel.
- Shop at different stores.
- Go to lunch or on breaks with different people.

want to see the program, videotape it for viewing later. Or, watch the early morning news offered on stations in most cities.

If you are a shift worker or work nights, try the following tips for a better sleep period:

- Make sure that the room in which you sleep is dark and quiet. Use heavy window covering to block out light.
- Make sure that the room is cool, approximately 65° F.
- Make sure that your mattress is comfortable and supportive, and is large enough so that you can move around comfortably.

Find a Hobby

Most people who participate in a hobby that they enjoy (e.g., gardening, ceramics, painting, dancing, photography) find that it relaxes them by providing a mental diversion (as discussed earlier). Whether you look for an active or a sedentary activity depends on your time, desires, and capabilities. The key is to do what you want to do and like.

Take a Humor Break

Read, watch, or listen to something humorous. In the workplace, take a break with some of your peers and share humorous experiences that you have had in dealing with customers. You might even learn some new customer service strategies.

Be a Realist

You are not superwoman or superman, so don't try to act as if you are. Recognize that you cannot do everything yourself or take on all opportunities offered to you. Trying to do so can ultimately cause you to burn out mentally, can lead to serious health problems, and can reduce your effectiveness and efficiency in dealing with people and situations. Use some of the time-management strategies discussed in Chapter 11 to assist in improving your performance while decreasing your stress.

Take a Mental Trip

Close your eyes and relax as you think of pleasant events or locations. Instead of listening to loud, reverberating music, try something light, instrumental, or low-key as you relax.

Smile

The old adage "Laughter is the best medicine" has merit. Try to find something humorous about the situations you encounter at work and home. This can help reduce tensions. Lighten up. Don't take everything people say seriously or personally.

Looking for the reasons why you feel stressed may help you find ways to relieve the stress. Coping with stress is important if you are to remain healthy.

Take a few minutes when you are feeling stressed to give yourself a mental break. To do this, follow the steps outlined below.

1. Find a straight-backed chair and sit comfortably, not rigidly (depending on where you are, you can lie on the floor).
2. Mentally prepare yourself by telling yourself that you are going to take the next few minutes out of your hectic schedule "for you."
3. Relax your whole body be settling into the chair and allowing it to support you.
4. Close your eyes in order to block out visual stimulation or other distractions.
5. Start breathing slowly and deeply. As you inhale, say to yourself, "I am . . ." and, as you exhale, ". . . relaxed."
6. Continue this slow, rhythmic breathing and repeating of the phrase for the duration of the activity.
7. To conclude, discontinue the phrase *I am relaxed* but continue to breathe deeply for a few moments. As you end the activity, slowly and gently extend and stretch your legs, feet, arms, hands, and whole body.
8. Open your eyes slowly.

Note: Depending on your location and musical taste, you may want to play some mellow, instrumental relaxation music in the background.

7   Workplace Violence

Concept: Since 1980, changes in the workplace as well as external factors such as substance abuse, shifting values and beliefs, violence on television and in the movies, and a general trend to lash out at others have made workplace violence a familiar phrase. You should learn to recognize the danger signals and how to address them.

No chapter on stress would be complete without a discussion of **workplace violence.** Prior to 1980, workplace violence was virtually unheard of. Since then, the culture of the workplace has changed dramatically because of many factors addressed in other parts of this book (e.g., diversity, organizational restructuring, downsizing, technology, and increased job demands). Other external factors are adding fuel to this smoldering fire (substance abuse, shifting societal values and beliefs, illegal drugs, violence on television and in movies, and a general trend for people to lash out at others in the form of verbal or physical assault, as in the case of so-called **road rage**).

Violence in the workplace is nearing epidemic proportions and is creating a true crisis. According to research by the National Institute for Occupational Safety and Health (NIOSH), "Violence is a substantial contributor to occupational injury and death, and homicide has become the second leading cause of occupational injury or death. Each week, an average of 20 workers are murdered and 18,000 assaulted while at work or on duty. Nonfatal assaults result in millions of lost workdays and cost workers millions of dollars in lost wages." Moreover, NIOSH found that "Workplace violence is clustered in certain occupational settings: For example, the retail trade and service industries account for more than half the workplace homicides (56%) and 85% of nonfatal workplace assaults. Of any occupational group, taxicab drivers are at the highest risk of being the victims of homicide. Workers in health care, community services, and retail settings are at

LEADERSHIP INITIATIVE 10.2

With the rise in the instances of workplace violence, it is prudent for managers, human resource personnel, and employees to work together. By helping people recognize contributing factors and danger signs, and by rehearsing security and emergency escape measures, serious injury and death can potentially be avoided.

---

increased risk of nonfatal assaults."[3] Statistically, the persons in greatest potential peril are employees whose jobs involve routine public contact and the exchange of money. Obviously, these figures indicate that this is an issue to be concerned about.

Preventing Workplace Violence

Each employee must take a proactive role in dealing with and preventing workplace violence. A key to prevention is to conduct yourself in a professional manner at all times, keeping in mind the positive communication skills described in this book. By doing so, you are less likely to escalate a situation into an emotional confrontation or provoke a violent reaction from others. Also, it is important to educate yourself on strategies for recognizing danger signals and how to address them. At the very least, talk to your supervisor about the organization's approach to dealing with violence and plan an escape route from the work area, in case you ever need it.

Recognizing Potential Offenders

During the past few decades, many law enforcement and private organizations have sought to create a profile of potentially dangerous people in the workplace. The following characteristics are offered to aid your awareness, not to make you suspicious of someone who fits the profile. Also, keep in mind that many factors, such as problems in someone's life, could trigger violent behavior. Some general characteristics of offenders are:

- White male who is between 35 and 45 years of age.
- Has a history of job changes.
- Takes constructive feedback or criticism poorly.
- Is interested in firearms and other weapons.
- Identifies with or talks about violence.
- Is a loner who has few friends and little family contact.
- Fails to take responsibility or blame when errors occur.
- May use drugs and/or alcohol.

Identifying Warning Signs

Many people who are prone to violence exhibit telltale behaviors that, when viewed in their totality, should be a warning signal for you and those around you. By being vigilant, you can possibly head off trouble by changing your approach

---

[3]U.S. Department of Health and Human Services, National Institute for Occupational Safety and Health, Current Intelligence Bulletin 57, Publication DHHS (NIOSH), Publication No. 97–100, July 1996.

in dealing with a possible offender, or at least reporting the behavior that you observe to a supervisor, team leader, human resources, and/or security. The following are possible indicators that someone could become violent under the certain circumstances.

History of violence. If someone discloses to you that in the past he or she has been involved in violent criminal acts or domestic violence, or has had verbal or physical confrontations with others, you may want to be alert. Typically, past behavior is a good indicator of future behavior. This is especially true if the person seems to brag about the past negative or antisocial behavior. For example, suppose that you are in the cafeteria of your organization and a male coworker brags about the fact that over the weekend he got into an argument in a local nightclub. He says that he had to hit some guy for looking at his date. He then gives a gloating blow-by-blow description of the ensuing fight, which caused the other person to go to the hospital. It is wise to listen silently, excuse yourself at the earliest opportunity, and steer clear of this person as much as possible in the future.

Romantic obsession. Many stories are based on the theme of obsession. In such scenarios, the stalker pursues his or her prey relentlessly even when the other person hasn't the slightest interest. In these stories, often someone is hurt or killed as a result of the obsession. This is a strong message. If someone seems to have such an obsession with you or someone else in your workplace, seek assistance immediately by reporting it to your supervisor or team leader and your human resources department.

Alcohol or chemical abuse. Substance abuse can send someone over the edge. If a coworker shows signs of being under the influence of alcohol or drugs, confidentially report the matter to your supervisor or team leader immediately. In some serious situations when a coworker's activities off the job are negatively influencing his or her on-the-job performance, you may want to inform your supervisor or team leader. It is unfair to you, your customers, and the organization if your coworker cannot do his or her job because of outside activities. If a customer appears to be under the influence of alcohol or drugs, politely excuse yourself and seek assistance from your supervisor or team leader immediately.

Depression. Depression is a major contributor to suicides and workplace violence. Certainly, it can negatively affect job performance and the ability to deliver quality customer service. If someone you know seems to be depressed, it may be time to speak to this person confidentially and encourage him or her to seek assistance. Many times, depression can be brought on by personal problems (e.g., a relationship, financial, or legal problem) or by workplace issues (e.g., dissatisfaction, disciplinary actions, termination, or poor relationships with others). In extreme cases, you may also want to alert your supervisor or team leader.

When customers appear to be depressed, provide cordial, friendly service and get them out of the area as quickly as possible without provoking an emotional reaction.

Threatening behavior. Take all threats seriously. When someone becomes verbally and/or physically threatening, harassing, or belligerent, it is a cry for help and should not be ignored. Even if he or she apologizes, recognize that something is not right. If you receive a threat face-to-face, in writing, or over the telephone, report it immediately to your supervisor or team leader.

Mental conditions. Obviously, you are not a psychiatrist and should not try to act like one in diagnosing a person's behavior. However, if you deal with people day in and out in your job, you can probably recognize unusual behavior. For example, you should be concerned when you notice coworkers who stop paying attention to their hygiene or appearance, have serious mood swings, become withdrawn, complain about a supervisor, their job, customers, or the organization excessively and dramatically, and/or display empathy for people who commit violent acts. You should also closely monitor customers who send cues such as erratic gestures, talking to themselves, responding to or asking questions illogically, or referring to imaginary people or objects. Such people may be harmless, but you can never tell what is affecting their behavior. They might be mentally ill, or they might be under the influence of some substance. Keep your distance, and quietly seek assistance.

As you have discovered through experience and by your study of this chapter, stressors are possible and likely in everyone's life. Your task or goal will be to find ways to control the effects of stress so that you can work with your customers more efficiently and effectively.

Chapter Summary

Stress is costly and unproductive in the workplace and in your personal life. Throughout this chapter, you have explored what stress is, its causes and costs, the factors that contribute to increasing stress, the strategies for reducing or eliminating it, and the trend toward workplace violence. A key way to reduce stress and violence is through education. Using the material in this chapter can help make you more productive and possibly improve the quality of your life. By identifying and eliminating stressors in your life, you can enhance the enjoyment you receive from your job and deliver higher-quality service to your customers.

SERVICE IN ACTION   Darden Restaurants   ·   CHAPTER 10

http://www.darden.com

Darden Restaurants, Inc., is the largest casual dining restaurant company in the world with net earnings in 2003 of $232.3 million. It operates more than 1,200 company-owned Red Lobster, Olive Garden, Bahama Breeze, and Smokey Bones restaurants in North America, and employs more than 140,000 people.

The Darden framework is built on core values of "Integrity and Fairness, Respect and Caring, Diversity, Always Learning/Always Teaching, Being 'of Service,' Teamwork and Excellence," supported by three strategic imperatives—leadership development, service and hospitality excellence, and culinary and beverage excellence.

A major key to Darden's success story in a volatile industry, where restaurants often fail and close, is that today's society supports the concept upon which the company's restaurants are built—casual dining. In addition, many things have changed in the United States in recent decades. Factors such as growth in real disposable income, an increasing number of women in the workforce, and the aging of the population combined with changing lifestyles that place a premium on the timesaving and social reconnection benefits of dining out provide the perfect formula for Darden's success.

Key Terms and Concepts		
acknowledgment	eustress	personal factors affecting
burnout	fight or flight syndrome	stress
distress	job factors affecting	stressors
environmental factors	stress	road rage
affecting stress	job stress	workplace violence

Quick Preview Answers

1. T	5. T	9. T
2. F	6. T	10. F
3. T	7. F	11. F
4. T	8. F	12. T

Chapter Review Questions

1. How does stress benefit you?
2. Describe the fight or flight syndrome.
3. What are some signs of stress?
4. What are five environmental factors that cause increased stress?
5. What job factors cause increased stress levels?
6. What are some personal factors that contribute to high stress levels?
7. What are some communication strategies that can help reduce stress?
8. What are some strategies for maintaining your sanity in the workplace?
9. What are some characteristics of the typical violent offender in the workplace?
10. What are some warning signs that someone in the workplace might become violent?

Search It Out

Search the Internet for Information on Stress or Workplace Violence

Log onto the Internet to search for sites that contain articles and/or information related to any of the following:

Causes of workplace stress
Strategies for reducing or eliminating workplace stress
Research on stress
Research on workplace violence
Identifying workplace violence
Strategies for preventing workplace violence

Note: A listing for additional research on specific URLs is provided on the Customer Service website at **<http:/www.mhhe.com/lucas05>.**

Collaborative Learning Activity

Oral Presentation on Stress or Workplace Violence

Based on the topics in this chapter, research and write a five- to ten-page paper on workplace stress or workplace violence. Prepare a 15- to 20-minute presentation based on the paper and using some form of visual aid (e.g., overhead projector, PowerPoint, slides, flip charts, pictures, charts).

Face to Face

Dealing With Stress at Southside Memorial Hospital

Background

Southside Memorial Hospital is a state-of-the-art medical facility located just inside the city limits of Houston, Texas. The hospital will soon be merging with a competitor, Houston General Hospital. Many of the patients who visit the hospital each day are Hispanic, Vietnamese, or Laotian. In addition to the new multimillion dollar cardiovascular care unit, the hospital provides typical inpatient and outpatient care to over 60,000 patients a year. On a normal day, the emergency room sees 90 to 100 patients with complaints of everything from colds and flu to lacerations, head trauma, and gunshot or knife wounds. The atmosphere in the emergency room is usually tense, with a steady stream of patients entering, being processed, diagnosed, and sent to appropriate areas of the hospital for further evaluation and diagnosis or treatment. For the past four hours, there has been a problem with the air-conditioning unit for the emergency room waiting area and the temperature is now above 90° F. There are 10 to 20 people in the waiting room.

Your Role

You are the triage nurse at the front desk in the emergency room. You have been with the hospital for eight years but have recently been thinking of leaving because you were passed over for a position as emergency room supervisor and because of the merger with Houston General. Your primary job is to oversee and orchestrate the processing of everyone who enters the emergency room. This includes the initial discussion of the patient's needs, providing and collecting registration and insurance forms, logging the patient in, and ensuring that he or she is seen by appropriate medical staff members as soon as possible. The position requires a high degree of medical knowledge, patience, interpersonal communication skills, and compassion.

You have worked a double shift today because of a flu epidemic. You are tired, your feet hurt, you haven't eaten in eight hours, your 13-year-old daughter (you are a single mother) called earlier to tell you that she came home from school because she was sick, and you believe that you are also coming down with the flu. Also, during the past hour, there has been an influx of people into the emergency room. You have had to deal with screaming children with colds, or with objects stuck up their nose, and with people who did not want to be in the emergency room. You have also screened a woman in labor, a teenage boy who cut his foot badly while using a lawnmower, a man with severe back strain, an elderly woman who appears to be senile (she imagines that people are coming to get her; you think that she has broken her hip), and a man who had an 11-inch spike driven through his forearm in an occupational accident.

At 8:42 P.M., you receive a radio message from an incoming ambulance informing you that a patient is being brought in who is highly agitated, belligerent, and possibly under the influence of alcohol or some other substance. He has lacerations to his forehead and shoulder from an automobile accident. As the vehicle arrives, you meet the paramedics at the emergency room door along with an orderly and a member of the security team. While you are attempting to assess the man's injury, he pushes your hand away saying he doesn't need any help from some overweight cow. He then tries to get off the gurney he is strapped to.

Critical Thinking Questions

1. What are some of the stressful environmental factors in this scenario?
2. What are some of the stressful job factors present in this scenario?
3. What are some of the stressful personal factors in this scenario?
4. How would you handle the situation with the patient who has just arrived? Explain.
5. What could go wrong in this situation?

PLANNING TO SERVE

CHAPTER 10

In order to reduce your stress level and improve your ability to more effectively provide quality service to customers, create an action plan that will potentially lead to a more efficient and relaxed quality of life.

First, create a list of three or four action items or goals related to stress. For example, "I plan to examine the list of stressors that I developed earlier in the chapter to determine the ones over which I have control. I will then list one to three strategies for better management of each factor."

Once you have your list of goals, create a list of people or other resources that can help you achieve your goals. Next, approach those individuals and explain what you are attempting to do. Solicit their assistance in helping you reach your goals.

Finally, set specific dates for reevaluating each goal to determine where you are in relation to achieving it. Make adjustments, as necessary. Put these dates on your calendar or in another prominent place where you see them regularly to remind you to continue working toward your goals.

Managing Your Time

From the Frontline Interview

Steve Tanzer is a managing partner in Global Performance Strategies LLC, a human resource consulting and training company. He has been dealing with customers in the business world for over 30 years. During that time, he has dealt with individual consumers and large corporate clients, representing multimillion dollar purchases.

1 In your experience with customers, what is a prime observation that you have made related to them?

I have found that even though each customer is unique in many ways, each is also similar in one very important way . . . he or she is "the customer" with purchasing power and decision-making authority.

A fundamental expectation by the customers is that the product or service they purchase will meet or exceed their expectations. If not, they look to the company (service provider) to resolve the problem. This is where a company establishes its true credentials with a customer. How a customer is handled in the "after-sale" situation will determine if the person is a long-term customer, or one who has a story to tell about how bad he or she was treated by a company with which the customer will no longer do business.

2 Related to time management when dealing with customers, what are some of the biggest time robbers you face each day?

**STEVE TANZER,
Managing Partner,
*Global Performance
Strategies LLC***

To me, the chief time robber is the emotional customer. This type of customer might be unhappy and very emotional over the product or service because it did not work as expected. These types of situations must be defused before any suitable solution can be put in place. To calm these customers down requires special training and skills for the employee who comes in contact with the customer. Failing to train employees in dealing with difficult and emotional customers could lead to greater long-term damage being done and waste even more time.

3 What are some strategies that you use to reduce the amount of time you lose each day?

When dealing with a customer I make them my top priority. By doing this, it will overall reduce the time I have to spend with them. Dealing with a situation immediately is crucial. By doing so, I only have to deal with it once. If I let a customer see he or she is important, I can gain a customer for life.

An example of this level of customer service was observed recently with a purchase my wife made at a major retail store in Sanford, Florida. After purchasing a high-end lipstick, it broke, requiring her to go back to the store. The saleslady immediately handled the return, but when all was done she did one thing more which set her apart from other professionals . . . she apologized for the inconvenience of having to return to the store. She recognized the extra time it took for

> *"There's never enough time to do it right, but there's always time to do it over."*
> *Jack Bergman, former VP, Jordache Enterprises, Inc., 1987*

Chapter Learning Objectives

After completing this chapter, you will be able to:

- Realize how time reality and perceptions of time differ.
- Recognize the need for effective time management.
- Prioritize daily tasks.
- Apply techniques that save time while serving customers.
- Use time usage criteria to reclaim time.

---

my wife to return to the store and make the exchange, plus the loss of use of the lipstick. Her apology demonstrated that she understood how important the customer is.

4 How have you seen technology assist and/or detract from efficiency of time usage?

Technology is only as good as the person who uses it. If you fail to take your calls live rather allowing voice mail to handle them you are misusing technology. If e-mails are never answered or left to "when you get to them" again, it is another misuse of the technology.

Unfortunately, incorrect use of technology can lead to a loss of productivity time for you. The question then becomes, "How do you regain this lost time?" The answer is two-part:

First, learn to master time or it will master you. Take a time management class and use a time management tool . . . this will pay you enormous dividends.

Second, if technology is part of your tool kit, use it correctly.

5 In your experience, what can service providers do better to utilize their time when dealing with customers?

Preparation and practice! A service provider can be in control of time if she or he is prepared and knows how to do a job well. This means having training, tools, and time management skills.

It goes without saying that organizations have the responsibility to ensure their customer service people are properly trained and empowered to resolve the customer's problem. But it is the service providers who ultimately have the responsibility to execute the work and decide how they use the tools and techniques they have been given. If done properly their time is well spent and efficient. If done improperly then time becomes a negative issue and they will fall far below the norm for their work group.

6 What advice about time management can you give to someone entering a customer service job today?

Three thoughts come to mind.

First, know the work environment you will be entering. All customer service groups are *not* equal. The one you pick will ultimately decide if you can be successful at your work.

Second, knowledge and training are key elements. You should take all the training available from your employer. Continuous learning will help you be the best at what you do and how efficient you are at doing it.

Third, become a master of time management. This is a skill that will serve you well in your personal and professional life. Take a formal class in time management and select a time management system (e.g., Daytimer®, Franklin Covey®, or whatever) to help you become its master. If you don't become its master, time will master you.

Critical Thinking

What is your reaction to Steve's comments and suggestions? In what way have you experienced similar challenges when trying to manage your time in a service environment?

Quick Preview

Before reviewing the chapter content, respond to the following questions by placing a "T" for true or an "F" for false on the rules. Use any questions you miss as a checklist of material to which you will pay particular attention as you read through the chapter. For those you get right, congratulate yourself, but review the sections they address in order to learn additional details about the topic.

_____ 1.   Increased self-satisfaction is one of the positive results of effective time management in the workplace.

_____ 2.   The way you use time has little effect on your stress levels.

_____ 3.   One technique for prioritizing your time is to schedule key events and then review the information regularly.

_____ 4.   Time tends to pass more slowly when the mind is not actively engaged or proactively performing and being stimulated.

_____ 5.   Tasks that could contribute to customer satisfaction and ultimately lead to improved performance should be a top priority, as should those regulated by law or established by policy or customer demand.

_____ 6.   Being prepared by having information and materials available to help serve customers is one technique for saving time while serving customers.

_____ 7.   You should look for opportunities to engage customers so that they will not become bored and dissatistifed and go to a competitor.

_____ 8.   Using a "take a number" system for waiting customers is one way to stimulate your customers mentally.

_____ 9.   When providing service by traveling to different locations or customer sites, you have virtually no control over your time because of unexpected delays.

_____ 10.   You should always confirm appointments before leaving to attend them even though you spoke with the person with whom you are meeting when you scheduled the meeting.

_____ 11.   To save time on the telephone, you should have a list of objectives before you call.

_____ 12.   When calling someone, you should screen or identify the person who answers before you begin speaking.

_____ 13.   Voice mail systems are a universally accepted tool for effective time management.

_____ 14.   To better manage your e-mail, prevent messages from accumulating, and save time, you should answer e-mail messages as soon as they arrive.

_____ 15.   Three criteria for examining time usage are necessity, appropriateness, and efficiency.

Answers to Quick Preview can be found at the end of the chapter.

1   Why the Need for Effective Time Management?

Concept: Time management is not just a workplace issue. Learning to apply skills that you use to manage your time away from the workplace to the workplace can make you more efficient.

This chapter focuses on increasing your awareness of the need for effective **time management**. By thinking about factors that inhibit effective productivity, and coming up with strategies for improving time usage, you can gain insights into ways to handle a variety of personal and workplace situations. Also, by better managing your time, you can improve your job performance and better serve your customers. One important thing to remember about time management is that it is not just a workplace issue. If you learn to manage your time outside the workplace, you can apply that skill to your job. On the other hand, if you mismanage your time outside the workplace, the problems will probably follow you to the job.

Four important positive results can come from effective time management in the workplace:

1. Elevated productivity through a more efficient approach to accomplishing tasks and dealing with customers.
2. Reduced stress levels, which can benefit you personally and can also make life easier for those around you since you will probably be calmer and seem more in control.
3. Increased self-satisfaction from confidence in your ability to get the job done professionally and in a more competent manner.
4. Improved quality of life, for good time management habits on the job can expedite the accomplishment of tasks and reduce the amount of overtime or extra hours needed to "catch up." This is time you can spend doing the things you enjoy in life either on or off the job.

As you read in Chapter 10, customer service is a very rewarding but stressful profession. With all the tasks and responsibilities that the average service provider must attend to, there are often not enough hours in a day to effectively balance work with personal life. Moreover, dealing with internal and external customers can be trying, to say the least. Many customers are a joy to serve; others are not. Even so, it is your job to smile, act professionally, and make a valiant effort to assist all of them to the best of your ability. Sometimes you are successful; sometimes you are not. Whatever the outcome, a key factor often influencing your actions (and inactions in some instances) is time. The amount of time you have or do not have has an important effect on your actions. In a workplace that has downsized, restructured, merged, and made all kinds of other adjustments, there never seems to be enough people or hours to get everything done. Add to this the fact that, in many cases, your customers are just as stressed and rushed as you are, and you have a formula for possible service breakdown. This potentially volatile combination can often lead to confrontation and customer dissatisfaction if you are not careful and cannot manage your time effectively. This is why your ability to manage time and tasks effectively is so crucial. If you can learn the skill of time management, you can squeeze out precious minutes throughout the day. Knowing how to manage your time can lead to fulfilling workplace experiences, satisfied customers, and self-satisfaction.

2   Where Does the Time Go?

Concept: Everyone has the same amount of time every day of the year. How you manage that time makes the difference.

As you saw from the opening quote for this chapter, there never seems to be enough time to get everything done that you have to do. As the workplace gets more chaotic and your responsibilities grow, you need as many tools as possible to gain control of your time and be more productive.

Time Reality

Everyone has the same amount of time each day (86,400 seconds, 1,440 minutes, or 24 hours). Some people use their time more efficiently than others do. Depending on the type of work and home environments in which you find yourself, your stress may increase because of your difficulties in using time effectively. For example, if you work in production areas (e.g., sales, telemarketing, or call centers) where you are held accountable for production rates, have timed standards for productivity, or work at a hectic pace, time can seem like your enemy. Or, high levels of stress may be caused by too few people handling too many tasks. In these environments, employees often have to work extended amounts of overtime or on weekends in order to meet established goals or standards. The frequent result is that they have little time to think before they speak. This is why a good system for time management and effective time management strategies can come in handy. Even if you can squeeze out a few minutes here and there, those precious minutes can help you efficiently deal with your **time reality** and more effectively serve your customers or accomplish other tasks.

Time Perception

Time can move quickly or slowly, depending on the circumstances and whether you view an event as positive or negative. Take a look at some of the following examples of **time perception** to see whether you agree.

Slow Time Passage	Fast Time Passage
Being on telephone hold (no music or announcements)	On a rollercoaster or amusement ride
In the dentist's chair	At an enjoyable lunch meeting
In the doctor's office	Taking a test (e.g., for a driver's license)
In a slow-moving bank line	
Waiting for popcorn to pop at a movie theater	Speaking with a service provider who bills by the hour (e.g., lawyer, consultant, plumber)

Notice in the situations in column 1, time seems to pass slowly when the mind is not actively engaged or proactively performing and being stimulated. Time seems to go quickly when the mind is involved in some sort of mental activity. The lesson to be learned is that you should try to engage your customers so that they will not become preoccupied with time. Likewise, plan your own events so that you do not experience nonproductive or "down time." When people have time on their hands, the mind gets busy doing other things. In a customer situation, often the customer's mind starts focusing on the fact that it is bored or that it's taking you a lot of time to provide service. Also, an unusual thing starts happening in such situations: the customer's internal clock starts speeding up. Ten seconds can seem like a minute. If you don't believe this, try an experiment. The next time you call a service provider and are put on hold before speaking with someone (e.g., a technical support line, bank or retail customer service, doctor's office), have a stopwatch handy. Start the stopwatch the moment you are put on hold. Without looking at the stopwatch, mentally track time until someone answers. Then stop the watch, but don't look at it. Have a pencil ready and make a note of how long you thought you were on hold. Now look at the stopwatch. If you are like most people, you will have

Working with your group, add to the list of slow and fast time passages given earlier. Try to think of specific customer service situations, possibly ones that you have experienced as a customer. Be prepared to discuss your answers.

perceived that you were on hold longer than you actually were. This is usually the result of boredom.

This phenomenon is one of the reasons organizations put music or announcements on the telephone hold function. They are engaging the customer's mind. Some companies even play occasional messages such as "Your approximate wait time is . . . ." Many times, if you check the time, you will find that the wait time is much longer than the message indicates.

3 Prioritizing Your Time

Concept: Use a system to prioritize your time.

Being able to prioritize is an important skill. Planning events, activities, and tasks on a yearly, monthly, weekly, and daily basis—that is, **prioritizing time**—can be rewarding from the standpoint of allowing you to be more proactive in preparing to deal with situations. Such planning can reduce your need to be a **crisis manager**. It is important on and off the job because, if you do not manage your personal life well, you may carry over the personal stress into the workplace. This is not only inefficient; it is also unfair to your employer, peers, coworkers, and external customers.

After you have scheduled key events and tasks using some type of scheduling system (e.g., time management software, written planning system or calendar, or electronic scheduling device that can download information into your computer), review the information regularly to avoid forgetting something.

One way to manage events, rather than having them manage you, is to create a list of activities each day and assign a value to each based on importance. The key is to be consistent and prioritize each day. Some people make planning the last activity of their workday. When they arrive in the morning, they are ready to begin rather than spending time preparing.

Guidelines for Setting Priorities

Three guidelines can help you in determining what tasks to do first. That is, they can help you create a realistic and achievable list of daily tasks. As you learned when you read about goal setting in other chapters, goals must be attainable. Use the following standards as a guide when **setting priorities**.

Judgment. You are the best judge of what you can accomplish in any given day. You know your strengths and what has to be done. When selecting priorities, remember that the ones having the most impact on customers and others should be placed high on your list. On the other hand, do not put so many priorities on a daily list that you will not get them done. If this happens, you might become discouraged and give up. When you find that you have more high priorities than you have time, you may need to ask for help or guidance from your boss. Many times, simply asking helps develop your relationship with others. They feel respected and trusted by your gesture, as long as you don't appear to be unloading your tasks onto them. Also, consider other resources that you might use to accomplish tasks (e.g., technology, outside vendors, customers).

Relativity. Assigning priorities is a matter of relativity. Some tasks and projects are readily rated higher than others are rated. You should be guided by the question "What is the best use of my time?"

Many people fill their daily schedule with frivolous or easy tasks and with tasks that they like to do. This produces a hollow feeling of accomplishment, for they may get a lot done and enjoy doing it, but they have not added a lot of value to customer service or the organizational goals. Keep in mind when setting priorities in the workplace that your No. 1 focus should be your customers and activities that support them.

Timing. Reality and deadlines have a way of dictating priorities. The starting time of a project or task also may establish priorities. Once you begin a task, there must be enough time to finish it. If this is not possible, you may have to reprioritize or seek assistance.

Be realistic about the time it will take to complete a task. Make sure that you schedule that much time, plus a little extra, on your daily planning sheet. Also, consider your peak time period for performance (your circadian rhythm, which you read about in Chapter 5). Each person typically has a period of the day in which he or she has more energy and can get more done. Capitalize on your peak period and schedule high-priority tasks during that time, if possible.

Prioritizing System

To set up your own priority system, list all your pending activities and then group them according to their level of importance. How you assign value to a task is not as important as long as you use the same format each day. Many people use an A, B, C system, and others use a 1, 2, 3 format. Here are suggested criteria for assignment:

Priority A—Must do or critical items. Some things must be done because of management directives, local, state, or federal regulations, importance to customers or clients, deadlines, or opportunities they provide for your success or advancement (e.g., state tax reports, actions requested by a customer, application for a position in the organization with a specific cutoff date for submission).

Priority B—Should do. Items in this category are of "medium" value. Although they may contribute to customer satisfaction and improved performance, they are not essential or do not have critical deadlines (e.g., mailing an unsolicited information kit to a customer about a new product or developing a proposal for changing an existing system or process).

Priority C—Nice to do. This is the lowest category and includes tasks that are not a direct link to customer satisfaction. They may even be fun or interesting but could be omitted or left undone. Postponing or scheduling such priorities until a slower time period will likely have little or no impact on customer service (e.g., meeting with team members to brainstorm ideas for a more efficient layout of cubicles, cleaning old e-mail files, or neatly lining up the products on a shelf).

Note: As you go through your e-mail and voice mail messages at the times you have scheduled throughout the day, prioritize them, and add them to your list of things to do.

4   Saving Time While You Serve

Concept: Prepare your daily schedule to make your calls or other appointments a priority. Use your time to good advantage between appointments.

In addition to prioritizing, many strategies can save time and result in a better quality of customer service. A key to effective service is to allocate enough time to handle customer issues. With experience, you will get better at doing this and at estimating how much time you need for various situations. Until then, talk to other, experienced service professionals, your boss, and your customers to find out how long a task should normally take. Also, observe other service providers as they serve you. Make mental notes of the efficient and effective things you hear and see, and avoid those things you perceive as ineffective time management techniques.

Finally, be prepared to serve by having available the information and materials you need (e.g., know your company's policies and procedures, know the products and services offered, be familiar with the various forms, and have pencil or pen handy) so that you do not have to search for something. Failure to be ready to serve wastes your time and that of your customers.

In addition to the tips you have just read, you can do some specific things in various situations to provide service while managing time effectively. As you read through the following sections, think of how you might apply the techniques described and what other ones you might use.

Time Management in Face-to-Face Situations

Time is an important element in a service provider's daily life. Whether you deal with complaints, counter service (e.g., post office, bank, supermarket), sales (e.g., car dealership, insurance agency, electronics store, department store), deliver service (e.g., plumbing, lawn service, appliance repair), or are in any type of job in which you sell or assist customers, time management comes into play. All the interpersonal communication skills described in this text are crucial in the delivery of professional service. By building effective relationships, you have a better chance of ensuring that interactions between customers and others in the workplace will be positive. Thus you will need your conflict-resolution skills less.

Some techniques for **time management face-to-face** that you may want to consider are:

Recognize the value of a customer's time and show a service orientation. Recognize the customer's presence nonverbally by smiling, and gesture with an index finger to indicate that you will be available in about a minute. If you are serving via the telephone, offer to call the customers back rather than keep them on hold.

Get the customer busy. If you need to do other things or wait on other customers, try to get a waiting customer actively involved in doing some task. For example, if a customer will need to fill out a form (e.g., a new patient in a doctor's or dentist's office, someone returning or exchanging a product at customer service, or an applicant for a job or license), give the customer a pen and form and let him or her get started while you serve another customer. This occupies the customer while you handle another customer—and the form gets filled out without causing you to wait until later.

Give the customer something to read. Depending on the situation and the type of organization, you might give the customer new product brochures to read while he or she waits. This not only occupies the customer's mind but may

LEADERSHIP INITIATIVE 11.1

To provide useful material that can occupy waiting customers, create a listing of frequently asked questions (FAQs) about your organization, product(s), and service(s). This can provide answers and information that might interest your customers while informing them. Query employees and customers for possible questions and then create answers for your handouts.

Having customers take a number organizes the wait time for service. *How would you organize the wait time in a retail business?*

answer questions that you won't have to answer later.

Have the customer take a number. Many organizations with high customer walk-up traffic volume (e.g., fast-food establishments, discount stores, motor vehicle offices, utility companies) use tear-off number dispensers to alert customers when it is their turn to be served. These ticket systems are also helpful during peak sales and service seasons (e.g., back to school, Christmas, going out-of-business or clearance sales). Such systems were designed to let customers know where they are in the line for service, keep customers moving, and save service providers the unpleasant and time-consuming task of having to deal with angry customers who think that other customers have been served out of turn.

Taking a number also gives customers some mental stimulation (unless service is really slow and they must wait for an unacceptable length of time to be served). Taking a number gives them something to do—watch the numbers of other customers get called until their own turn arrives.

If your organization has such a system, be sure that you are alert to people entering. Notify new customers to take a number for better service and to prevent confusion later over whose turn it is for service. Also, with such a system, be careful not to fall into the practice of thinking of your customers only as numbers. Instead of shouting out "Number _____," a more appropriate approach would be to say something like, "May I help the customer with ticket number _____?" Then, as the person approaches, try to make eye contact, smile, and offer a greeting such as "Good morning. How may I assist you?"

Time Management on the Run

You have probably heard the saying "There just aren't enough hours in the day." This is especially true if your job involves traveling to a client's site or if you work at or travel between remote locations (e.g., branch offices). Transit time can take a big chunk out of your day. In such situations it is important to recognize how to best use your time. Here are a few tips for **time management on the run**:

Prepare in advance. Make sure that you schedule your appointments far enough in advance to allow for emergencies. Gather the materials and information you will need well before the scheduled date and time. Waiting until the last minute could cause trouble, especially if something you need is not readily available. It can also cause a late departure which can then impact subsequently scheduled meetings or events.

Plan visits during non-rush-hour traffic. If possible, schedule client or customer visits when traffic is not snarled and transit times can be reduced. Often, when you drive to other locations, something will slow you down (e.g., malfunctioning traffic lights, accidents, trains, vehicle breakdowns). You can grumble and accept lost productivity time, or you can be prepared by having alternative routes in mind and making sure that your vehicle is well maintained. Also, you can use the last tip in this section—listen to audiotapes to make the most of your downtime.

Group appointments. Setting up more than one appointment in the same geographic area can save you and your customers time, effort, and frustration while reducing your travel miles. You can use the "group" approach when customers or vendors come to your site for meetings. Also, try to schedule meetings or return phone calls for one part of a day (e.g., the morning). For example, if you get all your meetings taken care of in the morning, you can then focus on other customer-related activities during the rest of the day without being interrupted.

Confirm your appointments. Take the time to e-mail or call your customer or client before leaving for an appointment. You will thus avoid an unnecessary trip if there was a change of plans and you were not notified, or someone forgot to note the meeting on his or her calendar. Your time, and the customer's, is precious; treat it as such.

Invest in a mobile phone. In today's changing world, cell phones have become indispensable. Use your phone when you leave one client location for the next one to verify an appointment. Do remember safety and don't operate the phone while driving.

Listen to audiotapes. Travel time is a great opportunity to catch up on the latest books on tape that you never seem to have time to read. You can also listen to taped notes from customers or meetings while you are traveling. Additionally, you can record information about various regular clients (ones you see or speak with periodically) and play them back on your way to appointments with them (e.g., past products or service used, organizational facts and statistics, names of key people in the organization). This mental rehearsal can assist you to be better informed and appear more competent.

Time Management and Technology

As you read in Chapter 9, there is much to consider in a workplace full of changing technology. As a result of technology, you may need to learn how to use all the technical tools available to help you better serve your customers. You may also have to struggle just to keep up with all the changes and upgrades; this is one of the big **time wasters** facing many organizations and service providers. The technology is needed to stay competitive, but it takes valuable time to install and maintain the equipment and software and to train employees to use it effectively. Some aspects of **time management and technology** follow.

Telephone Management

In addition to the interpersonal skills discussed in Chapters 3 to 5 and the basic guidelines for using the telephone that were covered in Chapter 9, effective **telephone management** takes planning and skill. Additional strategies for increasing effectiveness and better managing your time when using the telephone are described below.

Establish objectives before making your calls. If you are in sales, your objectives might have to do with total number of sales per hour or gross or net sales volume. If you work in an outbound call center that sets up appointments or qualifies credit prospects, you might also have a specific number to attain. Representatives handling inbound customer service calls or help desks might have time limits per call. Whatever measure the organization or you use, it should be decided before you start making calls.

If you are simply calling a customer or vendor or returning a call, you should have a clear goal in mind related to your reason for calling and what you want to get from the call.

Prepare for the call by making a list of topics you wish to address. This involves knowing to whom you want to speak and having a clear understanding of the reason for your call. Further, have any support materials (e.g., letters, files, materials, statistics) right by the phone for easy access during the conversation. If you need answers to specific questions, write them down and leave space on the page for the responses. Also, put your questions or comments in the order of importance to you in case your conversation is cut short; at least you will get the most important information from your call recipient. If you are making a formal sales call, you may even have a structured script that you use as a guideline with each customer. By having such things written down, you are less likely to forget to ask a question, give information, or fail to meet your objectives.

Screen your caller as soon as someone answers the telephone, unless he or she gives a name right away. Do not assume that you have the correct party on the telephone and immediately start talking or selling. You are wasting time (yours and that of the person on the telephone) if it is the wrong person. This is especially important if you are making a business-to-business call in which you phone another company to get or give information or to resolve a complaint. If you do not briefly define your reason for calling and then ask with whom you should speak, you may waste valuable time explaining everything to the wrong person, who will say, "I'm sorry, you'll need to speak to . . ." or transfer you and have you repeat the conversation to another person.

If your main job is to receive customer calls, use an efficient and customer-focused telephone technique. For example, get the name of the person and other pertinent information you will need to answer his or her questions, access customer records, and move the call along early in the conversation. However, try not to sound impersonal. It is often best to get account information after you greet your caller. Keep in mind what you have learned about personalizing a call by using a salutation (e.g., "Good morning"), giving the name of your organization and your name, and then offering to assist. Many providers use a somewhat impersonal greeting that can sound mechanical and uncaring to a customer (e.g., "ABC Company, may I have your account number?"). This approach does not recognize the customer as a person, and it implies "I only care about getting through this call as quickly as possible." In

Emergency operators receive special training on call screening in order to get essential information quickly. *What training or techniques would help you better get to your customers' needs in a timely manner?*

many organizations, you may not have a choice on what greeting you use since you are held accountable for "talk time" or time spent on each call. If you do have flexibility, go for the personalization. It can pay off by avoiding negative situations that take time to resolve.

Measure your activity periodically to determine how well you are doing at meeting your objectives. Most call centers have software that tracks such activity.

Keep the customer informed by returning to the call every 20 to 30 seconds if you have placed someone on hold. If appropriate, offer to call the customer later. This approach saves the customer time and keeps you from having to continually come back on the line for an update.

Be efficient and service-oriented by avoiding transferring customers numerous times to different people. Use the standards of your organization related to transfers. If none exist, use two transfers as your maximum number before you personally assume responsibility for a call and handle a customer situation. Transferring a customer more than twice is not efficient and frustrates the customer while sending an unprofessional message about the organization and its employees.

Voice Mail Management

Voice mail systems and telephone answering machines were developed to increase efficiency by helping callers and call recipients save time. Unfortunately, owing to abuses on both sides, many people detest these inventions. This is really a shame because with proper **voice mail management** these systems are effective. Not only do they help organizations reduce staff costs and save time by using technology for simple information collection and dissemination, but they also assist service providers by gathering valuable customer information that allows the provider to do research and better assist customers.

The abuse part comes when call service providers decide to send all their calls to voice mail even though they are sitting at their desks working next to the telephone. The systems were not designed to replace you or take all your calls. You may have legitimate reasons to let the machine answer your calls even though you are at your workstation (e.g., you are in a meeting with a customer or discussing some business-related matter with a coworker, you are working on a project that has a tight deadline, or you are preparing for an upcoming meeting or other function). In general, though, these systems should be a backup, not a replacement, for you.

Callers also abuse the systems by either hanging up when they realize that they have reached a machine or leaving inadequate information. As you read in Chapter 9, at a minimum when you call someone and reach a voice mail, you should leave your name, the time and date of the call, your phone number (including area code if appropriate), and a *brief* message. If you fail to leave a message, you have wasted your time and will have to call again; moreover, the service provider cannot return your call or help you.

Take ten minutes to develop a list of typical time wasters for service providers. Share these and discuss additional possibilities with others.

The systems were not designed to allow you to deliver a sales presentation. In some cases, the memory or tape length for recording messages is limited. If you leave long, drawn-out messages, you could irritate and offend your recipient by tying up all the recording space with your message. In that case you may never hear from the recipient, or you may receive a very terse response. Review Chapter 9 for information on leaving messages on voice mail and setting up your outgoing message for maximum efficiency.

E-Mail Efficiency

E-mail is a very quick and inexpensive way to get in touch with others inside and outside your organization. However, as you read in Chapter 9, you should observe e-mail etiquette. To use e-mail efficiently, you should respond to messages in a timely manner. This does not mean that you must stop what you are doing to respond every time a message arrives. That would be a poor **e-mail management** strategy, for you will probably lose your train of thought by stopping continually. Instead, check and return e-mails at scheduled times throughout the day.

All the techniques described in this section and in Chapter 9 can help show your customers that you are a professional, are organized, and know how to use technology to help you manage time well. The techniques can also save you time because you will not have to go searching for people, information, or items before you can serve a customer. In addition, you will avoid spending time in dealing with an emotional or dissatisfied customer who reacts negatively to your lack of organization or inability to provide service in a timely manner.

5 Strategies for Reclaiming Time

Concept: Examine each of your activities according to the following criteria: necessity, appropriateness, and efficiency.

Before you can implement **strategies for reclaiming time** that is typically wasted during the day, you must evaluate how you use time. After you have measured the time you spend on tasks, you can begin evaluating how well you use your time. To do this evaluation, use copies of Figure 11.1 to track your daily activities for a week. Once you have done so, examine your time usage based on the following three criteria:

> *Necessity.* Scrutinize each activity to be sure that it is necessary and contributes in some way to better customer service. Sometimes people go on using material that has outlived its usefulness (e.g., monthly reports—because they have always been done in a certain manner or format). If the activities you perform serve a useful purpose, continue doing them; just try to streamline and make them as efficient as possible (e.g., developing a form letter for regularly occurring messages, automating a process or file and otherwise using some of the technology discussed in Chapter 9). Doing this type of self-evaluation will help you reduce your tasks to only those that are essential.

LEADERSHIP INITIATIVE

11.2

If your organization does not have a policy for standardization of telephone service, you may want to create one. At a minimum, typical procedure guidelines include number of transfers allowed per call, length of time to leave someone on hold, and maximum number of rings prior to answering a call. Additionally, standards for outgoing messages and telephone greetings should be included.

FIGURE 11.1
Time Record Sheet

Date _____

To better determine how you use your time throughout the day, make five copies of this form. For the next five days, record your daily tasks in 15-minute increments (e.g., met with client, spoke to customer on telephone, responded to e-mails, lunch, drove to customer site). At the end of each day, list the types of activities on a separate sheet of paper and total the minutes spent for each.

Start and End Times		Activity	Comments
_____	_____	_____	_____
_____	_____	_____	_____
_____	_____	_____	_____
_____	_____	_____	_____
_____	_____	_____	_____
_____	_____	_____	_____
_____	_____	_____	_____
_____	_____	_____	_____
_____	_____	_____	_____
_____	_____	_____	_____
_____	_____	_____	_____
_____	_____	_____	_____
_____	_____	_____	_____
_____	_____	_____	_____
_____	_____	_____	_____
_____	_____	_____	_____
_____	_____	_____	_____

Appropriateness. Once you have identified essential functions, determine who should be doing them (e.g., what person or department) and adjust your workload accordingly. Sometimes, you might do this by simply asking a peer to switch duties (with team leader or supervisory approval). In other instances, you might want to prepare a formal recommendation for your supervisor, asking that your job description be changed and listing the reasons such a change is warranted.

Efficiency. The third criterion in examining your tasks is to consider how efficiently you are currently performing. If you feel that things are going well, step back and look again—objectively. Ask yourself, "Is there a better way of doing this?" You may even want to ask some of your peers for input. You should continually improve in carving out more saved time during your day.

Think about how you use your time during the day and at night. Do you spend it as effectively and efficiently as you could? Evaluate your record in Figure 11.1. How can you improve your use of time?

Chapter Summary

As you know from experience, and have read in this chapter, time management is a valuable skill to acquire and use. With so many things to do each day, it seems that our lives become more chaotic and less productive. Using the skills described in this chapter can help. The personal time record sheet, described in Figure 11.1, will help you become more aware of how you use your time. By developing a prioritization system and using it regularly, recognizing the importance of good time usage strategies in face-to-face encounters, over the telephone, and when using technology, and then using the techniques described outlined in this chapter, you will regain and control more of your time. To be successful, you must continually search for ways to improve efficiency in your work area, master the available technology to deliver customer service, and enhance the systems you use to gather information and deliver it to others in a variety of settings.

SERVICE IN ACTION   American Express Company **CHAPTER 11**

http://www.americanexpress.com

American Express Company was founded in 1850 and has grown to be a financial giant. Among other things, American Express provides customers with access to global travel and financial and network services. Some of the more recognizable products offered by the company include individual and corporate charge and credit cards and Travelers Cheques. Those are just the tip of the financial iceberg for American Express. It also offers financial planning, brokerage services, mutual funds, insurance, and other investment products. Part of these financial offerings include accounting and tax preparation services to small businesses, investment management services and pension and other employee benefit plans, and financial education services to employees at their places of work. The company provides banking services to wealthy individuals, retail customers, corporations, and financial institutions outside the United States. In addition, American Express is one of the world's largest travel agencies.

One of the key factors driving the American Express success story has been the diversification of products and services and the partnerships forged with organizations and governments. In the past, American Express offered traveler's checks through the AAA organizational network, and they recently signed an agreement to become the "official card" of the British Virgin Islands. For the annual fee paid by individuals and companies to use the American Express Card, customers gain many benefits. Customers receive such things as frequent flyer points, rebates on long-distance telephone services, and discounts and perks at restaurants, entertainment facilities, car rental agencies, gas stations, grocery stores, COSTCO warehouses, and many other locations.

Key Terms and Concepts	crisis manager	telephone management	time management
	e-mail management	time management	on the run
	prioritizing time	time management and	time perception
	setting priorities	technology	time reality
	strategies for reclaiming	time management face-	time wasters
	time	to-face	voice mail management

Quick Preview Answers

1. T	6. T	11. T
2. F	7. T	12. T
3. T	8. T	13. F
4. T	9. F	14. F
5. F	10. T	15. T

Chapter Review Questions

1. What are some reasons for practicing good time management?
2. What are four major positive results of good time management in the workplace?
3. What are three standards for prioritizing activities?
4. What are the three priority levels for daily activities?
5. What can you do to save time while serving a customer?
6. What are some time management techniques you can use in face-to-face service situations?
7. How can you increase time efficiency when providing service "on the run"?
8. What telephone time management techniques can assist in providing better service?
9. What techniques for voice mail usage can help save time?
10. How can e-mail be used effectively to add to, not detract from, available time?
11. What are three criteria for measuring time usage and reclaiming time?

Search It Out

Search the Internet for Information on Time Management Skills

Option 1: Log onto the Internet to research products, training programs, publications, and articles related to improving time management skills. Create a bibliographic list, make copies of the list, and share it with your peers and instructor in class.

Option 2: Research articles and websites related to time management. Try to develop a list of at least ten different time-saving strategies other than the ones described in the text. Also, develop a list of time wasters in your personal life that ultimately can affect your ability to perform effective customer service.

Note: A listing for additional research on specific URLs is provided on the Customer Service website at **<http://www.mhhe.com/lucas05>**.

Collaborative Learning Activity

Researching Wait Times

As a class, come up with a list of businesses in which customer wait times are typical (e.g., supermarkets, retail stores, call center support lines, doctors' offices, amusement parks, barber shops or hair salons, banks, car washes). Each person can select a business category, or teams can do research. Your research can be done in one of three ways:

- Personal experience.
- Secondhand experience (observing or interviewing others).
- A combination of both personal and secondhand experience.

During a two-week period, contact (or observe) people in your selected industry type and answer the following questions about each experience:

- What was the average wait time?
- What were you or other customers typically doing during the wait time?
- Was the wait time similar in the various organizations?
- What strategies did organizations use to reduce or minimize wait times?
- What were the actions or emotional levels of customers during their wait (e.g., exhibiting impatience, fidgeting, complaining to service providers or other customers, showing signs of frustration, sighing, looking at watch)?

At the end of two weeks, be prepared to discuss your observations and experiences with other students.

Face to Face

Handling Change at a Call Center

Background

You are the team leader of a call center team made up of six customer service representatives. The team members have an average experience level of about one year. Your organization provides support to customers who purchase small electronic appliances and devices through retail stores and catalogs. The company also has a website where customers can view product descriptions, place orders, e-mail your center with questions and comments, and request catalogs and other information through an online information fulfillment system. A unit within the call center provides third-party service support for companies that contract with your organization. Your facility is also equipped with a TTY system to assist the hearing-impaired, fax-on-demand, and other typical call center technology (e.g., e-mail, voice mail). A typical day for a representative in your unit involves answering customer calls directed from the ACD system, responding to e-mails and voice mails, and handling routine administrative functions (e.g., completing and filing forms, attending team meetings, dealing with last-minute assignments, fulfilling internal customer requests for information).

Things have been hectic in the call center for the last three months. Rumor of a merger is spreading. Several employees have resigned, and you have not been able to find suitable replacements. Your manager transferred to another unit last month (you have heard that her decision to leave was based on her concern that her position would be eliminated if the merger went through). A senior team leader is now running the center until management decides how to proceed.

Also, for the past two weeks, your team has been beta-testing a new customer information tracking telephony system (trying it out to discover whether the functions work as designed and whether it meets current organizational needs, learning the applications, and so on). Representatives from the company that designed the software for your organization are on site. During the last few days, on a number of occasions the system has disconnected customers, wiped out information on computer screens as representatives were talking to clients, and blocked representatives from entry into certain areas of the program. The problem has not been resolved, and there have been numerous complaints by irritated customers. One customer even telephoned the CEO's office because he had been unable to resolve a problem after three attempts. A memorandum has arrived requesting an explanation and asking you to take immediate action to rectify the situation.

Your Role

Your name is Pat Wilson, and you have been working in the call center for almost two and a half years. Earlier, you worked in the mailroom for your organization, in the customer care center (call center) for another organization, and in a fast-food restaurant for about a year. You are also a part-time student at the local community college, taking courses dealing primarily with customer service. You enjoy your work and interactions with customers and hope someday to become a call center manager. Therefore, you are reluctant to say no when someone asks you to take on a new assignment.

Because of all the changes, team members are getting anxious and coming to you with questions and concerns. You are responsible for employee training and working with the software representatives to overcome the glitches. You have also played a key role in preparing and delivering presentations to update senior management on the progress of the telephony system testing. In the last meeting the senior vice president responsible for the call center took you aside and stressed the importance of the project to the organization. She did not say so, but she implied that the success of the testing could have a serious impact on the merger.

On top of all this, you handle phone calls and perform the typical representative duties outline above, must write performance appraisals for three team members this week, have examinations in your college courses in a week, are working on a proposal for streamlining voice mail responses, and have decided to set up a new filing system in your work area.

Critical Thinking Questions

1. From a time management standpoint, what issues are you dealing with?
2. How should you prioritize the tasks you must handle?
3. Why did you prioritize the tasks in question 2 the way you did?

PLANNING TO SERVE

CHAPTER 11

Time can be your best friend or worst enemy in the service profession. To make sure that your time is used wisely and that you are prepared to provide excellent service to your customers, think about the things that typically cause you to waste valuable time on the job and list them.

Next, think about strategies that can help you reduce or eliminate each of these wasters and list them.

Finally, make a list of resources (e.g., people, books, websites) that can help you improve your time management skills.

Enhancing Customer Relationships

Encouraging Customer Loyalty

From the Frontline Interview

Dr. Collins has been a dentist in private practice for four years, during which time he has learned the importance of marketing and dealing with a staff and his patients. Prior to that, he was in the U.S. Navy.

1 What is customer loyalty to you and do you believe there is such a thing? Please explain.

Yes, I do believe there is such a thing. Customer loyalty means that the customer appreciates and values what you do for him or her and trusts and likes you enough that he or she chooses to come to see you instead of someone else. It also means that the customer would recommend you to family and friends.

2 What do you believe to be the biggest challenge for service providers in building customer loyalty?

DR. FAY H. COLLINS III, D.D.S. PA, *Private Practice*

I think that the biggest challenge today is establishing the initial trust level in a society that generally is becoming more cautious of the intentions of others.

3 What techniques or strategies do you believe to be most effective in establishing and holding customer loyalty?

Genuinely caring about the customer and making the customer feel or know that he or she is important to you is essential. It is important to talk to the customer and ask how he or she is doing and how you can serve him or her better. Bottom line . . . know your customer.

I have learned that internal marketing is more effective for bringing in the type of patients that I enjoy working with. I have initiated a referral awards program in which I thank my existing patients with some sort of gift whenever they refer a friend.

Chapter Learning Objectives

After completing this chapter, you will be able to:

- Establish and maintain trust with customers.
- Develop the characteristics that will enhance customer loyalty.
- Recognize the provider's responsibility for establishing and maintaining positive customer relations.

- Help customers feel important.
- Select strategies to enhance customer satisfaction and build loyalty.

I have also been exploring more emotional-based marketing with external customers, and I'm starting to see positive results. One thing that I have learned is that patients obtained through external marketing (solicited) are more fragile, from the standpoint of loyalty, than ones obtained through internal sources (referrals).

4 What are some of the things you have seen service providers do that discourages customer loyalty?

A number of factors are contrary to good customer service. Things such as sign-in sheets, long waits, not handling complaints or requests in a timely manner, and not recognizing a customer when she or he comes into the office can all lead to a breakdown in customer loyalty.

5 From your perspective, what is the most important thing to remember when dealing with a customer?

Listen to customer needs. Whatever is important to my patients is important to me.

6 What advice related to building customer loyalty would you give someone just entering the customer service profession?

Talk to your customer and find out if you are satisfying his or her needs. Ask how you can make things better for the person, if possible.

Critical Thinking

Dr. Collins mentions "trust" a number of times. What role do you believe that trust plays in building customer loyalty? Why?

Quick Preview

Before reviewing the chapter content, respond to the following questions by placing a "T" for true or an "F" for false on the rules. Use any questions you miss as a checklist of material to which you will pay particular attention as you read through the chapter. For those you get right, congratulate yourself, but review the sections they address in order to learn additional details about the topic.

_____ 1. Customer satisfaction and loyalty are the result of effective product and service delivery, resolution of problems, and elimination of dissatisfiers.

_____ 2. The number of customers with major problems who continue to do business with an organization if their complaint is resolved is about 9 percent.

_____ 3. One way to take responsibility for customer relationships is to personalize your approach when dealing with customers.

_____ 4. Customers usually decide to purchase or repurchase from a supplier based on the quality and performance of the products and services.

_____ 5. Many customers return to organizations because of relationships established with employees even though comparable products and services are available elsewhere.

_____ 6. As customers develop long-term relationships with an organization, they tend to become more tolerant of poor service.

_____ 7. Projecting an enthusiastic "I'm happy to serve you attitude" is one way to have a positive effect on customer relationships.

_____ 8. Customers usually exhibit six common needs that must be addressed by service providers in order to ensure customer loyalty.

_____ 9. Using a customer's name is a good way to personalize your relationship with a customer.

_____ 10. Trust is not a major concern for most customers.

_____ 11. Handling complaints quickly and effectively is a good strategy for aiding customer retention.

_____ 12. An important step often overlooked in dealing with customers is follow-up.

Answers to Quick Preview can be found at the end of the chapter.

1   The Role of Trust

Concept: Trust is the most important criteria for a relationship. Trust depends on many factors; communicating effectively, keeping your word, caring, and trusting your customers are some of these factors.

Customer loyalty is an emotional rather than a rational thing. It is typically based on customer interest in maintaining a relationship with your organization. Often, customer interest is created and maintained through one or more positive experiences which lead to a relationship.

Relationships are built on **trust**! The most important thing to remember about trust is that, without it, you have no relationship. This applies to all human situations, not just the customer service environment. For customers to continue doing business with you, they must trust you and your organization. Trust has to be earned, and it does not happen overnight. Only through continued positive efforts on the part of everyone in your organization can you demonstrate to customers that you are worthy of their trust and thereby positively affect customer retention. Through actions and deeds, you must deliver quality products, services, and information that satisfy the needs of your customers. Even when you win trust, it is very fragile. An inappropriate tone, a missed appointment, failure to follow through on a promise, a lie, or a misleading statement to a customer are just some of the ways you can destroy trust quickly.

In a June 2001[1] poll by Harris Interactive, five dimensions of trust were identified that help explain why customers trust one organization over others. These types of trust can be used by organizations to create systems and staffing strategies that foster trust. The dimensions are:

- Personal experience.
- Organizational knowledge (of the company).
- Deference (trust of companies in general).
- Reference (what one learns about a company from others).
- Glitz (advertising, packaging, and high pricing).

To gain and maintain trust, you and the organization must actively work toward incorporating the values and beliefs you read about in other chapters into daily actions. Failure to do so can send a message that you are not trustworthy or that you act according to a double standard of saying one thing but doing another. You must exhibit trustworthiness in words and actions, for although it takes a long time to gain trust, it can be lost in seconds. Once trust is gone, if you do not react quickly to correct the situation, you may never regain total customer confidence. Here are some basic strategies to gain and develop customer trust:

Communicate Effectively and Convincingly

If you cannot articulate or explain clearly (verbally and in writing) information customers can comprehend and act upon, they will not believe in you. You must provide more than facts and figures; you must send a message of sincerity, knowledge, and honesty.

As you communicate, project your feelings and emotions by being positive and enthusiastic. Let customers know that you are human and approachable. Also, communicate frequently and keep customers informed. This is especially important when they are awaiting a product or service that has been delayed. If you fail to update them regularly, they may become frustrated and could cancel their order, complain, take their business elsewhere, and tell others about their disappointing experience.

Display Caring

Emphasize to your customers that you have their best interests at heart. Work to demonstrate that you are willing to assist in satisfying their needs. Asking questions that uncover their needs and then taking positive action to satisfy them can do this. It can also be accomplished through passionate efforts to solve problems. Remember that their problem is your problem. Too often, service providers send a message that customers are not really that important. This can happen when service

[1]Humphrey Taylor, "Why Some Companies Are Trusted and Others Are Not: Personal Experience and Knowledge of Company More Important Than Glitz," <http://www.harrisinteractive.com>, June 20, 2001.

providers adopt a "next" mentality and treat customers as if they were numbers, not people. For example, think about the difference wording can make. Which of the following sends a more caring message to a group of customers standing in line as they wait for service?

1. A provider calls out "Next."
2. A provider looks over to the next person in line, smiles, and motions the person over with a waving hand gesture while saying, "May I help the next person in line?"

If you chose No. 2, you are on your way to providing caring service.

Be Fair

Make sure that you treat all customers with respect and consistency. If you give special discounts to established or return customers, do so discreetly. Failure to exercise discretion in these cases could cause other customers to be offended and take their business elsewhere. People like to feel that they are special. If a customer believes that another customer is getting special treatment, you could have problems. Such perceptions might even lead to legal action, if customers perceive they are being discriminated against.

Admit Errors or Lack of Knowledge

You are human and are expected to make mistakes. The key is to recover from errors by apologizing, accepting responsibility, and then quickly and appropriately solving the problem or getting the necessary information. One of the biggest mistakes a service provider can make is to deny accountability in dealing with a customer. When you or your organization or the products or services it sells cause customer inconvenience or dissatisfaction, take responsibility and work toward an acceptable resolution with the customer. To do otherwise is courting disaster. In some cases, even if a customer incorrectly perceives that you contributed to his or her dissatisfaction, it may be wise to take responsibility.

A story about the power of such action has been circulated for years. It involves the highly successful department store Nordstrom. As the story goes, a disgruntled customer brought a used car tire into a Nordstrom's store and complained that it was defective. After some discussion, the manager cheerfully accepted the tire and refunded the customer's money. This may not seem too unusual, except that Nordstrom does not sell automobile tires! So, why would the manager take such an extreme action? Think about the word-of-mouth publicity (how many people in your class now know this story from just reading it?) and the customer loyalty that likely resulted from it. Whether the event actually took place or someone made it up is irrelevant. The point is that taking unusual actions to solve ordinary customer problems can pay dividends long into the future.

In another classic example of taking responsibility for a problem, in 1982 an unknown person or group contaminated bottles of Extra-Strength Tylenol with cyanide. Seven people used the product and died. Upon finding out about the situation, the parent company (Johnson and Johnson) immediately called a press conference to announce the total recall of the product from store shelves (approximately 264,000 bottles). Johnson & Johnson started a major media campaign to reassure the public that its other products were safe. The company also helped lead the way in developing tamper-resistant packaging. The cost—millions. The result—walk into any store that sells over-the-counter drug products and look for Extra-Strength Tylenol. Tylenol is right there with all its competitors and is a strong seller. How did Johnson & Johnson pull this off? The actions of the company in taking responsibility for a situation that was not of its making communicated strong values and concern for public safety, and the public remained loyal as a result.

Other companies have not fared so well in the face of adversity. For example, think about the Exxon oil tanker *Valdez*, which spilled more than 200,000 gallons of crude oil along the Alaska coastline in 1989. This disaster caused major environmental as well as financial losses into the millions of dollars. This does not include the almost $3 billion Exxon has spent cleaning up the environmental damage and paying legal settlements. The company was slow to react, however, and did not, at first, take responsibility. As a result, it is still the object of litigation and jokes. From a trust standpoint, people harbor resentment over the incident, and, in protest, many people will not patronize Exxon gas stations.

Trust Your Customers

Most customers are not out to cheat or "rip you (or your organization) off." They do want the best value and service for their money and expect you to provide it. Make a good-faith effort to accomplish this and deal effectively with customers by communicating openly, listening objectively to their questions and concerns, providing service to the best of your ability, showing compassion for their needs, and demonstrating that you are their advocate when things go wrong (if appropriate).

One of the most common mistakes service providers make in dealing with customers who have a complaint or problem is to verbally acknowledge and agree but nonverbally send a message of skepticism. For example, suppose a customer comes in to complain about a defective product she purchased. As she is describing the symptoms of the problem, you use some of the paralanguage discussed in earlier chapters (e.g., "Uh huh," "I see," "Hmmm"); however, the inflection you use or your tone of voice communicates questioning or doubt (e.g., "I seee?" or "Hmmm?"). How do you think the customer might feel or perceive you at that point?

If you seek trust, communicate it.

Keep Your Word

Customers have many choices in selecting a service provider. If they feel you cannot be depended upon to take action, they simply leave, often without complaint or comment. When you tell customers you will do something, do it. Do not promise what you cannot deliver; many people take your word as your bond. Break the bond, and you risk destroying the relationship. If feasible following service, contact your customer to make sure that he or she was satisfied and that your service met expectations. This follow-up can be an informal call or a more formal questionnaire. Always strive to *under*promise and *over*deliver. Suppose that a customer drops off film to be processed at your store on Tuesday. The store guarantees that the photos will be ready on Saturday. If possible, develop the film before Saturday, and call to tell the customer it's ready. When he or she comes to pick it up, give a coupon for a discount on the next roll of film.

Provide Peace of Mind

Be positive and assertive. Assure customers through your words and actions that you are confident, have their best interests at heart, and are in control of the situation. Let them know that their calls or messages, questions, and needs will be addressed professionally and in a timely manner. Reassure them that what they

LEADERSHIP INITIATIVE 12.1

Effective supervisors are continually examining their organization's systems and practices, talking to employees and customers, and looking for ways to improve customer relationships.

Using some of the tools outlined in this chapter, leaders can gather information that can head off potential problems and possibly reduce customer dissatisfaction.

purchase is the best quality, has a solid warranty, will be backed by the organization, and will address their needs while providing many benefits. Also, assure them that their requests and information will be processed rapidly and promises will be met. All of these things can lead them to the belief that they made the right decision in selecting you and your organization and that you will take care of their needs.

2 The Importance of Customer Relationship Management (CRM)

Concept: Long-term relationships are the ones that sustain organizations.

Why bother building relationships with customers? The answer would seem obvious—so that you can stay in business. However, when you examine the question further, you may find that there are more reasons than you think.

At one point in history, business owners knew their customers personally. They know their customers' families, what their religious affiliation was, and what was happening in their lives. That was then, and this is now. The society is more mobile; people live in large metropolitan areas where relationships are distant. Large multinational organizations provide the products and services once provided by the neighborhood store. All this does not mean, however, that the customer-provider relationships can no longer exist.

Additionally, with B2B (business-to-business), customers are often companies. This makes managing **customer relationships** more difficult because of the number of contacts you might have in an organization and the varying requirements or needs each might have. Also, much of business-to-business service is delivered through technology. Many service organizations use customer **relationship management** software to better keep track of customer needs and to record service provided. Even so, CRM remains CRM and is a crucial element of customer loyalty.

Typically, many service providers look at customer interactions from a short-term perspective. They figure that a customer calls or comes in (or they go to the customer), they provide service, and then the customer goes away. This is a short-sighted viewpoint in that it does not consider the long-term implications. This is not the way to gain and sustain customer loyalty.

A more customer-focused approach is to view customers from a relationship standpoint. That does not mean that you have to become intimate friends with all your customers; it simply means that you should strive to employ as many of the positive relationship-building skills that you have learned as possible. By treating both internal and external customers in a manner that leads them to believe that you care for them and have their best interests at heart, you can start to generate reciprocal feelings. Using the interpersonal communication skills you have learned throughout this book is a great way to begin doing this. People usually gravitate toward organizations and people with whom they have developed rapport, respect, and trust, and who

Relationships are a crucial part of customer service. By working to build trust and getting to know customer needs, service providers can increase their effectiveness. *What techniques do you use to build rapport and trust with customers?*

treat them as if they are valued as a person. Relationships are developed and enhanced through one-on-one human interaction. This does not mean that people who provide service via technology cannot develop relationships. Those relationships develop on a different level, using the nonverbal skills addressed in Chapters 4, 6, and 8.

Remember that long-term customer relationships (**customer retention**) are the ones that sustain organizations. Seeking out new or replacement customers through advertising and other means is a very costly proposition. This is because in addition to having to find new customers, you and your organization have to educate and win them over. You have to prove yourself to newly acquired customers. More than likely, new customers are also going to be more apprehensive, skeptical, and critical than customers who have previous experience with your organization. For these reasons, it is imperative that you and every other member of your organization work to develop loyalty on the part of those customers with whom you have an existing relationship.

Benefits of Customer Relationship Management

- Less need to obtain new customers through marketing since current customers are aware of offerings and take advantage of them.
- Reduced marketing costs since direct mail, follow-up, and other customer recruitment activities are reduced.
- Increased return on investment (ROI) since marketing can target specific customer needs.
- Enhanced customer loyalty due to pricing and product service offerings that meet current customer needs.
- Elevated profitability due to increased sales, customer referrals, and longer customer retention during life cycle.
- Targeted marketing based on statistics of which customers buy more and on high-ticket item sales.

By providing excellent customer service and dealing with dissatisfaction as soon it is identified, you can help ensure that customers remain loyal and keep coming back. The following equation conveys this idea:

$$
\begin{aligned}
&\text{Effective product/service delivery} \\
+\ &\text{Proactive relationship building} \\
+\ &\text{Elimination of dissatisfiers} \\
+\ &\text{Resolution of problems} \\
+\ &\text{Follow-up} \\
=\ &\text{Customer satisfaction and loyalty.}
\end{aligned}
$$

Think about a service provider with whom you deal frequently and with whom you have established a better-than-average customer-provider relationship. Perhaps you have been dealing with the organization for a long period of time or visit frequently.

Reflect on the relationship and make a list of positive customer service behaviors exhibited by this person. Then review the list and make it a personal goal to replicate as many of these behaviors as possible when dealing with your own customers.

FIGURE 12.1

The Importance of Customer Loyalty

Source: Technical Assistance Research Program, or TARP, 1300 Wilson Boulevard, Suite 950, Arlington, Virginia 22209.

For almost three decades, the research firm TARP has conducted various studies to determine the impact of customer service. The research has revealed the following:

- It will cost an organization at least five times more to acquire a new customer as it will to keep an existing one.
- On average, 50 percent of consumers will complain about a problem to a frontline person. In business-to-business environments, this figure jumps to 75 percent.
- For small-ticket items, 96 percent of consumers do not complain or they complain to the retailer from whom they bought an item. For large-ticket items, 50 percent complain to frontline employees, and 5 to 10 percent escalate the problem to local managers or corporate headquarters.
- At least 50 percent of your customers who experience problems will not complain or contact your organization for help; they will simply go elsewhere.
- Customers who are dissatisfied will tell as many as 16 friends about a negative experience with your organization.
- The average business loses 10 to 15 percent of its customers per year because of bad service.

Traditionally, customers will remain loyal to a product, service, or organization that they believe meets their needs. Even when there is an actual or perceived breakdown in quality, many customers will return to an organization that they believe sincerely attempts to solve a problem or make restitution for an error. According to the **Technical Assistance Research Program (TARP)**, many organizations have found that, when complaints were acted upon and resolved quickly, most customers returned to the organization (see Figure 12.1).

The bottom line is that you and other employees must realize that customer service is everyone's business and that relationships are the basis of that business.

Cost of Dissatisfied Customers

Many research studies have been conducted to try to determine the **cost of dissatisfied customers**. Too often, service providers look at the loss of a sale when a customer is dissatisfied as a single event. However, as you saw in the last section, one dissatisfied customer can cost your organization a lot.

To get an idea of what one negative customer experience can cost your organization over a ten-year period, consider the following example:

Ms. Ling comes in to return a product that she paid $22 for over a month ago. She explains that the product did not fit her needs and that she had been meaning to return it since the date she purchased it, but kept forgetting. She also explains that she comes in at least once a week to make purchases. Your company has a three-day return policy, your manager is out to lunch and you do not have

Think of how you would expect to be treated if you were a customer of the company you work for currently. List behaviors that you would expect to encounter from customer service employees.

the authority to override the policy. Ms. Ling is in a hurry and is upset by your inability to resolve the issue. She leaves after saying, "You just lost a good customer!"

Let's assume that Ms. Ling spends at least $22 a week in your store and calculate the potential loss to your organization.

$22 × 52 (number of weeks in a year) = $1,144

10 (number of years) × $1,144 = $11,440

16 (number of people statistically told of a negative experience) × $11,440 = **$183,040**

These numbers are the bad news. The good news is that you and every other employee in your organization can reduce a large percentage of customer defections by providing quality service.

3 Provider Characteristics Affecting Customer Loyalty

Concept: Personal characteristics of a service provider may affect customer loyalty, positively or negatively.

According to the 2003 J. D. Power and Associates Sales Satisfaction Index (SSI) study, "more than one-fourth of the people who walked out of a new-vehicle dealership without buying said they didn't like the way the salesperson handled their business."[2]

Many of your personal characteristics affect your relationships with customers. In customer service, some circumstances are beyond your control; however, your personal characteristics are not. Some of the most common qualities of service providers that affect customers are described in the next sections.

Responsiveness

Customers typically like to feel that they are the most important person in the world when they come in contact with an organization (see Figure 12.2). This is a human need (remember Maslow's hierarchy and the need for esteem?). If customers feel that they are not appreciated or not welcome by you or another service provider, they will likely take their business elsewhere. However, they will often first complain to management and will tell anyone who will listen about the poor quality of service they received.

A simple way to demonstrate responsiveness is to attend to **customer needs** promptly. If you get an e-mail or voice mail message, respond to it immediately, if possible. If that is not possible, try to respond within 4 hours, or certainly within 24 hours. If you have face-to-face customer contact, greet customers quickly (within 10 to 15 seconds), even if you are busy with someone else. If nothing else, smile and gesture that you will be with them momentarily.

[2]American Woman Road and Travel, <http://www.roadandtravel.com>.

FIGURE 12.2
Addressing
Customer Needs

Everyone has needs that must be met in some fashion. Here are six common customer needs, along with strategies to satisfy them.

Need	Strategies for Satisfying the Need
To feel welcome	Use an enthusiastic greeting, smile, use the customer's name, thank the customer, be positive
To be understood	Listen actively, paraphrase, ask key questions, give positive feedback, empathize
To feel comfortable	Use an enthusiastic welcome, relieve anxiety through friendly communication, explain your actions calmly, ensure physical comfort (e.g., seats, refreshments)
To feel appreciated	Thank the customer, follow up, go beyond service expectations, provide "special" offers, remember special details about the customer (e.g., birthdays, favorite colors, facts about their families)
To feel important	Use the customer's name, personalize service, give special treatment when possible, elicit opinions, remember details about him or her (e.g., last purchase made, last visit, preferred styles or foods)
To be respected	Listen, don't interrupt, acknowledge the customer's emotions and concerns, take time to serve, ask advice, elicit feedback

Once you do get to serve the customer, and before getting to the business at hand, greet the customer with a smile and start the interaction on a friendly note in one or more of the following ways:

Be enthusiastic. Use open body language, vocal cues, and gestures that you have read about previously in this book, coupled with some of the techniques described below to let your customers know that you are glad they have chosen you and/or your organization.

Use the customer's title and name. If you know the customer's name, use it. Remember, though, not to assume familiarity and start using the customer's first name unless you are given permission to do so.

Show appreciation. "Thank you for coming to _____." "It's nice to see you this morning." "You have bene very patient while I assisted that other customer. Thank you."

Engage in small talk. "Isn't this weather terrible?" "Is this your first visit to our store?" "Didn't I see you in here last week?" (Say this only if you recognize the customer. If he or she answers yes, thank the person for returning to the store.)

Compliment. "You look like you're having a good day" (assuming the customer is smiling and does look happy). "That color really looks nice on you." "That's a beautiful necktie."

Adaptability

In a continually evolving world, you will undoubtedly have many opportunities to deal with customers who have different beliefs, values, perceptions, needs, and expectations. You will also encounter people whose personality styles differ from yours. Each of these meetings will provide an opportunity for you to adapt your approach in dealing with others. By doing so, you increase the likelihood of a suc-cessful interaction as well as a satisfied customer emerging from the encounter. Taking measures to adapt your personality style to that of your customers in order to communicate with and serve them effectively is a smart move. Keep in mind that you cannot change the customers; however, you can adapt to them and their approach to a situation.

Another, more subtle way to show your ability to adapt relates to technology. By quickly learning and mastering new technology systems provided to you by the organization, you can respond faster and more efficiently to customer needs. This is especially true, for many of your customers will likely be very technology-literate. If you cannot match their expectations, or at least demonstrate knowledge and effectiveness in using technology, you might frustrate them and drive them away. In turn, you might create negative word-of-mouth publicity about your organization and its employees.

Communication Skills

As you have read earlier in this book, your ability to obtain and give information, listen, write, and speak effectively, as well as deal with emotional situations are keys to successful customer service. By using a variety of effective interpersonal techniques, you can determine customer needs. The most successful service providers are the ones who have learned to interact positively with and build rap-port with customers. To help ensure the most effective service possible, you should continually strive to improve your ability to interact and communicate with a va-riety of people. The better your skills are, the more likely you will be able to ad-dress different situations that arise in the workplace.

Decisiveness

Decisiveness relates to being able and willing to make a decision and take neces-sary actions to fulfill customer needs. Taking a wait-and-see approach to customer service often leads to customer dissatisfaction. Just as you probably do, customers value their time. By keeping them waiting while you run to someone else for a de-cision or answer can be frustrating. Granted, such a situation is sometimes created by a management style that makes it necessary to get certain approvals (e.g., for checks, returns or refunds, or discounts). However, these are internal issues that should be resolved *before* the customer encounters them. If you face such barriers, think of alternative ways of handling them, and then approach your supervisor with suggestions for improvement. Your ideas may make your life easier by re-ducing the chances of a frustrating and unproductive service encounter.

Once you have supportive systems in place, gather information effectively by using the listening techniques discussed in Chapter 5, carefully and quickly ana-lyze the situation, and then make a decision on how to solve the problem.

Enthusiasm

As discussed earlier, attaining and maintaining a level of excitement about your customers, products, services, organization, and job that says "I'm happy to help you" is an important step toward establishing a relationship.

If you are enthusiastic about serving your customers, they will often respond by loyally supporting you and the organization. People typically react positively to enthusiastic employees who appear to be enjoying themselves as they work. This should not be interpreted as meaning that providers should act unprofessionally or create an environment in which they have fun at the expense of customer service or attention to their customers. Find a good balance between fun and professionalism. Southwest Airlines has succeeded in finding the right mix. Employees dress casually, are recruited based partially on their personality, and often use jokes and games on flights to reduce some of the stress of air travel in a security-conscious industry. They have been rewarded with continued corporate profits while other airlines often report losses.

The long-term benefit is that if you and your organization can generate return customers through enthusiasm, the potential for organizational growth and prosperity exists. This in turn sets the stage for better benefits, salary, and workplace modifications that lead to higher employee enthusiasm. So, all the elements are connected, and all contribute to successful customer service.

As a side note, many employees and employers are trying to find ways to make the workplace less stressful and more enjoyable for themselves and customers. Several resources listed in the Bibliography will help in this quest.

Ethical Behavior

With a heightened incidence of actual or alleged corporate wrongdoing (e.g., Enron and Martha Stewart), customers have been sensitized and made wary of organizations, their leaders, and practices. For that reason it is crucial that you and your peers guard against any words or actions that might raise scrutiny or customer skepticism.

Establishing and maintaining high legal, social, and ethical standards in all interactions with customers are imperative. Failure to do so can lead to loss of reputation and business, and/or legal liability. Some positive examples of **ethical behavior** are the following:

- A company that voluntarily recalls a product that it discovered was defective or potentially dangerous.
- A manager who notifies a customer when he or she finds out that an employee has lied to or deceived the customer.
- An employee who reports a theft carried out by another employee.
- A cab driver who finds a wallet in his taxi and turns it in.

  Some negative examples are:

- Providing or substituting an inferior product for an advertised name brand item.
- Providing inferior products or repairs on a service call.
- Lying to a customer about a warranty.
- Failing to adhere to local, state, or federal regulations (e.g., dumping hazardous waste, such as petroleum or pesticide products, in unauthorized areas or collecting sales taxes but failing to report the taxes).

Initiative

Taking an action related to your job or customer service without having to receive instructions from others is a sign of initiative. Such actions also help to ensure that your customer's needs are identified and met in a timely fashion. Too many service providers take the "It's not my job" or "I can't do that" approach to dealing with customer situations. This can lead to customer dissatisfaction because the provider seems to be lazy or uncaring. To counter such impressions, you should take responsibility when a problem arises. By building a strong knowledge base (as described in the next section) and using the skills discussed in this book, you will have the tools you need to deal effectively with various situations without having to turn to others for assistance. This can expedite service and enhance your reputation in the eyes of your customers, peers, and supervisors.

Knowledge

Your customers expect you to know what business your organization is in. With all the products and service variations available to customers, the high level of technology, deregulation of industries, and innovations coming on the market daily, customers depend on service providers to educate and guide them in making purchases and decisions. Taking time to learn about policies, procedures, resources, products, services, and other information can help you provide total customer satisfaction in an efficient and timely manner.

Many organizations provide training and literature to help employees become more knowledgeable and to stay current. Take advantage of such resources, if they are available in your organization. If the organization you work for does not provide training or resources, take the initiative to ask supervisors or team leaders for materials and information. Also, develop a network with other employees throughout the organization and use that network to gain access to information. You, your organization, and your customers will ultimately benefit from your initiatives.

Training is usually provided by most organizations to increase employee knowledge and effectiveness with customers. *What training do you think would be useful to you in a new position in customer service?*

Perceptiveness

Recognizing the need to pay close attention to verbal and nonverbal cues, cultural factors, and the feelings or concerns of others is important. If necessary, you may want to review these topics in Chapters 4 and 8. By staying focused on customers and the signals they send, you can often recognize hesitancy, interest in a product or adamant rejection, irritation, anxiety, and a multitude of other unspoken messages. Once you have identified customers' signals, you can react appropriately and address their needs.

One way you can address customer needs is to anticipate them. Suppose that a customer makes a comment like "Man, is it hot outside. My lips are parched." You might offer a cold drink or direct the customer to a cafeteria or soft drink machine. Or, you might offer a chair to someone who is accompanying a customer while he or she shops and tries on clothing. Such small gestures show that you are astute in noticing their needs and nonverbal cues. Remember, sometimes the little things mean a lot. Moreover, in both of these examples, by taking care of the customer's basic needs, you might encourage him or her to shop longer.

Planning Ability

Planning is a crucial skill to possess when operating in today's fast-paced, changing customer service environment, especially in technology-based environments. To prepare for all types of customer situations, you and your organization must have a strategy. This often involves assessing various factors related to your organization, industry, products, services, policies and procedures, resources, and customer based. By being proactive and in thinking about such factors, you will be able to provide better service to your customers.

Also, you should consider alternative strategies for dealing with unusual situations (**contingency plans**). Such alternatives are helpful when things do not go as originally planned (e.g., a computer database fails, service is not delivered as promised, or products that were ordered from another organization for a customer do not arrive as promised).

Figure 12.3 shows the **Planning Process Model**, the basic steps of which are:

Set a goal. In a customer service situation, the obvious goal is to prevent problems from occurring. You also want to successfully address customers' needs, have them leave the service experience satisfied, spread positive word-of-mouth advertising, and return in the future.

Examine and evaluate the situation. In this phase of planning, you should look at all possible factors that could affect a customer interaction (e.g., the environment, policies, procedures, your skills and authority level, management support, and the customer). With these factors in mind, work with your peers and supervisor or team leader to establish criteria for selecting acceptable actions. For example, it might be acceptable to use voice mail if you are dealing with a customer; however, it is not all right to forward incoming messages to voice mail so that you can meet with a peer on a non-work-related issue.

Identify alternatives. Meet with peers and supervisors or team leaders to develop a list of alternatives for dealing with various customer situations. Consider the advantages and disadvantages of each option.

Select the best alternative. After reviewing all the options, select the one (or more) that best addresses the targeted goal of providing quality service to customers. Do not forget to measure this choice against the criteria you established earlier.

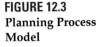

FIGURE 12.3
Planning Process
Model

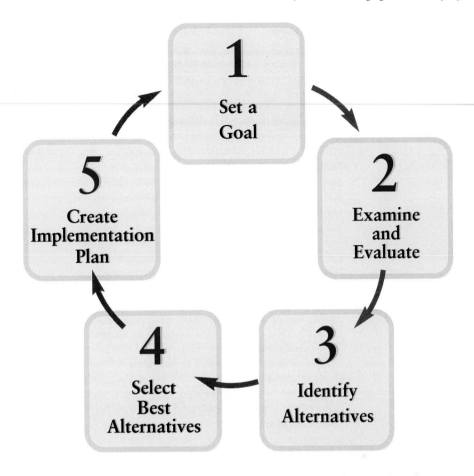

Create an implementation plan. Working with peers and supervisors or team leaders, decide which resources (human and otherwise) will be needed to deliver effective service. Also, develop a system for evaluating success. For example, a customer wants two items, but you have only one in stock. You apologize for not being able to fulfill the customer's needs. Is this "success"? Or, would you be successful if, in addition to the apology, you called other stores, located another item, and had it delivered to the customer's house at no cost?

Problem-Solving Ability

If a customer has a problem, you have a problem. Remembering this simple concept can go a long way in reminding you of your purpose for being a service provider. You exist (in your job position) to address the needs of your customer. To do this when a customer is dissatisfied or has a concern, you should take responsibility for the problem instead of trying to place blame and defer the issue to someone else. What or who created the problem (e.g., the weather, you, the customer, the manufacturer) doesn't matter. Your goal is to identify and implement appropriate solutions to the extent that you are authorized to do so. Otherwise, you should seek assistance from the appropriate person based on your organization's policy. To accomplish sound problem solving, you will need a process for gathering and analyzing information. As with the planning process discussed earlier, you should take some specific steps in finding a solution to a customer problem. These steps are described in the following sections. The **Problem-Solving Model**

FIGURE 12.4
Problem-Solving Model

- **Identify the problem.** Common sense dictates that before you can fix something, you have to find out in what way it is broken. However, many service providers do not seem to recognize this fact. Instead, they plunge into applying a standard solution because the problem resembles another one that the provider handled for another customer. Not only does this potentially waste time and other organizational resources, but it can also frustrate and anger the customer. This is especially true if the customer's problem is not adequately resolved.

  To effectively identify a problem, you must listen actively, ask questions to determine what did and did not work, and to determine the customer's expectation, paraphrase to the customer your understanding of the issue, and then go to the next step.

- **Analyze the problem.** In the second step of problem resolution, you should carefully evaluate what the customer has told you and get any additional information that will help you in understanding contributing factors and customer expectations for resolution of the problem.

- **Identify alternatives.** This step can significantly reduce the chance that you will provide a solution that does not satisfy your customer. Reflect on what you learned from the customer when you were identifying the problem and then determine what product and/or service options you have available to offer. For example, did the customer specify a certain brand, feature, color, or size? If so, providing an alternative may not be an acceptable option. However, if the customer was not specific, offering a compatible product or service might work.

- **Evaluate alternatives.** This step involves having a thorough knowledge of available products and services as well as knowing the warranty information, features, and benefits of each product and service. This knowledge can help you decide which of the alternatives available, if any, might be appropriate to offer.

  If the customer is with you or on the telephone, trying to determine an alternative may simply be a mental process of selecting possible solutions or options. With your goal being to meet customer needs and expectations, the more alternatives you can come up with, the better your chances for a successful resolution of the problem.

- **Make a decision.** Having identified the best alternatives, you can now offer specific suggestions to your customer. In some cases, this might result in a compromise. For example, assume that you are a host in a restaurant where reservations are required. A customer calls and wants a dinner reservation at 8 P.M., but no tables are available because a large party is being served at that time. So, you offer 7:30 as a compromise and offer free cocktails or wine. In offering this alternative, you may be able to satisfy the customer's desire to have dinner around 8 o'clock, and you have done a quick service recovery by offering the drinks.

- **Monitor the results.** Once a decision has been made, it is important to follow up with your customers to ensure their needs have been met. If not, go back to the first step in the model (identify the problem) and start over. You can follow up by simply asking a customer how the solution is working the next time you see him or her. For example, "Ms. Chin, how did the room we moved you into this morning suit your needs?" Such a question can uncover additional issues or confirm satisfaction. You can also use satisfaction surveys (telephone or e-mail), e-mail, or letter follow-up.

discussed in Chapter 7 can also be applied when you are trying to encourage and maintain customer loyalty (see Figure 12.4).

Problem resolution is not difficult if it is approached systematically. If you have done the planning described earlier and know what options are available and what authority you have, it becomes much easier.

Professionalism

As you have read in previous chapters, projecting a positive personal image, through manner of dress, knowledge, appearance of your work area, and your mental attitude, is a crucial element in communicating an "I care" image to customers

Working in teams of three or four members, decide on a course of action to resolve the problem posed in the following scenario:

You have been a cashier at Gifts Galore for a little over two months. A customer comes into your gift shop and wants to return a lamp that she says she purchased from your store as a gift for a wedding. Apparently, she discovered later that the recipient already had a lamp exactly like the one she bought. She tells you that she remembers the salesperson, Brittney, because her daughter's name is spelled the same way. You know that Brittney used to work at the gift shop, but quit about the time you started. The customer has no receipt, and you do not recognize the product as one that your store sells. You are empowered to make exchanges and give refunds up to a product value of $50. The customer says the lamp was $49.95 before tax. Store policy says that the customer must have a receipt if a refund is to be made. What questions would you ask to clarify the situation? How would you handle the problem?

and potential customers. By paying close attention to such factors, you better position yourself to establish and maintain a strong customer relationship. This is especially true where attitude is concerned. Attitude can mean success or failure when dealing with customers and can be communicated through the various verbal and nonverbal cues you have read about in other chapters.

4 Be Responsible for Your Customer Relationships

Concept: Take responsibility for good customer relationship management by personalizing your service, listening, keeping an open mind, and respecting your customers. Ask for input from your customers.

Taking a concerned, one-on-one approach to working with customers helps satisfy immediate needs while building a basis for long-lasting relationships. Customers tend to enjoy dealing more with people who they believe are caring and have their best interests at heart. To interact with someone they like is a pleasant experience. Take the time to personalize your customer interactions and to make each customer feel special. This can lead to enhanced trust and helps ensure that the customer returns.

You have reviewed some of the following points in other chapters. They are reviewed and expanded here because they are solid skills and go a long way toward building customer loyalty and, ultimately, customer retention. Take the actions described in the next sections to make your customers feel special.

Personalize Your Approach

Think of the theme song for the television show *Cheers*. The idea of the theme song was that *Cheers* was a great place to go because "everyone knows your name." Do you remember the social need in Maslow's hierarchy of needs? For the most part, people are a social species and need to be around others to grow and flourish. Helping your customers feel accepted can create a bond that will keep them coming back.

To create a social bond with customers, you will need to take time to get to know your regular customers and serve them individually. Recognizing them and using their name while interacting goes a long way toward creating that bond. For new customers, immediately start using the positive interpersonal communication skills you have learned. Treating customers as individuals and not as a number or one in a series is a very important step in building rapport and loyalty.

Listen Actively

In Chapter 5 you learned specific strategies for effective listening. By practicing active listening skills and avoiding distractions while determining customer needs and providing service, you can send the "I care" message discussed earlier. At the same time, you can discover the customer's needs and work toward satisfying them.

Keep an Open Mind

To develop and maintain an open mind, make it a habit to assess your attitude about your job, customers, products, and services before making contact with your customers. Make sure that you are positive, objective, prepared, and focused. Don't let negative attitudes block good service. Many service providers, even the more seasoned ones, go through slumps during which they feel down about themselves, their job, supervisors, organizations, customers, and so on. This is normal. Customer service is a stressful job, and external and internal factors (e.g. circadian rhythm, workload, and personal problems) influence one's perceptions of people and the world in general; however, guard against pessimism.

If you are facing personal problems that seem overwhelming, contact your supervisor, human resources or personnel department, or any other appropriate resource (e.g., Employee Assistance Program [EAP] representative) to help you sort out your problems. Failure to do so could lead to poor customer service or a less than professional image.

Individualize Service

Each customer is unique and has his or her own desires and needs. For that reason, every situation you handle will be slightly different. As you read in Chapter 8, you should view each person as an individual and not deal with customers based on preconceived ideas. By addressing a customer as an individual, listening so that you can discover his or her needs and problems, and then working to satisfy the needs or solve the problems, you potentially create a loyal customer. A simple way of accomplishing individualized service is to ask what else the customer would like. For example, in the case of a restaurant server who uses such a question, a customer might respond, "Do you have any _____?" If the item is available, the server could cheerfully reply, "We certainly do. I'll get it for you right away." If the item is not available, the server might reply, "I'm sorry we do not have _____. However, we do have _____. Would that be acceptable?"

Remember: Be positive and tell the customer what you can do, not what you cannot do.

Show Respect

Even if you don't agree with a customer, respect his or her point of view or need and provide the best possible service. In return, the customer will probably respect and appreciate you and your efforts. A variation of an old adage may help put this concept into perspective: *The customer may not always be right, but he or she is still the customer.*

If you lose sight of the fact that it is the customer who supports the organization, pays your salary, provides for your benefits, and gives you a job, you may want to examine why you are working in your current position. By acknowledging the value of your customers and affording them the respect and service that they deserve, you can greatly improve your chances of having a satisfied customer. Some easy ways to show respect to customers include:

Take a few minutes to think of other ways that you can show respect for a variety of customers (e.g., older, younger, people with disabilities, or of various cultural backgrounds). Discuss how these can positively influence service.

- When addressing the customer, use his or her last name and title. (If you are on the telephone, write down the customer's name along with other pertinent information.)
- Stop talking when the customer begins to speak.
- Take time to address the customer's questions or concerns.
- Return calls or e-mail messages within reasonable amounts of time.
- Show up on time for scheduled meetings.
- Do what you promised to do, and do it right the first time, within the agreed-upon time frame.

Elicit Input

Some people actually encourage rewarding customers who complain. In their 1996 book, Janelle Barlow and Claus Moller focused on the concept that "a complaint is a gift." The authors stressed that complaints provide feedback that can enable service providers and organizations to rapidly shift resources to fix things that are not working well in an effort to satisfy the customer. If you think about it, that makes sense.

Many times, service providers do not take the time to ask for feedback because they are afraid that it may not be good. In other instances, they simply do not think of asking or care to do so. To increase your own effectiveness and that of your organization, actively and regularly seek input from your customers. No one knows better than the customer what he or she likes or needs. Take the time to ask the customer, and then listen and act upon what you are told. By asking customers questions, you give them an opportunity to express interest, concerns, emotion, and even complaints. There are many ways of gathering this information (e.g., customer satisfaction cards, written surveys, and service follow-up telephone calls). The key is to somehow ask the customer "How well did we do in meeting your needs?" or "What do you think?"

There are many ways to gather information about customer satisfaction levels. Some of the more common include (see **<http://www.mhhe.com/lucas05>** for samples):

- *Customer comment cards* are simple 5" × 7 " (approximately) card stock questionnaires that quickly gather customer reactions to their service experience(s). These cards are commonly found on restaurant tables and at point-of-sale locations (e.g., cash registers). They typically consist of four or five closed-end questions that can be answered with yes/no or short answers and have a space for general comments.
- *Toll-free numbers* are often used to obtain customer opinions following a service encounter. Customers are provided a toll-free number on their sales receipt and encouraged to call within 24 hours. As a reward, they are often given discount coupons, bonus frequent guest/user points, or other small incentives.

Reflect on a recent interaction you had with an internal or external customer as a provider (over the telephone, in person, via e-mail, or through any other means). Immediately after that interaction, if someone had handed the customer a piece of paper and asked him or her to write down impressions of the treatment received from you, what would he or she likely have said? Why do you believe the customer would have said this?

Note: If you do not deal with customers, think of a situation that you recently experienced as a customer and answer the questions based on your experience. Record your perspective of what your customer's comments would have been, along with anything you could have done differently to improve the situation. Be as objective as you can.

- *Verbal comments* can be elicited from customers and logged in by service providers. By asking customers for feedback on their experience(s) and paying heed to them, immediate service adjustments can be made.
- *Follow-up telephone surveys* can be done by employees or consultants using a written list of questions. The key is to be brief, not impose on customers, and ask questions that will gather pertinent information (e.g., open-ended questions).
- *Service contact surveys* that are mailed or e-mailed (with permission) to people who have contacted an organization for information, to make a purchase, or use a service can gather more in-depth information.
- *Exit interviews* conducted by greeters, hosts, or hostesses as customers leave a facility. These are typically one or two quick questions (e.g., "How did you enjoy your stay?" "Were you able to find everything you needed?" or "What can we do to make your next visit more pleasurable?"). The key is to log in responses for future reference.
- *Shopper/customer surveys* that can yield a wealth of information. These are typically longer and more detailed than a comment card. They can be given to a customer as he or she leaves or can be sent to customers later (get names and addresses from checks written). Offer discount coupons or other incentives for returned surveys and provide self-addressed, stamped envelopes.
- *Focus groups* of six to eight internal or external customers can be formed to do in-depth, face-to-face or online (chat) surveys. Often organizations conducting these provide snacks and gifts (e.g., $50.00) for each participant. Ask open-ended questions related to the organization and product(s) and service(s) provided. Often, trained marketing or other facilitators are used to conduct such sessions. They also analyze responses and provide reports to management along with recommendations for improvement.
- *Sales and service records* can provide a wealth of information. They can reflect whether customers are returning and what products and services are being used most, and can show patterns of purchases.

Use Effective Closing Statements

Just as you would likely part company with a friend by saying good-bye, you should leave on a positive note with customers. After all, this is your final opportunity to convey your appreciation and show that you value the relationship you have established with them. Some typical approaches to accomplishing this are: "May I assist you with something else?" "If we may assist in the future, please let us know." "Please come again." "I look forward to serving you again, Ms. Ramirez. I'll see you at your next appointment."

5   Making the Customer Number One

Concept: Make a good first impression by establishing rapport; then identify and satisfy your customers' needs. Follow up to obtain repeat business.

The days of a customer adopting one product or company for life are long gone. With easy access and global competitiveness, customers are often swayed by advertising and a chance at a "better deal." Quality levels and features between competing brands and organizations are often comparable. The thing that separates competitors is their level of service. It is not unusual for customers to switch back and forth between products or organizations simply because of pricing. This is sometimes referred to as service **churn.**

Most people like to feel that they are important and valued. By recognizing and acting on that fact, you can go a long way toward providing solid customer service, reducing churn, and building a strong relationship with customers. By being an "I care" person, you can generate much goodwill while meeting customer needs.

Every time you encounter a customer in person or over the phone, you have an opportunity to provide excellent service. Some companies call a service encounter the **moment of truth** or refer to them as **contact points,** in which the customer comes into contact with some facet of the organization. At this point you and other service providers have an opportunity to deliver "knock your socks off" service, as Kristin Anderson and Ron Zemke discuss in several of their books on customer service. Each customer encounter moves through the following stages, although sometimes the order varies. At each step, you have another opportunity to provide excellent customer service.

Customer loyalty is won by providing extra service for the customer. Organizations must assess individual needs and determine how to meet those needs better than the competition does. In this case, customers who have mobility impairments or limitations will keep coming back to this establishment because they have provided transportation for those with disabilities. *How can you provide extra service for customers with special needs?*

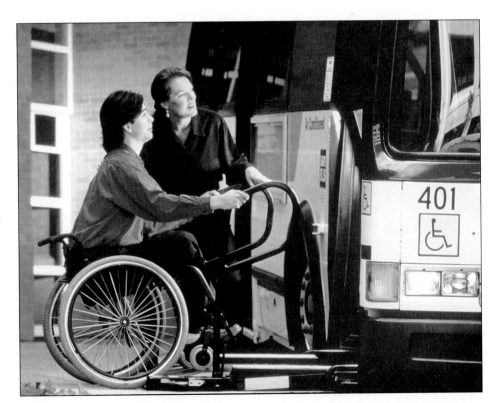

Make Positive Initial Contact

First impressions are crucial and often lasting. To ensure that you put your best effort forward, remember the basics of positive verbal and nonverbal communication—giving a professional salutation, projecting a positive attitude, and sincerely offering to assist. This is crucial because the average customer will come into an initial contact with certain expectations. If the expectations are not met, you and your organization can lose **relationship-rating points** that can ultimately cost the organization a customer. Such points are like the ones on performance appraisals used in many organizations to evaluate and rate employee performance (see Figure 12.5). Use this scale frequently to evaluate your rating as you deal with various customers.

Establish Rapport

Customers react to and deal effectively with employees who they perceive as likable, helpful, and effective. Throughout your interaction, continue to be helpful, smile, listen, use the customer's name frequently, and attend to the customer's needs or concerns. Also, look for opportunities to generate small talk about non-business-related matters. When something goes wrong, people who feel a kinship with service providers typically give higher ratings on the **relationship-rating point scale** than people who do not feel this connection.

Identify and Satisfy Customer Needs Quickly

Use the questioning, listening, observing, and feedback skills outlined in this book to focus on issues of concern to the customer. By effectively gathering information, you can then move to the next phase of customer service.

FIGURE 12.5
Relationship-Rating Point Scale

Exemplary (4) Service that is out of the ordinary and unexpected falls into this category. Examples: An auto repair shop details a customer's car after replacing a transmission. A beauty salon owner provides a free Swedish massage to a regular patron on her birthday. A restaurant server provides a complimentary meal and a coupon for a discount on a future visit to a customer who had to send her steak back twice to be cooked properly.

Above Average (3) Service in this category goes beyond the normal and may pleasantly surprise the customer, but does not dazzle or surprise the customer. Example: A regular customer at a bar gets a free second drink from the bartender. A clerk at a bank gives a customer a free wall calendar at the end of the transaction. A customer's son, who just received his first haircut, is given a lollypop by the barber.

Average (2) Service at this level is what is expected by a customer. Examples: A customer drops off laundry and when it is picked up, his shirts are starched as requested, on hangers, and in a plastic garment bag. A grocery store bagger asks, "Paper or plastic?" and then proceeds to comply with the customer's request. An accountant finishes a client's tax return on time, as promised.

Below Average (1) Service provided at this level is not as expected and disappoints customers. Examples: A newspaper deliverer brings a replacement paper after a customer calls to complain, leaves it on the doorstep, rings the bell, and departs without apologizing. A patient waits in a doctor's waiting room 15 minutes or longer beyond her scheduled appointment, and when she is finally seen, no one apologizes. A call center representative gives a customer a $15 credit on service because the customer had to call back three times to have a problem resolved.

Unsatisfactory (0) Service at this level is unacceptable and typically leads to a breakdown in the customer-provider relationship. Examples: A customer's cat is neutered by a veterinarian when taken in for a flea dip. A plumbing company that advertises "immediate emergency service" takes over four hours to send a repairperson to fix a leaking pipe in a wall; all carpeting in the living room is being saturated, and one wall is crumbling. A contracted tree-trimming worker cuts a large section from a tree that crashes through the garage roof and onto a brand-new car.

On a sheet of paper, list each of the initiatives for making customers No. 1 that you just read about. Then, develop an action plan for addressing each of them in your customer contacts. Be specific about exactly what you will do or say to address each strategy. Use the following initiatives and specify your actions and the expected customer response.

Make positive initial contact.

Establish rapport.

Identify and satisfy customer needs quickly.

Exceed expectations.

Follow up.

Encourage customers to return.

Exceed Expectations

As you can see on the relationship-rating point scale, customers typically expect that, if they pay a certain price for a product or service, they will receive a specific quality and quantity in return. This is not an unusual expectation. The average customer looks for value. As you read in earlier chapters, today's customers tend to be better-educated consumers who recognize that if they cannot fulfill their needs in one place, they can easily access the same or similar products and services on the Internet or by visiting a competitor. Therefore, you need to exceed a customer's expectations. Many terms are used to describe the concept of exceeding expectations—knock-their-socks-off service, positive memorable customer experiences, E-plus service, customer delight, dazzling service, fabled service, and Five Diamond or Five Star service. All these phrases have in common the concept of going above and beyond customer expectations—*under*promise and *over*deliver. By going out of your way not only to satisfy a customer but also to "wow" them by doing, saying, or offering the unexpected related to high-quality service delivery, you can exceed expectations. The result could be the reward of continuing patronage by the customer.

An example of unexpected service or going the extra mile follows. A customer bought flooring tiles from a home product warehouse and took them home. Upon opening the box, he discovered that several tiles were broken. After the customer called the store, an employee delivered the replacement tiles and assisted the customer in laying them.

Follow Up

Service professionals regrettably often overlook this step although it can be one of the most crucial in establishing long-term relationships. Follow-through is a major key in obtaining repeat business. After you have satisfied a customer's needs, follow up with the customer on his or her next visit or via mail, e-mail, or telephone to ensure that he or she was satisfied. For external customers, this follow-up can be coupled with a small thank-you card, coupons for discounts on future purchases, small presents, or any other incentive to reward their patronage. You can follow up with internal customers by using voice mail or e-mail messages, leaving Post-it notes on their desks, inviting them for coffee in the cafeteria, or any other of a number of ways. The prime objective is to let them know that you have not forgotten them and appreciate their business and support.

Encourage Customers to Return

Just as with your initial impression, you need to close on a high note. Smile, remind the customer you are available to help in the future, give an opportunity for last-minute questions, and invite the customer to return.

6 Enhancing Customer Satisfaction as a Strategy for Retaining Customers

Concept: Do the unexpected; deal with one customer at a time; handle complaints efficiently. These are just some of the things you can do to enhance customer satisfaction.

Building good relationships in order to increase **customer satisfaction** is valuable because it can lead to repeat business—the key to keeping a business productive and profitable.

Satisfaction is a big factor for many customers in remaining loyal. According to a national customer satisfaction survey (the American Customer Satisfaction Index), by the University of Michigan, a recent review of customer satisfaction in the United States shows a slight rise in the level of general customer satisfaction. There had been a steady decline that began in 1994 (when the numbers were first tracked) through 1997. Since then, there has been a slow increase to 73.8 percent in 2003.

Based on the University of Michigan study, there is definitely room for improvement in delivering customer service. In your own organization, your efforts could be a deciding factor in customer ratings for the quality of service rendered.

Keeping customers can be difficult in a competitive, global marketplace because so many companies have joined in the race for customers. By providing a personal, professional strategy, you can help ensure that customers return. Some tips that can help provide quality service to customers are given in the following sections.

Pay Attention

As you listen, focus all your attention on the customer so that you can identify and address his or her needs. If you are serving in person, use positive nonverbal cues (e.g., face the customer, smile, use open gestures, make eye contact, stop doing other things, and focus attention on the customer) and language. Ask open-ended questions to determine the customer's needs. Also, use the active listening techniques discussed in Chapter 5 to ensure that you get all the information you need to properly address the customer's needs or concerns.

Deal With One Customer at a Time

You cannot effectively handle two people (on the phone or in person) simultaneously. When more than one call or customer comes in at the same time, seek assistance or ask one customer to wait (or ask whether you can get back to him or her at a later time). Then, give personalized attention to the other customer.

Know Your Customers

This is crucial with long-term customers, but it is also important with everyone. You may see or talk to hundreds of customers a week; however, each customer has only one or two contacts with you. Although you might not recall the name of everyone you speak with during a day, your customers will remember what was said or

LEADERSHIP INITIATIVE   **12.2**

One effective way to enhance service potential and reward employees at the same time is to host a departmental strategy session. Order pizza or other food for lunch and spend the time brainstorming ideas for ways to make customers No. 1.

agreed upon previously, and expect you to do the same. For that reason, use notes or your computer to keep a record of conversations with customers. You can review or refer to these notes in subsequent encounters. This avoids having customers repeat themselves, and they will feel "special" because you remembered them.

Give Customers Special Treatment

As you read earlier, you should try to take the time for a little small talk once in a while. This will help you learn about your customers and what's important to them (potential needs). Occasionally, paying them compliments also helps (e.g., "That's an attractive tie," or "That perfume is very pleasing").

Service Each Customer at Least Adequately

Take the necessary time to handle your customer's questions, complaints, or needs. If you have a number of customers on the phone or in person, service one at a time and either ask to get back to the others or get help from a coworker, if possible. You might also suggest alternative information resources to customers, such as fax on demand or your website, online information system, or interactive voice response. This may satisfy them and help reduce the calls or visits from customers, because they can now get the information they need from alternative sources.

Do the Unexpected

Do not just provide service; provide exceptional service. Provide additional information, offer suggestions that will aid the customer, send articles that may be of interest, follow up transactions with calls or letters to make sure that needs were met, or send cards for special occasions and to thank customers. These are the little things that mean a lot and can mean the difference between a rating of Average or Exemplary on the relationship-rating point scale. Read the article in the following box quickly to see an example of this concept in action.

Give 'Em the Extra Pickle!

An example of doing the unexpected came when Bob Farrell, founder of Farrell's Ice Cream Parlor restaurants, responded to a customer complaint a number of years ago. Farrell received a letter from a regular customer of many years. The customer had been ordering hamburgers with an extra pickle since he started patronizing Farrell's. At some point, the man went to Farrell's and ordered a hamburger but was told by a new server that the extra pickle would cost an additional 25 cents. When the man protested, the server conferred with her manager and happily reported that the extra pickle would cost only 5 cents. At that point the man left and wrote Farrell, who wrote back enclosing a free coupon, apologizing, and inviting the customer back.

The lesson to be learned here is that when you have a loyal customer whom you might lose because of enforcement of a trivial policy, you should be flexible. When policies inhibit good service and negatively affect customer relationships, they should be pointed out to management and examined for possible modification or elimination.

Handle Complaints Effectively

Treat complaints as opportunities to redeem missed service expectations, and handle them effectively. Acknowledge any error on your part, and do everything possible to resolve the problem quickly and to the customer's satisfaction. Thank the customer for bringing his or her concerns to your attention.

Sell Benefits Not Features

An effective approach to increasing sales is used by most salespeople. They focus on benefits and not features of a product or service. A feature differs from a benefit in that it is a descriptive aspect of a product or service (e.g., has a shorter turn radius, has 27 options, or comes in five different colors).

Show each customer how your product, service, or information addressed his or her needs. What benefit will result? Stress that although other organizations may offer similar products and services, yours fits their needs best (if they do) and how. If your product or service doesn't fit their needs, admit it, and offer any available alternatives (such as referral to a competitor). Your customers will appreciate your honesty, and even if you can't help them, they will probably return in the future because you are trusted.

Know Your Competition

Stay abreast of what other, similar organizations are offering in order to counter comments about them. This does not mean that you should criticize or belittle your competitors or their products and services. Such behavior is unprofessional and will likely cause the customer to lose respect for you. And when respect goes, trust goes.

Staying aware of the competition has the additional benefit of helping you be sure that you can describe and offer the products, services, and features of your organization that are comparable to those being offered by others.

In 2003, the Marriott hotel chain recognized a need to compete with cheaper reservation rates being offered on the Internet. Marriott announced its "Look No Further Best Rate Guarantee" that matched reservation rates for its hotel (excluding Ritz-Carlton) no matter where the customer found them. The hotel chain did this to remain competitive and fill rooms.

7   Strive for Quality

Concept: A customer's perception of quality service is often one of the prime reasons for his or her return.

A final strategy for helping to increase customer loyalty relates to the quality of service you and your organization provide. So much is written these days about quality—how to measure it and its significance—that there is a temptation to think of it as a fad. In the areas of customer service and customer retention, thinking this way could be disastrous. A customer's perception of quality service is often one of the prime reasons for his or her return.

Terms such as **total quality management (TQM)** and **continuous quality improvement (CQI)** are often used in many industries to label the goal of improvement. Basically, quality service involves efforts and activities that are done well and that meet or exceed customer needs and expectations. In an effort to achieve quality service, many organizations go to great lengths to test and measure the level of service provided to customers.

On a personal level, you can strive for quality service by working to achieve an Exemplary rating on the relationship-rating point scale. Your organization's ability to deliver quality service depends on you and the others who provide frontline service to customers. If you do not adopt a professional attitude and continually strive to improve your knowledge, skills, and efforts in dealing with customers, failure and customer dissatisfaction can result.

A number of years ago, Texas A&M researchers developed a five-dimensional model, called **RATER** (for reliability, assurance, tangibles, empathy, and responsiveness), to describe quality service. The model, along with strategies for its implementation, is described below:

Reliability. The ability to provide what was promised, dependably and accurately.

IMPLEMENTATION STRATEGY: Make sure that you correctly identify customer needs, promise only what you can deliver, and follow through to ensure that the product or service was received as promised.

Assurance. The knowledge and courtesy of employees, and their ability to convey trust and confidence.

IMPLEMENTATION STRATEGY: Take the time to serve customers one at a time. Provide service assertively by using positive communication techniques and describing products and services accurately.

Tangibles. The physical facilities and equipment and the appearance of personnel.

IMPLEMENTATION STRATEGY: Maintain workspaces in a neat, orderly manner, dress professionally, and maintain excellent grooming and hygiene standards.

Empathy. The degree of caring and individual attention provided to customers.

IMPLEMENTATION STRATEGY: Listen for emotions in your customers' messages. Put yourself in their place and respond compassionately by offering service to address their needs.

Responsiveness. The willingness to help customers and provide prompt service.

IMPLEMENTATION STRATEGY: Project a positive, can-do attitude. Take immediate steps to help customers and satisfy needs.

Chapter Summary

Build enduring, strong customer relationships based on the principles of trust, responsibility, loyalty, and satisfying customer needs. These are all crucial elements of success in an increasingly competitive business world. Retaining current customers is less expensive and more effective than finding and developing new ones. The key is to provide courteous, professional service that addresses customer needs. Although many factors potentially affect your ability to deliver quality service, you can apply specific methods and strategies to keep your customers coming back.

Too often, service providers lose sight of the fact that they are the organization and that their actions determine the outcome of any customer-provider encounter. By employing the strategies outline in this chapter, and those you read about previously, you can do much to ensure customer satisfaction and organizational success.

SERVICE IN ACTION   Barnes & Noble, Inc.   CHAPTER 12

http://www.barnesandnoble.com

As of the end of 2002, Barnes & Noble, Inc., was one of the largest booksellers on the Internet and had over 2,000 book-stores and video game and entertainment software stores. According to the company's annual report, the December 2002 Jupiter Media Matrix rated the Barnes & Noble.com website as the ninth most trafficked shopping site and among the top 50 largest Web properties on the Internet. The company employs over 50,000 full-time and part-time employees and its sales operations grossed $5 billion.

Some of the strategies that have made this organization a sales superpower include offering a wide array of products to its customers. Even the less-than-avid reader is enticed to come to Barnes & Noble. Bookstores are no longer just that. They are now destinations where people go to meet for re-freshments, relax, unwind, and browse the shelves. In addition to a staggering number of books, magazines, music CDs, and other entertainment items, you will find items such as toys, gift cards, newspapers, trade journals, and other objects of interest to a diverse customer base. These are all located in a serene setting of background music in well-organized and comfortable stores which feature cafés serving specialty cof-fees, soft drinks, and pastries. They also offer children's story reading, meet the author events, and writer group meetings.

The Barnes & Noble.com website has created a reposi-tory for finding current and out-of-print publications, as well as many other products. Through their affiliate program, the company encourages other company websites to link to theirs with the promise of a percentage for every sale funneled through to Barnes & Noble. One such company is Creative Presentation Resources, Inc at **<http://www.presentationre-sources.net>**. This organization markets training aids, toys, in-centives, videos and other items that can enhance a learning environment for corporate trainers, educators, and presen-ters. The affiliate relationship with Barnes & Noble provides an added value to their customers while providing a possible revenue stream at no investment to the company.

Key Terms and Concepts

churn
contact points
contingency plans
continuous quality
   improvement (CQI)
cost of dissatisfied
   customers
customer loyalty
customer needs

customer relationships
customer retention
customer satisfaction
ethical behavior
moment of truth
Planning Process Model
Problem-Solving Model
RATER Model
relationship management

relationship-rating points
relationship-rating point
   scale
Technical Assistance
   Research Program
   (TARP)
total quality
   management (TQM)
trust

Quick Preview Answers

1. T
2. F
3. T
4. T

5. T
6. F
7. T
8. T

9. T
10. F
11. T
12. T

Chapter Review Questions

1. How can you build customer trust?
2. What are some key reasons why customers remain loyal to a product, a service, or an organization?
3. What are some of the provider characteristics that affect customer loyalty?
4. What are the steps in the Planning Process Model? Describe.
5. What are six common customer needs?
6. What are ways for service providers to take responsibility for customer relations?
7. What are some techniques for making the customer feel that he or she is No. 1?
8. What was the purpose of the RATER model developed at Texas A&M?

Search It Out

Search the Web for Information on Loyalty

Log on to the Internet to search for additional information related to customer loyalty. Select one of the following projects:

Go to the websites of organizations that deal with customers and service. Identify research data, articles, bibliographies, and other reference sources (e.g., videotapes) related to customer loyalty and create a bibliography similar to the one at the end of this book. Here are a few sites to get you started:

<http://www.ICSA.com>
<http://www.SOCAP.com>
<http://www.CSR.com>
<http://www.e-satisfy.com>
<http://www.Amazon.com>
<http://www.Barnes&Noble.com>
<http://www.Borders.com>

Go to various search engines to locate information and articles on *customer loyalty.* To find information, enter terms related to concepts covered in this chapter or locate Websites dealing with such issues. Here are a few to get you started:

Customer loyalty
Customer satisfaction
Customer retention
Customer Service Review magazine
Total quality management in customer service
Cost of customer service
<http://www.customercare.com>

Note: A listing for additional research on specific URLs is provided on the Customer Service website at **<http://www.mhhe.com/lucas05>.**

Collaborative Learning Activity

Building Loyalty

Here are two options for activities that you and others can use to reinforce the concepts of building loyalty that you read about in this chapter.

1. Working with a partner, think of times when you have both been frustrated or dissatisfied with service received from a provider. Make a list of characteristics the service provider(s) exhibited that had a negative impact on you. Once you have a list, discuss the items on the list, and then honestly say whether either (or both) of you exhibit any of these negative behaviors when dealing with others. For the ones you answered yes, jointly develop a list of strategies of improve each behavior.

2. Take a field trip around your town. Walk through and/or past as many establishments as possible. Look for example of actions that organizations are doing to encourage and discourage customer loyalty. List the examples on a sheet of

paper and be prepared to discuss them in groups assigned by your instructor when you return to class. Some examples of encouragement might be free samples of a product being distributed at a food court, discount coupons, acceptance of competitor coupons, or free refills on drinks. Negative examples might be signs that say "Rest rooms for customers only" or "No change given," and policies that allow discounts only on certain days and no refunds on purchases (exchanges only).

Face to Face

Assessing the Need for Reorganization at Get Away

Background

After over nine years in business, the Get Away travel agency in Des Moines, Iowa, is feeling the pinch of competition. During the past 14 months, the owners, Marsha Henry and Consuela (Connie) Gomez, have seen business profits dwindle by 18 percent. Neither Marsha nor Connie can figure out what has happened. Although travel reservationists have had to deal with airline fee caps, customers making more reservations on the Internet, and the fact that many industry travel providers are cutting back, competing agencies don't seem to be suffering as much as Get Away. The problem is especially worrisome because Marsha and Connie recently took out a second mortgage on their office building so that they could put more money into promotion and customer acquisition efforts. The more efforts they make at gaining exposure, the more customers they lose, it seems. Recently, they lost a major corporate client that accounted for over $100,000 in business a year. Out of desperation, they have decided to hire you, a seasoned travel agency manager, to try to stop their descent and turn the operation around.

Your Role

As the new manager at Get Away, you have been given the authority to do whatever is necessary to salvage the agency. By agreement with Marsha and Connie, they are delaying the announcement of your hiring to other agency employees. Your objective is to objectively assess the operation by acting as a customer.

Your first contact with the agency came on Thursday, when you placed a phone call to the office, posing as a customer. The phone rang 12 times and was curtly answered with "Hello. Please hold (click)." After nearly five minutes, an agent, Sue, came on the line and stated, "Sorry for the wait, we're swamped. Can I get your name and number and call you right back?" Two-and-a-half hours later, you got a call from Tom. He said that Sue had gone home for the day, and he was doing her callbacks. Sue would follow up when she came in the next day. You asked a friend to make a similar call on Wednesday, and she met with similar results.

On Thursday, you stopped by the office at 2:55 P.M. Of three agents who should have been there, only Claudia was present. Apparently Tom and Sue were still at lunch. Two customers were waiting as you arrived. Claudia greeted you with a small smile and asked you to "Take a number and have a seat." You looked around the office and saw desks piled high with materials, an overflowing trash can, and an empty coffeepot in the waiting area bearing the sign "Please have a cup on us." In talking to your fellow "customers," you learned that one had been there for over 45 minutes. Both were irritated at having to wait, and eventually, one left. You left after 30 minutes and passed Tom and Sue, who came in laughing. You thought you detected an odor of alcohol on Tom. Neither acknowledged you. From the office, you proceeded to a meeting with Marsha and Connie.

Critical Thinking Questions

1. What impressions of the travel agency did you have as a result of your initial phone call?
2. How did your office visit affect you?
3. What will you tell Marsha and Connie about employee professionalism?
4. What customer needs are being overlooked in this scenario?
5. In what ways can this situation be improved?

PLANNING TO SERVE

CHAPTER 12

To help enhance customer retention and foster customer loyalty efforts of any organization, think about the following questions:

1. What are some strategies that can be used to show customers that their business is valued?

2. What obstacles exist to customer loyalty and how might they be removed?

3. What are some of the things that impact customer loyalty positively in many organizations?

4. What are some things that differentiate organizations and which can be accentuated to build customer retention and loyalty?

Service Recovery

From the Frontline Interview

Nick Crnich is a Senior Sales Representative for RR Donnelley (a provider of printing and related services to the merchandising, magazine, book, directory, and financial markets) and has been with the company for 32 years. Throughout that period, he has been in customer service and sales-related positions, working with elementary and high school (El-Hi) publishers, Bible, reference, and higher education publishers. He has worked with very small organizations and multi-national corporations. In his current position, he interacts daily with the internal customers in the Customer Care and Estimating teams, Scheduling/Production Control, Strategic Planning, and Business Unit Management.

NICK CRNICH,
Senior Sales
Representative,
RR Donnelley

1 **What is service recovery to you in your industry?**

I look at service recovery as an event where the customer's specifications and expectations are not met.

The cause of a breakdown (or nonconformance) can occur when a mechanical process fails, when communication on specifications/expectations fails, or when a decision is made to accept nonconforming product and continue the manufacturing process.

Customers often leave after a service breakdown because they feel that their supplier does not truly care about the customer's products, or the supplier is unwilling to implement a process to guard product quality. This is important because customers invest time, effort, and dollars to create the best product they can envision. A failure can occur when a supplier does not respect that vision and the customer's efforts or when a supplier does not respect the end user. In the case of McGraw-Hill Higher Education, the latter would be professors and students.

2 **In working with dissatisfied customers, what are some of the most important things to remember related to resolving their issue and maintaining the relationship?**

That our customers are not the end customer. They will take the product, which we have manufactured, and sell that book in the open market. The publishers are investing in our production abilities. They expect a partner, not just a supplier. They want someone who cares as passionately about the quality and appearance as they do. Publishers want someone who will meet the agreed upon schedule, so that the end users can have confidence that the books will be available for classes on time. When there is a failure, the supplier needs to respond quickly and informatively. They need to keep the customer posted every step of the way. Both the salesperson and the entire manufacturing organization must be sensitive to the customer's situation and of the same mindset: this is our partner and we need to respond quickly to deliver the expected product to the end user.

Chapter Learning Objectives

After completing this chapter, you will be able to:

- Define what a service breakdown is.
- Discuss the causes of service breakdowns.
- Determine why customers leave following a service breakdown.

- Identify strategies for preventing customer dissatisfaction.
- Implement a frontline service recovery strategy.
- Spot roadblocks to service recovery.

3 What are some issues or pitfalls that service providers encounter related to service recovery?

When a service provider acts slowly, the customer feels that they are "going it alone." Also, when a provider does not give details of a failure, the customer feels the provider does not know what went wrong or why. If that is the case, they do not know how to control their process of manufacture. The customer might also suspect dishonesty.

4 How does the way you and others deal with service recovery impact your organization and your customers?

I try to be truthful with all of my customer/partners. I advise them that, at some time, we *will* have a service failure. But, I also advise them that the true measure of the relationship and partnership between the customer and their supplier is how quickly our entire organization responds and fixes the situation. It cannot be just lip service from the Sales Representative. The philosophy of *service recovery* has to be embraced by the entire organization to be a positive.

5 What are some of the strategies you use to recover from a service breakdown?

We encourage feedback/criticism from our customers. We need to know when we have failed to meet expectations. And, even in the least nonconformance, we need to respond quickly. Although the sales representative is the immediate "face" for the supplier, we prefer to have our team introduced during the process of manufacture, so that the customer knows that there are many employees looking out for their best interests. And, those are the same people who will truly respond to a service failure.

6 What advice, related to dealing with dissatisfied customers and regaining their confidence and support, would you give someone entering the customer service?

I suggest the following:

- Do it right the first time.
- Welcome/encourage complaints.
- Respond quickly.
- Treat customers honestly and fairly.
- Keep customers informed.
- Keep one point of contact (usually Sales). But, whoever receives the complaint, they own the complaint and will be the point in resolution of the complaint.

Additionally, I encourage all service providers to remember the following points:

- You are making promises to your customers.
- You have to have a team that is enabled to deliver on those promises (training, equipment, processes, etc.).
- You need to keep your promises.
- A service failure is a broken promise.
- The team needs to respond, recover, and deliver on that promise.

Critical Thinking

Based on what Nick has said, why do you think service recovery is so important in the service process? What do you believe are some of the keys to successful service recovery?

Quick Preview

Before reviewing the chapter content, respond to the following questions by placing a "T" for true or an "F" for false on the rules. Use any questions you miss as a checklist of material to which you will pay particular attention as you read through the chapter. For those you get right, congratulate yourself, but review the sections they address in order to learn additional details about the topic.

_____ 1. Service recovery occurs when a provider is able to make restitution, solve a problem, or regain customer trust after service breakdown.

_____ 2. Service breakdowns are rare in most organizations.

_____ 3. Thirteen percent of customers who have service problems tell three to five other people.

_____ 4. Organizational factors related to policies or procedures are rarely the basis for service breakdowns.

_____ 5. A good strategy for organizational success is to focus on the "average" customer.

_____ 6. Competency in communicating can eliminate the need for service recovery.

_____ 7. To effectively serve your customers, you need a strong knowledge of products, services, organizational structure, and organizational goals.

_____ 8. Service breakdowns always occur as a result of service provider error.

_____ 9. In the follow-through phase of recovery, negotiations take place when the organization and customer make a commitment to take specific actions.

_____ 10. One key strategy for preventing dissatisfaction is to learn to think like a customer.

_____ 11. The primary purpose of any good service recovery program should be to return the organization-customer relationship to a normal status.

Answers to Quick Preview can be found at the end of the chapter.

1 What Is Service Recovery?

Concept: When service breaks down, the customer expects that customer service representatives will take action to solve the customer's problem.

Effective **service recovery** occurs when an organization or service provider is able to solve a customer problem, make restitution, or regain trust following a breakdown in service delivery. Many times your customers have expectations that they will receive products, services, or other deliverables at a certain level. When they get something else, they can become frustrated, angry, and/or dissatisfied.

The challenge is to recognize that some customers will not tell you they are dissatisfied. That is where the ability to read their nonverbal cues and ask effective questions, as you read in Chapters 3 and 4, is paramount to your success. If you do not identify a customer's problem and take immediate steps to recover or make amends, you could lose a valuable customer, who may then tell others who might also defect or, if they are potential customers, stay away.

So in a way, you sometimes have to be part fortune teller, part detective, and part problem solver in order to deliver effective customer service. And, if you become really good at the service recovery technique, you may even be able to turn a negative situation into an additional sale or upgrade in products and services.

2   What Is a Service Breakdown?

Concept: Service breakdowns occur whenever any product or service fails to meet the customer's expectations.

Service breakdowns occur daily in many organizations. They happen whenever the product or service delivered fails to meet customer expectations. In some cases the product or service delivered may function exactly as it was designed, but if the customer perceived that it should work another way, a breakdown occurs. Here are some possible breakdowns:

- A waiter serves a meal containing an ingredient not expected by the customer, or one that the customer specified should not be added. A note of caution: If you are in food service, be vigilant in monitoring orders when customers ask that certain ingredients not be used. Check food and drinks before you deliver them to your customer to be sure that the staff did not forget the special request. Also, do not simply remove a food item if it was placed on a plate inadvertently. Some people have severe allergies to certain foods that could cause serious illness and even death—and a huge liability for you and your organization.
- A hotel room is not available when the customer arrives. (In some cases a stated check-in time may exist and the customer may be early. Make every effort to accommodate the customer if this happens.)
- A car repair is not completed at the time promised, or is done incorrectly.
- An additional cash register is not opened even though there are eight to ten customers waiting in a line and cashier staff are available in the store. (Some companies have signs stating that they will open another register if more than a certain number of customers are waiting.)
- A patient arrives for a scheduled doctor's appointment to find that the doctor left town on a personal emergency the day before but no one called the patient to reschedule.
- According to the customer, room service food was cold when delivered (e.g., not at the degree of warmth desired or expected).
- A coworker expects your assistance in providing information needed for a monthly report, but you failed to get it to her on time or as agreed.
- A manufacturer does not receive a parts delivery as you promised, and an assembly line has to be shut down.
- A garment you needed for a meeting returns from the laundry with broken buttons and cannot be worn.

In any of the situations described, customers may have not received what they were promised, or at least they perceived that they did not. When such incidents occur, there is a breakdown. Unfortunately, most such situations go unreported by customers. Moreover, when they are reported, often they are not effectively handled by businesses. TARP, a customer service research and consulting firm in Arlington, Virginia, has published numerous surveys on the topic of complaint

What examples of service breakdown have you experienced or can think of? List them and then discuss them with classmates. After discussing your lists, brainstorm ways that the organization did or could have recovered.

handling in the United States. A landmark study commissioned by the U.S. Office of Consumer Affairs in 1979 and updated in 1986 demonstrated the value of effective customer complaint resolution. These findings have been validated since 1986 throughout various industries (see Figures 13.1, 13.2, and 13.3).

3   Causes of Service Breakdowns

Concept: Service breakdowns can occur for a number of reasons. For the customer, however, the customer service provider represents the organization when the service breaks down. The provider must identify the cause and remedy the situation to the customer's satisfaction.

Human beings make mistakes; this is a fact. Mistakes are often glaring to customers, who can be very unforgiving at times. The best you can hope for when something goes wrong is that you can identify the **cause of the service breakdown** and remedy the problem quickly to your customer's satisfaction. By accomplishing this, you may maintain the customer loyalty as discussed in Chapter 12.

Many reasons exist for you and your organization to take action to remedy a situation that has gone wrong. Some typical events necessitating service recovery action are:

- A product or service did not do what it was expected to do.
- A promise was not kept.
- A deadline was missed.
- Customer service was not adequately provided (the customer had to wait too long or was ignored).
- A service provider lacked adequate knowledge or skills to handle a situation.
- Your actions or those of the organization inconvenienced the customer (e.g., a lab technician took blood during a patient's visit, but the sample was mishandled, requiring the patient to return for a retest).
- A customer was given the "runaround" (was transferred to various employees or departments and required to explain the situation to each individual).
- The customer was treated unprofessionally or in a rude manner (or perceived that this was the treatment).

Numerous factors in the service process can lead to a failure to meet customer expectations, and they can all influence service recovery. Generally, these factors fall into three categories—organizational, employee, or customer.

Organizational Factors

Organizational factors relate to processes, procedures, policies, and structures that, when not functioning effectively, can detract from service quality. As a frontline provider, you play a crucial role in implementing many of these practices. As such,

FIGURE 13.1
**What Complaint
Research Shows**

Source: TARP, 1300 Wilson
Blvd., Suite 950, Arlington,
VA 22209.

The median number of people customers who have a small problem will tell is 5, if the problem is appropriately resolved, and 10 if they are not satisfied.

The median number of people customers who have a large problem will tell is 8, if the problem is appropriately resolved, and 16 if they are not satisfied.

In 1,000 companies surveyed, on average, 50 percent of consumers and 25 percent of business customers who have problems never complain.

Three principal reasons why people do not complain:

(1) Complaining wasn't worth their time and effort.

(2) They believed that complaining wouldn't do any good; no one wanted to hear about their problems.

(3) They didn't know how or where to complain.

FIGURE 13.2
**Many Customers
Do Not Complain**

Source: TARP, 1300 Wilson
Blvd., Suite 950, Arlington,
VA 22209.

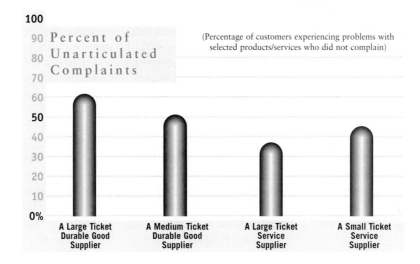

FIGURE 13.3
**Many Customers
Are Not Happy
With Businesses'
Response to Their
Complaints**

Source: TARP, 1300 Wilson
Blvd., Suite 950, Arlington,
VA 22209.

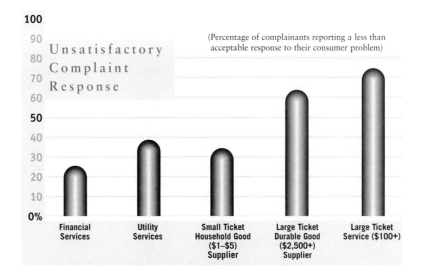

you become the organization in the eyes of a customer. When a customer yells at you because he or she perceives that something did not go as promised or expected, he or she is usually yelling at the organization through you. That is why you must control the tendency to take the anger personally. Instead, continue to listen objectively to what he or she has to say in order to get the information needed to solve the problems. Even so, there are some factors over which you have no direct control but that affect you and your customers. These include the following.

Human Resources

The screening, selection, training, performance appraisal, and compensation of employees who interact with customers are crucial. Managers should take care to develop and periodically update a job description that focuses on the competencies required for the position. This will help ensure that the right person is hired for a job and that employees are being recognized for what they do.

You can help in this regard by openly discussing your regular job tasks with your supervisor. Often, over time, employees take on tasks because it is easier for them to do so than to ask someone else, or because job responsibilities evolve when changes are made in procedures and systems. Your supervisor is usually aware of these modifications, but since they are minor, no change is made to your job description. Over time, your responsibilities may evolve far beyond the written job description. This is why you need to know what your job description defines as your duties and bring major changes to the attention of your supervisor. This is important because your performance is typically evaluated based on established goals and your job description.

Moreover, job descriptions are used to recruit and hire additional staff. It is to your advantage for your supervisor to have an accurate picture of the skills required so that he or she can adequately screen applicants and choose the best-qualified person to do the job. This is to your advantage since, if a person is hired based on an outdated job description, you may end up training this person on the job.

From a training standpoint, most large organizations spend millions of dollars each year training and updating employee knowledge and skills. Such efforts help companies stay competitive. Also, many organizations continually evaluate and modify compensation and benefit packages. They do this because all these factors affect employee morale and ultimately can create customer satisfaction, or dissatisfaction, depending on how they are handled.

Organization and Structure

Relationships between members of departments or cross-functional teams are typically clearly defined. Reporting structure, levels of empowerment (what employees are authorized to do and what decisions they are allowed to make), and integration of functions are examples. This may not be true in your organization. If necessary, go to your supervisor and ask for an explanation of the reporting hierarchy, as well as the customer-provider chain (people or groups to whom you supply and from which you receive products, information, and services). A thorough understanding of these relationships is important in making it possible for you to provide the best service possible to your customers. Such knowledge also allows you to follow up in cases of service breakdown and to recognize the limits of what you can and cannot do to satisfy customer needs or complaints.

Processes and Programs

The way complaints are handled, sales or promotional tools are used, products and services are delivered, and billing, advertising, and consumer-customer communications work falls into this category.

As a frontline provider, you must have a thorough knowledge of special sales and promotions and how all these systems function in service delivery. This allows you to respond consistently and correctly to customer questions or complaints. Failure to understand these processes can lead to miscommunication and customer dissatisfaction.

Product and Service Design and Delivery

Factors in this category are quality levels, available options, variety of offerings, performance, and availability. These factors often determine whether customers get what they perceive they deserve or need.

To effectively promote, sell, or service products or provide quality service levels, you need a comprehensive knowledge of what your organization offers. You must have a knowledge of processes related to these areas and also be able to discuss them clearly. Remember that you represent the organization, and your customers expect you to have answers.

Internal Communications

Internal communications involve the means for communicating within the organization to share information, elicit support, offer guidance, and train employees. Communication can be achieved through newsletters, meetings, bulletin boards, e-mail, voice mail, and various publications.

Since communication among members of your organization is crucial to your success, you need to be able to freely and regularly exchange product and service information, and to network with others through a variety of methods. The more access you have to data, the better informed you become, so that you are more capable of handling a variety of customer encounters.

Technological Support Systems

As you read in Chapter 9, computers, software, telecommunications, and other technology, along with the technical support staff to maintain the processes, are crucial in today's service environment. All of these resources play an integral role in allowing the exchange of information, problem solving, effective customer service, and keeping your organization competitive. In the age of the **information highway,** you need to be competent in using technology-based information systems, in order to gain and provide information to deliver quality service effectively and efficiently.

Customers don't want to hear "I'm sorry. I can't bring up your file. My computer is down." You need to know how to access information or quickly find someone

Technology has enhanced the way service providers do their jobs. *What improvements have you witnessed in the service sector as a result of technological changes?*

who can. In addition, educating yourself on alternative information sources is helpful. Speak with your supervisor or team leader and peers to find out whether other ways exist for accessing information when technology fails. If such files or systems exist, learn to use them. If not, suggest them if appropriate. At the very least, ask your supervisor what you should do or say if technology fails.

Standards

Standards are tenets or guidelines that affect the way employees view the organization and how they behave. They also influence the way people outside the organization perceive you and the organization. For example, do you and your company truly value customers? Do systems, products, and services support efforts to satisfy the most demanding customer? If you answered "yes," then you are on your way to flourishing in a competitive service market. If not, start analyzing what might need improvement and make recommendations for change to your supervisor or team leader. By focusing on the average customer, the organization is saying "We're happy to just get by with average service and results." Customer perception could be that your organization and/or you don't really care about satisfaction, but just profit and survival. This perception can lead to customer defection.

Employee Factors

These elements relate to your own abilities, competencies, knowledge levels, and expertise in dealing with others:

Communication Skills

Your verbal, nonverbal, and written communication and listening skills will often determine whether you'll have to initiate a service recovery strategy. For example, if you effectively communicate usage instructions for a piece of equipment you sell, a customer may not have difficulties once he or she gets home. This avoids customer frustration and reduces complaints. It can also result in time and effort saved for you and the customer, as well as in money saved and good customer rapport maintained.

Knowledge

To effectively serve your customers, you need a strong knowledge of products, services, organizational structure and goals, processes, procedures, and how to effectively provide service. Also, a sound understanding of some of the issues discussed in Part 2 of this book (e.g., interpersonal communication skills, diversity, and technology) is very helpful in gaining and maintaining a solid customer-provider relationship.

Through your knowledge, you will be able to quickly and effectively identify needs and offer the right solution to address customer needs and concerns.

Attitude

The way you perceive your organization, self, job, and customers determines much about the quality of service you provide. For example, an upbeat, positive focus will allow you to look forward to and enjoy each customer encounter (positive and negative). Your positive attitude will help you make a sincere effort to identify and satisfy customer needs.

Technical Skills

Your ability to safely and efficiently use equipment and systems that support service (e.g., computer, telephones, facsimile machines, photo copiers, and other job-related machinery and equipment) is important from an efficiency and safety standpoint and also from a service perspective. As you have read, technology can greatly enhance your ability to provide quality service to more customers, and to do it more quickly. Since technology is so commonplace, your customer expects that you will have access to and know how to operate various types of equipment. You may depend on heavy equipment to do your job and provide products or services to customers (e.g., construction equipment, power tools, electric pumps). Through knowledge and expertise in using such equipment, you will be able to provide products and services to your customers promptly and without service breakdowns.

Customer Factors

There are times when customer actions or inactions can lead to a service breakdown, as described in the following sections.

Failure to Use Product or Service Information Correctly

No matter how meticulous your explanations are, customers sometimes fail to listen to or follow instructions for proper product or service usage. By disregarding or missing key information relayed verbally or in writing, they increase the likelihood of improper use, and therefore dissatisfaction. They also increase the possibility of damage or injury. Subsequently, they may lodge a complaint of defective product or ineffective service.

Your objective in providing exceptional service, while raising your rating on the relationship-rating point scale, should be to practice active listening and read your customer's nonverbal cues in order to determine his or her level of understanding. Use effective open-ended questions, as were discussed in previous chapters. Only through your vigilant efforts can problems and misunderstandings be identified and corrected before the customer develops a problem or becomes dissatisfied.

Failure to Follow Through

Sometimes a customer buys a product or service and has a problem that necessitates recovery efforts. In these instances, negotiations often take place in which the customer and organization agree to take specific actions. Sometimes, the customer may not live up to his or her part of the bargain. For example, suppose a customer buys a new computer from your organization, has trouble getting it to function properly, and calls to complain. He talks to a technical support representative who informs him that the company stands behind its product warranty. The representative also asks the customer to write down error messages that appear on his computer monitor for the next two days so the problem can be better diagnosed, and then bring the unit to the store for repair. Two days later the customer shows up at the store with the computer but has forgotten to write down the error messages. This type of customer behavior and failure to follow through can be frustrating, but it may be unavoidable in some instances. When such events occur, the customer may still become dissatisfied and may even blame the organization or you. Either way, everyone loses. About the only thing you can do before and after such an event occurs is to practice effective communication skills and try to emphasize the importance of the customer following through with instructions and requests.

With a partner, discuss strategies or actions you can take that will aid customers and reduce the possibility that they will become dissatisfied by their own actions or failures. Write them down for future reference.

4   Reasons for Customer Defection

Concept: Failing to meet the customer's needs, handling problems inefficiently, treating the customer unfairly, and using inadequate systems are reasons for the customer to leave you and go elsewhere.

Following a service breakdown, there is often a possibility that you may never see the customer again. This is potentially disastrous to your organization, because it costs five to six times as much to win a new customer as it costs to retain a current one. And, as we saw earlier in this chapter, a dissatisfied customer is also likely to tell other people about the bad experience. Thus, you and others in your organization must be especially careful to identify **reasons for customer defection** and remedy potential and actual problems before they negatively affect customers.

Poor service and complacency. If customers perceive that you and/or your organization do not sincerely care about them or about solving their problems, they may go elsewhere. If a concern is important enough for the customer to verbalize (formally or informally) or to write down, it is important enough for you to take seriously. You should immediately address the problem by listening, gathering information, and taking appropriate action. Customer comments might be casual, for example, "You know, I sure wish you folks stocked a wider variety of rose bushes. I love shopping here, but your selection is so limited." In this instance, you might write down the customer's name, phone number, and address and then follow up with your manager or buyers about it. Also, practice your questioning skills by asking, "What color did you have in mind?" or "What is your favorite color?" If the customer has a specific request, you could pass that along. You or someone else should try to obtain the item and then contact the customer to discuss your efforts and findings. Sometimes the obvious solutions are the ones that are overlooked, so be perceptive when dealing with customers and look for little clues such as these. It could mean the difference in continued business and word-of-mouth advertising by your customer.

Inappropriate complaint resolution. The key thing to remember about complaint resolution is that it is the *customer's* perception of the situation, not yours, that counts. If customers believe that they were not treated fairly, honestly, in a timely manner, and in an appropriate fashion, or if they are still dissatisfied, your efforts failed. Remember that only a small percentage of your customers complain. Second attempts at resolution by customers are almost unheard of.

Unmet needs. As stated in Chapter 12, customers have very specific needs to which you must attend. When these needs are not addressed or are unsatisfactorily met, the customer is likely to seek an alternative source of fulfillment.

One way in which leaders can help reduce service breakdowns is to review the factors that cause them and ensure that there are no negative elements in place in the organization. It is important to continually look at what competitors are doing (benchmarking) to recover from service breakdowns and at least match their efforts.

So often, service providers make the mistake of trying to project their personal needs onto others. Their feeling is that "I like it, so everybody should like it." However, as you read in Chapter 8, today's diverse world requires you to be more knowledgeable and accepting of the ideas, values, beliefs, and needs of others. Failure to be sensitive to diversity may set you, your organization, and your customers on a collision course. Remember what you have read about trust and how quickly it can be destroyed in relationships.

Unfair treatment. When customers *perceive* that they have been treated unfairly or, worse—dishonestly—they are likely to leave. They may do so angrily and follow up with formal complaints or retaliation (e.g., in the form of letters to advocacy groups, senior management, or local news media, or even a lawsuit).

Inadequate systems. When breakdowns occur at crucial points of the service chain, you can expect customer dissatisfaction and desertion. Typical failures occur in order taking, billing, shipping, 800 numbers, e-mail, Internet response, inventory control, and customer service. To help reduce or eliminate such failures, look for potential problem areas and work with others in the organization to fix them before the customer comes into contact with them.

5 Strategies for Preventing Dissatisfaction

Concept: Focusing on the customers' needs and seeking ways to satisfy their needs quickly while exceeding customer expectations are ways to prevent dissatisfaction.

The best way to deal with a service breakdown is to prevent it from occurring. Here are some specific **strategies for preventing dissatisfaction.**

Think Like the Customer

Learn to use the interactive communication techniques described in this book. Once you've mastered them, set out to discover what customers want by observing nonverbal behavior, asking specific questions, and listening to their comments and responses. Learn to listen for their unspoken as well as verbalized needs, concerns, and questions. Think about how you would like to be served under the conditions you are dealing with and act accordingly.

Pamper the Customer

Make customers feel special and important. Treat them as if they are the center of your attention and that you are there for no other purpose than to serve them. Do the unexpected, and take any extra effort necessary to meet and exceed their needs. Even if you can't satisfy all their wishes, if you are positive, enthusiastic, and show initiative, customers can walk away feeling good about the encounter.

Think about the techniques described in this book for focusing on the customer. What additional strategies can you think of?

Respect the Customer

Before you begin focusing on customers' problems, take time to listen and show that you support them and their viewpoint. By using a people-centered approach to problem analysis and problem solving, you can win the customer over. With both of you working together, you can define the problem and jointly reach an acceptable solution.

Focus on the Customer

When a customer takes the time to share a concern, complaint, or question, take the following actions:

React to remarks or actions. Let customers know that you heard what they said or received their written message. If the information is given in person, remember to use the verbal, nonverbal, and listening skills discussed earlier in this book. Smile and acknowledge their presence and comments. If you can't deal with them at that moment because you are serving another customer, let them know when you will be available. If customer comments are in writing, respond quickly. If a phone number is available, try calling to speed up the response and then follow up in writing.

Empathize. Let customers know that you are concerned, that you do appreciate their views, feelings, or concerns, and that you'll do your best to serve them. Really try to "feel their pain" and act as if you were resolving a personal issue of your own. Chances are you will then put more effort into it and appear more sincere.

Take action. Once you've gathered enough information to determine an appropriate response, get agreement from your customer and then act. The faster you act, the more important the customer will feel.

Reassure or reaffirm. Take measures to let customers know that you and the organization have their best interests at heart. Stress their value to you and your commitment to resolving their complaint. Part of this is providing your name and phone number, and telling them what actions you will take; for example, "Mrs. Lupe, I appreciate your concern about not receiving the package on time. My name is Bob Lucas, my number is 407 555-6134, and I will research the problem. Once I've discovered what happened, I'll call you back. If it looks as though it will take more than a day, I'll call you by 4 P.M. tomorrow to update you. Is that acceptable?"

Follow up. Once a customer transaction is completed, make sure that any necessary follow-up actions are begun. For example, if appropriate, make an additional phone call to customers to be sure that they received their order, they are satisfied with your actions, or simply to reassure them and provide an opportunity for questions. If you promised to take some action, do so and coordinate with others who need to be involved.

Exceed Expectations

Go the extra mile by giving your customers the exemplary service you read about in Chapter 12. Strive to get the highest rating possible on the relationship-rating point scale. To do so, work hard to understand what the customer wants and expects. Observe customers, monitor trends, and talk to customers. Constantly look for ways to go beyond the expected or what the competition provides. Provide it faster, better, and more efficiently than others, and exceed customer expectations. Do things for your customer that set your service attitude apart from that of other providers. Some things cost little or nothing and return your "investment" many times over through goodwill and positive word-of-mouth publicity. To raise your rating and please your customers, try some of these simple strategies:

> *Auto repair technician:* "After I rotated and balanced your tires, I checked and filled all your fluids, free of charge."
>
> *Clothing salesperson:* "While you try on that outfit, I'll go pick out a couple of other blouses that would suit you perfectly."
>
> *Bank customer service representative:* "While you are waiting for a loan officer, can I get you a cup of coffee?"
>
> *Hotel operator:* "Along with your wake-up call, I'll have some coffee or tea brought up. Which would you prefer?"
>
> *Restaurant host:* "The wait for a table is approximately 30 minutes. Can I get you a complimentary glass of wine or soft drink from the bar?"
>
> *Travel agent:* "Since this is your honeymoon cruise, I've arranged for a complimentary bottle of champagne to be delivered to your room along with a book of discount coupons for onboard services."
>
> *Call center representative:* "Because you were on hold so long to place your order, I'm taking 10 percent off your order."
>
> *Dentist:* "For referring your friend to us, I've told my receptionist to take $25 off your next cleaning fee."
>
> *Plumber:* "While I was fixing your toilet stopper, I noticed that the lift arm was almost rusted through, so I changed it too, at no charge."

6 Implementing a Service Recovery Strategy

Concept: The job of a service provider is to return the customer to a satisfied state. Not listening, poor communication, and lack of respect are roadblocks to service recovery.

The primary purpose of any good service recovery program should be to return the customer-provider relationship to its normal state. When this is done well, a disgruntled customer can become one who is very loyal and who acts as a publicist for the organization.

Typically, there are five phases to the service recovery process (see Figure 13.4):

1. *Apologize, apologize, apologize.* Showing sincere remorse throughout the recovery cycle is crucial. *Listen* carefully. Empathize with the customer as he or she explains and *do not* make excuses, interrupt, or otherwise indicate (verbally or nonverbally) that you do not have time for the customer. You want to retain the customer and have an opportunity for recovery. You must demonstrate that you care for the customer and that he or she is *very* important to you and your

FIGURE 13.4
Service Recovery Process

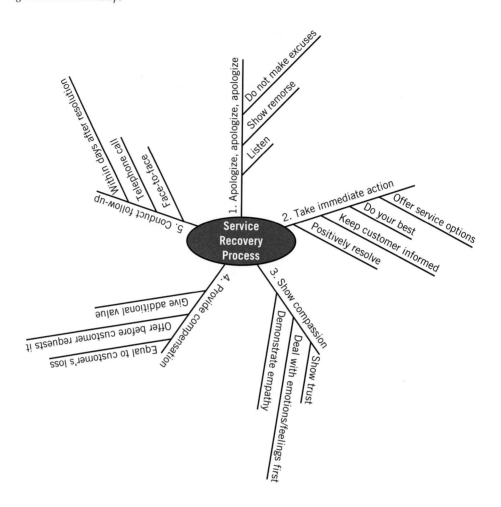

organization. Interestingly, many service providers do not accept responsibility and/or apologize when customers become dissatisfied. Such an apology should come immediately after the discovery of the customer's dissatisfaction and should be delivered in person, if possible. The phone is a second option. Written apologies are the last choice.

2. *Take immediate action.* As soon as your customer has identified a problem, you must set about positively resolving it. As you proceed, it is crucial that you keep the customer informed of actions, barriers encountered, or successful efforts. Even if you are unable to make a quick resolution, the customer may be satisfied if he or she perceives your efforts as sincere and ongoing. You must convince customers through your actions and words that you are doing your best to solve the problem in a timely manner. Also, do not forget what you read earlier in the book about avoiding having to say no without offering **service options**. Remember that your customers want to hear what you *can* do for them, not what you cannot.

Certainly, there may be time when even though you want to give customers exactly what they want, you will not be able to do so because of regulations or **prohibition** (e.g., local, state, or federal laws or regulations). In such cases, it is important to use all the interpersonal skills discussed throughout this book (e.g., active listening, empathizing, and providing feedback) to let customers know that you are prohibited from fulfilling their needs. It is also important to explain the "why" in such situations rather than just saying, "I'm sorry, the law won't let me do that." This type of response sounds as if you are not being truthful, do not want to assist, and are hiding behind an invisible barrier.

An example of a prohibition would be when the sister of a patient goes to a doctor's office to get a copy of her brother's medical records. Without specific permission, this would be against the law, because of a patient's right to privacy and confidentiality between patient and doctor. If you were the receptionist in a doctor's office and someone made such a request, your response might be: "Ms. Ramsey, I apologize for your inconvenience in coming in for nothing. I know it's frustrating. However, although I would love to assist you, I cannot because of state regulations that protect a patient's privacy and confidentiality. If you can get me a signed medical release from your brother, I would be happy to copy his file for you. Can you do that? And, so you won't have to make another trip in here, if you have a fax number, I can get them to you that way." In this instance, you have empathized with the customer, stated what you cannot do, explained why, and offered a way to resolve the problem along with a recovery strategy (e.g., fax).

In another situation, you may want to help a customer but cannot because your abilities, time constraints, resources, or the customer's timing of a request prevent fulfillment. Here are some examples of such situations, along with possible responses to your customer:

Your abilities. You work in a pet supply store, you are the only person in the store, and you have a severe back injury that prevents you from lifting anything over 25 pounds. A customer comes in and buys 50 bags of chicken feed, each weighing 100 pounds. She asks that you help her load the bags onto her truck.

YOUR RESPONSE: "Ms. Saunders, we appreciate your business. I know your time is valuable and I'd love to help you. However, I have a back injury and the doctor told me not to lift anything over 25 pounds. I'm the only person working here during the lunch hour. If you can come back in half an hour, I'll have two guys who will load bags for you in no time. Would that be possible? For your inconvenience, I'll even take $10 off your order total."

Time constraints. You work in a bakery and a distraught customer comes in at 3 P.M. Apparently he had forgotten that he was supposed to stop by on the way to work this morning to order a chocolate cake for his daughter's first birthday party, which is at 5 P.M. He wants you to make him a two-layer chocolate cake.

YOUR RESPONSE: "Mr. Simon, that first birthday party sounds exciting, and I want to help you make it a success. However, realistically, it just cannot be done. We sold our last chocolate cake half an hour ago, and if I bake a new one, it will still have to cool before I can decorate it. You will never make it by five o'clock. I know it's frustrating not to get exactly what you want. However, since your daughter is only one year old and won't know the difference in the type of cake, can I suggest an alternative? We have virtually any other kind of cake you could want, and I can put on chocolate icing and decorate it for you in less than 15 minutes. Would that work?"

Available resources. You are in North Carolina, near the coastline. A customer comes into your lumberyard in search of plywood to board up his house a day before a major hurricane is predicted to hit the area. Since the impending hurricane was announced on the news, you have been overwhelmed with purchases of plywood and sold out two hours ago.

YOUR RESPONSE: "Mr. Rasheed, I can appreciate the urgency of your need. Unfortunately, as you know, everyone in town is buying plywood and we sold out two hours ago. However, I do have a couple of options for you. I can call our store in Jacksonville to find out whether any plywood is left. If there is some, I can have it held if you want to drive over there. The other option is that we have a shipment on the way that should arrive sometime around 3 A.M. I'll be here and can hold some for you if you want to come back at that time. Would either of those options work for you?"

Timing. It is April 13 and you are an accountant. With the federal tax filing deadline two days away, you and the entire staff of your firm have been working 12- to 14-hour days for weeks. A regular customer calls and wants to come in the next couple of days to discuss incorporating her business and to get some information on the tax advantages for doing so.

YOUR RESPONSE: "Ruth, it's great that you are ready to move forward with the incorporation. I think you will find that it will be very beneficial for you. However, with tax deadlines two days away, we are swamped and there is just no way I can take on anything else. Since your incorporation is not under a deadline, can we set up our meeting some time around the first of next week? That will give me time to wrap up taxes, take a breather, and then give you the full attention you deserve."

In all of these instances, you show a willingness to assist and meet the customers' requests even though you are prevented from doing so. You also partner with them and offer alternatives for consideration. This is important, since you do not want to close the door on customer opportunities. Doing so will surely send customers to a competitor.

There might be other occasions when you or your organization do not meet a customer's request even though it is possible to do so. In such cases, company restrictions keep you from fulfilling the customers' request. In this type of situation, you sometimes hear service providers hide behind a phrase such as "Policy says." The reality is that someone in the organization has decided for business reasons that certain actions cannot or should not be taken. If you encounter such "policies" that prohibit you from delivering service to customers, bring them to the attention of your team leader or management for discussion. These restrictions will most likely cost your organization some customers and result in bad word-of-mouth publicity. An example of such a situation, along with a possible response, is described below:

Situation. You work in a gas station in a major tourist area that has a policy that prohibits accepting out-of-town checks. A tourist from another state has her family with her and fills her car with gas. She then comes to you to pay for her purchase. She tells you that she has only personal checks and $2 in cash with her. She is leaving town to return home at this time.

YOUR RESPONSE: "I know that this is an inconvenience, and I apologize. However, because of problems we've had in the past, we do not accept checks from banks out of this area. We will gladly accept major credit cards, travelers' checks, or cash. Does anyone else in your car have a credit card or cash? We also have an ATM machine where you can use a bank debit card to get cash."

3. *Show compassion.* To help the customer see that your remorse and desire to solve a problem are genuine, you must demonstrate empathy. Expressions such as "I can appreciate your trust," "I understand how we have inconvenienced you," or "I can imagine how you must feel" can go a long way in soothing and winning the customer over. Before you can truly address the customers' problem, however, you must deal with their emotions or feelings. If you disregard their feelings, customers may not give you a chance to help resolve the breakdown. Also, keep in mind what you read about trust in an earlier chapter: you must give it to receive it.

4. *Provide compensation.* Prove to customers that they are valuable and that you are trying to make up for their inconvenience or loss. This penance or symbolic self-punishment should be significant enough that the customer feels that you and your organization have suffered an equal loss. The value or degree of your atonement should equal the customer's loss in time, money, energy, or frustration. For example, if a customer's meal was cooked improperly and the customer and others in the party had to wait, you might give the customer a free meal. If you forgot a vegetable that was ordered and it came much later, a free dessert might suffice. The key is to make the offer without the customer having to suggest or demand it.

   Not only must the recovery compensate original loss, it should give additional value. For example, if a customer had an oil change done on his or her car and oil was spilled on the carpet, an appropriate gesture might be to give the oil change free and have the carpet cleaned at your company's expense. This solution compensates for inconvenience and lost time while providing added value (saving the cost of the oil change).

5. *Conduct follow-up.* The only way to find out whether you were successful in your recovery efforts or whether the customer is truly satisfied is to follow up. The preferable methods are face-to-face questioning or a phone call. This contact should come within a few days after the complaint was resolved. It could take the form of a few simple statements or questions (e.g., "I am following up in case you had any additional questions" or "I'm calling to make sure that _____ is now working as it should be. Is there anything else we can do to assist you?").

   This last step in the recovery process can be the deciding factor in whether the customer returns to you or your organization. It is the phase that reemphasizes, the message "We truly care."

7   Roadblocks to Service Recovery

Concept: Service recovery depends on the provider recognizing a roadblock and taking steps to remove it so that recovery steps can begin.

From time to time, you may find your recovery efforts blocked by your own actions or inactions or those of others in your organization. Some of the **roadblocks to service recovery** attempts are described in the next sections:

Not listening. As we discussed in the chapter on listening, you must take an active role to listen effectively. Not only must you receive data, but you must also analyze and act upon it. Many service providers go through the motions of listening, but they fail to do so accurately or actively. This can send the message, "I really don't care about you."

LEADERSHIP INITIATIVE

13.2

To help prevent putting employees and customers on a confrontational course, supervisors should develop effective service recovery strategies. These practices should be coordinated with frontline employees who deal daily with customers and who know what they want or request most often when service breaks down. Once strategies have been decided upon, each employee should be trained on how to best implement them and informed of his or her level of authority in providing compensation.

Lack of respect. Closely tied to listening is the matter of customer respect. Your actions or inactions related to customers and their problems can lead to a perception that you are being rude or disrespectful. Either way, you and the organization lose as customers desert to a competitor.

Poor or inadequate communication. The quality and amount of communication between you and your customer can be the determining success factor. You should make every effort to constantly update and consult with the customers. If they feel neglected or left out, further dissatisfaction and loss of business loyalty could follow.

Inadequate or outdated materials or equipment. Trying to provide service excellence without the necessary tools is frustrating and almost impossible. It also can destroy a customer relationship and trust. For example, you may be calling a customer from a list provided by the marketing department in order to update an address or to sell the customer new services or products. You may be unaware that others have already called the customer, that the customer has already made a purchase from another service representative, or that the customer had received a mail-order solicitation that had a different (and better) offer for the same products and services. Your frustration goes up and your credibility goes down in such a situation.

Lack of training. It's very difficult to perform at exceptional levels when you do not have the knowledge and skills required. Whenever you identify gaps in your knowledge or skill, you should approach your boss with a request for training. This training might be informal (e.g., audiotapes, self-study courses, Internet courses, or written materials) or formal (e.g., classrooms, one-on-one coaching, or conferences). The format is not as important as the results—you improve your skills to better interact with and serve your customers.

Work conflicts. No matter how much you care and want to provide quality service, you may fail if you overcommit or if your organization overextends its human resources. It's impossible to be everything to everyone. When work scheduling causes employees to be pulled in too many directions, failure is probable. To avoid this breakdown, constant monitoring of workload is required. Recommendations to your team leader or supervisor for schedule changes, job sharing, or reapportionment of workload might be appropriate.

Chapter Summary

Whenever a customer experiences an actual or perceived breakdown in service, prompt, appropriate recovery efforts may be your only hope of retaining the customer. In a profession that has seen major strides in quality and technology as well as increased domestic and global competition, service is often the deciding factor. Customers expect and often demand their rights and to be treated in an exemplary fashion. When they are disappointed, they simply go elsewhere. Your role in the process is to remain vigilant, recognize customer needs, and provide service levels that will keep them coming back.

SERVICE IN ACTION Office Depot CHAPTER 13

http://www.officedepot.com

Office Depot, Inc., was founded in 1986 and is headquartered in Delray Beach, Florida. In less than 20 years, Office Depot has become one of the world's largest sellers of office products and an industry leader in every distribution channel, including stores, direct mail, contract delivery, the Internet, and business-to-business electronic commerce.

As of 2003, there were over 43,000 employees throughout the world working for 1,059 Office Depots and its subsidiaries operating in 12 countries. There are also 22 domestic delivery centers and 13 regional call centers, plus state-of-the-art Internet sites. All of this contributes to the generation of $11 billion annually in revenue. Viking Office Products, a wholly owned subsidiary of Office Depot, currently operates one of the industry's leading direct-mail marketers of office products worldwide.

The company's International Division has direct-mail, contract, Internet, and retail operations in 20 countries outside the United States and Canada. In addition, it sells office supplies and services through joint venture operations and licensing agreements in seven countries.

One reason for the phenomenal growth of the company is its approach to customer service, which is summed up in its value statement found on the Office Depot website:

. . . Fanatical Customer Service

- We impress our customers (internal and external) so much that they want to buy again.
- We give higher priority to people than to tasks.
- We do it right the first time but "wow" our customers on recovery when we miss.

Key Terms and Concepts

causes of service breakdowns
information highway prohibitions
reasons for customer defection

roadblocks to service recovery
service breakdowns
service options

service recovery standards
strategies for preventing dissatisfaction

Quick Preview Answers

1. T
2. F
3. T
4. F

5. F
6. T
7. T
8. F

9. T
10. T
11. T

Chapter Review Questions

1. What is service recovery?
2. What is meant by the term *service breakdown?* Define.
3. What are some of the organizational factors that can lead to service breakdown?
4. Which employee-related factors can contribute to service breakdown? List them.
5. Why do customers defect?
6. What are some strategies for preventing customer dissatisfaction? List them.
7. When a service recovery strategy is implemented, what are the five steps that should be taken?
8. What are some of the roadblocks to service recovery?

Search It Out

Search the Internet for Service Recovery Information

Visit a variety of websites in order to locate additional information on service recovery. Look for articles, books, research studies, or specific organizational strategies for handling service recovery. To locate the information, select some of the key terms mentioned in this chapter to prompt various search engines. Here are some of the terms you may want to try:

Service recovery
Customer satisfaction
Customer retention
Service breakdowns
Customer dissatisfaction
Customer defection

Also, try these sites as a starter:

<http://www.tarp>
<http://www.ICSA>
<http://www.SOCAP>

Note: A listing for additional research on specific URLs is provided on the Customer Service website at **<http://www.mhhe.com/lucas05>.**

Collaborative Learning Activity

Role-Playing Failure to Address Needs

To give you some practical experience in using the techniques described in this chapter, you will interact with others in your group. Your instructor will assign one or more of the following activities.

Option 1: Pair up with another student and develop several scenarios in which a customer's needs or concerns have not been addressed. Role-play these scenarios, with each of you alternately taking the role of service provider and customer. Be sure to incorporate tips and strategies discussed throughout this book.

Option 2: Working with your classmates, develop a list of open-ended questions based on information related to service recovery that was covered in this chapter (similar to the type of questions in the From the Frontline interview at the beginning of this chapter). Use the questions to conduct an informal survey of friends, peers, and relatives. Try to determine what works and what does not work in service breakdown situations. Discuss your thoughts with other members of the class and then use this information to improve your own service efforts.

Face to Face

Handling Service Breakdowns at AAA Landscaping

Background

You are the owner of AAA Landscaping, a small company in Orlando, Florida, that specializes in resodding and maintenance of lawns. Much of your business is through word-of-mouth advertising. Once a contract is negotiated, portions of it are subcontracted out to other companies (e.g., sprinkler system repair and pesticide services). Recently, you went to the home of Stu Murphy to bid on resodding Stu's lawn. Several other bids were obtained, but yours was the lowest. You arranged for work to begin to remove old grass and replace it with St. Augustine grass sod.

As part of the contract, Stu had asked that some basic maintenance be done (e.g., hedge and tree trimming, hauling away of old decorative wooden logs from around flower beds, and general sprucing up of the front area of the house). Also, fertilizer and pesticide were to be applied within two weeks. The contract was signed on Wednesday, and the work was to be completed by Saturday, when Stu had planned a party.

Your Role

You were pleased to get the contract worth over $1,200. This is actually the third or fourth contract in the same subdivision because of word-of-mouth advertising. The initial sod removal and replacement, weeding, and pruning were completed on Saturday, and you received full payment on Monday.

Later in the week you received a call from Stu stating that several trees were not trimmed to his satisfaction, debris covering decorative rocks along hedges was not removed as agreed, and bags of clippings had been left behind. Because of other commitments, it was several days before you sent someone out to finish the job. A day later, Stu left another message on your answering machine stating that there was still an untrimmed tree, the debris remained, and the clippings were still in the garage. You didn't get around to returning his call. Over a week later Stu called again, repeating the message he'd left before and reminding you that the contract called for pesticide and fertilizer to be applied to the lawn. You called back and said that someone would be out later in the week. Again, other commitments kept you from following through. Stu called on Saturday and left a fourth message on your answering machine. He said that he was getting irritated at not getting callbacks and action on his needs. Without returning Stu's call, you responded by sending someone out on Tuesday to take care of the outstanding work.

It's been several days since the work was completed, and you assume that Stu is now satisfied since you have heard nothing else from him.

Critical Thinking Questions

1. Based on information in this chapter, how have you done on providing service to Stu? Explain.
2. What were Stu's needs in this case?
3. Could you have done anything differently?
4. Are you sure that Stu will give a good recommendation to neighbors or friends in the future? Why or why not?

PLANNING TO SERVE

CHAPTER 13

In an effort to head off potential service breakdowns and an ultimate need to provide recovery, answer the following questions. Use your responses as a guide or checklist when serving customers.

1. What actions or circumstances have you noticed lead to service breakdowns in organizations where you were either a customer or service provider?

2. What are some effective service recovery strategies that you have witnessed service providers use?

3. When you were a customer and service broke down, what recovery strategies were effectively used to help "make you whole?"

4. When you were a customer and service broke down, what ineffective recovery strategies did you experience?"

PART FIVE

Customer Service for the Twenty-First Century

CHAPTER FOURTEEN Focusing on the Future

Focusing on the Future

Before reviewing the chapter content, respond to the following questions by placing a "T" for true or an "F" for false on the rules. Use any questions you miss as a checklist of material to which you will pay particular attention as you read through the chapter. For those you get right, congratulate yourself, but review the sections they address in order to learn additional details about the topic.

_____ 1. A longer life expectancy and a decline in the birthrate will contribute to a shortage of entry-level employees in the future.

_____ 2. The downside of an aging society is that customers will require fewer personal services.

_____ 3. Technological changes are occurring so rapidly that continual training, retraining, and education on software and delivery systems are needed.

_____ 4. Evolving technology has changed the roles and needs of customers.

Chapter Learning Objectives

After completing this chapter, you will be able to:

- Identify service challenges of the future.
- Use your knowledge of the changing demographics in the United States to be better prepared to provide service.

- Realize the impact of global competition on business.
- Build skills for future career growth.
- Plan to meet the challenges of the future.

_____ 5. During the past three decades, little has changed from a legal standpoint with respect to customer service.

_____ 6. Global competition has provided new career opportunities in customer service.

_____ 7. To meet today's business challenges, schools are improving programming and keeping pace with changes.

_____ 8. To keep up with competition, a leading-edge company might spend over $4 million a year on employee training.

_____ 9. Some of the minimum skills for success in the customer service field are communication, creative thinking, and interpersonal skills.

_____ 10. Even though organizations are changing, the responsibility for leadership still rests with managers.

Answers to Quick Preview can be found at the end of the chapter.

1 Future Challenges

Concept: By being aware of changes, you can better prepare yourself to serve your customers in the future.

Although no one can predict the future with any degree of certainty, economists, **futurists,** and business analysts can spot trends and make fairly accurate projections. Bookshelves are lined with publications containing insights and research on industry, economic, business, and demographic changes over recent decades. Some consistent patterns of change that have surfaced and that will directly affect your job and the customer service field are outlined in this chapter. By recognizing and understanding these trends, you can better prepare yourself for the inevitable changes. You can also build skills to better serve your customers.

2 Shifts in Demographics

Concept: Society has changed dramatically over the last decade. Many changes that involve the population are related to its age, gender, ethnic background, and wants and needs, as well as income level, and will affect customer service.

For several decades, U.S. government analysts have been tracking **shifts in demographics** of the United States and other countries (see Figure 14.1). According to the U.S. Census Bureau, people are living longer. The median age of the U.S. population in 2000 was 35.3, the highest it has ever been, and up from 32.9 in 1990, while the average life expectancy for men was 74.1 years of age and women, 79.5 years.[1] For the first time in the history of the census, the 65-and-over population increased at a slower rate than the overall population. These trends will mean more customers demanding service and, coupled with the decline of births as a result of the **baby bust** (people born to baby boomers after 1964), will contribute to a strain on a service system already suffering from an acute shortage of entry-level employees. Like most other countries, the population continues to diversify (see Figures 14.2 and 14.3). The number of people in the 15- to 19-year-old age group saw some growth between 1990 and 2000 (approximately 2.5 million), while the group from 20 to 34 years of age declined by nearly 3½ million.

These population shifts are not restricted to the United States and are having major ripple effects throughout the world as countries struggle to deal with a world different from previous ones in relation to the age makeup of their societies. One of the big challenges is the number of people who are 65 or older. The ratio of older people to total population differs between developed countries and developing countries; for example, the United States is aging faster than developing countries. The obvious implications politically and economically by the middle of the twenty-first century are potentially dramatic in that some countries have an abundance of younger, yet inexperienced people, whereas traditionally dominant societies have fewer people to step into the shoes of those more senior as they die off. By way of comparison, the United States is thirty-second on a list ranking countries with high populations of people age 65 and older. More than one-third of the world's oldest people (80 and above) live in three countries: China (11.5 million), the United States (9.2 million), and India (6.2 million).[2]

---

[1]Center for Disease Control, National Center for Health Statistics, *National Vital Statistics Reports,* Vol. 51, No. 3, December 19, 2002.

[2]K. Kinsella, and V. A. Velkoff, *An Aging World: 2001,* U.S. Census Bureau, November 2001, p. 5.

FIGURE 14.1
Fast Facts From the Census Bureau

Source: U.S. Census Bureau.

Service providers can benefit in marketing and service from tracking demographic trends such as the following:.

- The number of males (138.1) edged closer to the number of females (143.4) bringing the ratio of males to females up to 96.3.
- The average household size was 2.59, down slightly from 2.63 in 1990.
- The number of nonfamily households rose at twice the rate of family households (23 versus 11 percent).
- 4 percent of all households are multigenerational (different levels of parents and children).
- Families maintained by women with no husband present increased three times as fast as married-couple families.
- In 2002, 72 percent of mothers with children age 1 and older were in the workforce.
- The largest five-year age group is the 35- to 39-year-olds (22.7 million).
- The five fastest-growing U.S. counties (with 10,000 or more population) are:
  Rockwall, Texas
  Loudoun, Virginia
  Henry, Georgia
  Forsyth, Georgia
  Flagler, Florida
- Between 1999–2000, 1.7 million people moved to the United States from abroad.

FIGURE 14.2
U.S. Resident Population as of September 2003

Source: U.S. Census Bureau.

	Total	Percentage of Population
Total resident population	291,950,153	100.0%
Males	138,053,563	49.1%
Females	143,368,343	50.9%
White	211,460,626	75.1%
Black	34,658,190	12.3%
Asian	10,242,998	3.6%
American Indian & Alaskan Native	2,475,956	0.9%
Hispanic/Latino	35,305,818	12.5%
Native Hawaiian & Other Pacific Islanders	398,835	0.1%

A pressing service impact of these numbers in the United States is that there are fewer younger entry-level people who traditionally begin their careers in the workforce in service jobs at theaters, fast-food restaurants, car washes, delivery services, department and grocery stores, and similar businesses. To compensate, organizations are moving toward using technology to handle many functions (e.g., telemarketing calls, information collection, ticket sales, greeting customers, and product dispensing via machines), and in some cases are exporting lower-level service jobs (e.g., call centers) to less-developed countries where annual salaries can be as little as $2,000. They are also recruiting older workers who have retired and workers from other countries. Many of the workers who will come to the United States will likely be from Latin America where there is a growing population of younger workers who have fewer work opportunities. This influx will create the need for managers and workers to better understand Hispanic and Portuguese cultures and languages.

FIGURE 14.3 **Projected Resident Population of the United States as of July 1, 2050**

Source: National Projections Program. Population Division, U.S. Census Bureau, Washington, D.C. 20233, <http://www.census.gov/population/www/projections/np_p4.g.f>.

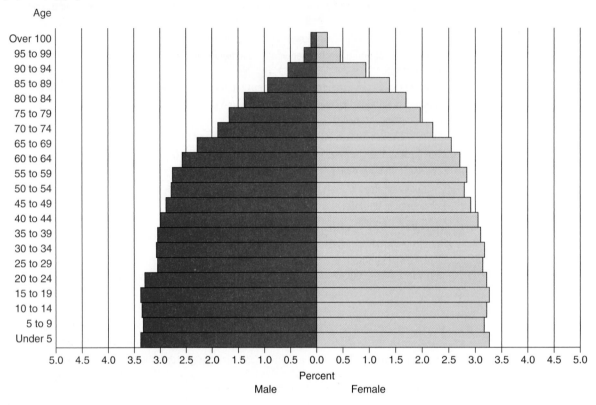

These strategies are impacting the United States as service providers are displaced and incomes are severed, resulting in reduced buying power and less need for products and services. Thus, a cycle is created in which there are fewer people earning money, reduced demand for items and services, and a strain on the governmental systems that people turn to when unemployed or underemployed.

Another impact caused by the aging or **graying of the** United States **population** is that you will be serving more people who are older. The number of people 65 years and older is expected to grow by almost 40 million in 2010 and to 69 million by 2030 (when surviving baby boomers become 65+). At that point, approximately 20 percent of the U.S. population will be over the age of 65. Additionally, the fastest-growing age group is the 85+ population. As a group, they are expected to grow fivefold by the year 2050.[3] Because of this projected growth, the skills discussed in Chapter 8 related to dealing with diverse individuals will come into play for those in the service sector.

In many cases older customers will want and need more services to ease their life (e.g., laundry, yard care, car maintenance, assisted living, and personal shopping) and many will also seek employment to offset their medical and living expenses. As this older group grows, they will have a significant impact on the

[3]U.S. Department of Commerce, Economics and Statistics Administration, Bureau of Census, *Population Projections of the United States by Age, Sex, Race, and Hispanic Origin: 1995–2050* (P25–1130), p. 1.

FIGURE 14.4   U.S. Age Distribution in Percent: 1990 and 2000

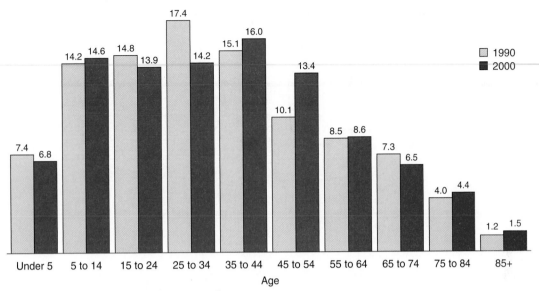

Source: U.S. Census Bureau, Census 2000 and 1990 census.

commerce and workforce, depending on where they are located. Figure 14.4 shows the population by age distribution between 1990 and 2000 and Figure 14.5 shows the dispersion of persons 65 years and older throughout the United States between 1995 and 2025. This distribution will take a toll on business from the standpoint of number of customers and eligible workers, as well as on society through social services (e.g., health care, human services, and other support systems). The latter will be true for those optimistic people in the aging group who believed that the Social Security system would be there as a retirement base or who did not adequately save for retirement, and for the lesser educated.

As a result, some retirees will return to work (or remain in the workforce longer) in order to compensate for a lack of savings or income. Others will do so because they are better educated, earn more money, and are less willing to quit their careers early or simply to fulfill a need to interact with others in the workplace and feel productive. Bureau of Labor Statistics forecasts have indicated that between 2000 and 2010, there will be a 33 percent increase in the number of people ages 65 to 74 in the workforce.

The Impact of Education on Society

The **impact of education on society** is great, particularly when related to income and retirement readiness. For example, statistically, men with a high school diploma or less have experienced a loss of income in the years between 1963 and 1997. The numbers have improved somewhat since then. This is a problem from a service standpoint because buying power is reduced significantly when people attain a lower level of education. According to the National Center for Education Statistics (NCES), over the last decade, between 347,000 and 544,000 10th- through 12th-grade students left school each year without successfully completing a high school program. Between October 2001 and October 2002, about 400,000 young adults left school. Of those numbers, less than 12 percent are young women while

FIGURE 14.5
Percent of Total State Population 65 Years and Over: 1995–2025

Source: U.S. Bureau of the Census, Population Division, PPL-47.

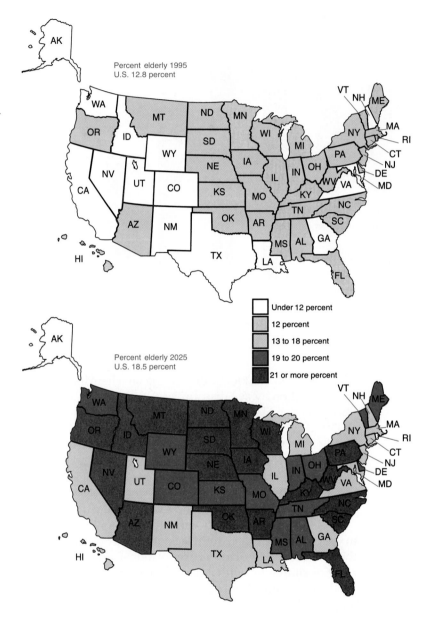

15.8 percent are young men. The unemployment rate in 2002 was 16.9 percent for this dropout group. Men who did attain a high school diploma have seen their salary shrink from $28,914 in 1963 to $25,453. On the other hand, women with the same educational level have seen their salary grow from $11,028 to $13,407 during the same period.[4]

On the upside, the Bureau of Labor Statistics reports that over 65 percent of the high school graduating class of 2002 was enrolled in college or university by the fall. This equates to a 3. 5 percent increase from a year earlier and is the highest rate since 1998. Additionally, the "total college-level job openings between 1998–2008 will be nearly equal to the number of college-educated entrants to the labor force . . .

[4]U.S. Department of Labor.

FIGURE 14.6 **Households Age 25 and Older by Educational Attainment (Mean Income Earnings)**

Source: Census Bureau, Current Population Surveys, March 1991 and 2001.

Educational Attainment	Number of Households (in millions)	Percent Change (1991–2000)	Mean Household Income (2000)	Percent Aggregate Income	Percent Change (1991–2000)
Less than high school diploma	15.8	−19.5%	$32,356	8.0	−7.5%
High school diploma	30.8	2.0	$46,226	23.9	12.3
Some college	8.2	63.0	$55,850	8.5	80.1
Associate degree	27.0	29.3	$61,399	42.2	54.0
Bachelor's or higher	17.5	33.4	$93,060	25.2	61.2
Graduate degree	9.5	22.3	$98,795	17.0	44.5

a primary reason is the large number of retirements expected from workers on the leading edge of the 'baby boom' generation . . . who are college educated."[5] More than in the past, a larger percentage of the current graying population of baby boomers are college-educated. As a result, many baby boomers earn more income than their predecessors did. Since 1963, the median income levels have risen for men and women who have a bachelor's degree or higher. According to the Census Bureau, the aggregate income of college-educated households jumped 54 percent between 1991 and 2000, compared with a 12 percent increase for high school graduates. As a result, the 27 percent of households with a bachelor's degree or higher now take home 44 percent of all aggregate household income. This means that the college-educated group will have more disposable income than in the past and will likely use it for a variety of services that allow them to enjoy more free time and/or retirement. Figure 14.6 provides more information on the relationship between education level and earning potential.

Women Have Experienced Increases in Income at All Educational Levels

In 2001, women who worked full-time, year-round, earned 76 cents for every $1 earned by their male counterparts. Although the gap in gender earnings leaves room for improvement, it represents the highest female-to-male earnings ratio in history. Similarly, there has been movement toward gender parity among husbands and wives in married-couple families. In 2002 women who earned more than their spouses increased to 28 percent. The long-term impact of this increased earning power will be to elevate women's lifetime earning potential. This is a particularly important development, because women, on average, live eight to ten years longer than men. This means they will need that increased lifetime earning power to sustain themselves in their later years and to purchase more personal goods and services.

More Women, Minorities, and Immigrants Entering Workforce

An additional demographic shift impacting customer service professionals is the increase in number of women, minorities, and immigrants entering the workplace. This shift is being fueled to a great extent by the increasing birthrate in virtually all demographic groups. The birthrate had decreased slightly at the end of the twentieth century. Projections are that the numbers will continue to go up until around the year 2011

[5]C. Fleetwood and K. Shelley, "The Outlook for College Graduates, 1998–2008: A Balancing Act," *Occupational Outlook Quarterly*, Bureau of Labor Statistics, Fall 2000, p. 3.

Think about the advertisements you have seen on television and heard on the radio in the last couple of years.

What types of background songs are the advertisements using? (Give specific examples of songs.)

What population group do you think they are targeting? Why?

Do you believe that this is a smart marketing strategy? Why or why not?

when they are expected to exceed the highest number of births ever achieved in the twentieth century. Much of the growth can be attributed to such factors as the children of baby boomers (who in many cases delayed starting a family until later in life) beginning to create their own families. As a result of increased births, coupled with increased immigration, the U.S. population is expected to grow by about 29 million people through 2020 and 80 million by 2050. Of that population growth through immigration, census projections are that each year two of ten people will be Hispanic, three of ten Asian and Pacific Islander, two of ten non-Hispanic white, and one of ten black. Births would account for two of five people being non-Hispanic white, with the remainder being equally distributed among Hispanic, black, and Asian and Pacific Islanders.[6]

These changes mean that you will be servicing and working with a larger, more diverse group. For that reason, the ability to speak a second language (e.g., Spanish) and to have a sound knowledge of the differences outlined in Chapter 8 of this book, related to cultural differences and nonverbal communication cues, will be extremely important to your success and that of your organization.

3 Technology Implications

Concept: Technology has and will continue to affect customer service. Being aware of the latest technology and how to use it efficiently can help you become a more effective service provider.

As you read in Chapter 9, at no time in history have the **technology implications** been more prominent in businesses or more complex inasmuch as nearly one-half of the U.S. population has access to the Internet and 42 percent have computers. Changes are occurring so rapidly that you will have a continual need to train, retrain and educate yourself on software and delivery systems, including computer hardware, telephone systems, fax machines, and other business and industrial equipment.

Technology has changed the roles and needs of customers. Often customers actively participate in the design and delivery of goods and services tailored to fit their needs and preferences. For example, customers are requiring manufacturers to use shorter and more tailored production runs that produce merchandise in a more timely manner and will be customized to the needs of the individual rather than aimed at a mass market. Customers are also getting actively involved in such activities as the design of their own homes and insurance packages. Providers are

[6]J. C. Day, *Population Projections of the United States by Age, Sex, Race, and Hispanic Origin: 1995–2050,* U.S. Bureau of Census, Current Population Reports, P25–1130, U.S. Government Printing Office, Washington, D.C., 1996, p. 2.

LEADERSHIP INITIATIVE

14.1

By helping employees understand trends in society and the potential impact on business and service, managers can create an informed environment in which service providers are better prepared to deal with virtually any customer situation. Surprises and crisis management can also be reduced or eliminated.

For may customer service jobs, skill in using technology will increase your value as a source of information for current and future customers. *How can you keep abreast of changes in technology?*

reducing wait times and service effectiveness by accessing such innovations as iris-reading technology, which can scan the customer's eye to verify identification (much like a password does).

Future customer service will also involve a broader use of telecommunications. As you saw in Chapter 9, by tapping into the technological capabilities of many computer systems, organizations will be able to reach many more customers. Through other computer capabilities, such as enhanced information storage capabilities, catalogs and product service information will become more readily available to consumers. As the Internet becomes faster and more sophisticated it will drive e-commerce to new heights and will potentially change the face of the economy in the United States and the world. Since Internet commerce (**e-commerce**) involves both consumer-based retail transactions and business-to-business transactions (e.g., Internet access services, financial services, client and support operations) and accounts for 93 percent of e-commerce, the potential revenue is enormous (see Figure 14.7).

Other sources of revenue generation that will likely continue to be popular and expand are the television shopping networks and infomercials. Through these sources, viewers see products and services displayed and described and then call in to order or obtain information. Certainly, as technology continues to be develped and refined, other options for delivery will evolve.

Think about new types of businesses that you have seen open in your community in the past couple of years and that focus on personal customer service.

What products and/or services do they provide?

What population group is most likely to use these products and/or services?

FIGURE 14.7
E-Commerce Fast Facts

Source: U.S. Census Bureau.

The travel industry generated nearly one-fourth of its total revenue online in 2001.

In manufacturing, e-shipments of computer and electronic equipment declined 6 percent ($5 billion), while total shipments fell by 16 percent ($81 billion).

Merchant wholesalers' online growth was particularly strong in drug proprietaries and druggists' sundries, where online sales grew 24 percent ($19 billion) and total sales grew 20 percent ($33 billion).

Nonstore retailers—businesses ranging from television shopping networks to Internet shopping sites—accounted for 75 percent ($26 billion) of online retail sales, a growth of 21 percent from 2000–2001.

In the electronic shopping and mail-order houses industry, three merchandise groups were the major source of the strong growth in e-sales: furniture and home furnishings grew 70 percent; clothing and clothing accessories, 56 percent; and office equipment and supplies, 37 percent. Total sales fell in all three groups.

In the services sector, the securities and commodity contracts intermediation and brokerage industries saw a 37 percent decline ($2 billion), while total revenues fell 13 percent ($37 billion).

Information sector service industries experienced strong growth in e-revenues, which grew 12 percent ($1 billion), while total revenue rose 3 percent ($24 billion).

4   A Changing Legal Environment

Concept: Many laws have been enacted to protect consumers to ensure that they are treated well. Knowing these laws will enable you to serve your customers well and within the law.

A **changing legal environment** has dramatically affected the face of American business during the last part of the twentieth and into the twenty-first century. Consumer protection has become increasingly important. Legislators as well as advocacy groups have paraded before Congress and the public to demand that customers be treated well. Also, organizations that seek to cheat, defraud, or violate consumer rights and the law are dealt with harshly, often paying millions of dollars in reparation. Examples are the actions taken against the tobacco industry and producers of silicon breast implants by various states and individuals. Not only are the litigants seeking to stem the production and distribution of products viewed as hazardous, they are also seeking financial reparation for those harmed by such products.

Starting with enactment of legislation such as the **Civil Rights Act of 1964** (which prohibited discrimination based on race, color, gender, religion, or national origin), the **Americans With Disabilities Act of 1990** (which ensured access by disabled people to telecommunications, transportation, the workplace), and consumer protection laws that protect against telephone, mail, Internet fraud, and harassment, changes in customer service have occurred. Ignorance of the law is not an acceptable defense; therefore, many companies that might otherwise have discriminated or abused consumer rights have been forced to change their operating practices.

LEADERSHIP INITIATIVE   14.2

To assist and remind employees of the laws governing the workplace, supervisors can provide job aids in the form of lists or booklets that outline current federal, state, and local laws and regulations. Key provisions of each and penalties for violation can be bulleted for quick reference and as a reminder of the need for compliance.

As you read in Chapter 8, some groups have special needs. Effectively serving those needs and complying with the laws affecting these groups require an increased awareness and improved skill level. Many organizations now make awareness training for laws affecting customer service part of the orientation of new employees. If your employer doesn't provide such training, you would be wise to check with your local library, the Internet, and/or publications that deal with workplace issues and consumer rights and read about pertinent laws.

5   The Role of Training and Development

Concept: Through the advancement of skills and knowledge as well as the reshaping of attitudes and opinions, organizations are realizing that training pays off in increased revenues and lower expenditures per customer.

In past decades, hard work and sweat often led to career advancement, sometimes into the executive office, but that isn't necessarily the case today. Because of the continued competitiveness of business on a global level, the increased use of technology, and the need for solid people skills, a solid education is now the best ticket upward. As you read earlier in this chapter, there is a direct correlation between education and income. If you want to excel, you'll need to invest in yourself (time and money) to gain needed skills. The other alternative is to find an employer who will make a commitment to your knowledge growth and provide regular training or educational opportunities.

Many employers realize that workers coming into the workforce today are not adequately prepared for the tasks that face them. In some cases, the educational system is failing to provide the skills and training necessary to meet today's business challenges. The result is a decrease in job and promotion opportunities and an increased pressure for training to be the responsibility of the individual and the organization.

Recognizing the importance of the **role of training and development,** many organizations are now investing in their most important resource—employees. As a result, millions of dollars are being spent to upgrade skills and prepare customer service representatives and others to create and maintain a customer-focused environment. Through the enhancement of knowledge and skills and efforts to reshape attitudes and opinions related to the "correct" way to serve customers, organizations are realizing a huge return on investment in the form of higher revenue and lower expenditures per customer. According to ASTD, many companies spend 1.9 percent of payroll ($761.00 per employee) on employee training with each employee getting 23.7 hours of training.[7]

[7]C. Thompson, E. Koon, W. H. Woodwell Jr., and J. Beauvais, *Training for the Next Economy: An ASTD State of the Industry Report on Trends in Employer-Provided Training in the United States,* ASTD Research Department, Alexandria, Va., 2002.

Training employees to improve their knowledge and skills is important to the success of an organization. *What skills do you need to improve, and how can you get this training?*

Why are employers investing so heavily in this type of training? Quite simply, it's good business; if they don't do it, their competitors are likely to overtake them in the marketplace. A better-trained staff can more effectively and efficiently use systems and equipment while providing quality customer service.

Why should you care about additional training and learning? Studies consistently show a correlation between education and job security and salary.

6   Skills for Success

Concept: Among the skills for success that you need to acquire and perfect are reading, writing, computation, communication, the ability to work with others, and the ability to solve problems.

Change will continue to be the workplace norm. To get ahead of others today and in the future, you'll need specific abilities and skills. Skills that work today may not work tomorrow. Today's consumer does not accept the status quo or minimal standards. You must be versatile enough to handle the unusual, tailor product and service delivery to the individual customer, and interact with a variety of customers in many situations. The following skills are the minimum you'll need to be successful in the future.

Basic Skills (Reading, Writing, and Computation)

Service employees spend much of their working day reading forms, correspondence, directions, and technological support materials. They also answer memorandums and letters and share information in writing with others. Failure to communicate concisely creates misunderstandings and projects a negative image of you and your organization.

Computation skills are also crucial for many service workers, who need to do basic math computation (addition, subtraction, multiplication, and division) and compute measurements and distances. The following strategies can help you strengthen **basic skills** necessary for success.

Strategies for Improvement

- Spend one hour a day reading a book, magazine, newspaper, or other publication.
- Attend a speed-reading workshop or course.
- Attend a basic grammar and/or business writing and proofreading course.
- Ask someone whom you believe to be a skilled writer to coach you and provide feedback on your writing.
- When faced with a problem, analyze the pros and cons before making a decision.
- Attend a refresher math course.
- Purchase books on mathematical problem-solving activities and practice doing the exercises.

Communication Skills

As you read in Chapters 3 to 5, the ability to ask questions correctly, provide feedback, listen, read nonverbal cues, and share ideas effectively is a key to successful customer service. Since these are "life" skills, you can practice them anywhere and gain in your personal as well as professional relationships. Preview the following strategies for improving your **communication skills** and select a few to work on.

Strategies for Improvement

- Regularly elicit feedback and ideas for improvement from others on your communication style and effectiveness.
- Identify at least five people whom you believe to have excellent communication skills. Have lunch with or network with them, and informally interview them about how they got to be such good communicators. This will enhance your knowledge, strengthen your relationships with these people, and make them feel good about their skills.
- Read books and articles on effective interpersonal communication (see Bibliography).
- Attend a course on interpersonal communication at a local school or college.
- Develop a list of ways that you can provide feedback to others.
- Practice these skills regularly in a variety of situations.

Creative Thinking Skills

To become a valued asset, you need to be able to go beyond normal paradigms (the way you typically view things). By breaking out of the traditional way of thinking, looking for new ways of doing things, and focusing on excellence, you move ahead of many coworkers who satisfy themselves with the status quo. Try the following tips for improving your **creative thinking skills.**

Strategies for Improvement

- Look at everything with which you come into contact (e.g., processes, procedures, policies, forms, products, services) from the standpoint of how it can be improved. Make recommendations to your supervisor.
- Read books or articles on creativity.

The challenges of the future will require new skills and approaches to serving customers. *What have you done to acquire critical thinking, problem-solving, and decision-making skills that can help you in working with customers?*

- Attend seminars or college courses on the topic.
- Develop an "idea file." Write down and keep ideas for future development or action.
- Network with others to share ideas for improvement.
- Challenge yourself with puzzles and exercises that stretch your mind.

Interpersonal Skills

At no time in the history of business in the United States has the skill of working effectively with others, especially those who are different from yourself, been more important. Many companies have now adopted a team environment—employees work together on projects or tasks as a group, are accountable for results as a group, and are rewarded as a group. An inability to function in such an environment can lead to personal, team, and organizational failure while also alienating customers.

In the customer service arena, your ability to deal with others in a variety of situations can determine whether you succeed. You must be able to communicate and relate with a variety of personality and cultural styles, be willing to share information and interact with others, and deal with changing situations. Some ways to strengthen your **interpersonal skills** follow.

Strategies for Success

- Volunteer to serve on a cross-functional team or committee in order to practice your communication and networking skills.
- Read books and articles on interpersonal skill building.

- Join a professional organization and get involved on committees or a board of directors.
- Actively participate in workplace group activities and committees.
- Attend after-work functions to get to know coworkers in a different environment.
- Target one knowledgeable, experienced person to serve as your career mentor (someone who can guide and coach you). Meet with your mentor and ask for tips on success and advancement.

Leadership Skills

As organizations continue to change, employees will be required to assume new roles and exercise leadership not normally associated with their jobs. At some point, you will need to assume control of a situation or project in order to bring about a resolution or satisfy a customer. Often, you will be expected to do this in the absence of guidelines or directives from supervisors. Preview the following strategies for improving your **leadership skills** and select ones that will assist your growth.

Strategies for Success
- Before approaching others with an idea or proposal, list advantages on a piece of paper. Use them to defend your idea.
- Identify prominent historical leaders. Read their autobiographies and use their successful behaviors.
- Take the time to build relationships and gain influence.
- Read literature on leadership.
- Attend workshops or courses on the topic.
- Get actively involved in professional organizations by volunteering to chair committees or serve on a board of directors. You gain leadership experience and exposure by doing so.

Negotiation Skills

Many of the daily encounters you'll have with customers, vendors, coworkers, and bosses will test your **negotiation skills**—that is, your ability to compromise, collaborate, accommodate, and work toward a situation both parties can live with (win-win problem solving).

Strategies for Success
- Practice compromise and sharing skills with others rather than always trying to win or be right.
- Read articles or books on the topic.
- Attend negotiation workshops or courses.
- Observe others in sales or negotiation situations. Make mental notes of their positive and negative actions. Use their positive techniques when you perform similar tasks or encounter similar situations.

Problem-Solving Skills

As the workplace evolves, employees are being asked to do more with less (e.g., less money, fewer resources) while maintaining quality service. Your employer will likely look to you to recognize problems, develop resolution strategies, and implement them. How well you can do this is crucial. The following suggestions, coupled with what you read in Chapters 7 and 12, can get you started in developing or honing your **problem-solving skills.**

Strategies for Success

- Volunteer to participate on committees that are established to solve problems or develop or redesign new products or processes.
- For every problem or challenge you encounter, try to come up with at least two possible solutions.
- Attend courses or workshops on problem solving.
- Read books, articles, or other publications on problem solving.
- Find information on organizations that have overcome adversity to regain market share after a loss of prestige or customer trust or respect (e.g., Coca-Cola after the failed 1985 introduction of the New Coke product, Tylenol after the 1982 tampering incident). Study how the decisions made turned the situations around.

Technical Skills

Since so much of the customer service function is tied to various aspects of technology, you'll need to adapt to and master a variety of **technical skills**. In order to process information and serve the customer, you'll access various sources of information stored in computers. You will also need to operate a variety of machinery, equipment, and technology in order to be successful.

Strategies for Success

- Read magazine articles, books, and other publications about the latest changes or inventions in the technology used in your profession.
- Attend courses that teach the operation and use of technology related to your job.
- Take courses on various software programs to expand your knowledge about the capabilities of the software products and to enhance your skills.
- Spend time surfing the Internet just to gain experience on navigating and on locating data.
- Practice, practice, practice.

A Final Thought About Customer Service

Throughout this book, we've reviewed problems and strategies related to better serving the customer. We've looked at trends and how they do or will affect you as a customer service provider. Knowledge of all of those topics is crucial for the delivery of service excellence. However, the key component of the process is the customer. Never lose sight of the fact that the customer is your reason for existence in the workplace. Focus all your energies on understanding and responding to the customer and his or her needs. A good summary of what customer service is can be found on walls of offices all over the country. It is reprinted here. You may want to make a copy of it and post it on your work area wall as a reminder of your purpose.

> *The customer* is the most important person in any business.
>
> *The customer* is not dependent on us—we are dependent on the customer.
>
> *The customer* is not an interruption of our work—the customer is the reason for our work.

The customer does us a favor when he or she calls—we are not doing the customer a favor by serving.

The customer is part of our business—not an outsider.

The customer is not a cold statistic—he or she is a flesh-and-blood human being with feelings and emotions like our own.

The customer is not someone to argue with or match wits with.

The customer is a person who brings us his or her wants—it is our job to fill those wants.

The customer is deserving of the most courteous and attentive treatment we can provide.

The customer is the lifeblood of every business.

Like this operational motto, this book contains only words aimed at expressing concepts and ideas. It is up to you to decide whether the strategies and techniques you've read about are valuable. If you decide that they are, you'll then have to develop an action plan for implementation. This book is not the crucial link with your customer—you are!

7 Building for Tomorrow

Concept: Developing a plan for action to improve customer service is a goal worthy of your consideration.

Reflect on what you've experienced throughout this book and then turn to the Personal Action Plan in the "Planning to Serve" feature of this chapter (page 391) and develop your own action plan. Refer to it regularly and share it with others so that they can encourage you to achieve your goals.

Chapter Summary

For years, some American organizations took a relaxed approach to doing business in which they disregarded the rise of their competitors. In recent decades, as competition from Asia, Europe, and elsewhere has gained momentum, companies in the United States that were previously satisfied with status quo began to pay attention. Recent decades have brought about the realization that traditional product and service leaders won't remain leaders in the face of strong competition. This awareness has served as a wake-up call to those organizations. Is it too late for those companies to regain their competitive edge? Time will tell, but the fact that awareness and focus are now centered on creating true customer-focused cultures is a good indication that there is a strong chance of success in the future.

SERVICE IN ACTION   JCPenney Company, Inc.   CHAPTER 14

http://www.jcpenney.com

James Cash Penney opened his first Golden Rule Store in the mining town of Kemmerer, Wyoming, in 1902. Eleven years later, Penney incorporated under JCPenney, Inc.

At the heart of Penney's dream was customer satisfaction. His stated goal was "to serve the public, as nearly as we can, to its complete satisfaction." This vision has been carried out for over 100 years of innovative consumer marketing and retailing to the point that JCPenney is an American icon. By valuing customers, associates, communities, investors, products, and services, JCPenney has become one of the most trusted retailers in America.

Over the years, JCPenney has grown and diversified its marketing efforts. As one of the early leaders in the catalog business, Penney brought products to peoples' home via home delivery. In 1998, Penney launched its Internet site in combination with the catalog division. Both of these are supported by the largest telemarketing network in the United States. Currently, there are nearly 1,100 JCPenney stores in all 50 states, Puerto Rico, and Mexico. The company also operates 50 Renner department stores in Brazil and the most recent venture has been the purchase of the Eckerd drugstore chain. To some extent, the latter was purchased as an investment in the future since the aging baby boomer population (people born between 1946 and 1964) will eventually require more drugs and health-related products to maintain their quality of life.

Key Terms and Concepts	Americans With Disabilities Act of 1990	creative thinking skills	leadership skills
	baby bust	e-commerce	negotiation skills
	basic skills	futurists	problem-solving skills
	changing legal environment	graying of the population	role of training and development
	Civil Rights Act of 1964	impact of education on society	shifts in demographics
	communication skills	interpersonal skills	technical skills
			technology implications

Quick Preview Answers

1. T
2. F
3. T
4. T

5. F
6. T
7. F

8. T
9. T
10. F

Chapter Review Questions

1. What are some of the major challenges that lie ahead for customer service professionals?
2. How will projected changes in the demographic makeup of society affect the customer service profession from the perspective of the customer? From the perspective of the customer service professional?
3. How will technology affect the way service is delivered in the future?
4. In what ways have you seen laws affect the delivery of service in the United States?
5. How might the economy affect service delivery?
6. What are some of the key projections for growth in the service economy?
7. How important will education and training be in the future?

8. What global factors have affected and will continue to affect customer needs and service delivery?

9. What are some of the key skills you'll need to be successful as a customer service professional in the future?

10. What are some steps you can take to prepare for the customer service job of tomorrow?

Search It Out

Search the Internet for Customer Service Articles

Log on to the Internet and search for information on trends related to customer service. Be prepared to discuss your findings in class. Search for some of the following topics:

Consumer rights
Legal environment related to customer service
Employee training and education
Technology in customer service
Changing demographics
Economic shifts
Product tampering

Note: A listing for additional research on specific URLs is provided on the Customer Service website at **<http://www.mhhe.com/lucas05>.**

Collaborative Learning Activity

Emphasizing Education

Team up with several other people to form a discussion group. Spend some time talking about what you believe the role of schools is today and how well the schools are preparing young people for the work world. Share specific personal examples from your own educational background or that of someone you know.

PLANNING TO SERVE   CHAPTER 14

PERSONAL ACTION PLAN
Now that you have completed this text and course, think about how you will apply what you have learned. Respond to the following list and use the action plan to enhance your skills and prepare you to better serve your current or future customers.

Make a list of skills I will work on during the next three to four weeks.

Indicate my goal(s) in addressing this issue. List three goals.

Decide which resources or reference materials I will need to accomplish my goal(s).

Choose the person I will enlist to help coach, guide, and/or encourage me.

Determine my target date for completion and improvement.

Indicate when I will know I have reached my goal(s).

Reader's Customer Service Survey

Name _____

Title _____

Organization/School _____

Your mailing address (for your free booklet) _____

City/State/ZIP _____

Phone (   ) _____

Customer feedback is crucial for delivering effective service and addressing specific needs. For us to make necessary additions, deletions, or corrections to this book, we need your help. Please take a few minutes to provide feedback in the following areas and return this questionnaire to the address at the end of the survey. In exchange for your thoughts and time, we'll send you a free booklet on effective interpersonal communication techniques.

(Photocopy the questionnaire if you prefer.)

Thank you.

1. Describe yourself in terms of customer contact experience:

   ___ Entry level (up to 1 year)   ___ Midlevel (2–5 years)   ___Senior (5 + years)

2. Are you currently working in a frontline customer contact position?
   Yes _____   No _____

3. The information provided in this book was clearly written and easy to read.

   1_____ 2_____ 3_____ 4_____ 5_____ 6_____ 7_____
   Strongly   Neutral   Strongly
   Disagree   Agree

4. The techniques outlined in this book are realistic and useful.

   1_____ 2_____ 3_____ 4_____ 5_____ 6_____ 7_____
   Strongly   Neutral   Strongly
   Disagree   Agree

5. The supplemental materials (figures, role-play activities, questions, references) added value to the text.

   1_____ 2_____ 3_____ 4_____ 5_____ 6_____ 7_____
   Strongly   Neutral   Strongly
   Disagree   Agree

6. The design of this book was logical, efficient, effective, and easy to follow.

1_____ 2_____ 3_____ 4_____ 5_____ 6_____ 7_____
Strongly   Neutral   Strongly
Disagree   Agree

7. The level of information was well targeted to entry-level to midlevel customer contact personnel.

1_____ 2_____ 3_____ 4_____ 5_____ 6_____ 7_____
Strongly   Neutral   Strongly
Disagree   Agree

8. The text included real-world examples and scenarios to which I could relate.

1_____ 2_____ 3_____ 4_____ 5_____ 6_____ 7_____
Strongly   Neutral   Strongly
Disagree   Agree

9. I can apply information or ideas learned directly to my current or future job.

1_____ 2_____ 3_____ 4_____ 5_____ 6_____ 7_____
Strongly   Neutral   Strongly
Disagree   Agree

10. I plan to use this book as a reference in the future.

1_____ 2_____ 3_____ 4_____ 5_____ 6_____ 7_____
Strongly   Neutral   Strongly
Disagree   Agree

11. This book met my overall needs and expectations.

1_____ 2_____ 3_____ 4_____ 5_____ 6_____ 7_____
Strongly   Neutral   Strongly
Disagree   Agree

12. I will recommend this book to others.

1_____ 2_____ 3_____ 4_____ 5_____ 6_____ 7_____
Strongly   Neutral   Strongly
Disagree   Agree

13. What chapter was most valuable to you? Why?

14. Please tell us one thing related to customer service that you would like to have seen added to this book.

15. In your mind, what is the most critical issue facing customer service professionals today?

16. What other topics related to customer service are of interest to you?

17. Were there any typographical or other errors noted in the text?

Send to: Bob Lucas, President
Creative Presentation Resources, Inc.
P.O. Box 180487
Casselberry, Florida 32718-0487
(800) 308-0399/(407) 695-5535   FAX: (407) 695-7447
Email: blucas@presentationresources.net
www.presentationresources.net

A

acculturation   Adjustment or adaptation to a new and different culture.

acknowledgment   A communication technique for use with customers who have a complaint or are upset. It involves recognizing the customer's level of emotion before moving on to help resolve the issue.

Added Value And Results For Me (AVARFM)
The concept of showing someone what he/she will gain from taking a certain action or buying in to an idea. The concept helps reinforce "why" someone should accept what is being offered or proposed.

Americans With Disabilities Act of 1990   A United States federal act signed into law in July of 1990 guaranteeing people with disabilities equal access to workplace opportunities.

angry customers   Customers who become emotional because either their needs are not met or they become dissatisfied with the services or products purchased from an organization.

appearance or grooming   Nonverbal characteristics exhibited by service providers that can send a variety of messages that range from being a professional to having a negative attitude.

articulation   Refers to the manner or clarity in which verbal messages are delivered. Synonyms include *pronunciation* and *enunciation.*

assertiveness   Involves projecting a presence that is assured, confident, and capable without seeming to be aggressive or arrogant.

assigning meaning   The phase of the listening process in which the brain attempts to match a received sound or message with other information stored in the brain in order to recognize or extract meaning from it. (See also **comprehending.**)

attending   The phase of the listening process in which a listener focuses attention on a specific sound or message being received from the environment.

attitudes   Emotional responses to people, ideas, and objects. They are based on values, differ between individuals and cultures, and impact the way people deal with various issues and situations. (See also **values.**)

automatic call distribution (ACD) system   Telecommunications system used by many companies in their call centers and customer care facilities to capture incoming calls and route them to available service providers.

automatic number identification (ANI) system
A form of caller identification system similar to home telephone caller ID systems. ANI allows incoming customers to be identified on a computer screen with background information so that they can be routed to an appropriate service representative for assistance.

B

B2B   Refers to business-to-business customer service.

baby boomer   A term applied to anyone born between 1946 to 1964. People in this age group are often called boomers.

baby bust   Term applied to period following the baby boom in which the birthrate was down because boomers delayed or forwent having children in order to take advantage of alternative life choices such as a career.

basic skills   Term that refers to the skills needed to be successful in the workplace and life. Examples are reading, writing, and computation skills.

behavioral styles   Descriptive term that identifies categories of human behavior identified by behavioral researchers. Many of the models used to group behaviors date back to those identified by Carl Jung.

beliefs   Perceptions or assumptions that individuals or cultures maintain. These perceptions are based on past experiences, memories, and interpretations and influence how people act and interact with certain individuals or groups.

biases   Beliefs or opinions that a person has about an individual or group. Often based on unreasonable distortions or prejudice.

blind transfer   The practice of transferring an incoming caller to another telephone number and hanging up once someone answers without announcing who is calling.

body language   Nonverbal communication cues that send powerful messages through gestures, vocal qualities, manner of dress and grooming, and many other cues.

burnout   A category of stress that encompasses personal exhaustion, lack of enthusiasm, reduced productivity, and apathy toward the job and customers.

C

call center Also known as *customer care centers.* A collection of customer service representatives in an area which uses telephone equipment, computers, and other technology to receive and make calls and service customers. Two versions exist—inbound (incoming calls to an organization) and outbound (making calls to current and potential customers or conducting survey work).

causes of service breakdowns Occurs when customers are not satisfied with the service or product provided by an organization. (See also **service breakdowns.**)

changing legal environment An evolving workplace and society creates the ongoing need for updated and new legislation to help manage business and behavior.

channel Term used to describe the method through which people communicate messages. Examples are face-to-face, telephone, e-mail, written correspondence, or facsimile.

Chicano culture Refers primarily to people with a heritage based in Mexico. (See also **Hispanic origin** and **Latino culture.**)

churn The process of a customer switching between products or companies, often simply to get a better price, rebate, or warranty.

circadian rhythm The physiological 24-hour cycle associated with the earth's rotation that affects metabolic and sleep patterns in humans as day displaces night.

Civil Rights Act of 1964 Major legislation passed to guarantee rights and prevent workplace discrimination based on age, sex, race, religion, and national origin.

closed-end questions Inquiries that typically start with a verb and solicit short one-syllable answer (e.g., yes, no, one word, or a number) and can be used for such purposes as clarifying, verifying information already given, controlling conversation, or affirming something.

clusters of nonverbal behavior Groupings of nonverbal behaviors to indicate a possible positive or negative intent (e.g., crossed arms, closed body posturing, frowning, or turning away could indicate negative intent while smiling, open gestures with arms and hands, and friendly touching could indicate positive message intent).

collective cultures Members of a group share common interests and values. They see themselves as an interdependent unit and conform and cooperate for the good of the group.

communication skills Strategies used by people to communicate verbally and nonverbally in order to exchange messages and information.

comprehending The phase of the listening process in which the brain attempts to match a received sound or message with other information stored in the brain in order to recognize or extract meaning from it. (See also **assigning meaning.**)

concept of time Term used to describe how certain societies view time as either polychronic or monochronic.

conflict resolution style The manner in which a person handles conflict. People typically use one of five approaches to resolving conflict—avoidance, compromise, competition, accommodation, or collaboration.

congruence In communication, this relates to ensuring that verbal messages sent match or are in agreement with the nonverbal cues used.

contact points Instances in which a customer connects with a service provider or some other aspect of an organization.

contingency plans Back systems or procedures that are implemented when regular ones break down or fail to function as intended.

continuous quality improvement (CQI) (See **total quality management.**)

cost of dissatisfied customers Phrase that refers to any formula used to calculate the cost of acquiring a new customer or replacing a current one as a result of having a dissatisfied customer leave an organization.

cottage industry Term adopted in the early days of customer service when many people started small businesses in their homes or cottages and bartered products or services with neighbors.

creative thinking skills Phrase referring to the ability to look at things in more abstract or global terms as opposed to a linear, step-by-step manner.

crisis manager A person who waits until the last minute to address an issue or take an action. The result is that others are then inconvenienced and have to shift their priorities to help resolve the issue.

culture Refers to a set of fundamental beliefs, ideas, practices, attitudes, and norms for a group, which guide behaviors within the group.

cultural diversity Refers to the differences and similarities attributed to various groups of people within a culture.

customer expectations The perceptions that customers have when they contact an organization or service provider concerning the kind and level and quality of products and services they should receive.

customer-focused organizations   Companies that spend energy and effort on satisfying internal and external customers by first identifying customer needs then establishing policies, procedures, and management and reward systems to support excellence in service delivery.

customer friendly systems   Refers to the processes in an organization that make service seamless to customers by ensuring that things work properly and the customer is satisfied.

customer loyalty   Term used to describe customers who return to a product or organization regularly because of the service and satisfaction they receive.

customer needs   Motivators or drivers that cause customers to seek out specific types of products or services. These may be marketing-driven based on advertising they have seen or may tie directly to Abraham Maslow's Hierarchy of Needs Theory.

customer relationship management (CRM)   Concept of identifying customer needs: understanding and influencing customer behavior through ongoing communication strategies in an effort to acquire, retain, and satisfy the customer. The ultimate goal is customer loyalty.

customer relationships   The practice of building and maintaining ongoing friendships with customers in an effort to make them feel comfortable with an organization and its service providers in an effort to enhance customer loyalty.

customer retention   The ongoing effort by an organization to meet customer needs and desires in an effort to build long-term relationships and keep them for life.

customer satisfaction   The state of a person feeling that his or her needs have been met by an organization.

customer service   The ability of knowledgeable, capable, and enthusiastic employees to deliver products and services to their internal and external customers in a manner which satisfies identified and unidentified needs and ultimately results in positive word-of-mouth publicity and return business.

customer service environment   Made up of and influenced by various elements of an organization. Examples are delivery systems, human resources, service, products, and organizational culture.

customers with disabilities   Descriptive phrase that refers to anyone with a physical or mental disability.

D

decisive style   One of four behavior style groupings characterized by a direct, no-nonsense approach to people and situations.

decoding   The stage in the interpersonal communication process in which messages received are analyzed by a receiver in an effort to determine the sender's intent.

deliverables   Products or services provided by an organization.

delivery system   The method(s) used by an organization to provide services and products to its customers.

demanding or domineering customers   Customers who have definite ideas about what they want and are unwilling to compromise or accept alternatives.

deregulation   Occurs when governments remove legislative or regulatory guidelines that inhibit and control an industry (e.g., transportation, natural gas, and telecommunications).

difficult customers   People who challenge a service provider's ability to deliver service and who require special skills and patience.

dissatisfied customer   Someone who either does not or perceives that he or she does not receive promised products or services.

dissatisfiers   Elements of the service environment that inhibit satisfaction of customer needs and ultimately can result in reduced customer loyalty.

distress   Pain or worry brought on by either internal or external physical or mental strain.

diversity   The different characteristics, values, beliefs, and factors that make people different, yet similar. (See also **cultural diversity**.)

downsizing   Term applied to the situation in which employees are terminated.

E

e-commerce   An entire spectrum of companies that market products and services on the Internet and through other technology, and the process of accessing them by consumers.

elderly customers   Customers who are typically past retirement and who sometimes require special communication and relationship skills to service.

e-mail   Electronic mail system used to transmit messages around the Internet.

e-mail management   System of providing organizational guidelines for effective use of e-mail systems.

emotional icons or emoticons   Humorous characters that send visual messages such as smiling or frowning. They are created with various strokes of the computer keyboard characters and symbols.

emotional messages of color   Research-based use of color to send nonverbal messages through advertisements and other elements of the organization.

Emotion-Reducing Model   Process for reducing customer emotion in situations when frustration or anger exists.

employee expectations   Perceptions about positive and negative aspects of the workplace.

employee roles   Task assignments that service providers assume.

empowerment   The phrase used to describe the giving of decision-making and problem-resolution authority to lower-level employees in an organization. This precludes having to get permission from higher levels in order to take an action or serve a customer.

encoding   The stage in the interpersonal communication process in which the sender decides what message will be sent and how it will be transmitted along with considerations about the receiver.

enunciation   See **articulation.**

environmental cues   Any aspect of the workplace with which a customer comes into contact. Such things as the general appearance of an area, clutter, unsightly or offensive items, or general disorganization contribute to the perception of an environment.

environmental factors affecting stress   Refers to the workplace, organizational, and societal elements that impact a service provider's mental and physical state.

environmental time wasters   People, items, or other factors that interfere with one's ability to accomplish planned tasks and to use time effectively.

ethical behavior   Expected performance that sends a message of being trustworthy and honest, and having the intent to provide quality service.

etiquette   Includes the acceptable rules, manners, and ceremonies for an organization, profession, or society.

eustress   A term coined by psychologist, Dr. Hans Seyle, to describe positive stress that people sometimes experience when they set goals or objectives to achieve. It provides stimulation and exhilaration that are essential for personal expansion and growth.

expectations of privacy   The belief that personal information provided to an organization will be safeguarded against inappropriate or unauthorized use or dissemination.

expressive style   One of four behavior groups characterized as being people-oriented fun-loving, upbeat, and extroverted.

external customers   Those people outside the organization who purchase or lease products and services. This group includes vendors, suppliers, and people on the telephone, or others not from the organization.

external obstacles   Factors outside an organization or the sphere of one's influence that can cause challenges in delivering service.

F

face   Refers to the concept of esteem in many Asian cultures.

facsimile (fax) machine   Equipment that converts printed words into electronic signals and allows them to be transmitted across telephone lines then reassembled into text message on the receiving end.

Father of Listening   A term sometimes attributed to Dr. Ralph C. Nichols because of the extensive amount of research he conducted and his contributions to understanding how humans listen.

faulty assumptions   Service provider projections made about underlying customer message meanings based on past experiences.

fax on demand   Technology that allows information, such as a form, stored in a computer to be requested electronically via a telephone and transmitted to a customer.

feedback   The stage of the interpersonal communication process in which a receiver responds to a sender's message.

feel, felt, found strategy   A process for expressing empathy and concern for someone and for helping them understand that you can relate to their situation.

fight or flight syndrome   A term used by scientists to describe the body's reaction to stressors in which the heart starts pumping the chemical adrenaline into the blood stream and the lungs start taking in more oxygen. This provides the fuel needed to deal with the situation (See also **stressors.**)

filters   Psychological barriers in the form or personal experiences, lessons learned, societal beliefs, and values through which people process and compare information received to determine its significance.

foreign-born population   Refers to people not born in a given country.

forms of address   Titles used to address people. Examples are Mister, Miss, or Doctor.

futurists   People who look at current trends and events and make predictions of future ones.

G

gender   The grammatical classification of words in relation to their sex or lack of it (e.g., masculine, feminine, or neuter).

gender communication   Term used to refer to communication between genders.

gender roles   Behaviors attributed to or assigned by societal norms.

globalization   The term applied to an ongoing trend of information, knowledge, and resource sharing around the world. Due to a more mobile society and easier access to transportation and technology, more people are traveling and accessing products and services from international sources than ever before.

global terms   Potentially inflammatory words or phrases used in conversation. They tend to inappropriately generalize behavior or group people or incidents together (e.g., always, never, everyone, everything, all the time).

graying of the population   Refers to the large aging population throughout the world due in part to the large number of baby boomers who are moving into retirement years.

H

hearing   A passive physiological process of gathering sound waves and transmitting them to the brain for analysis. It is the first phase of the listening process.

hearing disabilities   Conditions in which the ability to hear is diminished below established auditory standards.

help desk   Term used to describe a service provider trained and assigned to assist customers with questions, problems, or suggestions.

Hierarchy of Needs Theory (see also **Maslow**)   was developed by Dr. Abraham Maslow. In studies done, Maslow identified five levels of needs that humans possess—physiological (basic), safety, social, esteem, and self-actualization.

high touch customers   Refers to people who want and require a lot of personal contact and assistance from service representatives instead of desiring to use technological service mechanisms such as the Internet, telephone, and e-mail.

Hispanic origin   Refers to people who were born in Mexico, Puerto Rico, Cuba, and Central or South America. (See also **Latino culture** and **Chicano culture**.)

hostile work environment   A phrase that legally defines a work environment in which offensive behaviors (e.g., ethnic, racial, or other offensive jokes are told; inappropriate and/or unsolicited touching occurs; or certain groups are excluded from workplace opportunities) occur.

human resources   Refers to the employees of an organization.

hygiene   The healthy maintenance of the body through such practices as regular bathing, washing of hair, brushing of teeth, cleaning of fingernails, and using commercial products to eliminate or mask odors.

I

I or we messages   Messages that are potentially less offensive than the word "you," which is like nonverbal finger pointing when emotions are high.

impact of culture   Refers to the outcome of people from various countries or backgrounds coming into contact with one another and potentially experiencing misunderstandings or relationship breakdowns. (See also **culture**.)

impact of education on society   Refers to the outcome of people with various educational or societal backgrounds coming into contact with one another and potentially experiencing misunderstandings or relationship breakdowns.

importance of relationships   Focuses on the need for service providers to build strong bonds with customers.

inclusive   The concept of ensuring that people of all races, genders, religious and ethnic backgrounds, as well as a multitude of other diverse factors, are included in communications and activities in the workplace.

indecisive customers   People who have difficulty making a decision or making a selection when given choices of products or services.

individualistic cultures   Groups in which members value themselves as individuals who are separate from their group and are responsible for their own destiny.

inflection   The change in tone of the voice as one speaks. This quality is also called pitch and adds vocal variety and punctuation to verbal messages. (See also **pitch**.)

informational overload   Refers to having too many messages coming together and causing confusion, frustration, or an inability to act.

information highway   A term coined to address the easy access of information through the World Wide Web (Internet) and associated technology systems.

inquisitive style   One of four behavioral groups characterized by being introverted, task-focused, and detail-oriented.

interactive voice response (IVR) system   Technology that allows customers to call an organization 24 hours a day, 7 days a week to get information through recorded message or computer by keying a series of numbers on the telephone keypad in response to questions or prompts.

internal customers   People within the organization who either require support and service or provide information, products, and services to service providers. Such customers include peers, coworkers, bosses, subordinates, or people from other areas of their organization.

Internet call back   Technology that allows someone browsing the Internet to key a prompt on a website and have a service representative call a phone number provided.

Internet telephony   Technology that allows people to talk to one another via the Internet as if they were on a regular telephone.

interpersonal skills   The skills used by people to relate to and communicate effectively with others. Examples are verbal and nonverbal communication skills and the ability to build trust, empathy, and compassion.

J

jargon   A form of slang that typically pertains to one or more industries or professions. (See also **slang.**)

job factors affecting stress   Refers to the elements of a job that frustrate or pressure someone.

job stress   Term coined to describe the impact of the internal and external elements of the workplace that cause service providers to feel mentally and physically pressured or to become ill.

K

KISS principle   Refers to the practice of **K**eeping **I**t **S**hort and **S**weet when performing a task or doing something.

L

lag time   The term applied to the difference in the rate at which the human brain can receive and process information and at which most adults speak. (See also **listening gap.**)

Latino culture   Refers to people of Hispanic descent. (See also **Hispanic origin** and **Chicano culture.**)

leadership skills   Related to the ability to effectively encourage, support, and guide others.

learning organizations   A term used by Peter Senge in his book *The Fifth Discipline* to describe organizations that value knowledge, education, and employee training. They also learn from their competition, industry trends, and other sources, and they develop systems to support continued growth and development in order to remain competitive.

learning style   Refers to how a person gains and processes information. Involves the five senses.

listening   An active, learned process consisting of four phases—receiving/hearing the message, attending, comprehending/assigning meaning, and responding.

listening gap   The difference in the speed at which the brain can comprehend communication and the speed at which the average adult speaks in the United States. (See also **lag time.**)

low touch customers   People who are adept at helping themselves and often prefer to not be involved personally with a service representative. They are often comfortable with using technological service mechanisms such as telephone answering systems, Internet, and e-mail.

M

manners   See **etiquette.**

Maslow, Abraham   A psychologist, author, and educator who did extensive studies following World War II to determine worker motivators. His classic Hierarchy of Needs Theory is still prominent in the workplace today.

media blending   Technology that allows a service provider to communicate with a customer via telephone while at the same time displaying information to the customer over the computer.

mentees   The recipients of the efforts of mentors and are typically less experienced.

mentors   Individuals who dedicate time and effort to befriend and assist others. In an organization, they are typically people with a lot of knowledge, experience, skills, and initiative, and have a large personal and professional network established.

message   A communication delivered through speech or signals, or in writing.

miscellaneous cues   Refers to factors used to send messages that impact a customer's perception or feelings about a service provider or organization. Examples are personal habits, etiquette, and manners.

mission   The direction or focus of an organization that supports day-to-day interactions with customers.

mobility or motion impairment   Physical limitations that some people have requiring accommodation or special consideration to allow access to products or services.

modesty   Refers to the way that cultures view propriety of dress and conduct.

moment of truth   A phrase popularized by Scandinavian Airlines President Jan Carlzon in his popular 1987 book by the same title. A moment of truth is defined as any instance when a customer comes into contact with any element or representative of an organizational.

monochronic   Refers to the perception of time as being a central focus with deadlines being a crucial element of societal norm.

mutual time wasters   Events or obstacles that can be created by the actions and inactions of anyone involved in a situation.

N

needs   See **customer needs.**

negotiation skills   Refers to the ability to confer with others in an effort to have them compromise on an issue.

networking   The process of building interpersonal relationships and sharing resources with others.

Nichols, Ralph G.   Researcher who conducted many studies to examine the nature and effect of effective listening. He is sometimes referred to as the Father of Listening by experts in his field.

noise   Refers to physiological or psychological factors (physical characteristics, level of attention, message clarity, loudness of message, or environmental factors) that interfere with the accurate reception of information.

nonverbal feedback   Messages sent to someone through other than spoken means. Examples are gestures, appearance, and facial expressions.

nonverbal messages (cues)   Consist of such things as movements, gestures, body positions, vocal qualities, and a variety of unspoken signals sent by people, often in conjunction with verbal messages.

North American Free Trade Agreement (NAFTA)
A trade agreement entered into by the United States, Canada, and Mexico among other things to help eliminate barriers to trade, promote conditions of fair trade across borders, and increase investment opportunities, and promote and protect intellectual property rights.

O

objections   Reasons given by customers for not wanting to purchase a product or service during an interaction with a salesperson or service provider (e.g., "I don't need one," "I can't afford it," or "I already have one").

online information fulfillment system   Technology that allows a customer to access an organization's website and click on desired information without having to interact with a service provider.

open-ended questions   Typically start with words like who, when, what, how, and why and are used to engage others in conversation or to gain input and ideas.

organizational culture   Includes an element of an organization that a customer encounters. (See also **customer service environment.**)

ownership of property   Refers to how people of a given culture view property.

P

paralanguage   Consists of voice qualities (e.g., pitch, rate, tone, or other vocal qualities) or noises and vocalizations (e.g., "Hmmm" or "Ahhh") made as someone speaks, which let a speaker know that his or her message is being listened to and followed.

paraphrase   The practice of a message receiver giving back in his or her own words what he or she believes a sender said.

pauses   A verbal technique of delaying response in order to allow time to process information received, think of a response, or gain attention.

perception checking   The process of clarifying a nonverbal cue that was received by stating what behavior was observed, giving one or two possible interpretations, then asking the message sender for clarification.

perceptions   How someone views an item, situation, or others.

personal factors affecting stress   Refers to issues that someone has related to family, finances, or other elements of a life that can create pressure or frustration.

personal obstacles   Factors that can limit performance or success in life. Examples are disabilities, lack of education, or biases.

pet peeves   Refers to factors, people, or situations that personally irritate or frustrate a service provider and which, left unchecked, can create a breakdown in effective service.

pitch   Refers to the change in tone of the voice as one speaks. This quality is also called inflection and adds vocal variety and punctuation to verbal messages. (See also **inflection.**)

Planning Process Model   Five-step process for helping a customer resolve problems.

Platinum Rule   Term coined by speaker and author Tony Alessandra related to going beyond the step of treating customers the way you want to be treated, to the next level of treating them the way they would like to be treated.

polychronic   Refers to the perception of time as a fluid commodity that does not interfere with relationships and elements of happiness.

positive wording   Focuses on using terminology that is less likely to evoke emotion or cause relationship breakdowns when dealing with others.

posture   Refers to how one sits or stands in order to project various nonverbal messages.

predictive dialing system   Technology that automatically places ongoing calls and delivers incoming calls to the next available service representative in a call center.

primary behavior pattern   Refers to a person's preferred style of dealing with others.

prioritizing time   Relates to how someone decides the importance of various tasks and the order in which they are dealt with.

problem solving   The system of identifying issues, determining alternatives for dealing with them, then selecting and monitoring a strategy for resolution.

Problem-Solving Model   The process used by a service provider to assist customers in determining and selecting appropriate solutions to their issues, concerns, or needs.

problem-solving skills   Refers to the aptitude that a service provider has for determining the true cause of an issue and finding appropriate resolution.

process improvement   Refers to the process of continually evaluating products and services to ensure that maximum effectiveness, efficiency, and potential are being obtained from them.

product   Something produced or an output by an individual or organization. In the service environment, products are created to satisfy customer needs or wants.

prohibitions   Local, state, or federal regulations that prevent a service provider from satisfying a customer's request even though the provider would normally do so. (See also **service options.**)

pronunciation   See **articulation.**

proxemics   Relates to the invisible barrier surrounding people in which they feel comfortable interacting with others. This zone varies depending on the level of relationship a person has with someone else. (See also **spatial cues.**)

psychological distracters   Refers to mental factors that can cause a shift in focus when interacting with others. Examples are state of health and personal issues.

R

rapport   The silent bond built between two people as a result of sharing of common interests and issues and demonstration of a win-win, I care attitude.

rate of speech   Refers to the number of words spoken per minute. Some research studies have found that the average rate of speech for adults in Western cultures is approximately 125–150 words per minute (wpm).

RATER Model   A system of evaluating the level of service received.

rational style   One of four behavioral groups characterized by being quiet, reflective, task-focused, and systematic.

reasons for customer defection   Refers to the causes of customer dissatisfaction or the reasons customers look elsewhere for products or services.

receiver   One of the two primary elements of a two-way conversation. Gathers the sender's message and decides how to react to it.

relationship-rating points   Values mentally assigned by customers to a service provider and his or her organization. They are based on a number of factors starting with initial impressions and subsequently by the quality and level of service provided. (See also **relationship-rating point scale.**)

relationship-rating point scale   The mental rating system that customers apply to service and service providers. Ratings range from *exemplary* to *unsatisfactory,* with *average* being assigned when service occurs as expected.

relationship management   The process of continually monitoring interactions with a customer in order to strengthen ties and retain the customer. (See also **customer relationship management.**)

respect for elders   A value held by people from many cultures.

responding   Refers to sending back verbal and nonverbal messages to a message originator.

ripple effect   Related to time management, this occurs when someone drops a project or issue into an environment and the "ripples" or waves that begin as a result wash over other people or situations. This often results in a negative impact in the form of having to react quickly or deal with the resulting issue(s) and being taken away from a planned agenda.

roadblocks to service recovery   Issues or things that can impede correction of a service problem and, ultimately, delay satisfying a customer.

road rage   A term used to describe the practice of a driver or passenger in a vehicle verbally and/or physically assaulting others as a result of the frustrations experienced while driving (e.g., driver failing to signal, cutting into a lane abruptly, or tailgating).

role of training and development   Refers to the importance of activities designed to increase employee knowledge and skills within an organization.

rude or inconsiderate customers   People who seem to take pleasure in being obstinate and contrary when dealing with service providers and who seem to have their own agenda without concern for the feelings of others.

RUMBA   An acronym for five criteria (Realistic, Understandable, Measurable, Believable, and Attainable) used to establish and measure employee performance goals.

S

salutation   The greeting included in written communications (e.g., Dear Dr., Dear Sir, or Dear Human Resources Director).

screen pop-ups   Small screen images that are programmed to appear on someone's computer monitor when a website is accessed.

self-generated time wasters   Those things that people create themselves or are a part of them that reduce time usage effectiveness.

semantics   The scientific study of relationships between signs, symbols, and words and their meaning. The way words are used or stressed often affects their perceived meaning.

sender   One of the two primary elements of a two-way conversation. Originates messages to a receiver.

service breakdowns   Situations when customers have expectations of a certain type or level of service which is not met by a service provider.

service culture   A service environment made up various factors, including the values, beliefs, norms, rituals and practices of a group or organization.

service delivery systems   The mechanisms or strategies used by an organization to provide service to customers.

service economy   A term used to describe the trend in which businesses have shifted from primarily production and manufacturing to more service delivery. As part of this evolution, many organizations have developed specifically to provide services to customers.

service industry   A term used to describe businesses that are engaged primarily in service delivery. Service sector is a more accurate term since many organizations provide some form of service to their customers even though they are primarily engaged in research, development, and manufacture of products.

service measurement   Techniques used by organizations to determine how well customers perceive the value of services and products received.

service options   Alternatives offered by service providers when an original request by a customer cannot be honored because of such restrictions as governmental statutory regulations, nonavailability of products, or inability to perform as requested. (See also **prohibitions.**)

service philosophy   The approach that an organization takes to providing service and addressing the needs of customers.

service providers   Technology companies that provide relay services for customers by linking their computers through the company's server. Customers can then access the Internet system in order to receive and transmit information.

service recovery   The process of righting a wrong or correcting something that has gone wrong involving provision of a product or service to a customer. The concept involves not only replacing defective products, but also going the extra step of providing compensation for the customer's inconvenience.

service sector   Refers to organizations and individuals involved in delivering service as a primary product.

service strategy   A combination of systems and practices coordinated to help an organization determine how it will conduct business and remain competitive.

setting priorities   The process of deciding which factors or elements have greater importance and placing them in a hierarchy.

shifts in demographics   Changes in the societal makeup of a country or the world.

silence   Technique used to gain attention when speaking, to allow thought, or to process information received.

slang   Informal language or words developed by adapting existing words or creating new ones, usually without regard for contemporary rules of grammar. (See also **jargon.**)

Small Business Administration (SBA)   United States governmental agency established to assist small business owners.

small talk   Dialogue used to enhance relationships, show civility, and build rapport.

spatial cues   Nonverbal messages sent on the basis of how close or far someone stands from another person. (See also **proxemics.**)

standards   Acceptable levels of quality used to gauge acceptance of a product or service.

stereotypes   Generalizations made about an individual or group and not based on reality. Similar people are often lumped together for ease in categorizing them.

strategies for preventing dissatisfaction   Techniques used to prevent a breakdown in needs fulfillment when dealing with customers.

strategies for reclaiming time   Techniques used to eliminate time wasters and to become more effective and efficient.

stressors Factors in a person's life that cause them to react positively or negatively to a situation that caused the pressure. (See also **fight or flight syndrome.**)

style manuals Written guidelines produced by some organizations that outline how correspondence and presentation materials will be organized and look. This is done to ensure a consistent, professional image in all written materials used to conduct business.

subcultures Groups within a cultural group. Behavioral characteristics, language patterns, modes of dress, beliefs, or other tangible and intangible factors (e.g., within the American culture found in the United States, there are a variety of ethnic, religious, and other smaller groups) that often identify such groups. (See also **culture.**)

T

talkative customers Customers exhibiting extroverted behavior who are very people-oriented.

TARP See **Technical Assistance Research Program.**

Technical Assistance Research Program (TARP) An Arlington, Virginia-based firm specializing in customer service research studies for call centers and many other industries.

technical skills Aptitudes and knowledge that allows effective use of technology.

technology implications Potential impact on service through the use of various equipment and systems.

telecommuting A trend seen in many congested metropolitan areas and government offices. To reduce traffic, pollution, and save resources (e.g., rent, telephone, and technology systems) many organizations allow employees to set up home offices and from there electronically communicate and forward information to their corporate offices.

telephone management Strategies for the effective use of the telephone and associated equipment in communicating.

teletype (TTY) (also known as telephone device for the disabled [TDD]) A typewriter-type device used by people with hearing disabilities for typing messages back and forth via telephone lines.

templates Predesigned style sheets that can be used to prepare letters, forms, memorandums, or other such routine documentation. Many computer software programs come with such features programmed into them for quick reference.

thought speed The rate at which the human brain processes information.

time allocation Amount of attention given to a person or project.

time management The systematic practice of categorizing daily activities, identifying and eliminating factors that interfere with efficiency, and developing effective strategies for getting the most out of the time available.

time management and technology Refers to the ability to use technology to improve effectiveness and efficiency in a service environment.

time management face-to-face Techniques for increasing time efficiency when dealing with customers.

time management on the run Strategies for using downtime effectively to accomplish small tasks or be creative.

time perception The manner in which time is viewed as being either polychronic or monochronic.

time reality Acceptance of the fact that each person has only a finite amount of time each day to accomplish tasks and to enhance its usage.

time wasters Events, people, items, and other factors that create unnecessary loss of time.

total quality management (TQM) A systematic approach to identifying and quantifying best practices in an organization and/or industry in order to make improvements in effectiveness and efficiency. Leading proponents of this process were W. Edwards Deming, Joseph Juran, and Philip Crosby.

total quality service (TQS) The service industry equivalent to total quality management (TQM) used in manufacturing firms. A main difference in the two is that TQS focuses on customers rather than systems and processes.

trust Key element in cementing interpersonal relationships.

two-way communication An active process in which two individuals apply all the elements of interpersonal communication (e.g., listening, feedback, positive language) in order to effect the effective exchange of information and ideas.

V

values Long-term appraisals of the worth of an idea, person, place, thing, or practice held by individuals, groups, or cultures. They impact attitudes and behavior.

verbal feedback The response given to a sender's message that allows both the sender and receiver to know that a message was received correctly.

verbal fillers Verbal sounds, words, or utterances that break silence but add little to a conversation. Examples are uh, um, ah, or you know.

vision disabilities   Condition resulting from reduced or lost visual acuity or ability.

vocal cues   Qualities of the voice that send powerful nonverbal messages. Examples are rate, pitch, volume, and tone.

voice mail management   System for creating outgoing messages and leaving messages on an answering system effectively.

voice quality   Refers to the sound of one's voice. Terms often attributed to voice quality are raspy, nasal, hoarse, and gravelly.

voice response unit (VRU)   System that allows customers to call 24 hours a day, 7 days a week by keying a series of numbers on the telephone keypad in order to get information or answers to questions.

volume   Refers to loudness or softness of the voice when speaking.

W

wants   Things that customers typically desire but do not necessarily need.

Welfare to Work Partnership   A national, nonpartisan, not-for-profit organization established by small, medium, and large businesses to help employ people formerly in federal assistance programs.

what customers want   See **wants.**

win-win situation   An outcome to a disagreement in which both parties walk away feeling that they got what they wanted or needed.

Workplace Investment Act of 1998.   A law signed by President William Jefferson Clinton to replace the Job Training Partnership Act of 1982. It provides resources to job seekers, including skill assessment, counseling, and job skills training.

workplace violence   A trend that has developed and escalated in the past decade. Spawned by many changes in the workplace, shifting societal values and beliefs, and a variety of other factors, violence is blossoming in the workplace.

Y

Y2K bug   The term applied to a programming error made in many software packages that would cause a computer to fail to recognize the year 2000 at midnight on December 31, 1999. In instances where the oversight occurred, computers would cease to function at that hour. Billions of dollars were spent to correct the error worldwide.

younger customers   Subjective term referring to anyone younger than a service provider. Sometimes used to describe members of generation X (born to baby boomers) or later.

BIBLIOGRAPHY

Abromovitz, Hedy G., and Les Abromovitz, *Bringing TQM on the QT to Your Organization,* SPC Press, Knoxville, Tenn., 1993.

Aguilar, Leslie, and Linda Stokes, *Multicultural Customer Service: Providing Outstanding Service Across Cultures,* McGraw-Hill/Irwin, Burr Ridge, Ill., 1996.

Alessandra, Tony, and Michael J. O'Connor, *The Platinum Rule,* Warner Books, New York, 1996.

Anderson, Kristin, *Great Customer Service on the Telephone,* AMACOM, New York, 1992.

Anderson, Kristin, and Carol Kerr, *Customer Relationship Management,* McGraw-Hill, New York, 2002.

Anderson, Kristin, and Ron Zemke, *Knock Their Socks Off Answers,* AMACOM, New York, 1995.

Arredondo, Lani, *Communicating Effectively,* McGraw-Hill, New York, 2000.

Axtell, Roger E., *Gestures: The Do's and Taboos of Body Language Around the World,* Wiley, New York, 1991.

Barlow, Janelle, and Claus Moller, *A Complaint Is a Gift: Using Customer Feedback as a Strategic Tool,* Barrett-Koehler, San Francisco, 1996.

Bayan, Richard, *Words That Sell,* Contemporary Books, Chicago, Ill., 1984.

Berko, Roy M., Lawrence B. Rosenfeld, and Larry A. Samovar, *Connecting: A Culture-Sensitive Approach to Interpersonal Communication Competency,* 2d ed., Harcourt Brace, Fort Worth, Tex., 1997.

Blanchard, Ken, and Sheldon Bowles, *Raving Fans: A Revolutionary Approach to Customer Service,* William Morrow, New York, 1993.

Broydrick, Stephen C., *How May I Help You? Providing Personal Service in an Impersonal World,* McGraw-Hill/Irwin, Burr Ridge, Ill., 1994.

Carr, Clay, *Front-Line Customer Service: 15 Keys to Customer Satisfaction,* Wiley, New York, 1990.

Chen, Guo-Ming, and William J. Starosta, *Foundations of Intercultural Communication,* Allyn & Bacon, Needham Heights, Mass., 1998.

Cleveland, Brad, and Julia Kayben, *Call Center Management on Fast Forward: Succeeding in Today's Dynamic Inbound Environment,* Call Center Press, Annapolis, Md., 1997.

Cohen, R., *Negotiating Across Cultures: Intercultural Communication in an Interdependent World,* U. S. Institute of Peace, Washington, D.C. 1997.

Coscia, Stephen, *Customer Service Over the Phone,* Telecom Books, New York, 1998.

Coscia, Stephen, *TELE-Stress: Relief for Call Center Stress,* Telecom Books, New York, 1998.

Currie, Marilyn, *Achieving Customer Loyalty: A Retailer's Guide to Creating and Sustaining a Service Strategy,* Retail Learning Initiative, Toronto, Canada, 1996.

Cusacki, Michael, *Online Customer Care: Applying Today's Technology to Achieve World Class Customer Interaction,* ASQ Quality Press, Milwaukee, Wis., 1998.

Davidson, Jeff, *The Complete Idiot's Guide to Managing Stress,* Alpha Books, New York, 1997.

Dawson, Keith, *The Call Center Handbook: The Complete Guide to Starting, Running, and Improving Your Call Center,* 2d ed., Telecom Books and Flatiron Publishing, New York, 1998.

Dee, David, *The Extra Mile: Building Profitable Customer Relations Every Time,* Dartnell Corporation, Chicago, Ill., 1994.

Dee, David, *Stand-Out Service: Talk Straight, Think Positive, and Smile!* Dartnell Corporation, Chicago, Ill., 1994.

Dee, David, *Phone Me, Fax Me, Beep Me: Teleconnecting Your Way to Success in the New Cyberspaced Workplace,* Dartnell Corporation, Chicago, Ill., 1998.

DeVito, Joseph A., and Raymond Zeuschner, *Essentials of Oral Communication,* 3d ed., Pearson, Needham Heights, Mass., 1999.

De Vries, Mary A., *The Complete Word Book: The Practical Guide to Anything and Everything You Need to Know About Words and How to Use Them,* Barnes & Noble, New York, 1999.

Dodd, Carley H., *Dynamics of Intercultural Communication,* 4th ed., Brown & Benchmark, Madison, Wis., 1995.

Edstrom, K.R.S., *Conquering Stress,* Barron's, Hauppauge, N.Y., 1993.

Eggland, Steven A., and Michael J. Britten, *Customer Service: Serve Us America,* Prentice Hall, Upper Saddle River, N.J., 2002.

Finch, Lloyd C., *Telephone Courtesy & Customer Service,* Crisp Publications, Los Altos, Calif., 1987.

Finch, Lloyd C., *Twenty Ways to Improve Customer Service,* Crisp Publications, Los Altos, Calif., 1994.

Finch, Lloyd C., *Success as a CSR,* Crisp Publications, Los Altos, Calif., 1998.

Fisher, Donna, and Sandy Vilas, *Power Networking: 55 Secrets for Personal and Professional Success,* MountainHarbour Publications, Austin, Tex., 1992.

Fisher, Judith E., *Telephone Skills at Work,* McGraw-Hill/Irwin, Burr Ridge, Ill., 1994.

Fisher, Judith E., *The Phone Book: Telephone Skills for Business Success,* McGraw-Hill/Irwin, Chicago, Ill., 1996.

Glanz, Barbara, *The Creative Communicator,* McGraw-Hill/Irwin, Homewood, Ill., 1993.

Gorman, Tom, *The Complete Idiot's Almanac of Business Letters and Memos,* Alpha Books, New York, 1997.

Green, Michael, and Jonathon G. Ripley, *Communicating for Future Business Professionals,* Prentice Hall, Upper Saddle River, N.J., 1998.

Greiner, Donna, and Theodore B. Kinni, *1,001 Ways to Keep Customers Coming Back,* Prima, Roseville, Calif., 1999.

Grey, John, *Men Are From Mars, Women Are From Venus,* HarperCollins, New York, 1992.

Griffin, Jill, *Customer Loyalty: How to Earn It How to Keep It,* Jossey-Bass, San Francisco, 1995.

Gundykunst, William B., *Bridging Differences: Effective Intergroup Communication,* 3d ed., Sage, Thousand Oaks, Calif., 1998.

Hanna, Michael S., and Gerald Wilson, *Communicating in Business and Professional Settings,* 4th ed., McGraw-Hill, New York, 1998.

Hanson, Peter G., *Stress for Success: Thriving on Stress at Work,* Collins, Toronto, Canada, 1989.

Hargrave, Jan, *Let Me See Your Body Talk,* Kendall/Hunt, Dubuque, Iowa, 1995.

Harris, Elaine K., *Customer Service: A Practical Approach,* 2d ed., Prentice Hall, Upper Saddle River, N.J., 2000.

Harvey, Eric, and The Walk the Talk Team, *180 Ways to Walk the Customer Service Talk: The How-To Handbook for Everyone in Your Organization,* Performance Systems Corporation, Dallas, Tex., 1999.

Hathaway, Patti, *Giving and Receiving Criticism: Your Key to Interpersonal Success,* Crisp Publications, Menlo Park, Calif., 1990.

Hecht, Michael L., Mary J. Collier, and Sidney A. Ribeau, *African American Communication; Ethnic Identity and Cultural Interpretation,* Sage Publications, Thousand Oaks, Calif., 1993.

Helmstetter, Shad, *What You Say When You Talk to Yourself,* Pocket Books, New York, 1986.

Hemsath, Dave, and Leslie Yerkes, *301 Ways to Have at Work,* Berrett-Koehler, San Francisco, 1997.

Hill, Norman C., *Improving Peer Relationships: Achieving Results Informally,* Crisp Publications, Menlo Park, Calif., 1996.

Hitchcock, David J., *Asian Values and the United States: How Much Conflict?* Center for Strategic & International Studies, Washington, D.C., 1994.

Ivy, Dianna K., and Phil Backlund, *Exploring GenderSpeak: Personal Effectiveness in Gender Communication,* McGraw-Hill, New York, 1994.

Jandt, Fred, *The Customer Is Usually Wrong!* Park Avenue Publications, Indianapolis, Ind., 1995.

Karr, Ron, and Don Blohowiak, *The Complete Idiot's Guide to Great Customer Service,* Alpha Books, New York, 1997.

Kenton, Sherron, and Deborah Valentine, *Crosstalk: Communicating in a Multicultural Workplace,* Prentice Hall, Upper Saddle River, N.J., 1997.

Kincaid, Judith W., *Customer Relationship Management: Getting It Right!* Prentice Hall, Upper Saddle River, N.J., 2003.

Kindler, Herbert S., *Managing Disagreement Constructively,* Crisp Publications, Menlo Park, Calif., 1996.

Knouse, Stephen B., Paul Rosenfeld, and Amy L. Culbertson, *Hispanics in the Workplace,* Sage Publications, Newbury Park, Calif., 1992.

Leathers, David G., *Successful Nonverbal Communication,* 3d ed., Allyn & Bacon, Boston, Mass., 1997.

Lebon, Paul, *Escape Voicemail Hell: Boost Your Productivity by Making Voicemail Work for You,* Parleau, Highland Village, Tex., 2000.

Leland, Karen, and Keith Bailey, *Customer Service for Dummies,* IDG Books Worldwide, Foster City, Calif., 1995.

Lickson, Charles P., *Ironing It Out: Seven Simple Steps to Resolving Conflict,* Crisp Publications, Menlo Park, Calif., 1996.

Lindsell-Roberts, Sheryl, *Business Writing for Dummies,* IDG Books, Foster City, Calif., 1999.

Lloyd, Sam R., *Developing Positive Assertiveness: Practical Techniques for Personal Success,* Crisp Publications, Menlo Park, Calif., 1995.

Locke, Don C., *Increasing Multicultural Understanding: A Comprehensive Model,* 2d ed., Sage, Thousand Oaks, Calif., 1998.

Lucas, Robert W., *Job Strategies for New Employees,* American Media, West Des Moines, Iowa, 1996.

Lucas, Robert. W., *Effective Interpersonal Relationships,* Mirror Press, Burr Ridge, Ill., 1999.

Lucas, Robert W., *How to Be a Great Call Center Representative*, American Management Association, Watertown, Mass., 2001.

Luhn, Rebecca R., *Managing Anger: Methods for a Happier and Healthier Life*, Crisp Publications, Menlo Park, Calif., 1992.

MacNeill, Dedra J., *Customer Service Excellence*, American Media Publishing, West Des Moines, Iowa, 1994.

Mallory, Charles, *How to Get Everything Done (And Still Have a Life)*, American Media Publishing, West Des Moines, Iowa, 1997.

Mayer, Jeffrey J., *Time Management for Dummies*, 2d ed., IDG Books, Foster City, Calif., 1999.

Mehrabian, Albert, *Silent Messages*, Wadsworth, Belmont, Calif., 1971.

Morris, Desmond, *Bodytalk: The Meaning of Human Gestures*, Crown Trade Paperbacks, New York, 1994.

Morrison, Terri, Wayne A. Conaway, and George A. Borden, *Kiss, Bow, or Shake Hands: How to Do Business in Sixty Countries*, Adams Media Corporation, Holbrook, Mass., 1994.

Neher, William, and David H. Waite, *The Business and Professional Communicator*, Allyn & Bacon, Needham Heights, Mass., 1993.

Nelson, Bob, *1001 Ways to Energize Employees*, Workman, New York, 1994.

Nierenberg, Gerald I., and Henry H. Calero, *How to Read a Person Like a Book*, Barnes & Noble, New York, 1993.

Pepper, Gerald L., *Communicating in Organizations: A Cultural Approach*, McGraw-Hill, New York, 1995.

Potter, Beverly A., *Preventing Job Burnout: Transforming Work Pressure Into Productivity*, Crisp Publications, Menlo Park, Calif., 1996.

Quinlan, Kathryn A., *Customer Service Representative*, Capstone Press, Mankato, Minn., 1999.

Raines, Claire, *Beyond Generation X: A Practical Guide for Managers*, Crisp Publications, Menlo Park, Calif., 1997.

Reardon, Kathleen K., *They Don't Get It Do They? Communication in the Workplace—Closing the Gap Between Women and Men*, Little, Brown, Boston, Mass., 1995.

Reynolds, Larry, *The Trust Effect: Creating the High Trust High Performance Organization*, Nicholas Brealey, London, England, 1997.

Samovar, Larry A., Richard E. Porter, and Lisa A. Stefani, *Communication Between Cultures*, Wadsworth, Belmont, Calif., 1998.

Sanders, Betsy, *Fabled Service: Ordinary Acts, Extraordinary Outcomes*, Pfeiffer, San Diego, Calif., 1995.

Satterwhite, Marilyn, and Judith Olson-Sutton, *Business Communication at Work*, Glencoe/McGraw-Hill, New York, 2000.

Senge, Peter M., *The Fifth Discipline: The Art and Practice of the Learning Organization*, Doubleday, New York, 1994.

Shelton, Nelda, and Sharon Burton, *Assertiveness Skills*, Mc-Graw-Hill/Irwin, Burr Ridge, Ill., 1994.

Simons, George, and G. Deborah Weissman, *Men and Women: Partners at Work*, Crisp Publications, Menlo Park, Calif., 1990.

Simons, George, with Amy J. Zuckerman, *Working Together: Succeeding in a Multicultural Organization*, Crisp Publications, Menlo Park, Calif., 1994.

Sterne, Jim, *Customer Service on the Internet: Building Relationships, Increasing Loyalty, and Staying Competitive*, Wiley, New York, 1996.

Swift, Ronald S., *Accelerating Customer Relationships: Using CRM and Relationship Technologies*, Prentice Hall, Upper Saddle River, N.J., 2001.

Tannen, Deborah, *You Just Don't Understand: Women and Men in Conversations*, Ballantine Books, New York, 1990.

Tannen, Deborah, *The Argument Culture: Moving From Debate to Dialogue*, Random House, New York, 1998.

Timm, Paul R., *Customer Service: Career Success Through Customer Satisfaction*, Prentice Hall, Upper Saddle River, N.J., 1998.

Whiteley, Richard C., *The Customer Driven Company: Moving From Talk to Action*, Addison-Wesley, Reading, Mass., 1991.

Willingham, Ron, *Hey, I'm the Customer*, Prentice Hall, Englewood Cliffs, N.J., 1992.

Wolvin, Andrew, and Carolyn G. Coakley, *Listening*, 5th ed., Brown & Benchmark, Madison, Wis., 1996.

Woods, Donald R., and Shirley D. Ornerod, *Networking: How to Enrich Your Life and Get Things Done*, Pfeiffer, San Diego, Calif., 1993.

Zemke, Ron, *Service Recovery: Fixing Broken Customers*, Productivity Press, Portland, Oreg., 1995.

Zemke, Ron and Chip Bell, *Service Magic: The Art of Amazing Your Customers*, Dearborn, Mich., 2003.

Zemke, Ron, Claire Raines, and Bob Filipczak, *Generations at Work: Managing the Clash of Veterans, Boomers, Xers, and Nexters in Your Workplace*, AMACOM, New York, 2000.

Index

Sickles Photo Reporting/Gettyimages   page 5

© Corbis   page 9

© Corbis   page 15

© Corbis   page 17

Courtesy of David Littlehale   page 28

© Corbis   page 37

© Corbis   page 43

© Corbis   page 47

© Corbis   page 49

Courtesy of Ginger Simpson   page 60

© Corbis   page 63

© Corbis   page 68

© Corbis   page 77

Photo 1, © Corbis   page 78

Photo 2, © Corbis   page 78

Photo 3, © Corbis   page 78

Photo 4, © Corbis   page 78

Photo 5, © Corbis   page 78

Photo 6, © Corbis   page 78

Photo 7, © Corbis   page 78

Photo 8, Scott T. Baxter/Gettyimages   page 78

John Lawlor/Gettyimages   page 81

Courtesy of Frank Ross   page 92

© Corbis   page 96

David Rosenberg/Gettyimages   page 100

© Corbis   page 105

Courtesy of Begum Tolgay   page 122

© Corbis   page 129

© Corbis   page 130

© Corbis   page 139

Courtesy of Jason Grimard   page 150

Michael Malyszko/Gettyimages   page 160

© Corbis   page 169

Courtesy of Christy Street   page 176

© Corbis   page 179

Dana White/PhotoEdit   page 189

Steve Niedorf Photography/Gettyimages
page 191

Courtesy of Karen Buchan, Webster University
page 204

Chris Ryan/Gettyimages   page 209

© Corbis   page 223

Courtesy of Ana Bertoli   page 238

© Corbis   page 243

© Corbis   page 252

© Corbis   page 256

Courtesy of Sharelle Rogers   page 268

© Corbis   page 272

© Corbis   page 281

Jeff Smith/Gettyimages   page 283

Courtesy of Steve Tanzer   page 296

Deborah Davis/PhotoEdit   page 304

© Corbis   page 307

Courtesy of Dr. F. H. Collins   page 316

© Corbis   page 323

© Corbis   page 329

Barros & Barros/Gettyimages   page 337

Courtesy of Nick Crnich   page 348

© Corbis   page 355

© Corbis   page 381

© Corbis   page 384

© Corbis   page 386